Key Thinkers in Psychology

Key Thinkers in Psychology

Rom Harré

SAGE Publications
London ● Thousand Oaks ● New Delhi

SAGE Publications Ltd
1 Oliver's Yard
55 City Road
London EC1Y 1SP

SAGE Publications Inc.
2455 Teller Road
Thousand Oaks, California 91320

SAGE Publications India Pvt Ltd
B-42, Panchsheel Enclave
Post Box 4109
New Delhi 110 017

British Library Cataloguing in Publication data

A catalogue record for this book is available from
the British Library

ISBN 1-4129-0344-0
ISBN 1-4129-0345-9 (pbk)

Library of Congress Control Number available

Typeset by C&M Digitals (P) Ltd., Chennai, India
Printed in Great Britain by TJ International, Padstow, Cornwall
Printed on paper from sustainable resources

Contents

Note: Throughout the book the names of major figures are given in bold type, while minor but still important contributors appear in italics.

Preface

The 20th century was rich in attempts to characterize and explain psychological phenomena and so to understand the human mind. These projects were undertaken by a huge and diverse cast of characters. Among the most important were Ivan Pavlov, Sigmund Freud, Alexander Luria, Ludwig Wittgenstein, Lev Vygotsky, Jean Piaget, Burrhus Frederick Skinner, Alan Turing, Noam Chomsky, Frederic Bartlett, Jerome Bruner and James Gibson. Each contributed a distinctive perspective on the nature of persons and their cognitive and emotional capacities. Some, such as Lev Vygotsky and Jerome Bruner, have left an enduring mark on our understanding of ourselves. Others, such as Burrhus Frederick Skinner and Raymond Cattell, influential in their time, followed trails that seem to have reached dead ends.

Choosing the people whose life and work has been of notable importance involved two decisions. A century is a somewhat arbitrary division of time. A cut-off point had to be chosen. I settled on the simple criterion that the major works by which a person influenced the development of scientific psychology should have been published in the 20th century. Under this principle the lives and work of Wilhelm Wundt and William James were reluctantly excluded. Sigmund Freud and Emile Kraepelin, though very active in the late 19th century, met this requirement for inclusion.

To select a cast of characters from those who are indubitably figures of the 20th century involves a second decision. The people I have chosen reflect a certain presumption on my part as to how psychology evolved in the 20th century and how it is likely to develop in the 21st. To choose about 40 influential thinkers from so many interesting people in the end must reflect one's personal perception of where psychology came from and where it is headed.

This book is an account of the lives and work of the people I take to have been major innovators in several important branches of psychology. I make no claims to comprehensiveness. There are several massive tomes devoted to the lives of psychologists, past and present. There are some excellent biographical articles on the web in various electronic encyclopaedias. References to these will be found in the Further Readings attached to each section, and the bibliography at the end of the introduction.

On looking over the cast of characters I have put together in response to the publisher's original suggestion for this project, it struck me that it did not include any women. This is not due to my testosterone-induced blindness. It was a noticeable feature of 20th century psychology. However, if we were to take the human sciences as a whole, rather than the narrow realm of psychology as it was understood in the last century, women made notable contributions. For instance, one would include Deborah Tannen (1991), whose academic location is linguistics. She showed how the patterns of men's and women's talk tended to lead to mutual incomprehension. The work of Hélène Cixous (1986), social and literary critic, displayed the gender patterning of Western literature. Catherine Lutz (1988), anthropologist, demonstrated the cultural specificity of repertoires of emotions. Bronwyn Davies (1989), educationalist, developed a research method based on phenomenological poetics, and tracked the development of the sense of gender in human development. Anna Wierzbicka (1992), anthropological linguist, demonstrated some of the universal features of human cognition. This list could be extended in various directions. The work of none of these women is in the received canon of 'scientific psychology'. So much the worse for that canon, one might well say.

There might also be thought to be an omission of a major branch of psychology, namely the psychology of the emotions, to which one might couple the psychology of the arts generally. In the last century studies in the psychology of the emotions have ranged from cultural-historical investigations, to ethological research into emotion displays as signalling systems, to the neurophysiology of arousal. However, no one individual stands out as a true innovator or a major influence on the way the field developed. With neither a commanding figure nor an especially innovative approach exclusive to the psychology of the emotions, the remit of this book leaves no place for any one representative. Of course, in any general history of psychology in the last century it would feature prominently.

In a masterly analysis of the history of scientific schools, Lewis Feuer (1963) showed how the development of a natural science, such as physics or chemistry, in one of the great centres of research, passed through an 80-year cycle. The story begins with the work of a 'Maverick Guru', whose innovations are resisted or ignored by the established leaders in the field. However, the promise of a new field of research attracts a generation of exceptionally talented disciples who take up the work of innovator. The cycle ends with minor variations of known results as successive generations of lesser talent are attracted to a now famous research programme. A similar pattern is discernible in the recent history of psychology. Through the lives of our cast of characters we will follow the progress of some of the great innovations of the 20th century as they rose into established paradigms, and sometimes declined into obscurity.

The life stories presented here are arranged in roughly chronological clusters around topics to which a major part of the life work of each of our characters was directed. The clusters are grouped under heads that suggest the content of the topics they cover. Of course, many of these exceptionally active and innovative people contributed to more than one domain of the official dimensions of academic psychology. Should Jerome Bruner be placed among the developmentalists or the cognitivists? Should Sigmund Freud be located as a psychopathologist or as a developmentalist? And so on. Cross references take us to and fro across the clusters.

Lists for further reading include a selection of major works, some secondary sources, and, wherever they exist and are accessible, biographies and autobiographies. References to some of the excellent articles and biographies available on the internet have been included.

Cross-references are indicated in bold with the full name of the author discussed in the section to which reference is made. The names of people who have made lesser but significant contributions to psychology are displayed in italics.

The book is based on a course given at American University, Washington DC during the spring semester 2004. To comply with the constraints of the semester a selection was necessary. The course comprised the lives and work of the following: Ivan Pavlov, Burrhus Frederick Skinner, Lev Vygotsky, Jean Piaget, Jerome Bruner, Gordon Allport, Erving Goffman, Alan Turing, Noam Chomsky, Wilder Penfield, Alexander Luria, Karl Pribram, Sigmund Freud, Ludwig Wittgenstein and Michel Foucault. Though in some sense arbitrary, this proved to be a workable selection. Other choices could certainly be made, and other course structures developed on the basis of the material in this volume.

A study like this depends very much on the ready availability of the relevant books. I would like to express particularly warm thanks to the staff of the Radcliffe Science Library in Oxford and of the Medical Library at Georgetown for their help and interest.

Rom Harré
Oxford and Washington DC, 2005

Introduction: A Sketch of Some Historical Trends

At the beginning of the 20th century the long standing presumption that an adequate understanding of how and why people behaved the way they did could be picked up from studies such as the law, the Greek and Roman classics, philosophy and, more informally, literature and the theatre, was being seriously challenged. Alongside the laboratories for studying chemical, physical and biological phenomena, there would be places dedicated to the investigation of psychological phenomena, in more or less the same way as the phenomena that comprised the domain of the natural sciences were being investigated. The vast resources of existing knowledge of the patterns of human thought and feeling were not to be set aside, but the nature of human mental life was to be investigated anew. Inevitably the methods adapted from those in use in research in the natural sciences led to controversy.

In the first half of the century the dominant paradigm in academic institutions was Behaviourism. Based on the principle that the whole range of human behaviour could be analysed into patterns of simple stimulus-response units, it encouraged an experimental methodology involving the manipulation of independent and dependent variables. Most of the research material came from studies of animals, where, it was presumed, the basic stimulus-response units could be more easily extracted than with human subjects. During and after the First World War statistical methods were imported into psychology (Danziger, 1990). Part of the strength of the behaviourist stance to psychology came from its evident similarity to the dominant philosophy of the time, Positivism. Both movements rejected the use of unobservable states and processes in scientific explanations. This connection was made explicit by **Burrhus Frederick Skinner** (pp. 15–24). The influence of behaviourist methodology continued to be important even when its main principles had been abandoned.

Mid-century saw a radical challenge to the dominant paradigm. This has come to be called the First Cognitive Revolution. It was initiated by **Jerome Bruner** (pp. 54–62) and others in the United States. Without consciously adopting a philosophical position, the architects of the First Cognitive Revolution can be seen in hindsight to be working out the consequences of following the Realist philosophy of science. They began to make use of hypotheses about cognitive states and processes that were not publicly or even privately observable. Psychologists once again entertained theories in the sense that chemists and physicists do. Behaviourism did not dominate European psychology to anything like the same extent as it did the work of American psychologists. Already in the 1930s **Jean Piaget** (pp. 34–43), **Lev Vygotsky** (pp. 26–34) and **Frederic Bartlett** (pp. 47–54) were working in ways that matched the insights of the First Cognitive Revolution of the 1950s.

However, matters did not rest there. Behaviourism and Cognitivism were aimed at discovering universal features of human cognition, emotion and perception. If there were a universal human nature it existed at a very high level of abstraction. The advocates of the First Cognitive Revolution, be they Europeans or Americans, drew attention to the fact that psychological phenomena were defined by their meanings for the people involved, rather than by properties of other kinds, such as those of their neurological correlates. Psychology as the science of meaning making would, of necessity, attend to the way people used languages and other symbolic systems to accomplish their ends. Cultural influences on thought and behaviour began to come to the fore. Even before the Second World War **Frederic Bartlett**, **William McDougall** (pp. 191–194) and **Lev Vygotsky** were prominent advocates of the necessity to pay attention to the possibility that people in different cultures differed psychologically from the subjects of most Western psychological research. It seemed that it might even be necessary to put the project of a universal human psychological science on hold, while attending to the distinctive ways individual people thought and acted. **George Kelly** (pp. 62–68) pioneered one way in which idiographic studies could be made to meet the demands of scientific method. **Gordon Allport** (pp. 167–172) pressed for a similar stance to be taken to personality.

A Second Cognitive Revolution seems to have been taking place in the last quarter of the 20th century. Attention to meanings as the basic psychological phenomena suggests some important limitations on the use of causal concepts to explain the temporal patterns of thought, action and feeling. Cognitive psychologists and their allies in Computational Psychology, such as **Marvin Minsky** (pp. 93–8), began to think in terms of rules and schemata, formal representations of the bodies of knowledge that had become the focus of cognitive psychology. It was a short step to the suggestion that at least some of the organizing principles of psychological processes came from narrative conventions, life as the living of a story line. Once again **Jerome Bruner** played a prominent role in this development.

The science of the mental life as the study of the ways human agents actively manage meanings in accordance with the rules and conventions that express both universal and local standards of propriety has become closely integrated with the findings of the neurosciences. After all, the most important mechanism with which we think, act and perceive is the human brain. From its beginning in Russia with the wartime work of **Alexander Luria** (pp. 105–113) and its subsequent development by **Wilder Penfield** (pp. 113–118), **Karl Pribram** (pp. 118–125) and others, neuroscience has been based on a methodology that links expressions of personal experience with states and processes of the brain and nervous system. The linkage of higher order cognitive processes and other kinds of behaviour to the neural mechanisms with which people execute their daily tasks is slowly being worked out. The psychology of perception is closely allied to cognitive neuroscience. **Richard Gregory** (pp. 148–154) argued for the thesis that perception is literally cognitive, while **James Gibson** (pp. 142–148) showed how perceptual systems are organized to extract invariants from the patterns of stimuli on the retina.

Looked at from a global perspective, there seem to be two main trends emerging as the new century opens. On the one hand there is an increasing depth and sophistication in the identification of the biological roots of human capacities. Neuropsychology and genetic psychology have developed rapidly. On the other hand there has been an equally striking spread of a cluster of approaches typified by cultural psychology. This loose collection of research methods and theoretical presuppositions has emerged as a new analytical frame within which to identify and classify psychological phenomena. It has its origins in the writings of such authors as **Lev Vygotsky**, and has been developed further in the work of **Jerome Bruner**, **Serge Moscovici** (pp. 216–221) and others. It is beginning to appear as the natural partner of neuroscience. Taking the two lines of development together, it seems to me that a new paradigm is emerging that displays a strongly Realist philosophy in keeping with similar developments in the way physics, chemistry and biology have shaken off the positivism of the mid 20th century.

Psychology, like any other science, is as much an arena for the creative use of ideas as it is for empirical research. There are two valuable readers to complement the contents of this book: Daniel Robinson's *Intellectual History of Psychology* (1986) and Ali Moghaddam's (2005) study of the leading ideas that have shaped psychology, perhaps supplemented by Graham Richards' (2002) *Putting Psychology in its Place*, Chapters 5 to 14. For more detailed topic-oriented accounts of the history of psychology the most recent edition of Thomas Leahey's *A History of Modern Psychology* (2004), Chapters 8 to 10, would make useful supplementary reading. Chapters 9, 10, 13 and 14 of Elizabeth Valentine's *Conceptual Issues in Psychology* (1986), though written some time ago, give a good general idea of some of the philosophical problems that have beset psychology.

References

Cixous, H. (1986) *The Newly Born Woman*. Manchester: Manchester University Press.

Danziger, K. (1990) *Constructing the Subject*. Cambridge: Cambridge University Press.

Davies, B. (1989) *Frogs and Snails and Feminist Tales*. Sydney: Allen and Unwin.

Feuer, L. S. (1963) *The Scientific Intellectual*. New York: Basic Books.

Leahey, T. H. (2004) *A History of Modern Psychology*. Upper Saddle River, NJ: Pearson Educational.

Lutz, C. (1988) *Unnatural Emotions*. Chicago: Chicago University Press.

Moghaddam, F. M. (2005) *Great Ideas in Psychology: A Cultural and Historical Introduction*. Oxford: One World Publications.

Richards, G. (2002) *Putting Psychology in its Place.* London: Taylor and Francis.

Robinson, D. N. (1986) *An Intellectual History of Psychology.* Madison, WI: University of Wisconsin Press.

Tannen, D. (1991) *You Just Don't Understand.* London: Virago.

Valentine, E. (1986) *Conceptual Issues in Psychology.* London: George Allen and Unwin.

Wierzbicka, A. (1992) *Semantics, Culture and Cognition.* Oxford: Oxford University Press.

Some Useful Biographical Collections

Boring, E. E. & Lindzey, G. (1967) (eds), *History of Psychology in Autobiography.* New York: Appleton Century Crofts.

Brinzmann, W. G., Luck, H. E., Miller, R. & Early, C. E. (1997) *A Pictorial History of Psychology.* Carol Stream, IL: Quintessence Publishing.

Kibble, G. A., Wertheimer, M. & White, C. L. (1991) *Portraits of Pioneers in Psychology.* Hove and London: Lawrence Erlbaum Associates.

Some excellent online biographical articles can also be found on *The Internet Encyclopedia of Philosophy* and *The Internet Encyclopedia of Psychology.*

PART ONE

From Behaviourism to Cognitivism

1

The Behaviourists

During the first half of the 20th century a radical shift appeared in the very conception of what a scientific psychology ought to encompass. From the time of the British empiricists of the 17th and 18th centuries to the German experimentalists of the 19th century, the legitimacy of people's reports of their subjective states was hardly ever questioned. However, in the 1920s the role of conscious states and processes as the prime sources of explanations of publicly observable behaviour was called into question. Not only were there doubts about the reliability of incorporating private experiences among the data of psychology, but, beginning with J. B. Watson (1919), the opinion began to spread that such data were redundant. Public behaviour could be explained by identifying the stimulus that triggered it.

However, in the first instance, human behaviour was far too complex to be studied by looking for stimulus-response patterns. Animals could serve as models for the study of behaviour in general. Not only were animals readily accommodated in experimental programmes, but it was presumed that their more primitive repertoires of responses could be analysed into simple elementary stimulus and response units. This presumption facilitated a certain kind of programme of experimental research.

The experimental study of stimulus-response patterns could be accomplished, it was assumed, by identifying elementary states of the environment and elementary responses and treating these as independent and dependent variables. An experiment would consist in manipulating the independent variable and observing the changes in the dependent variable. Show a dog some food and it will salivate. Thus we have an experimentally confirmed 'psychological' unit: food as stimulus elicits salivation as response.

During the first half of the 20th century a great many experiments based on this paradigm were carried out. Watson did little himself. The major figures behind a great deal of this work were **Ivan Pavlov** (pp. 8–15) and **Burrhus Frederick Skinner** (pp. 15–24). Both worked with animals – dogs, rats and pigeons. Both made systematic use of the methodology of independent and dependent variables. They differed on whether this route would lead to a comprehensive scientific psychology. However, both were willing to generalize their findings to the case of *Homo sapiens*.

In this way the programme of behaviourism was born. It flourished in the United States, particularly as it was developed by Edward Tolman (1932) and others. It had little influence in Europe, where anthropology and other descriptive approaches to understanding human life were generally more important at that time. We can see this in the work of **Frederic Bartlett** (pp. 47–54) and of **William McDougall** (pp. 191–194).

In eschewing any reference to mental processes behaviourists quite naturally began to see the stimulus-response patterns extracted from experiments in causal terms. Stimuli cause the emission of behaviours. The human being as active and responsible agent is implicitly expelled from psychology.

As the school of behaviourist psychology developed into a paradigm for a scientific psychology, it absorbed another trend that at first might seem alien to the very idea of a psychology. Influenced by the demands of the military and by business studies, psychologists began to subject their results to statistical analysis, requiring a population of subjects to take part in experiments (Danziger, 1990).

Long after behaviourism as a general psychology had been abandoned, the methodology of behaviourist research programmes continued and soon became an almost ubiquitous paradigm, practically defining what a scientific psychology should be. The three components – a causal metaphysics, an experimental methodology based on independent and dependent variables applied to a population and the use of statistics as the main analytical tool – made up a conception of psychology sometimes identified as the Old Paradigm. For the most part psychologists were simply unaware that the natural sciences they hoped to emulate made very little use of Old Paradigm methodology. The challenges to that methodology that emerged in the 1970s as the New Paradigm were partly animated by the idea of applying the actual methodology and metaphysics of physics and chemistry to the problems of psychology. Concepts like 'activity' and 'structure' made their appearance. Model making began to take precedence over experiments.

In this chapter we look closely at the lives and work of the pioneers of two versions of behaviourism, **Ivan Pavlov** and **Burrhus Frederick Skinner**.

References

Danziger, K. (1990) *Constructing the Subject*. Cambridge: Cambridge University Press.

Tolman, E. C. (1932) *Purposive Behavior in Animals and Man*. New York: Appleton-Century-Crofts.

Watson, J. B. (1919) *Psychology from the Standpoint of a Behaviorist*. Philadelphia: Lippincott.

Ivan Petrovich Pavlov (1849–1936)

By the beginning of the 20th century sufficient was known about the human brain and nervous system to support the idea of a psychology based on that system alone. La Mettrie's dream of a materialist and all embracing human science seemed to be a real possibility. At this time the key concept on which this hope was based was the 'reflex arc'. Sensory stimuli were carried to the brain, where they were processed, and appropriate neural instructions were sent to the muscles and other organs involved in behaviour. Could this 'arc' be the basis of the complex patterns of thought, feeling and action of the mature human being? Ivan Pavlov was the first to try to answer this question affirmatively.

Who was Ivan Petrovich Pavlov?

He was born on 26 September 1849 in the small town of Ryazan in Russia. His father was a priest, a man of some education. Ivan was the eldest of 11 children. When he was seven he fell from a balcony onto his head. He was severely injured and in consequence suffered from difficulties with his sight. He had trouble concentrating on 'academic' matters. In the event he had no formal schooling until he was 11. Helping his father in the garden, he learned a good deal of natural history. Assisting his mother in the house, he acquired an unusual range of manual skills for a young boy. In later life he put down his enthusiasm for the experimental aspect of physiology to the chores that fell to his lot as a child.

In 1860 he entered the Ryazan Theological Seminary. The teachers were mostly liberal in outlook and encouraged Ivan's interest in natural science. In later life Pavlov recalled Father Orlov in particular. The works of the most progressive thinkers of the time were in the local town library and Pavlov immersed himself in their writings, particularly the radical Russian author Dmitrij Ivanovich Pisarev (1840–1868) and the Englishman Samuel Smiles (1812–1904). Pisarev's political vision was dominated by the idea of the amelioration of society's ills by the use of science. From Smiles young Pavlov seems to have picked up the idea of a disciplined, almost moral attitude to the work of science. Both enthused young Ivan Petrovich with the idea of science as the major influence on social and political progress.

In 1870 he hoped to begin his studies at St Petersburg University to pursue his passion for science. However, his mathematical skills were weak. Somehow, he avoided the test in mathematics and passed his matriculation ordeal satisfactorily. His inclinations led him to study in the natural history section in the school of physical sciences. At this time he was as much filled with the idea of a science-led transformation of society as he was with enthusiasm for scientific knowledge for its own sake. His private reading led him to the Englishman George Lewes's popular works, particularly on biology, long passages from which he learned by heart.

His formal studies were dominated by the teaching of the great physiologist Ilya Fadeyevich Tsion (1842–1910), whose influence on Pavlov was lifelong. Under Tsion's supervision he carried out a detailed study of the pancreatic nerves, for which he was awarded a gold medal. Already he had been drawn into the idea of the nervous system as the main, indeed for a while he believed the only, means by which the internal organs were stimulated to perform their various functions. Picking up an old conceptual distinction, he distinguished between his 'nervic' theory of the management of the internal organs and the 'humoric' theory of chemical influences.

Taking his first degree in 1875, he was able to enter the Academy of Medicine, intending to pursue his physiological studies rather than to qualify as a doctor. He continued to work under Tsion's wing, and thus, fatefully for him, he became involved in one of the great academic scandals of the era. Tsion decided to end the custom of giving a pass mark to everyone who attended the Academy, the 'gentleman's C' grade. The subsequent student unrest was only put down by armed force, and a vicious campaign, fueled by anti-semitism, forced Tsion to resign. Pavlov resigned as well. Thus began a period of extreme poverty, shared by his new wife, Serafina Vassilievna Kartatievskaya, whom he married in 1881. She had known him as a student and has left a vivid memoir of his enthusiasm for intellectual debates.

Sergei Botkin, a student of Claude Bernard (1813–1878), the great French physiologist, became the director of the Veterinary Institute, and shortly thereafter Pavlov joined as his assistant. Scientific research was not well supported, and Botkin had very little to offer him. The salary was barely enough to live on, and there was scarcely anything for the expenses of research. Their laboratory was a tumbledown shed. Yet, in those 10 years, Pavlov not only brought 15 doctoral projects to fruition, but continued his own studies into neurophysiology. He describes his time there with characteristic generosity and enthusiasm. His duties to the clinic itself were minimal. Though he enjoyed working with the students on collaborative projects, he said later: 'from our discussions I gained the habit of "physiological reasoning" [later to emerge as a distrust of mentalistic explanations]. I progressed until no laboratory technique held any secrets for me.' During his years with Botkin, Pavlov worked on the pancreatic nerves, the nervous control of the heart, and began an interest in the control of gastric secretions. In 1883 he submitted his doctoral thesis, on the nerves of the heart, a development of Tsion's discovery of the accelerator nerve.

Though he now had a job that suited him, he and his wife could not afford an apartment, and while she stayed with relatives, he slept under the laboratory bench. Their first child, Mirtnik, was sickly and Serafina took him to relatives in the south. Ivan and his brother just managed to get together enough money for the fare. Unfortunately the child did not thrive and eventually died. Once, when Pavlov was utterly destitute, his students collected a fund for his everyday needs, but he spent the money on experimental animals (Cuny, 1964: 35). His second son happily survived. Notorious for the long hours he spent in the laboratory, nevertheless he disciplined himself to take proper vacations, taking up gardening with enthusiasm.

During this period his sense of his life project underwent a major change. As a youth he had been inspired by the political scientism of Pisarev, who had argued for a strict materialism, implying the dominance of physical science over all other disciplines. Pavlov had also taken up the ideas of Samuel Smiles, whose advocacy of honest work and personal industry affected him throughout his life. Now, a passion for science itself, rather than for any of its myriad consequences or its social uses, dominated his view of his own career. He returned again and again for inspiration to the writings of George Lewes, and to the essays of Claude Bernard. It seems fair to say that as Pavlov became more enthusiastic for the practice of science, he became indifferent to the political tides of the times, even to so extraordinary a series of events as the revolution of 1917.

His doctoral thesis was very well received. Not only did he win a second gold medal, but he was awarded a scholarship for study in Germany, spending the years 1884 to 1886 there. Carl Ludwig's laboratory in Leipzig was the Mecca of neurophysiologists the world over. And there he spent the major part of his two years abroad.

His maturing surgical skills enabled him to prepare experimental dogs in a remarkable way. He created fistulas (external permanent openings) to obtain samples from the salivary glands, the stomach, the liver, the pancreas and even the small intestines. This enabled him to follow the process of digestion in extraordinary detail, particularly to make exact measurements of the quantitative relationships between stimuli and gastric responses. The American army surgeon William Beaumont (1785–1853) had been able to begin serious work on the processes of digestion, through the chance of finding a servant with a fistula into the stomach, the result of a poorly healed wound.

In 1895 Pavlov's goal of a Chair in Physiology at St Petersburg was finally realized when, after various vicissitudes, he was appointed to the chair of physiology in the Military Medical Academy. Shortly afterwards he took on the direction of the physiology division of the Imperial Institute of Experimental Medicine.

His work was attracting considerable international attention. In 1904 he was awarded the Nobel Prize for his researches into the neural mechanism by which the secretion of gastric juices was stimulated. However, in his Nobel speech he devoted a good deal of space to his investigations of the conditioned (-al) reflex, which had only just begun. It was this work which was to prove so influential in psychology.

In St Petersburg, he drew around him a team of highly skilled and devoted assistants. Pavlov's bluff honesty was legendary, but so too was his willingness to acknowledge hasty judgements. The discovery of secretin by Bayliss and Starling in 1902, a chemical agent in the control of digestive secretions, threw his principle of exclusive neural control into doubt. He ordered his assistants to repeat the experiments. When they turned out to confirm the discovery, he accepted the finding, despite the complications it brought into the understanding of the nature of the system of digestive controls.

After the revolution of 1917, he gave his general but critical support to the new regime. In so far as it had emphasized the advancement of science it had his full commitment. However, he seems to have stood back from the 'social engineering' of the early Bolshevik regime that eventually went so tragically wrong. Over the years he had moved away from the dogmatic materialism of his youth, though he never ceased to be vigorously opposed to any idea of the mind as a mental substance, separate and detachable from the body.

A great many dogs were sacrificed in Pavlov's pursuit of knowledge. Strongly and publicly opposed to 'crude vivisection' of animals, he was a foremost defender of their humane use in scientific studies. He set up a memorial to his dogs on which he put the following inscription:

The dog, man's helper and friend from prehistoric times, may justly be offered as a sacrifice to science, but this should always be done without unnecessary suffering.

Thanks to a generous donation from Alfred Nobel in 1893, he was able to erect a purpose built set of laboratories in which to carry on the researches he had laboured to perform in the straitened conditions of his early years. However, as sometimes happens, despite the excellent conditions, the spark was no longer there, though his legendary industry lived on. In his later years he did not add to his scientific accomplishments in any major way. He died in 1936, still active in neurophysiological research.

What did he contribute?

As early as 1863, Ivan Sechenov had suggested that the apparent subjective worlds of animals and people alike are explicable physiologically. Pavlov came to very much the same conclusion, in his studies of what he called 'psychical excitation'. Here is an example he found particularly striking. If some pebbles are put in the mouth of a dog there is no salivation, but if the pebbles are ground up into sand, then there is a copious production of saliva. It almost seems as if the dog is assessing the situation and making a choice as to the best response. Yet, it is entirely a physiological phenomenon which takes place independently of the will or intentions of the subject. This example shows how wary we must be in attributing thought to animals in situations in which there is a neurophysiological explanation to hand.

Salivation is a natural reflex. Pavlov's great contribution was to introduce the concept of a conditional or artificial reflex, extending the domain of neurophysiology to cover non-natural responses. All organisms, including plants, respond to situations in the environment in some degree. However, those with complex nervous systems display a range of responses specific to the nature of the environmental conditions, as perceived by the animal in question. These are the natural reflexes. For example, a human being will blink when something approaches the eye. Why are these responses called 'reflexes'? The name comes from a hypothesis about the structure of the nervous system. A signal from the environment enters the nervous system along a certain pathway. This signal activates a centre in the brain from which emanates a signal to the relevant musculature, producing a movement. Thus, we have a natural or unconditional 'reflex' process in the nervous system. We now know that this picture of the nervous control of muscular movement is greatly oversimplified.

However, with higher animals and man, the nervous system is sufficiently complex to permit a range of responses to any given stimulus, and a range of stimuli will elicit any given response. What fixes these into established pairs, that we might call 'habits'? The answer is 'conditioning'.

As Pavlov notes:

the most fundamental and the most general function of the [cerebral] hemispheres is that of reacting to signals presented by innumerable stimuli of *interchangeable signification.* (Pavlov, 1927: 15, my emphasis)

This suggests the possibility of the same response to an environmental situation different from that in which it is naturally evoked. When that happens we say that the reflex is 'conditional', a direct translation of Pavlov's phrase *uslovnyi refleks*. With this phrase Pavlov marked the transition from a psychological or subjective account of behaviour, expressed in terms like 'psychic secretions', to a purely physiological account.

How is the conditioning of responses brought about? The process of conditioning a reflex is very simple. Just present the old stimulus with the new a few times, and the new stimulus will elicit the old response.

> if the intake of food by the animal takes place simultaneously with the action of a neutral stimulus which has hitherto been in no way related to food, the neutral stimulus readily acquires the property of eliciting the same reaction in the animal as would food itself. (Pavlov, 1927: 26)

There are two simple requirements for what soon came to be called a conditioned reflex to be established. The stimulus that is to become the signal in the conditioned reflex must overlap in time with the unconditioned stimulus. And 'the neutral stimulus must precede the unconditioned stimulus' (Pavlov, 1927: 27). Ringing a bell 374 times *after* food had been presented did not establish bell ringing as a conditioned stimulus. However, the sound of a metronome that was heard by a dog *at the same time* as food was presented led to a conditioned reflex. The sound of the metronome alone led to salivation and movements characteristic of dogs in the presence of food. This research links neatly on to the principles of associationism, enunciated by the British empiricists, particularly David Hume (1748). The very idea of 'causality', he had argued, was nothing but a habit of expectation, the result of the frequency with which a person had experienced a correlation between two types of events.

A conditioned reflex fades away if the response is elicited by the use of the conditioned stimulus alone. From time to time the original natural reflex must be activated. However, the phenomenon is one of inhibition rather than total extinction. One further discovery must be mentioned, the phenomenon Pavlov called 'irradiation'. In his researches using the metronome as a stimulus, he found that, at least for a while, other noises would also elicit salivation. Finally, with a view to the future of psychological research, Pavlov introduced the concept of a stereotype, a pattern of stimuli which 'evoke highly diverse conditioned and unconditioned effects. They must ... finally become systematized, equilibrated, and form, so to speak, a dynamic stereotype' (Cuny, 1964: 77).

Pavlov was well aware that the environment in which unconditioned reflexes were activated was very complex. There were a great many features which could be adopted into the system as the material of conditioned reflexes, including the footsteps of the assistants. Special equipment had to be developed to enable precise measurements to be made on one neutral stimulus at a time, while allowing access to the secretions which were the response. Pavlov had developed remarkable surgical techniques to establish fistulas to various organs in the digestive system, such as salivary ducts, isolated portions of the stomach and so on. Funnels were attached to the fistulas, to facilitate the collection and precise measurement of the quantity of the secretions elicited by this or that stimulus. He was able to investigate not only the qualitative patterns between the neutral stimulus and the conditioned response, but to gauge the strength of conditioning by measurement of the quantities of secreted fluids.

How did Pavlov come to carry out these researches? He gave a good deal of credit to the influence of Sechenov's book, much admired in his youth. However, by 1902 he seems to have decided to shift the research focus of his laboratory and the work of his assistants from the digestive tract to the nervous system, and, in particular, to the development and refinement of the study of conditional reflexes. If this was to replace the study of subjective states as the main explanatory system for human behaviour, then we are set on the road to behaviourism. The terminology changed as Pavlov's research programme became more widely known. 'Conditional' reflexes soon became 'conditioned' reflexes. The demonstration that the 'psychic secretions' could be explained purely physiologically, without any necessity to invoke mental states, intentions, judgements and so on, seemed to Pavlov to vindicate his programme for a scientific psychology, by generalizing the idea of conditioning from such matters as the secretion of gastric fluids to anything the organism might do. It is easy to see how Pavlov's discoveries tie in with the project of developmental psychology: 'Upbringing is conditioning pure and simple' (Cuny, 1964: 85).

Having turned over his laboratory to the study of those conditioned reflexes that he had identified with the illusion of cognition, of thinking and choosing, Pavlov wanted to go further. Were there other natural reflexes that could be elaborated by conditioning into something approximating human psychology? There were at least three possibilities. The first was the goal-seeking or grasping reflex. He argued that the simple motor reflex of grasping something in the hand transforms into a goal-seeking reflex, the stretching out and reaching for that which one has not yet got in one's hand. This is very like the psychic reflexes of the sight of food rather than its taste and texture in the mouth that were the earliest reflexes that informed his whole research programme. He even goes so far as to connect this reflex, through conditioning, to miserliness and greed.

The second was a reflex for liberty. He found that some of his dogs were simply untrainable unless they were free of constraints. They had a natural reflex to struggle against bonds. This too could be conditioned onto other stimuli and become part of such political activities as revolutionary fervour against oppression.

The third candidate was the unconditional or natural reflex for servility. Before **George Herbert Mead** (pp. 232–235) had taken this as the key to the maintenance of social order amongst wolves, Pavlov emphasized its importance in the life of dogs as it defused aggression between them. Living only with laboratory animals, he had not grasped the idea of animal hierarchies, but later work has shown how important submission rituals are in the lives of most animals.

Out of all of these discoveries Pavlov sketched the possibility of a psychology that both did justice to human life and also rested on a physiological foundation.

At the same time it allowed for the development of the individual human being beyond the endowments of nature by the conditioning of responses to non-natural stimuli and to the irradiation effect.

Further Reading

Primary Source

Pavlov, I. (1927) *Conditioned Reflexes: The Investigation of the Physiological Activity of the Cerebral Cortex*. London: Oxford University Press.

Secondary Source

Hume, D. (1951 [1748]) *An Enquiry Concerning Human Understanding* (Ch. 7). Oxford: Clarendon Press.

Biographies and Autobiographies

Cuny, H. (1964) *Ivan Pavlov: The Man and His Theories* (trans. P. Evans). London: Souvenir.
Gray, J. A. (1979) *Pavlov*. Brighton: Harvester.

Burrhus Frederick Skinner (1904–90)

Unlike Pavlov, who moved directly from the observation of behaviour to testable hypotheses about the workings of the nervous system and the processes mediating between environmental stimuli and conditioned responses, Skinner was a strict behaviourist. Only relations between types of stimuli and types of behaviour counted as contributions to an alleged 'scientific' psychology. He insisted that neither mental processes nor neural mechanisms ought to be adverted to in psychological explanations. Only the contingencies of the environment, past and present, should count. Unlike J. B. Watson (1925), who had banished all talk of a subjective realm of conscious experience, Skinner expanded the domain of behaviour to include private experiences, thoughts and feelings. However, the logic of conditioning applied to private 'behaviour' as much as to public behaviour. Subjective states were as much conditioned responses as were overt actions.

Who was Burrhus Frederick Skinner?

He was born on 20 March 1904 in the town of Susquehanna in northern Pennsylvania. His family was typically small town middle class. His father, William Skinner, came from a humble family, and worked his way through law school to set up a modestly prosperous practice. Relations between his parents were not idyllic. His mother seems to have somewhat condescended to her husband, and was in the habit of telling derogatory tales about him. Nevertheless, in Part II of his autobiography, Skinner paints a picture of a bountiful natural environment, counterbalancing the grubby railroad town. Young Fred went through the local school system. At the junior level the teachers managed to impart a good basic education, even though they had to teach more than one class in the same room. He describes the childhood of a somewhat awkward and naïve lad. There was little to do in Susquehanna so entertainments such as amateur theatricals flourished for a time. There are some surprises in the autobiography, particularly Skinner's interest and competence in music. He learned several instruments and played in various bands. As a youth, he was something of an autodidact. He reports feeling an intellectual gap opening up between his parents and himself, partly due to his ambitious reading. In his final year at high school his father was appointed attorney to a prominent railroad company. While the family moved to Scranton, Pennsylvania, Fred went off to Hamilton College, in Clinton, New York. He seems to have had an excellent education there, with a strong emphasis on literary studies. After his four years at college, he returned to the family home in Scranton, determined to be a writer. This was not without reason, since he had had some small successes in placing articles in various newspapers and magazines.

We can see how the life he had lived in Susquehanna could have formed a certain reforming zeal and resolve in young Skinner, perhaps scarcely consciously articulated. The town was depressing, and the relations in his family far from ideal. Around about was the idyll of nature. What stood between life as human beings were living it, and what it might become? Surely, the ingrained habits of the people. Change them, and the realization of utopia was sure.

Like **Sigmund Freud** (pp. 270–280), he developed an itch for personal fame, though in quite what capacity it would eventuate took him some time to decide. His year-long experiment as a novelist and short story writer after he left Hamilton College was not a success. Yet his autobiography reveals a sensitive and intelligent young man. It is attractively written in a clear and engaging style. There is a huge contrast between the kind of crass, simplistic psychological theories he developed and promulgated and the literary ambitions and promise of the young Hamilton graduate. How did this split come about?

Random reading took him to **Ivan Pavlov** (pp. 8–15) and J. B. Watson (1925), from whom he adopted a lifelong enthusiasm for the kind of positivistic behaviourism he made his own. Yet his autobiography discloses a mind sensitive to the nuances of literature, forever wanting to break free of these preconceptions, yet driven back by what in hindsight we can see was a distorted idea of what made an investigation scientific.

After some vicissitudes Skinner entered Harvard as a graduate student. He seems to have found some of the course work taxing, and to some of it he was markedly unsympathetic. However, he was obviously bright and enthusiastic and a fellowship allowed him to spend the next five years at Harvard experimenting on various aspects of conditioning. I think it fair to say that the work he did for his doctorate and in the years immediately following contained the essential core of his psychology, both theoretical and empirical. He came under the influence of William Crozier, an enthusiastic and proselytizing convert to hardline positivism, who eschewed any hypotheses as to the mechanisms that might be mediating environmental influences and behaviour. Persons, too, had no part to play in psychology. 'A scientific analysis of behavior', Skinner said later (1974: 203), 'must, I believe, assume that a person's behavior is controlled by his genetic and environmental history rather than by the person himself as an initiating, creative agent'. It follows that people can be controlled by controlling their environmental history.

In the early part of 1936 Skinner accepted the offer of a teaching post at the University of Minnesota. In July of the same year he met Yvonne Blue, who had majored in English at Chicago. A fairly rapid courtship followed, and, after some drama, they married and took up life in Minneapolis. Their two daughters were born there. During the Second World War, Skinner took up the idea of training pigeons to peck at a mark to guide a missile on to a target. The project was abandoned with the advent of radar, but it is said it worked.

He was convinced that this was how organisms, including human beings, learned, acted, and indeed did everything that they did. The rest of his long and active life was devoted to suggesting and sometimes trying out ways in which the idea of development as training by operant conditioning could be put to practical use. Shortly after the end of the Second World War, the Skinners moved to Bloomington, Indiana. In 1948 he returned to Harvard as a professor in the Department of Psychology. Here he had a platform from which he sought to promulgate the plans for his reforming projects. Back at Harvard, Skinner continued his experimentation with pigeons, but more and more his attention turned from the generalization of the results of these experiments to programmes for reshaping human beings towards a utopian society of his own devising.

His projects included the invention of a crib in which a baby would have the advantage of a well-planned and appropriate environment in which to develop. Though widely believed, it is not true that the crib was a version of the experimental apparatus he had used to study rats and pigeons. He did not experiment on his younger daughter along Skinnerian lines. At least, inhabiting the crib, she did not get a cold until she was six, so he says. So much the worse for the fine-tuning of her immune system!

Of greater moment was the teaching machine, which he developed during these years. The idea was to apply the principles of operant conditioning to human learning. The growth of knowledge as the result of the critical interplay between tutor and pupil in a long running conversation had no part in this scheme. Moreover, it presupposed that there was a body of knowledge conceived as a repertoire of responses to be transmitted to the learner, by whatever method was most effective. The movement for teaching machines reached the national level and even attracted grants from governmental sources. Its demise was a great blow to his ambitions.

From the days of Governor Winthrop and the Massachusetts Colony, there has been a strand of moral authoritarianism in American life. Skinner made no secret of his belief that people could be brought to act morally, as he understood it, by the widespread use of his methods. Moral struggle was to be replaced by good habits, inculcated by training. As his conviction of the rightness of his conception of psychology grew, Skinner adopted an almost messianic ambition to redesign the human world and to redeem its evils by the universal application of the techniques of operant conditioning. He expounded his moral and political views in two extraordinary works.

In 1948 he published *Walden Two*, a fictionalized account of a utopian community led by Frazier, a benevolent but authoritarian figure, whose character Skinner admitted had been modelled on himself. The members of the society were conditioned into socially admirable ways of acting, at least according to the standards of upstate, small town Pennsylvania. Much later came *Beyond Freedom and Dignity* (1971), in which he argued against the spirit of the moral revolution of the 1960s, the idea that the moral life demanded a personal choice among alternative ways of being. Instead, he offered an educational regime, based on his conception of learning by conditioning, that would result, he believed, in ingraining tendencies to 'good behaviour'. They would be unassailable, because they would not depend on the vagaries of personal reflections. However, the paradox of *Walden Two* was clear: who trains the trainers?

I think it fair to say that Skinner suffered from the blindness of enthusiasm, which so easily crosses over into arrogance. His three volumes of autobiography reveal a certain degree of self-satisfaction combined with a sort of naiveté, a wonder that a lad from Susquehanna should have uncovered the secret of human life. In generalizing from pigeons to people, he quickly ran into well-grounded opposition. His attempt to comprehend the origin and uses of language within his scheme was famously ridiculed by **Noam Chomsky** (pp. 68–77). His projects for the moral development of human kind earned him the support of a small but enthusiastic band of disciples. For most people the authoritarian regime of *Walden Two*, and the simplistic ideals of his utopia, were not only unrealistic but morally dubious as well. His project for a 'new world' not only earned him a reputation for naiveté, but the disapproval and even the hatred of many others who valued individual conscience and personal responsibility as the core of the moral life. On his last visit to Oxford, it was thought desirable to scatter some plain-clothes police amongst the audience in case he might be attacked. Fortunately nothing untoward occurred, though at other universities his reception was not so good natured.

How could Skinner have failed to be aware of the limits of his system and the crudity of his psychological concepts? Philosophical presuppositions certainly played an important part. His commitment to positivism prevented him from attending to the enormous complexity of developmental processes and patterns, while his reforming zeal blinkered him to the many alternative ways of conceiving of human development that were in play in his time. His technique of redescribing complex thought patterns in the simple catch-all terms of his theory contributed to his self-deception. His temperament was a factor too. His autobiography reveals a man virtually impervious to criticism, evident, for example, in his lack of serious response to Chomsky's lethal review of *Verbal Behavior*. It had already surfaced when as a graduate student he resisted the attempts by Edwin Boring to get him to include some hints at explanatory mechanisms in his doctoral dissertation. How did he come to this pass?

In his autobiography he acknowledges that 'from the very first, I believed in a science of behavior and in behaviorism as the philosophy of that science' (1983: 410). Everything turns on what one's philosophy allows a science to be. The crippling effect of the positivism inherent in behaviourism forced Skinner to search for his 'science' in the shallows of human life. This masked the existence of the depths all around him, exacerbated by his habit of lumping the naive with the sophisticated and calling them all by the name of the simplest item in the cluster.

His sense of the importance and significance of his work was also a factor in how closed his mind seems to have been. For example, after he had recorded the first example of a curve displaying the extinction of a conditioned response, he says that he crossed the streets with great care, so that he should not be killed in a street accident before he could tell someone of his discovery. This scientific egocentrism is evident too in the cursory references we find in his writings to Pavlov and the extensive Russian studies of the phenomena of condition(al)ed reflexes, even though Skinner knew that Pavlov was carrying on parallel investigations in what had then become Leningrad.

Skinner's later years were spent partly in travelling, when he often found himself in situations in which he had to defend the scientific status of his 'rat/pigeon to person' generalization. The moral standing of his claims for operant conditioning as a moral and political device, and radical behaviourism as a universal account sufficient to explain all of human life, were often publicly criticized. But objections from far and near seem to have had no effect whatever on his self-confidence. The key move of redescription, concealing the psychological generalization of the simplistic 'rat/pigeon to people' move, was his usual response. To take one example, if one abandons niceties, one's scientific theories are indeed 'shaped by the subject matter'. The final years of his life were devoted to completing his autobiography, in part a defence against the many objections against his work. One has to say that though he was notably candid in recording these doubts, he was singularly ineffective in rebutting them. He died on 18 August 1990.

What did he contribute?

The way that Skinner created the theoretical basis on which the whole edifice rested was, in a fundamental way, lexical. He lumped together a wide variety of very diverse psychological states, processes and so on, and labelled the totality so constructed with a simple and powerful name. For example, the activities of the experimenter were all lumped together as 'control'. Then he chose the simplest phenomenon in the group, one that displayed some aspects of the pattern of a satisfactory response. Then, he declared that this was to be the archetype for all the rest of the items in the cluster. In his case the archetype was the conditioning of rats and then, under the impetus of war, pigeons.

Boring had already spotted the weakness of Skinner's way of creating theory. He had expressed doubts in critical comments on the draft of his doctoral thesis. He noted that Skinner had given a 'very broad, strange, almost bizarre meaning to the word *reflex*' (Skinner, 1979: 73). Furthermore, Boring wanted him to discuss what intervened between stimulus and response. Skinner's response was to insist on his aim of creating 'a science of behavior'. It soon becomes evident that the constraints which his positivism forced on him as to what a science should comprehend quickly became metaphysical dogmas. The expulsion of thinking *and* physiology from his positivistic conception of the project of psychology meant that at best he would come up with a bit of natural history and at worst a pseudo-science.

Almost without exception the empirical basis of his universalistic claims was the upshot of his long-running programme of conditioning experiments. Just as Pavlov had done, he thought of development as training an animal to make the appropriate – that is, for him, the rewarding – responses to contingencies in the environment. Unlike Pavlov, who sought the physiological links that mediated behaviour, the physiological and/or cognitive mechanisms that would have raised Skinner's studies to the status of a science were not allowed to intrude, thanks to his commitment to positivism. The authoritarian programme of social amelioration and the organization of his utopia, *Walden Two*, developed directly from this way of theorizing. Here was development as conditioning applied, member by member, to a whole society.

Pavlov had studied the conditions under which a response could be conditioned on to a prior state of the environment, rich in contemporaneous possibilities. Skinner realized that the complementary question had not been answered. Under what conditions would an action from amongst a variety of possible behaviours be preferred by an animal by virtue of the consequences of that action? To investigate this he devised an apparatus that rewarded only one of the many types of action that a confined animal would 'emit'. In a way rare in psychology, Skinner's thought was driven by the apparatus he invented. The equipment he devised included a gadget that recorded the rate with which a rat responded to a stimulus. With the help of this apparatus, Skinner made the discovery that in one way or another dominated the rest of his life. A rat, and he soon generalized this to any organism, is conditioned on behaviour that operates on the environment from a range of unstructured random movements, one of which is selectively reinforced by the effects it has for the animal involved. He called this *operant conditioning*.

In classical or Pavlovian conditioning, a response is conditioned on a prior stimulus, rather than on something that happens after the stimulus. The bell rings, then the dog salivates. In operant conditioning only when the pigeon pecks the right place is it rewarded with corn. So it pecks at that spot more frequently than doing anything else that it might have done in the circumstances. That aspect of its behaviour is 'reinforced' by the reward. The second, and for him the most important discovery, was the patterns of rates of behaviours in various conditioning situations.

To understand the roots of Skinner's thinking, we need to look closely at the empirical work on which the whole edifice was based. What was in the experimental apparatus? Rats and pigeons! The 20 years that had passed between Skinner's arrival at Harvard as a graduate student and his return as a professor of psychology had been filled with animals pressing bars and pecking at targets. In a similar way the physiological psychology of Pavlov was, in effect, the psychology of dogs. There were no experiments with human subjects.

Let us now turn to examine Skinner's progress more closely. First in Minnesota and then in Indiana he expanded the research begun at Harvard. His aim was to find the conditions for the most effective methods for conditioning whatever behaviour he wanted into his animal and avian subjects. In the course of the programme he brought to light more and more of the conditions under which the most rapid and the most permanent conditioning occurred.

The key concepts in terms of which the experimental programme was conceived were an 'operant', or a spontaneously emitted behaviour, for example pecking at random, and 'shaping', the regime of rewards that led to the establishment of the 'correct' response from the original random repertoire. The overall concept that defined the relation between the experimenter and the subject was 'control'.

His research programme was directed to answering two main questions: What were the conditions under which a selected operant was most effectively reinforced? And, what were the conditions under which the established response was extinguished? These, it should be emphasized, were also Pavlov's questions. However, while Pavlov looked among the conditions prior to the response, the stimuli, Skinner looked for the conditions of conditioning among the consequences of the response that he wished to select, the reinforcers.

The experimental programme was driven by an apparatus, the Skinner box, in which a lever could be pressed to release a food pellet. A device recorded the *rate* at which an operant was 'emitted' by the animal. After some trial and error a rat would learn to press the lever more frequently than emitting any other behaviour. The rate at which one among possible operants was emitted would soon outrun the rate of less effective actions, under appropriate conditions of reinforcement. But if food was not forthcoming, the rat would press the lever more rapidly for a while, and then gradually cease to do so. This was the extinction curve that had so excited Skinner that he was determined not to die before he had passed on his discovery. He had found the behaviourist version of the old adage: If at first you do not succeed, try, try, try again. If that fails, give up.

In summing up the results of his experiments, Skinner declared that he had 'four processes – deprivation, satiation, conditioning and extinction – under some kind of experimental control' (Skinner, 1976: 95). Out of this sparse material he constructed his psychology, as he explored the many conditions, variation in which would affect the rate at which the selected operant was emitted and the rate at which the response was extinguished.

What did he add to our knowledge of the best way to train an animal, knowledge that could be put to use every day by dog handlers, horse trainers, lion tamers and so on? His experiments confirmed the commonsense belief that the consequences of an action were crucial to establishing it as a habit, for example 'praise a dog that sits on command'. His major contribution was the introduction of the measurement of rates at which habits were acquired and conditioned responses extinguished. By that means he was able to distinguish between more and less effective schedules of reinforcement.

One further and fundamental principle needs to be added to complete the story of what Skinner had now come to call 'radical behaviourism'. This was the thesis that all animal activity, human included, could be broken down into elementary units of behaviour. Boring was among the first to spot this presumption in Skinner's work, and to bring it into question, as Skinner himself reports in his autobiography. Skinner resolutely resisted the criticism, but it is, perhaps, the most fundamental mistake in the shaky underpinnings of Skinner's generalization of his point of view.

How did he move from the bar pressings of rats and the peckings of pigeons to the activities of human beings? It was not through experimentation. His method was the redescription of sophisticated human cognitive performances in terms of his stripped down and universalized categories. Mental states were without significant effect in the lives of human beings. 'States of mind may be interpreted as collateral products of the contingencies which generate behavior' (Skinner, 1976: 75). Here is just one example of many that illustrate his technique. In discussing the way a person shifts attention from one aspect of a situation to another, for example, from one instrument to another during a musical performance, he declared that certain 'mental or cognitive activities have been invented ... [to account for these phenomena] ... what is involved in attention is not a change of stimulus or of receptors but the contingencies underlying the process of discrimination ... the contingencies not the mind [or the person] make the discrimination ...' (Skinner, 1976: 116–17). We have already noted the key to Skinner's psychology in the lumping together of a great diversity of different cognitive activities and public intentional and habitual actions under a few catch-all terms, which carry with them the limiting of psychological processes to the contingencies reinforcing the emission of operants.

To give him his due, Skinner realized that the generalization of his results to the whole of the animal world, including people, required that the behaviour of the experimenter should be explicable within the same conceptual system as that of the subjects. The idea was famously ridiculed by Douglas Adams in the *Hitchhiker's Guide to the Galaxy* where it was disclosed that the white mice are experimenting on the psychologists. In the third volume of his autobiography (Skinner, 1983: 214–17) Skinner does turn to reflect on his own lifestyle from the point of view of radical behaviourism. He remarks that the quality of his lectures was under 'excellent audience control'. These remarks display the role in his methodology of renaming the commonplace: 'my lectures were appreciated so I continued to follow that same style' becomes 'my lectures were under excellent audience control'. In discussing his younger daughter's school report he translates 'lack of motivation' into 'lack of reinforcement'. Throughout his life, he was fond of pointing out that science too was a matter of the shaping of behaviour by reinforcement. If we allow enough latitude in what these words might mean, it is hard to disagree.

There is no doubt that people can be trained in the Skinnerian manner. However, the crucial issue is whether even in such cases hypothetical cognitive processes, or the neurophysiology that links stimuli and responses, can be ignored.

Further Reading

Primary Sources

Skinner, B. F. (1948) *Walden Two*. New York: Vintage Books.
Skinner, B. F. (1957) *Verbal Behaviour*. London: Methuen.
Skinner, B. F. (1971) *Beyond Freedom and Dignity*. Harmondsworth: Penguin.
Skinner, B. F. (1974) *About Behaviourism*. London: Cape.

Secondary Sources

Chomsky, N. (1959) Review of B. F. Skinner's *Verbal Behavior. Language*, **35**, 26–58.
Watson, J. B. (1925) *Behaviourism*. London: Kegan Paul.

Autobiography

Skinner, B. F. (1976–83) *Particulars of My Life (3 vols)*. New York: Knopf.

Reflections

There are deep differences between the outlooks of Pavlov and Skinner, despite their adherence to a certain methodology and use of exclusively animal models. Pavlov took for granted that a scientific psychology would encompass the generative mechanisms by means of which responses were brought about on the presentation of stimuli. As a materialist he took the second dimension to be neurophysiological. In the language of philosophy Pavlov was a *scientific realist*. Skinner, on the other hand, insisted that a scientific psychology must be confined to observable correlations between observable phenomena. He allowed personal observability as well as public observability to count. However, the second dimension of a scientific account of some domain of phenomena, the study of the generative mechanisms involved, he refused to countenance. In the language of philosophy Skinner was a *positivist*. *Positivism* lived on in academic psychology long after behaviourism had been dropped. As we shall see, the First Cognitive Revolution, initiated by Jerome Bruner and others in the mid-20th century, in rejecting behaviourism was built on the presuppositions of *scientific realism*.

2

The Developmentalists

Human beings are born in a state far from that which they will assume as adults. Babies can neither walk nor talk. Yet, after a decade or two each human being has developed a huge range of cognitive and practical skills, and for the most part has acquired a stable personality and character. What is more people are clearly differentiated into national and cultural types, through languages, cognitive and social styles, systems of belief and so on. Two major questions confront the developmentalist. How much of what a human being will become is already predetermined by virtue of inbuilt potentialities? How far and in what ways is the process of development dependent on the material and human environment of the growing child?

The 20th century saw a revival of the 17th century debate on the existence of 'innate ideas'. John Locke (1634–1704) vigorously insisted that the human mind begins as a *tabula rasa*, a clean slate on which experience inscribed the whole content of knowledge and skill. The behaviourists, most prominently B. F. Skinner, building on the researches of Ivan Pavlov, revived the idea that the mental and moral endowments of people are all acquired. In the 20th century, the new science of genetics offered a theoretical foundation for a revival of the innateness point of view. Strong claims have been made for the dominance of 'nature' over 'nurture'. Towards the end of the 20th century, more and more of those traits and skills that were once assumed to be the result of environmental influences have been claimed to be the result of the inheritance of certain clusters of genes, shaping patterns of behaviour by shaping the brain and nervous system, just as other clusters of genes shape other organs of the body.

Set obliquely to this debate, the role of the environment was seen very differently by the two leading developmentalists of the century, **Jean Piaget** (pp. 34–43) and **Lev Vygotsky** (pp. 26–34). For Piaget the material and social conditions of life impelled the developing child along a universal and predetermined sequence of stages in the course of which the cognitive skills of the mature human adult were brought to life, so to say. The sequence ran from thinking in concrete terms to the ability to handle abstract forms of thought. For Vygotsky the activity of the brain and nervous system, initially inchoate, was shaped into the patterns of mature thought by the acquisition of linguistic and practical skills appropriated from the local human environment, whatever that should happen to be.

The story of developmental psychology in the 20th century is made more complex by the influence of very different ways of regarding development, depending on how adult behaviour was to be interpreted. Should we see human behaviour as the result of active agents trying to achieve various goals according to local rules and conventions, or should we see what people do as the effects of causes? If the former, then developmentalists should be attending to how skills are acquired together with the associated bodies of knowledge. If the latter they should be attending to how children acquire a repertoire of trained responses, inculcated by processes of conditioning. As the century wore on, the 'skills' conception gradually overtook and began to overshadow the 'conditioned responses' school.

The 'learning as conditioning' school took its start from the work of the behaviourists, **Ivan Pavlov** (pp. 8–15) and **B. F. Skinner** (pp. 15–24), with his technique of 'operant conditioning'. The 'cognitive skills' school was led independently by **Lev Vygotsky** and **Jean Piaget**. Though **Jerome Bruner**'s (pp. 54–62) influence on the development of psychology in the 20th century was most marked in the advent of cognitivism, he made vital contributions to the approach pioneered by Vygotsky and Piaget.

Comparing a young child with an adult, it is clear that there are at least four domains in which a developmental transformation has come about. Manual skills are acquired and polished. Cognitive skills are gradually built up over decades. A third kind of development occurs, as human beings come to see themselves as men and women with a sense of ethnic identity. At the same time distinctive personalities and characters are established. How far are these aspects of personhood inborn and how much of them is learned?

Lev Semionovich Vygotsky (1896–1934)

Suppressed on the orders of Stalin, the work of Vygotsky was almost unknown in the West until the 1960s. Its first appearance was in the now well-known book *Thought and Language*, published in 1964. The main thesis of Vygotsky's developmental psychology was the priority of the social relations between children and their families over the progress of an isolated individual subject to instruction. The political atmosphere in the United States in the 1960s, even though the McCarthy era was past, made it difficult for psychologists in that country to take up Vygotsky's work with the enthusiasm it deserved. It can still be found under the label 'Marxist Psychology' in some contemporary encyclopaedias. Vygotsky's guiding principle, that the medium of human development was predominantly though not exclusively language, is certainly very different from the leading reductionist and materialist ideas of the Marxist-Leninism of the Stalinist era in which Vygotsky worked. The orchestrated attacks on his viewpoint, that began even before his death, turned on the clash between the official ideology, which held that material labour was the exclusive medium between man and nature, and Vygotsky's insistence that both material and verbal tools were essential to the formation of human beings in the framework of societal processes. On the other hand, it was as far as anything could be from behaviourism and the idea of development as conditioned responses to stimuli. Though Vygotsky was critical of many aspects of Piaget's work, seen from the point of view of behaviourism, the work of these two pioneers must have looked much the same.

Who was Lev Semionovich Vygotsky?

He was born on 17 November 1896, the second of eight children, in a prosperous middle class family in Orsha, a small town in Byelorussia. While he was still an infant his family moved to the larger town of Gomel, where his father had a senior position in a bank and represented an insurance agency. The town was completely destroyed in the Second World War, but a good deal of Vygotsky's early life has become known through the stories of his friend Semen Dobkin, as told to Levintin (1982). Though Lev Semionovich's mother was a trained and certified teacher, she devoted herself to the care of the family. We know from the reminiscences of Vygotsky's daughter Gita (Vygodskaya, 1995) that, according to her father, there was a vigorous intellectual conversation every day at the traditional Russian 'tea time'. Semion Vygodsky (as he spelled the name) was said to have been a man of ironic character and mordant wit. The family was sufficiently well off for young Lev to be privately educated, first by a tutor and later at a private Jewish secondary school. He seems to have owed a great deal to the tutor, Solomon Ashpiz, who developed his mind through searching conversations rather than through formal exercises. The family was Jewish, and suffered some of the restraints of the official restrictions placed on Jews in the Russia of the Tsars, and this is surely the reason why the boy did not attend the state schools. To his schoolmates at the Jewish gymnasium, he was 'the professor', though he seems to have been modest about his accomplishments.

His entrance to university was the source of a story reported by all his biographers, the lost bet. He had graduated from the gymnasium with a gold medal, and though the government restricted Jewish intake into the universities to a mere 3% it was sure that he would find a place. However, at that very moment, a new law was introduced, that Jewish students would be admitted by lot. Lev Semionovich was deeply discouraged by this news, but his friend Dobkin urged him to apply for a place nevertheless, and bet him he would win. When he did he paid the forfeit of a book of poems inscribed 'To Senya, in memory of a lost bet'.

He entered Moscow University just before the First World War, in the medical faculty. His father urged him to do this. He hoped that Lev Semionovich would enter a profession in which there was no official bar to the careers of Jews. Very soon he transferred to the Faculty of Law, a profession also open to Jews. The study of human beings talking and writing was evidently beginning to dominate his interests. While at school he had been very much involved in literary studies and in the theatre. The man's prodigious energy became apparent when he enrolled at another university, the unofficial but influential Shanyavskii People's University, to study these subjects too, as well as psychology and philosophy. He graduated in

1917, an ominous year in Russian history. The war with Germany had reached a disastrous end. The Russian state itself had collapsed with the revolution that began in St Petersburg. Finally, after a bitter civil war, the Bolsheviks came to power.

Lev Semionovich returned that year to Gomel, though the town was still under German occupation. The revolution had brought the anti-Jewish laws to an abrupt end, so a teaching post was now open to him. Altogether he spent seven years there as a teacher. Among his courses were psychology in the Teacher's Training College, literature in a high school, and history of art at the Conservatory. Even at this time, he displayed extraordinary energy. As well as his teaching, he took a great interest in adult education, and even founded a publishing company for producing cheap editions of the classics. The setting up of a psychology laboratory in the local Teacher's Training College furthered his interest in experimental psychology. At the same time he read widely, including poetry, fiction and psychology. Sometime in the latter part of his time in Gomel, the idea that there could be a new psychology that would transform the human race came to him. Just what that would consist of was still not clear, but it would be a psychology that centred around historical change and the centrality of language as a major instrument in the life of human beings.

The conditions of daily life in Gomel were appalling, with shortages of almost every necessity of life. Vygotsky's mother and sister both contracted tuberculosis and very soon Lev Semionovich too had fallen victim. He was never to be cured, though he spent only short periods in a sanatorium. Just before he returned to Moscow he married Roza Smekhova, who long outlived him. Their two daughters were born in Moscow.

In January 1924 Vygotsky went to Leningrad to attend the Psychoneurological Congress. His talk was a huge success, and on the strength of it he was invited to join the Psychological Institute in Moscow. He seems to have had an extraordinary effect on those around him, not only on audiences at his lectures but on individuals. Shortly after he came to Moscow he met **Alexander Romanovich Luria** (pp. 105–113), whose life and work we will encounter in the section on neuropsychology, and Alexei Nikolievich Leont'ev, the founder in later years of activity psychology. It was some time before these friendships matured into their famous collaborations. Luria's attachment to Freudian ideas was not congenial to Vygotsky, while Leont'ev remained uncommitted to Vygotsky's language oriented theoretical basis of the cultural/historical/instrumental version of the genetic/developmental point of view.

This was a period of lively optimism in the whole Soviet Union, in provincial towns like Gomel as much as in the great centres of Moscow and Leningrad. With Vygotsky's arrival in Moscow a group of colleagues and students coalesced around him. Their passionately pursed aim was the reconstruction of psychology on quite new lines. The key ideas had some antecedents in the West, for example in the writings of William James, but they took a form that owed a great deal to Vygotsky himself. The principles of the cultural/historical/instrumental method are simple to state but profound in their consequences.

The first idea was that the social life of human beings was the source of their individual psychological traits and capacities. This entailed a respect for different ethnicities, as the sources for different psychologies, though it did not preclude judgements as to their value in the scales of human development. The second idea seemed to lead away from the individual as the locus of psychological reality to the history of languages, cultures, material practices and so on that went into the formation of individual minds. However, it was the individual human being who was shaped by the confluence of natural maturation and the acquisition of language and other symbolic tools. The third idea was that human beings acquired a repertoire of skills, including linguistics capacities, which should be looked on as instruments in the creation and management of life. Research methodology must conform to these principles if it was to be capable of revealing psychological phenomena in all their depth. This was the cultural/historical/instrumental method.

Throughout his life, Vygotsky was interested in the problems created by human defects, crippling damage to the body as well as mental retardation. In Russia, the catch-all term 'defectology' was used for the study of the whole gamut of functional abnormalities. In the 1920s, he set up a Laboratory for the Psychology of Abnormal Childhood, which, after his death, became the Institute for Defectology. In addition to his regular lecturing he acted as director of a department for retarded children. Not only that, but he set about getting a training in medicine. This led to his final post, as Director of the USSR Institute of Experimental Medicine, though this post was just one among many places in which he laboured.

This was a man of amazing energy. His schedule involved several simultaneous careers, as teacher, researcher, and medical student. In addition he gave courses not only in Moscow, but also in other, far-flung parts of the Soviet Union, such as Uzbekistan, where he helped to found a Psychology Institute. However, his most important project was the creation of a new centre for psychology in Khar'kov in the Ukraine. Luria and Leont'ev moved there permanently while Vygotsky paid regular visits.

Throughout these years, until his death from tuberculosis in 1934, he conducted a vigorous research programme. He and his friends Alexander Luria and Alexei Leont'ev would meet every week in Vygotsky's apartment to plan out the research projects for the week ahead. He still managed to find the time to write reviews and papers by working into the small hours of the night, when he would not be interrupted. The living conditions for everyone in those years were miserable. The family occupied a one room apartment in a crowded block, hardly the conditions for a flourishing intellectual life, nor a suitable environment for someone suffering from tuberculosis. There can surely be no doubt that the frenetic pace of his life was a response to his realization that tuberculosis was sure to claim his life very soon, and yet, at the same time, his response to this intuition was hastening the end. After a serious haemorrhage, he entered the Serebryani sanatorium on 2 June 1934, and died a few days later. The many personal reminiscences that have survived picture a man of immense enthusiasm, passionately devoted to the idea of a new psychology as the source of a new humanity, stern in its defence, and yet always ready to take time to befriend and encourage those around him.

As S. E. Toulmin rightly said: 'Vygotsky was the Mozart of psychology.'

What did he contribute?

Vygotsky's emphasis on the phenomena of consciousness as the domain of psychology ought not to be interpreted as a return to Cartesianism. On the contrary, in accordance with the dictum of his favourite philosopher Spinoza, Vygotsky argued that 'the mental does not have an independent existence. According to Spinoza's definition thinking is not a substance, but an attribute' (quoted in Wertsch, 1985: 201). In particular, thinking is a form of action, but the tools are symbols.

The success of 19th century German experimental psychology in linking neurological stimuli with subjective states was bought, as Vygotsky emphasized, at the cost of deleting higher order cognitive functions from the research agenda. For example, in studying remembering as Ebbinghaus had done, by using the recall of nonsense syllables, the social/practical uses of the remembering function were simply excised. The German reaction to this was to turn to the phenomenology of subjective experiences. Vygotsky's goal was to study the higher order cognitive functions scientifically, that is objectively, in the sense of using public, interpersonal material as the foundations of research, rather than reports of introspection.

The sources of higher order cognitive processes like remembering, reasoning, classifying and so on were social, not psychic. He was hostile to Freud's assumption of a realm of unconscious mental activity invoked to explain behaviour. With his friend Luria, he emphasized the coordination of seemingly distinct functions into an integrated whole. Later, towards the end of his life, his medical studies were in part directed to the problem of understanding the disintegration and restoration, not only of distinct cognitive functions, but of the integration of the whole. This allied him, at least in part, to the Gestalt school of psychology, and in particular the work of **Wolfgang Köhler** (pp. 136–142).

To put Vygotsky's point of view at its simplest, language is the mediating tool of all higher order cognitive functions, and it is in the conversations in the family circle and amongst one's peers that psychological development occurs. In the family, the child is in intimate contact with the culture in which he or she will eventually find a place as a competent and respected member. The key to Vygotsky's psychology is the idea of a kind of psychological symbiosis. Let us imagine a situation in which a child is confronted by a task which is beyond its capabilities. It tries to perform the task but fails. Close by is someone else, more able. The second person, realizing what the child is trying to do, or perhaps even providing the child's uncertain aims with a more fully formed intention, fills in the missing moves needed to complete the task successfully. The child copies the supplementary moves next time it is confronted with a similar task. At the beginning of this process, the task and the child's capabilities are in the 'zone of proximal development'. The other person might be an adult, but it could be another child. Sometimes the complementation is mutual, as in Vygotsky's marvellous description of the way two sisters developed the sense of sisterhood by playing at 'sisters'. Sometimes there is a hierarchy of capabilities.

He expressed the basic developmental principle in a famous dictum:

Every function in the child's cultural development appears twice: first, on the social level, and later, on the individual level; first between people (interpsychological) and then inside the child (intrapsychological). This applies equally to voluntary attention, to logical memory, and to the formation of concepts. All the higher functions originate as actual relationships between individuals. (Vygotsky, 1978: 57)

What are these relationships? They are, no doubt, cases of psychological symbiosis, joint management of tasks in the zone of proximal development. It is important to realize that Vygotsky made no sharp division between material or physical tasks and intellectual ones. Material and symbolic tools had an essential part to play in both.

However, Vygotsky laid great emphasis on the role of language, not just as an attribute of individuals, but as the medium of interpersonal conversations. In these conversations, cognitive problems are solved and cognitive tasks performed. Appropriating the means, the individual becomes a competent individual performer. Is thought nothing but public and private speech? No – the biological individual is mentally active from birth and before, but not in a coherent and culturally recognizable way. Language and thought are two streams, the one social and the other individual, which flow together in the higher cognitive functions, such as reasoning, deciding and remembering (Vygotsky, 1962). Vygotsky introduced the idea of the acquisition not only of material tools but of cognitive tools, symbolic systems of which the most important was language.

Jean Piaget (pp. 34–43) had noticed that children at about the age of three display a marked 'egocentricity' in their speech. According to him, children speak only about themselves. They are not interested in whether others listen. Vygotsky's studies of speech in the zone of proximal development of higher cognitive functions showed that this interpretation was wide of the mark. Egocentric speech is the beginning of the differentiation of speech functions, into the public and the private. Egocentric speech becomes inner speech, and in the process displays the overriding character of inner speech, namely abbreviation. In its earliest manifestations egocentric speech is a device by which a child regulates and manages its actions. It is not talking of itself, but to itself, issuing instructions for example. Egocentric speech goes underground to become inner speech. It brings with it the activity managing function of 'egocentric' speech.

There is a direct link here to pedagogy. Interpsychological functioning must be so structured as to enhance the development of intrapsychological functioning. 'Instruction in the zone of proximal development "calls to life in the child, awakens and puts in motion an entire series of internal processes of development"' (Wertsch, 1985: 71).

There is also a link to the development of adult capacities in the course of introducing formal schooling to places where it had not previously existed. This also interested Vygotsky. With Alexander Luria he conducted a series of studies in central Asia, comparing the proficiency of literate people in cognitive tasks, such as syllogistic reasoning and classifying, with the performance of illiterates. The superior performance of literates showed, Vygotsky and Luria concluded, that they have 'decontextualized' the means of cognitive mediation, and are able to use language in a way which is independent of immediate contexts of use. The results of these studies were not published until long afterwards. The fact that it had emerged that the most politically active Uzbeks were not proficient in abstract thought was enough to ensure the postponement of publication and ultimately the suppression of the work.

How does Vygotsky's psychology differ from Pavlov's? Both emphasize the social role of signals. However, as we have seen, the conditioning of Pavlov's dogs depended on the maintenance of natural signals. Even when a conditioned response to something quite other than the natural stimulus had been established, the conditioning faded unless the natural response was re-activated. Vygotsky emphasized the importance of artificial signals, as the basis of human language, a feature which differentiated it sharply from anything in the animal world. It tied language to culture, a human construction. Once established it was stable, a permanent feature of the person, unless it was overridden by another phase of 'psychological symbiosis'. The defects that arose from damage to the brain would seriously impair the use of the symbolic system to manage a person's affairs.

So far we have touched on *appropriation* of higher cognitive processes from the cultural store, and the *mediation* of cognitive and material processes by symbolic tools, the 'instrumental aspect' making abstract and decontexualized thought possible. However there is a third aspect of Vygotsky's general position of even greater importance in relation to a possible science of psychology. This is the idea of *genetic development*. It is quite unlike the principles which we will encounter in the developmental psychology of **Jean Piaget** and at odds with the basic principles of **Ivan Pavlov** (pp. 8–15) and **B. F. Skinner** (pp. 15–24). For Vygotsky there is no one common process that is active at all stages of development, nor is there one explanatory principle that accounts for qualitative changes in consciousness and cognitive and practical skills during the maturation of a human being. Neither Piaget's repeated transformations of cognitive level by accommodation and assimilation, nor Skinner's repeated doses of operant conditioning, is adequate to account for the genesis of the fully human individual. At each moment in the development of a human being different principles and processes come into prominence. This is the 'historical' component in his threefold specification of psychology as a cultural/historical/instrumental discipline.

Vygotsky was in active intellectual contact with his European contemporaries. His critical essays pointing to the a priori elements in the 'personalism' of William Stern, to which he was generally sympathetic, and his strictures on the repetition of the steps up the one-way 'ladder' principle of Piaget still make excellent reading (Vygotsky, 1978). He was acquainted with Kurt Lewin, and the Gestalt psychologists, particularly Koffka, who took part in Luria's Vygotsky-inspired second expedition to central Asia to study the cognitive skills and modes of reasoning of people of different cultures and of little or no formal schooling.

The long running debate about what sort of data is required by psychology also drew his attention. He placed great emphasis on careful description, on qualitative data, warning against the fallacy of partitioning psychological phenomena into units which no longer had the meaning of the wholes from which they were dissected. It is fair to say that this warning has fallen on deaf ears among many 'mainstream' psychologists, intent on relating dependent and independent variables.

His attitude to literature is also worth remarking on. Acknowledging the depth of understanding of human beings attained by the great novelists and playwrights, he drew on literary material to enhance and enrich his psychological studies. In his discussion of the role of linguistic symbols in thinking he cites the famous passage from *Anna Karenina* (Tolstoy, 1878 [1992]) in which Kitty and Levin carry on a conversation in which their mutual love is disclosed and cemented by means of the initial letters of words alone. A little later in the same chapter he cites Dostoevsky's description of a conversation between six drunken workmen, in which only one vocable, the Russian equivalent of the well know universal English four-letter word, is used to carry on a complex conversational interchange. As Wittgenstein was later to declare, 'meaning is use' (Vygotsky, 1962: 140–4). Vygotsky's study of Shakespeare's *Hamlet,* the topic of his diploma dissertation, is still highly regarded in Russia as literary criticism. He continued throughout his life to be interested in the psychology of art, and published a full scale study of the topic.

It is clear that mainstream psychology as it has been practised in the United States has not yet assimilated the Vygotskian revolution, despite the slow spread of Vygotskian ideas in the various new paradigm movements of the last quarter of the 20th century. Social worlds are still presumed to be the joint products of individual actors, complex interactive patterns of psychological phenomena are mercilessly dissected and pressed onto the Procrustean bed of dependent and independent variables. Language still languishes on the periphery even of much that is presented as 'cognitive science'. One of the main points of *Thought and Language* is the criticism of analysis by decomposition: 'since it results in products that have lost the characteristics of the whole, this process is not a form of analysis in the true sense of the word' (Vygotsky, 1962: 45). We must carry our analysis through just as far as it results in a 'product that possesses all the basic characteristics of the whole' (Vygotsky, 1962: 46).

Further Readings

Primary Sources

Vygotsky, L. S. (1962) *Thought and Language* (trans. E. Hanfmann and G. Vakar). Cambridge, MA: MIT Press.
Vygotsky, L. S. (1978) *Mind in Society* (ed. M. Cole). Cambridge, MA: Harvard University Press.

Secondary Sources

Tolstoy, L. (1878) [1992] *Anna Karenina*. London: Donald Campbell.
Van der Veer, R. & Valsiner, J. (1991) *Understanding Vygotsky*. Oxford: Blackwell.
Vygodskaya, G. L. (1995) Remembering Father. *Educational Psychologist*, **30** (1), 57–59.

Biography

Wertsch, J. V. (1985) *Vygotsky and the Social Formation of Mind*. Cambridge, MA: Harvard University Press.

Jean Piaget (1896–1980)

The writings of Jean Piaget, extending over decades, present a complex amalgam of philosophy of science, massive observational studies of children at work and at play, and a subtle predilection for the skills and mores of the upper classes of the Europe he knew. His influence on Western thought in the 20th century was initially contested. Eventually it became a major influence on generations of psychologists. Educational practice was strongly influenced, at least for a while, by his basic thesis that cognitive development proceded along an ineluctable sequence of stages. Studies of moral development, using the idea of stages, were the work of *Lawrence Kohlberg*, his most influential follower. Piaget's emphasis on cognition and the cognitively oriented researches that he undertook stood in sharp contrast to the behaviourism of the United States with its roots in the idea of the conditioned reflex and the radical behaviourism of **B. F. Skinner** (pp. 15–24).

Who was Jean Piaget?

He was born near Lake Neuchatel in the French-speaking region of Switzerland on 9 August 1896, the eldest child in the family. His family background was pro-fessional middle class, like that of many of our cast of characters. His father, Arthur Piaget, was a university professor in a provincial town. Piaget père was painstaking and meticulous in his attitude to work. His penchant for detail seems to have been picked up by his son. There was evidently some tension between the parents, at least as seen by young Jean. He describes his mother, Rebecca Jackson, as 'very intelligent, energetic and fundamentally a very kind person ... [but] her rather neurotic temperament ... made family life somewhat troublesome' (Evans, 1973: 108). It is very clear that he allied himself with his father. He even goes so far as to declare that 'his mother's poor mental health' led him to take a (tempo-rary) interest in psychiatry, but he preferred the study of normality. His mother was strictly religious, but by encouraging him to attend religious instruction she managed to turn him against it.

While still a child, he took a great interest in biology. This developed into a long running series of researches into the classification of molluscs and their evolutionary connections. He was encouraged by the curator of the Neuchatel Museé d'Histoire. While still at high school he began publishing on the subject of molluscs. So mature was his biological work that some of his correspondents presumed him to be an adult. He was even offered a professional curatorship of a mollusc collection while he was still a schoolboy. Despite these successes, he seems to have suffered some kind of breakdown at the end of his school days, and spent a year recuperating in the mountains.

From this precocious childhood he brought into adult life a respect for science as a protection against the 'demon of philosophy', which he took to be the temptation to engage in ungrounded speculation. The gap left by his disenchantment with religious doctrine was more than made up by the biologically oriented philosophy of Henri Bergson, to which he was introduced by his godfather. About this time he experienced the first of the epiphanies that shaped his life. He decided that his life work should be the search for a 'biological explanation of knowledge'.

Entering the local university, he continued his studies in biology, and completed a doctorate on molluscs in 1918. He had already begun to reflect on general philosophical topics. Generalizing the biological point of view, he formulated a principle that dominated the rest of his life work: that there are emergent totalities that impose their form on their parts. The *structuralist* doctrine of emergent forms is hardly original, but it served him as a lifelong guide.

Almost immediately he began to interest himself in psychology. He worked for a while in Eugen Bleuler's clinic in Zurich. He tried psychoanalysis, but soon abandoned that for a wide variety of studies in Paris. Here he was the beneficiary of the first of a series of career preferments brought about by the patronage of influential people, in this case the Simon of the Simon-Binet test. Simon wanted to continue the work of the late Alfred Binet in psychological testing. Young Piaget was offered the job of developing a French version of the English tests, devised by the later controversial Sir Cyril Burtt, in Binet's school/laboratory. However, he soon turned from merely collecting children's answers to the prescribed test questions to discussing with them their reasons for what they had written or said. This was the second epiphany that shaped his life (Evans, 1973: 118). From then on he developed his ideas about how children reasoned by talking to them and following their thoughts in both natural and contrived situations. The focus on children's cognition was not the result of an interest in pedagogy or even developmental psychology as such. It was part of a much larger project: the project of *genetic epistemology*. How did knowledge grow?

As a young man, he read widely among philosophers and psychologists, yet we do not find Pierre Duhem in his professed catalogue of authors. Duhem's historical philosophy of science exactly matches Piaget's genetic epistemology. A physicist and philosopher of great eminence, Duhem is still known for his famous distinction between deep and narrow minds, typical of French scientists, who can handle abstract forms of thought, and broad and shallow minds, typical of English scientists, who can think only with the help of concrete imagery. Piaget's 'stages' seem to be an echo of this distinction.

The idea that children's cognition was everywhere more or less the same came to him through noticing that the French children in Binet's tests seemed to involve ways of thinking that were very similar to those of Francophone Swiss children of the same age.

In 1921 he returned to Switzerland to the Institut Rousseau, again as the result of patronage, a job arranged for him by Édourd Claparède (1873–1940). There he began systematic studies of the reasoning powers of schoolchildren, with the first of a flood of talented and enthusiastic assistants. His publication of book-length studies of the development of knowledge caused a furore, especially in the United States, where the behaviourist conception of development as training, mediated by the mechanisms of conditioning, was deeply entrenched. Throughout his life Piaget was unrattled by criticism, simply going on to pile up the empirical evidence for his conception of genetic epistemology. While at times this approach stood him in good stead, later in his career it militated against his willingness to repair errors and eliminate mistakes.

He married one of his students, Valentine Châtenay, in 1923. Their three children became the focus for an intensive study, the results of which also appeared in book-length monographs.

During the rest of his career he moved from one important job to another, becoming more and more involved in the public uses of psychology. He was successively Director of the International Bureau of Education, Director of the Psychology Laboratory at Geneva, and eventually a professor at the Sorbonne. During the latter part of his active institutional life he set up the International Centre for Genetic Epistemology. It is noteworthy that these shifts of venue had little obvious influence on his single-minded pursuit of his life project, the unravelling of the processes and stages of the genesis of knowledge.

His retirement from official duties meant no great change in his work, though he turned more and more to developing the general theory of structures. He died in Geneva on 16 September 1980.

What did Piaget contribute?

Piaget became fascinated by the way children at various ages actually thought. One of his major innovations, the 'Piagetian method' one might say, involved conversing with children to elicit childish ways of explaining and interpreting what they saw around them. Respecting children's thought styles rather than correcting their 'errors', errors only in relation to adult thought forms, opened up the possibility of tracking a schedule of developmental stages. Though he often used the word to describe his researches, Piaget did not conduct 'experiments' in the usual sense. The idea of demarcating complex behaviour and the environments in which it occurred into dependent and independent variables played no part in his empirical studies. His 'experiments' involved devising situations in which children were called upon to think, and talking to them about their cognitive activities.

To understand his project it is important to realize that Piaget was first and foremost a biologist, and thought like a biologist. If there was development, then there must be stages which are transcended sequentially. He followed the famous biological dictum that ontogeny recapitulates phylogeny; the development of the individual follows the same schedule as the evolutionary development of the species, in this case the culture itself, and specifically the development of the sciences. It is important to realize too that Piaget was a philosopher almost as much as he was a biologist, despite his protestations against the lure of philosophy. His project was to try to track and understand the development of knowledge. One of his best-known books has the revealing title *Behaviour and Evolution*. This does not herald a reduction of culture to biology, but the use of a common explanatory scheme to understand both the evolution of organisms and the growth of scientific knowledge. In psychology it appears as *genetic epistemology*, Piaget's term for his lifelong project.

'Genetic epistemology', he says (Evans, 1973: xlii), 'deals with the formation and meaning of knowledge and with the means by which the human mind goes from a lower level of knowledge to one that is judged to be higher.' The making of this judgement, he insists, is not the business of psychologists. Here, perhaps, we can see the unacknowledged influence of Duhem, for whom abstract thought is always 'higher' than concrete thought.

The second fundamental principle underlying the whole Piagetian project is 'structuralism'. 'In all fields of life (organic, mental, social) there exist "totalities" [structures] qualitatively distinct from their parts and imposing on them an organization' (Evans, 1973: 114). There is a general principle of equilibrium, according to which 'there is a reciprocal preservation of the parts and of the whole' (Evans, 1973: 114). He tells us that he came to his structuralist ideas before he took an interest in psychology. For example, he did not know then of the Gestaltists, Max Wertheimer and **Wolfgang Köhler** (pp. 136–142).

Asked to describe Piaget's contributions to developmental psychology, three main principles and leading concepts would no doubt be mentioned by most psychologists: development by stages, the processes of assimilation and accommodation and egocentrism. In a way, all three depend on two deep ideas. The first of these root ideas is the biological principle that understanding the way a being evolves is essential to truly understanding it. The second is the principle that children are actively exploring the environment, much as scientists do. They can be thought of metaphorically as making experiments and trying to understand the results. Both these ideas run contrary to those of **B. F. Skinner** (pp. 15–24), whose exemplary organisms are trained but do not evolve on their own initiative.

The key to displaying the nature of thought at each stage is the structuralist principle of invariance under a transformation. This principle appears first in the infant's gradual grasp of the idea that an object can exist unseen, 'object constancy'. It appears later as the gradual realization by the five-year-old that quantity of sub-stance is invariant under transformation of shape, 'conservation'.

The first idea of consequence for developmentalists would surely be the theory that there are *stages of cognitive development*. Each individual must pass through them in a certain order, the earlier stages being necessary conditions for reaching the later. First comes the sensori-motor stage, in which rudimentary manipulative skills become coordinated into complex capacities. According to Piaget, children from birth to about two years of age do not form mental or symbolic representations of objects. 'Experiments' on object constancy seemed to show that infants are unable to conceive of an object continuing to exist when it is out of sight. Much of Piaget's observations of the sensori-motor stage have been verified by other investigators, such as **Jerome Bruner** (pp. 54–62), but in ways that throw doubt on Piaget's principle that abstract cognition is not found among the very young. There is logic displayed by the child, but it is realized in actions, not in thoughts.

The next or pre-operational stage is marked by the way a child can think about something that is not currently in view, implying the development of a capacity for mental representation, and the beginnings of the acquisition of language as a system of symbols. The key addition at this stage is the 'semiotic function', by which language and other forms of representation make possible another level of intelligence. However, Piaget declared that this capacity involves a concrete image. He claimed that children in this stage are incapable of abstract, logical thought. Furthermore, he saw them as egocentric, seeing and understanding everything each from his or her own point of view.

The third stage is the concrete operational step, at which the child makes use of whatever is present concretely in the here and now in dealing with situations and problems, but with attention to the point of view of others. At this stage, chil-dren have mastered the concept of conservation. A material substance, such as a certain quantity of water, remains the same throughout various manipulations. At this stage, reasoning is carried on with the use of concrete rather than abstract symbols. At the final or formal operational stage, abstractions and formal schemata are used in the management of situations and the solving of problems. In short, abstract logic is the highest form of cognition (Gruber & Vonèche, 1977).

Piaget's conception of the process of cognitive maturation is equally well known. He thought that new skills were acquired in two steps, involving the twin processes of *assimilation* and *accommodation*, through which new experience comes to be incorporated as a permanent feature of the resources of the developing human being. In the process of *assimilation*, information presented to or picked up by the child is transformed to fit the pre-existing schemata with which he or she thinks about and acts in the world. This eventually leads to trouble. *Accommodation* is the process by which pre-existing schemata are modified to fit new experiences. The passage through the Piagetian stages is driven by the way that assimilation of new experience gives way to accommodation as the cognitive schemata are transformed to manage it successfully. This is the universal schedule of cognitive development, the Piagetian ladder.

The third widely known Piagetian thesis would no doubt be *egocentrism*. Young children, he claimed, cannot take the point of view of another person, but each sees the world only from its own point of view. This is characteristic, so Piaget claims, of children at the pre-operational stage. He thought that egocentrism was displayed both in the way two- and three-year-olds seem to talk to themselves, and in such seeming incapacities as to be able to appreciate the relativity of spatial perspective to the location of the observer.

Despite the empirical evidence that Piaget claimed to have accumulated to support these leading ideas, each has been subject to criticism. Doubt has been cast on the methods he employed in his experimental and observational work. Dubious presuppositions have been identified in the theoretical foundations of his research programme. It is sometimes said that fortune favours the prepared mind, but in Piaget's case the aphorism should be reversed. Piaget seems to have 'seen' stages in somewhat the same way as Percival Lowell 'saw' canals on Mars. Among many research reports that upset Piaget's stages we will concentrate on only two: his claims about the age/stage before which logical reasoning becomes possible, and his claims about the egocentricity of perspective taking, as in the 'three mountains test'.

The 'stages' principle, the trademark Piagetian idea, has been criticized from several points of view. I have already pointed out how closely Piaget's views tracked those of the philosopher Pierre Duhem. According to Duhem, the ultimate goal of the physical sciences was an abstract representation of the world and its constituent processes. Couple this with attitudes of the French-speaking upper middle class from which Piaget and his childish subjects came both in Paris and Geneva, and we can see how he might have taken for granted that a capacity for abstract thought was a higher as well as a later stage of cognition. Duhem's 'formalism' has been vigorously disputed by philosophers of science, on the grounds that the aim of science is to produce a working model of reality, a concrete representation of the material world. Mathematical descriptions of such models are a convenience but by no means a substitute for concrete modelling.

In a masterly summary of the evidence, Margaret Donaldson (Donaldson, Grieve & Pratt, 1983: Ch. 18) not only offers convincing examples of children under the age of six or seven reasoning deductively, but draws on Simon Hewson's insightful analysis of the source of Piaget's mistake. Here is a conversation with a five-year-old, shortly after the death of Donald Campbell in a boating accident and the visit to the school of Robin Campbell.

Child:	'Is that Mr Campbell who came here – *dead*?'
Teacher:	'No, I'm quite sure he isn't dead.'
Child:	'Well, there must be two Mr Campbells then, because Mr Campbell's dead under water.'

In a close analysis of several experiments that seem to support staging, Hewson showed that the difficulty is not in the inferential process, but in ambiguities in the procedures that are involved in the task. Bryant (1984) has demonstrated that, left to themselves, very young children can conduct measurement comparisons using an intervening standard perfectly competently. Again, his studies bear out Hewson's analysis. Piaget's conclusions are clearly in need of refinement.

The issue of the interpretation of the apparent 'egocentricity' of very young children was already opened up by **Lev Vygotsky** (pp. 26–34). It turns out there is something seriously wrong with the famous 'three mountains test', an experiment to test the thesis of egocentricity in perspective taking. Piaget's interpretations of the various 'experiments' he devised to test the principle of conservation or invariance of quantity through transformation of shape or arrangement have also been called in to question. Studies of invariance under transformation, the most basic principle of structuralism, were of great importance for Piaget, since each is a marker for a stage in his ladder of cognitive development.

Turning now to the 'three mountains test': a child is asked to look at a model of three mountains set in the middle of a table, the highest in the centre back, the next highest to the right and the lowest on the left. The mountains are differently coloured and each has a different object on the summit. After being given time to scrutinize the set-up, the young participant is asked to demonstrate with cut-outs how the scene would look to someone on the other three sides of the table. In the pre-operational stage children simply reproduce their own view, just as the scene looks from where the child itself is sitting. At a later age, a child will give the answer that an adult would judge to be correct. Piaget took this to be a clear indication of egocentrism, the child able to see the world only from its own point of view. A faceless doll was added to simulate another person.

Margaret Donaldson replicated the experimental task but in a quite different way (Donaldson, 1983: 246–50). Two toys, a policeman and a boy, were placed on a table, with a movable wall. The child was asked to place the wall so that the policeman could not see the boy, who wished to hide. Whether the policeman was on the same side of the table as the child, or on the opposite side, or on the ends, three- and four-year-olds all placed the wall in the line of sight of the policeman. In a second experiment, there were two policemen and a cross-shaped set of walls. Now the child had to hide the boy from both policemen, involving taking the perspectives of two other people. Even with a group that included three-year-olds, the majority of the children got the right answer. As Margaret Donaldson remarks, the results show that even three-year-olds are capable of well-coordinated, decentred thinking. It seems clear that in Piaget's experiment the child had not been presented with a clear enough question to give an adequate answer.

Further to the question of the reality of egocentrism, Vygotsky made a detailed record of the talk with which young children accompanied their activities. Sure enough, a great deal was in the first person. However, Vygotsky went on to consider the purpose of this talk, and to look at its role in the activities of the child. For the most part the use of the first person expressed an act of self-instruction, rather than an act of self-attention. It was not indicative of a self-contained world at all. This interpretation has been supported by other studies.

According to Piaget, an important marker of cognitive maturation is the ability to judge correctly whether something has survived unchanged in quantity through a sequence of operations. Here is a famous experiment: some water in a broad shallow glass is poured into a tall narrow glass. Is the quantity of water still the same in the second glass? Very young children tend to say that there is more water in the tall and narrow glass, despite having seen it being poured in from the short and shallow glass. Similarly, children shown some dots spread out in a line and the same number of dots tightly packed together tend to say that there are more dots in the first case. If one of two identical balls of clay is squeezed into a sausage shape, is there the same amount of clay in the two lumps? Very young children tend to say that there is not. These famous demonstrations seem to support Piaget's claim – but do they?

Critics, such as Peter Bryant (1984), have deconstructed the experiments in such a way as to bring out the way that in each case two quantitative rules are in conflict. The child has to choose between them. If the child is presented with a problem expressed in terms of one or other of the rules of quantity, 'greater length is more' and 'greater volume is more', it gets the correct answer. However, presented with a problem that seems to demand both rules, children are stumped. It is not that they do not understand about the conservation of amounts of water, but they are faced with two rules for judging quantity. Experience enables them to prioritize one over the other. Length measures give way to volume measures, though most of the time the length measure works well. More milk in my glass is proved by a rise in the height of surface of the liquid.

How was it possible for Piaget to miss such critical possibilities? Despite there being no explicit mention of Duhem's philosophy of science in his writings, Duhemist ideas seem to have dominated Piaget's thinking about cognition. If individual human development mirrored the history of science, then the 'child as scientist' must follow the same steps, from concrete to abstract representations – at least that was Duhem's ladder of history. In a way the ordering of the stages of Piaget's ladder was not determined by observation, but by a philosophical and cultural presumption.

Looking at the reports of his empirical studies, extensively reproduced in Gruber and Vonèche (1977), it becomes very clear that he did not realize the extent to which 'facts' are generated relationally. Much of his material comes from the answers children gave to his and his colleagues' questions. Despite the fact that he respected their answers, he seems not to have taken sufficient account of the contextual determination of the meaning of his questions. Unlike Vygotsky, he did not adopt the stance of the 'fly on the wall', and so he failed to record the independent cognitive activities of children. For example, young children do not think that rules are sacrosanct in all circumstances, as he claimed. Studies that have followed how children actually use rules and when they are willing to transform them have shown a remarkable subtlety. The children who answer 'No' to the question as to whether the rules of a game can be changed are expressing the adult principle that adopting or following different rules constitutes a different game (Linaza, 1984).

The influence of a truly social dimension to development, and even to adult cognition, seems to have been hard for Piaget to hold on to. His focus is always on the cognitive functioning of the individual child, even to the extent of misinterpreting the meaning of the use of the first person. In commenting on Mead's conception of the 'I' and the 'me', he seems to miss the Vygtoskian point entirely. He says that prior construction of the self, the self-aware, centred organization of thought, 'it is not there' (Evans, 1973: 19–20). But where is 'there'? The point common to **G. H. Mead** (pp. 232–235) and **Lev Vygotsky** (pp. 26–34) is that the self *is* there, in the conversational and other interactions between and among the people who are the child's actual community. In being treated as a self the self of an individual is in the zone of proximal development.

It has to be said that Piaget was unmoved by theoretical criticisms and experimental refutations of various aspects of his approach to child development. The brilliance of his observations and the sheer weight of his contribution, together with his unwavering opposition to behaviourism with its unrealistic reliance on explanations that cite only the processes of conditioning, brought many people under his spell. Almost all his fundamental principles have been brought into question to some extent. Instead of the ladder of stages, we have come to see development as a complex weave of skills and the capacity to manage the application of skills. Newly acquired skills can mask or disturb the uses of old cognitive capacities. Management of cognitive practices is crucially dependent on the apprenticeship relations to other more mature people, who are available in the child's immediate social and material surroundings at every age. Development is not, it seems, an individual process, but the result of lifelong symbiosis with others.

Piaget's influence has been enormous. To raise doubts as I have done may seem to be mere carping when set against the moral and intellectual value of his campaign against the sort of approach we have found in the writings of Skinner. Yet, it can hardly be denied that the way children develop must be correctly understood, so much depends upon it. Generations of children can be harmed by the use of defective educational methods, drawn from the writings of dominant and authoritative figures, if there are mistakes and misunderstandings in those writings. Cognitive development is not just training in 'correct' responses, as the Skinnerian approach suggests. Nor is it right to pace the steps in an educational programme until children are 'ready for them', as Piaget's development stages have been supposed to imply.

The most faithful application of Piaget's conception of cognitive development appeared in the work of *Lawrence Kohlberg* (1927–87), on the moral development of human beings. He identified a pre-conventional level, in which moral reasoning is driven by personal desires and the fear of punishment. At this stage moral decisions are based on what will be likely to achieve the former and avoid the latter. The conventional level is based on loyalty to the local norms of propriety, and conventional patterns of correct behaviour. The post-conventional or principled stage, in true Piagetian fashion, involves the use of abstract principles to arrive at solutions to moral dilemmas (Kohlberg, 1984). As his theory developed, Kohlberg added substages to the basic scheme, including a seventh level in which an abstract conception of duty is turned to in making moral decisions.

To try to assign people to stages, Kohlberg devised a 'test', based on the solutions that a person offers to a concrete but fictional moral problem, usually posed as a dilemma. The most widely used features a man, Heinz, whose wife is seriously ill. The family is unable to get the necessary medicine by legitimate means. The pharmacist will not give Heinz the drug, even though he knows it will save the woman's life. She urges Heinz to steal the drug. Would she still think it right if she were in the pharmacist's position? Kohlberg and his students devised a complex system for coding the answers to arrive at a location for each respondent on their scale of moral development. Other dilemmas involved mercy killing, and choosing whom to sacrifice among the survivors on a lifeboat.

Further Readings

Primary Sources

Evans, R. I. (1973) (Ed.) *Jean Piaget: The Man and His Ideas* (trans. E. Duckworth). New York: Dutton.
Gruber, H. E. & Vonèche, J. J. (1977) *The Essential Piaget*. New York: Basic Books.

Secondary Sources

Bryant, P. E. (1984) Piaget, teachers and psychologists. *Oxford Review of Education,* **10**, 251–260.
Donaldson, M. (1983) Children's reasoning. In M. Donaldson et al., *Early Childhood Development and Education* (pp. 246–250). New York and London: The Guildford Press.
Donaldson, M., Grieve, R. & Pratt, C. (1983) *Early Childhood Development and Education.* New York and London: The Guildford Press.
Kohlberg, L. (1984) *The Psychology of Moral Development: The Nature and Validity of Moral Stages*. San Francisco: Harper and Row.
Linaza, J. (1984) Piaget's marbles. *Oxford Review of Education,* **10**, 271–274.

Biographies and Autobiographies

Boeree, C. G. (2004) Jean Piaget. *Internet Encyclopedia of Psychology.*
Evans, R. I. (1973) (Ed.) *Jean Piaget: The Man and His Ideas* (trans. E. Duckworth). New York: Dutton.

Reflections

While both **Lev Vygotksy** (pp. 26–34) and **Jean Piaget** (pp. 34–43) were concerned with the development of cognitive capacities, their approaches differed in several fundamental ways. Even though Piaget did not lose sight of the influence of other people on human development, nevertheless the 'ladder of stages', the most important Piagetian concept, was personal and individual. He seems never to have realized how much it might have owed to the characteristics admired in the upper middle classes of France and Switzerland.

Vygotsky's emphasis was on cognitive skills which are in a process of development, that is in the 'zone of proximal development'. They mature because children are always in the living presence of other people, who act out things with them, embedding them in an ocean of talk. Every higher order cognitive process is first lived in company with others and only then can it be appropriated as a personal skill. Self-addressed talk is not a mark of egocentrism but a display of self-instruction. The cultural/historical/instrumental approach pioneered by Vygotsky still has a great deal to offer psychologists in the 21st century.

Piaget's empirical studies were evidently quite unlike those of the behaviourists. However, his close interaction with the children in his numerous research projects meant that he himself was a factor in the situation. His choice of questions framed the children's answers. This seems to have been a major factor in leading him to some erroneous conclusions in many of his 'conservation' studies. Nevertheless, much of enormous value remains even after his work has been subjected to critical evaluation.

3

The Cognitivists

Psychology is the study of thinking, feeling, acting and perceiving. The main focus of cognitive psychology during the 20th century was on the study of the mental processes of thinking, including reasoning, deciding, planning, calculating and remembering, independently of their likely grounding in the brain. Nevertheless, most cognitive psychologists bore in mind the key principle that the ultimate grounding of cognition must lie, somehow, in the way the brain and nervous system worked. Towards the latter half of the century the role of cognition in emotions, in perception and in social action began to gain attention.

Cognitive psychology is based on the principle that human beings acquire bodies of knowledge which are implemented in managing various tasks. This stands in sharp contrast with the behaviourist's picture of the person as the site of a myriad independent stimulus response units, acquired by some form of conditioning. The task of the cognitive psychologist is to create a representation of relevant bodies of knowledge and to develop a theory of how they are implemented in thought and action. A person's body of knowledge includes not only what he or she takes to be factual knowledge, though some of it may be wrong, but also procedural knowledge, how to do things. Both **William McDougall** (pp. 191–194) and **Serge Moscovici** (pp. 216–221) introduced the idea of bodies of social knowledge into their research paradigms for social psychology.

Behaviourism was not so overwhelming an influence in the United Kingdom and elsewhere in Europe as it had been in the United States. **Frederic Bartlett** (pp. 47–54) began systematic studies of the mental activity of thinking shortly after the end of the Second World War, having pioneered the study of remembering as the maintenance of a body of knowledge of what had happened in the past and how this changed over time. By the 1960s a vigorous programme of research into cognition had begun at Harvard. Led by the researches of **Jerome Bruner** (pp. 54–62), the philosophical basis of psychology began to shift. The cognitive psychology of Bruner and his colleagues was based on the principle that in order to complete an adequate explanation of the observable performances of thinking, remembering, deciding, classifying, perceiving and so on, hypotheses about factual and procedural knowledge, and of cognitive structures and processes of which one was not currently aware, were required.

From the point of view of philosophy of science, cognitivism is a striking example of a realist reaction against the positivism of behaviourism. Hypotheses about unobservable 'cognitive schemata', 'cognitive mechanisms' and so on were to be taken seriously. They are not only the formal bases of explanation, but also can be examined as possible representations of something that is taken to be as real as the phenomena they are meant to explain. The exact status of such unobservables has been the subject of a long-running debate, without undermining the methodological principle on which cognitive psychology has been based.

Since the relevant bodies of knowledge and many of the processes by which they are implemented in problem solving and other mental processes are unobservable, our understanding of them must be indirect. The natural sciences have learned to deal with the problem this raises by making use of the techniques of model building. What sort of models, that is plausible representations of hidden cognitive 'mechanisms', should we construct and test? The Center for Cognitive Studies, founded by Bruner and George Miller, inaugurated a research programme in which the new inventions in computing machines were drawn on, in ever greater detail, as sources for formal models of cognition. The development and critical reception of this way of modeling will be discussed in the next chapter. A more overtly mentalistic approach was taken up by **Noam Chomsky** (pp. 68–77), in his very influential studies of the workings of language. The task of the cognitively-oriented linguist was to create a representation of the knowledge that was required for a person to be able to carry on linguistic performances.

A fine line needs to be drawn, however, between heuristic models of cognitive processes, constructed to facilitate understanding of some complex psychological phenomenon, and realistic models, purporting to represent something real but unobservable. For example, Alan Baddely's 'loops', proposed as an imaginary mechanism to help us think about long and short term memory, are not meant to represent real neural structures (Baddeley, 1998). **Jerome Bruner**'s schemata, described in this chapter, are presented as psychological entities with a claim to exist in addition to the perceptual phenomena they help to explain.

I have chosen my cast of characters from a wide range of possible candidates, partly to bring out two major dimensions along which the cognitivism of the mid-century diverged. **Frederic Bartlett** focused on the content of remembering, and he made no attempt to construct formal models of the cognitive processes involved. **Noam Chomsky** moved very quickly to the use of a formal style of theorizing, his now well known formal representations of knowledge of syntax as clusters of rules. The sacrifice of content entailed by adopting a formal mode of representation ought to have been compensated for by a corresponding leap in generality. This 'leap' was particularly prominent in Chomsky's work, since he explicitly made claims for the universality of his deep grammatical forms.

In its 'classical' form cognitive psychology was based on the presupposition that the primary location of the relevant cognitive processes was an individual person. **George Kelly** (pp. 62–68) was responsible not only for the idea that individual people had their own, idiosyncratic ways of reasoning, but also for a technique by which the cognitive resources of individual people could be brought to light, represented in the constructs displayed by his method of repertory grid analysis.

The 'discursive' version of cognitive psychology, influenced by **Lev Vygotsky** (pp. 26–34) and the later writings of **Jerome Bruner**, has been based on the thesis that the primary location of cognitive processes is the symbolic interactions among the people jointly bringing various cognitive projects to fruition (Shotter, 1993). There is interpersonal as well as intrapersonal cognition. The former is mediated by language as the medium of collective thinking. A body of knowledge may even exist only in the interactions between members of a group.

By the end of the 20th century cognitive psychology had developed along two lines, depending on the status accorded to the processes of cognition. On the one hand, the hypothetical cognitive processes invoked in explanations were modelled by information processing activities in computational machines. On the other hand, the same processes have been interpreted in terms of neural networks and brain physiology. Building computational models of unobservable cognitive processes in addition to creating representations of bodies of knowledge made possible a further step in the realist account of cognition. Did any of these models suggest a second interpretation, as representations of neural structures and processes in the brain? The work of **Alexander Luria** (pp. 105–113), **Wilder Penfield** (pp. 113–118) and **Karl Pribram** (pp. 118–125), to be described in Chapter 5, has opened up possibilities of advances in neuropsychology suggested by computational models that have still not been fully explored. A complementary project has been based on developments in neuroscience that have encouraged the attempt to construct computational models that might bear some resemblance to the structures of the human brain. We will follow these developments in some detail in the work of **Alan Turing** (pp. 82–86) and **Marvin Minsky** (pp. 93–98).

References

Baddeley, A. (1998) *Human Memory: Theory and Practice.* London: Allyn and Bacon.
Shotter, J. (1993) *Cultural Politics of Everyday Life.* Buckingham: Open University Press.

Sir Frederic Charles Bartlett (1886–1969)

The basic principle of cognitive psychology, that unobserved mental processes must be presumed for a sound psychological explanation of many higher order human performances, seems to have been invented twice. There is no doubt that priority for this important innovation must go to Frederic Bartlett, who worked all his life at Cambridge University. This major step was already clearly set out in his book *Remembering* of 1932. It was not until the 1950s and 1960s that **Jerome Bruner** (pp. 54–62) and his colleagues at the Center made a similar step at Harvard.

Who was Frederic Charles Bartlett?

He was born on 20 October 1886 in Stow-on-the-Wold, in the Cotswolds district of Gloucestershire. Now one of the must-see towns of the tourist route around southern England, in those days it was a small place, servicing farming and with a few modest industries. Bartlett's father was a successful manufacturer of boots and shoes. After primary education in the local school, Frederic went on to Stow Grammar School. Unfortunately it closed before his secondary education was complete.

The remedy for such a contretemps, going off to boarding school, the usual educational route for the English middle classes, was prevented by Frederic falling seriously ill. He stayed at home, more or less educating himself. His father and the local vicar both possessed considerable libraries, so there was plenty of material available for a keen reader. University College, London offered external degrees, and it was through this route that Bartlett began his higher education. He took a broad range of subjects, including logic and ethics, and sociology. At that time, logic courses were still taught within the framework of a theory of thinking, rather than as the algebra of principles of correct reasoning. Logical laws were the 'laws of thought'. So a course in logic doubled as a course in cognitive psychology, as we should now call it. Bartlett took his MA in 1911.

For reasons that are not entirely clear, he then went up to St John's College, Cambridge, to begin his education afresh. He was much influenced by W. H. R. Rivers, who had worked in the German tradition of psychophysics, more or less in the style of Wundt, and who, like Wundt, had turned to cultural studies as the complement to psychophysics. Pursuing the study of culture, Rivers became one of the most distinguished anthropologists of the era. Though Bartlett never lost an intense interest in anthropology, he began work in experimental psychology under Cyril Burt, later suspected of manufacturing evidence to support his views on the inheritance of intelligence.

He took his degree with First Class Honours in 1914, the year of the outbreak of the First World War. His fragile health meant that he was excluded from active participation in the war, and he remained in Cambridge. However, Burt had then gone to take up a position in London, and the promising young Bartlett took over Burt's experimental psychology courses. One biographer remarks that this more or less chance event pushed Bartlett more towards psychology and further away from anthropology than perhaps he would have preferred.

During the war he turned his attention to practical research, in particular the detection of very faint sounds. The project was aimed at improving the capacity of the Navy to pick up the tracks of German submarines. This project had an unintended outcome. Bartlett married Mary Smith, his collaborator in the submarine research project.

Once the war was over both Rivers and Bartlett's other senior colleague, C. S. Myers, returned to Cambridge. However, Rivers died suddenly in 1922 and Myers retired almost immediately. This left Bartlett in charge. He became the director of the psychology laboratory, a post he held until taking up a chair in experimental psychology. This was established in 1931 with Bartlett as its first holder.

However, he did not remain faithful to psychology during his tenure of the directorship. He was drawn back from time to time to anthropology, publishing *Psychology and Primitive Culture* in 1923. During this time the major work that made his name came to fruition. This was *Remembering*, the cumulative record of a long series of studies of a cognitive process as such. It was published in 1932. As we will see, this book not only anticipated much that emerged from Harvard in the mid-20th century, but also laid the foundations for a kind of psychology that only now, in the 21st century, is coming back into fashion. Not only did it look at a psychological process in the real world, but the research was based on a very sophisticated methodology, the use of the indicative case, or 'instance of light', as Francis Bacon called it.

The Second World War again drew Bartlett away from academic psychology to practical research programmes. In particular his studies of high grade manual skills, carried out with Kenneth Craik, were important in refining the training programmes for pilots. As the laboratory facilities at Cambridge expanded under the demands of the war, he was able to enlarge the scope of this work, including the study of the effects of fatigue on skilled performance. At the end of the war it modulated into a new institution, the Applied Psychology Research Unit, under the directorship of Craik, whose tragic death shortly before the end of the war had a devastating effect on Bartlett.

Perhaps because of his close involvement with Craik in the study of motor skills, Bartlett turned to the study of thinking, as a cognitive skill. The method of research was similar to that he had developed for studying remembering. Once again we are presented with work that has its echoes nearly 50 years later. His *Thinking: An Experimental and Social Study* appeared in 1958.

Biographical memoirs are unanimous in describing Bartlett's powerful personal influence, and the extraordinary excitement of his twice weekly seminars. Here were gathered a group of students who were to become distinguished psychologists in their own right. The seminar also attracted faculty members, not only from psychology. Bartlett comes through from various accounts as a complex character, authoritarian at times, but with a mixture of outgoing charm and sudden withdrawal that is one of the ingredients in the charismatic personality.

His career was punctuated by unusual public recognition for a psychologist. He was elected to the Royal Society in 1932, and knighted in 1948. Despite his ill health as a youth, he continued to be active both in writing and research and in public service of various kinds after his retirement in 1952. He died in 1969, widely honored both at home and abroad. Thereafter his influence waned and for a time almost vanished. One could go for months without hearing his name, and his work was rarely cited. The influence he had exercised in the 1950s seemed as if it would be ephemeral. Yet, so powerful and forward-looking were his two major studies of *Remembering* and *Thinking*, that the new trends in psychology in recent years already seem like celebrations of Bartlett's work, even though they grew out of other sources and other dissatisfactions.

What did he contribute?

To understand the importance of Bartlett's innovations both in the topics he took up and the methods he employed in studying them one must bear in mind the perennial weakness of experimental psychology as it has often been practised. The attempt to base research on the methodology of dependent and independent variables fails for the most part to offer significant results in the psychological domain for two main reasons. It is usually impossible to detach a property from a complex structure in such a way that the property itself retains its identity when extracted. Even if such an abstraction were to succeed, the manipulation of the independent variable generally affects not only whatever is thought to be the dependent variable, but the whole interrelated structure of action and cognition itself. One reason for the failure of the psychological community to appreciate these insoluble problems in simple experimental designs is the ambiguity of the word 'variable'. As an algebraic symbol a variable is a generic term for which specific values can be substituted, independently of substitutions into other variables in a function. In reality, a variable in the algebraic sense can stand for or represent a generic property which can occur at different levels or intensities in different settings. Variables in this sense cannot be manipulated without affecting the whole of the system of which they form a part. For this reason this methodology is rare in the advanced natural sciences. It was useful for the study of simple electrical circuits and the movements of bodies described in the laws of elementary mechanics, but of limited value for anything more complex. For example, chemists are interested in discovering and modifying structures rather than manipulating variables such as temperatures and concentrations.

Natural scientists know this very well. As long ago as 1620 Francis Bacon pointed out that the choice of a striking or exemplary instance of a phenomenon is often a superior way to display the general character of a natural process than an induction over a great many instances. Darwin was a master of this method. It would make no sense to try to study the origin of species by identifying an independent variable, manipulating it to see if a new species arose! Instead Darwin displays the general principles of organic evolution by natural selection in a careful description of the beaks of the finches of the Galapagos Islands. This technique, the careful study of exemplary instances in detail, is the basis of Bartlett's methodology.

Bartlett carried out two large-scale studies of important psychological phenomena, remembering and thinking. Note well the choice of words: 'remembering' rather than 'memory', and 'thinking' rather than 'cognition'. The focus is on activity and what we would now call the practices of remembering and thinking.

At the time Bartlett began his classical study of remembering, the work of Hermann Ebbinghaus (1850–1903) was the major source of knowledge in this field. Ebbinghaus had subjected himself to a regime of learning strings of meaningless syllables, looking for relationships between such matters as the frequency with which he had seen or heard the material and the time between first acquaintance and attempted recall. The psychological process which he studied was deliberately divorced from both context and meaning. He was in search of the pure 'mechanism' of recall and recognition. Bartlett realized that these studies were practically worthless in attempting to understand how real people in real situations remembered real matters of interest.

Bartlett introduced two main research methods: the method of description and the method of repeated reproduction. The point of his researches was to track down the influences that shaped what was remembered, and to catalogue the kinds of changes that took place in 'remembered' material over time. He began his studies with the perception of faces, and showed how evaluation as well as plan or arrangement plays a major role in what someone claims to have perceived. Turning to remembering proper, the Method of Description (Bartlett, 1932: 37–48) requires the subject to look at a series of items and to recall them after various lapses of time. In every case there were both transformations, the shifting of a detail from one member of the series (of faces) to another, and importations, introducing details into the recollection from elsewhere than the remembered material. Furthermore, the longer the lapse of time the more imported material there would be.

The method of repeated reproduction is aimed at the same problem, how what is 'remembered' changes with time. In this study the subjects read through a complex Inuit story twice. Then each was asked to repeat the story at intervals ranging from 15 minutes after the first reading to as much as 2½ years later. Out of this came two conclusions of paramount importance. First of all there was a strong tendency for the form taken by the first reproduction for each person to persist through later repetitions. More important still was what Bartlett (1932: 84) called 'effort after meaning'. Accuracy of reproduction was a rare exception, and with repeated repetitions details became stereotyped. The presumed plot rather than the original story provided a source for the importation of details. In another study involving signs rather than words, he found that signs unrelated to material already used tended to be omitted in recall tasks.

The upshot of these and other studies showed that 'an individual does not normally take ... a situation [to be recalled] detail by detail and meticulously build up the whole. In ordinary instances he has an overmastering tendency simply to get a general impression of the whole; and on the basis of this, he constructs the probable detail. ... it is the sort of construction that justifies his general impression' (Bartlett, 1932: 206). Despite some reservations, Bartlett settled on the word 'schema' to express the idea of a coherent set of elements that influences remembering almost en masse. 'This and this and this must have occurred, in order that my present state should be what it is.' The leading influences on this way of thinking are schemata (Bartlett, 1932: 202). 'Condensation, elaboration and invention are common features of ordinary remembering, and these all very often involve the mingling of materials belonging originally to different "schemata"' (Bartlett, 1932: 205).

There is an irony worth recording in Donald Broadbent's obituary of Bartlett. Broadbent declared that the method of 'selecting significant incidents ... to illustrate general truths' made it difficult to select the truly significant. So much for Darwin's finches! He was wrong too to declare that Bartlett's concept of 'schema' was outmoded. Shortly thereafter it burst on the world in the cognitive psychology that came from the Harvard Center.

In another tour de force, anticipating some of the most interesting work on remembering of the late 20th century, Bartlett turned his attention to social practices of remembering with a group of people who were involved in the construction of a version of the past. The organization of the group has an influence on how and what is socially recalled. Summing up his results he remarks that 'the matter of recall is mainly a question of interest, while the manner of recall is chiefly one of temperament and character' (Bartlett, 1932: 256). 'Constructive recall, constructive imagination and constructive thinking differ in the range of material over which they move, and the precise manner of their control ... remembering is "schematically" determined' (Bartlett, 1932: 312).

Bartlett had always intended to push on with the use of his methodology to investigate the vast territory of 'thinking'. The book of that name, which summed up many years of work, has the same elegance and clarity as its illustrious predecessor, though it must be confessed that it is an inferior work overall. The basis of the 'thinking' study is the idea that thinking is a skill. We know a great deal about motor skills, so the project should be shaped by developing a research project into the degree to which the concepts appropriate to motor skills can be displaced into a research programme on mental or cognitive skills.

However, Bartlett was quick to point out that the similarities between motor and cognitive skills could only be used methodologically, as guides to what to look for in a research programme. Working along these lines he found four features that deserve to have an important methodological role. There is 'timing', which boils down to identifying the gaps in the sequence that need to be filled; 'halts', at which the next step is prepared; 'regions of no return', in which the whole of the subsequent action is already in train; and 'direction', to what end the sequence of steps is directed. Thinking is required 'when a process cannot be accounted for wholly by the immediate external environment' (Bartlett, 1958: 72).

Shaping the whole research programme is the distinction between thinking with closed systems and adventurous thinking. For the former kind of thinking 'the process begins when evidence or information is available which is treated as possessing gaps, or as being incomplete. The gaps are then filled up. ... This is done by an extension or supplementation of the evidence ... it carries it further ... there are always a series of intermediate steps' (Bartlett, 1958: 75). There seem to be two main ways that thinking proceeds. It may be by extrapolation, that is by extracting and following a rule. Or it may be by reinterpreting the evidence so the seeming gap is now filled. Either way the procedure is complete.

Adventurous thinking is characterized by the fact that at the early stages of this kind of thinking directional features of the structure are predominant. 'As thinking moves towards greater freedom ... the thinker is less and less concerned with the likelihood of items and more and more with that of packets or groups of items ... he is more "schematic" minded' (Bartlett, 1958: 111).

He went on to a series of case studies of the thinking evident in two examples of scientific research, the study of infective microorganisms and the experimental study of reaction times. It is not entirely clear just what Bartlett was trying to bring out in these examples. He makes much of the fact that experimental studies came late in the case of infectious diseases, long after a great deal of knowledge had been acquired by observation. In the case of reaction times he points out that the most important techniques of investigation came from elsewhere than the traditional means of study of the phenomena.

Summing up the characteristics of adventurous thinking as they are revealed in the case studies, Bartlett identifies four features: 'experimental thinking has to do with systems whose structure begins to appear … only after much search has been made' (Bartlett, 1958: 132). Secondly, since the investigator is in thrall to the available instruments, progress requires that instruments be brought into the field from the outside. The third requirement is to have a precise idea where a problem is sited. Finally, there is what he calls 'making openings', again a matter of realizing where techniques from outside the field can advantageously be brought in.

Another and perhaps more interesting topic for experimental study in the Bartlett style was the thinking displayed by a group of people with respect to group relations. The experiments involved the presentation of incomplete situations, and the subjects were asked to say how they would continue and what the likely outcome would be. The first major finding was that generalizing is very different in these cases from the way it appears in thinking in closed systems, more a matter of trying out how the extension of a rule 'feels'. The timing of contributions to group processes is also unlike that of thinking in closed systems. A suggestion rejected or ignored at one time may be taken up at some other moment. The persistence or point of no return aspect differs too, in that in closed systems it is the value of the reasoning rather than the prestige of the speaker that keeps a line of thought going (Bartlett, 1958: 185). Compromise is rarely achieved in everyday adventurous thinking, unless a third party intervenes.

These studies are rounded off by a somewhat sketchy account of the thinking of artists. One cannot but be struck by the flimsiness of the study of *Thinking* alongside the depth and solidity of the work on *Remembering*. At almost every point in the former one wants to say, 'Yes, now let's take that further.' There is an air of casualness and even perhaps fatigue in the writing.

Bartlett wrote extensively on anthropological topics, and made good use of them in some of his studies, notably the examples in *Remembering*. That book will be one of those to which the psychologists of the 21st century will surely return, when the works of others of our cast of characters are marked in the library catalogue as 'stored off campus'.

Further Reading

Primary Sources

Bartlett, Sir Frederic Charles (1932) *Remembering: A Study in Experimental and Social Psychology*. Cambridge: Cambridge University Press.
Bartlett, Sir Frederic Charles (1958) *Thinking: An Experimental and Social Study*. London: George Allen and Unwin.

Biography

Roediger, H. L. (2000) Sir Frederic Charles Bartlett: experimental and applied psychologist. In G. A. Kimbel & M. Wertheimer (Eds), *Portraits of Pioneers in Psychology* (pp. 148–161). Mahwah, NJ: Lawrence Erlbaum.

Jerome Seymour Bruner (1915–)

Bruner must be credited with a distinction almost unique among psychologists of abandoning a cherished position, not only once but twice. We have already seen how often psychologists, like other scientists, for example Piaget, have been resistant to criticism, sticking to a fixed position in the face of theoretical objections and empirical refutations.

In the 1950s, Jerome Bruner did a series of experiments which were widely taken to demonstrate that the behaviourist attempt to account for how we think, perceive and act in terms of meaningless patterns of conditioning is not only factually wrong but theoretically deeply confused. He was also able to show in a variety of studies that it is the meanings of experiences, not their conditioning history, nor the immediate sensory stimulus, that accounts for such phenomena as the recognition of words, the shapes of coins and the perception of the colours of suites of cards. It seems that there are cognitive processes that intervene between the stimulus and the act of recognition. They can be understood only if studied in terms of meanings.

With these and other studies he inaugurated the first cognitive revolution, the project of creating a psychology that was primarily concerned with people as meaning managers. However, that led to something he had not intended, the modelling of the mind as a computational device.

However, later in life, he returned to the key insights of the 1950s. It is not too much to say that he drew together a worldwide but fragmentary movement into a second cognitive revolution. The new element that infused his work in the 1980s was the idea that much of mental life is ordered by cultural narratives, storylines that people live out in their psychological and social activities.

Who is Jerome Seymour Bruner?

He was born on 1 October 1915 into a well-off middle class Jewish family in New York. 'Jerry' was the youngest of four children. He describes his family as 'nominally observant' in religious matters. This seems to have been the case with many such families in New York at that period, as their ties with the old world weakened, and the attractions of secularism began to draw young people of Bruner's age. A similar atmosphere is described by the playwright Arthur Miller, in his description of his childhood in that city. In his autobiography, Bruner (1983b) remarks on the sense of a childhood pretty much disconnected from the sort of person he believed himself to have become in later life. Born blind, he was not able to see until the age of two. His sight was restored by a series of operations. Later, the consequences of the death of his father when he was 12 threw him into another situation that ought to have left permanent psychic scars. To add to the troubles of a fatherless adolescence, his widowed mother moved house annually. Not only was the normal course of family life disrupted, but so also was his schooling. Yet to those who know him, he appears as an ebullient and confident man, overflowing with ideas.

He describes his mother as dutiful rather than affectionate. Both parents had come from Poland, his mother already a widow when she and Jerry's father married. Again, like many at that time, the prospect of being drafted into the Russian army spurred the elder Bruner and his brother Simon to emigrate to New York. Bruner père was soon established in the wool trade, with his own business. He died unexpectedly in 1927. However, he had set up a trust fund to provide for the education of his children. To make up for the sporadic schooling that he had received, Jerry had to spend a year preparing for the university entrance examinations at a 'crammer'. Having leapt that hurdle, he entered Duke University in 1933.

He quickly found his feet as a psychology major, completing the undergraduate courses early and beginning graduate work before taking his degree. However, he fell foul of the college authorities over the excessively authoritarian style of university management. He was rescued by **William McDougall** (pp. 191–194), and began work on animal experiments in McDougall's laboratory. Having to choose between animals and people as the places where 'psychology' happened, he chose Harvard and people over Duke and animals. He tells us that this was largely due to the influence of the writings of **Gordon Allport** (pp. 167–172). He began his graduate studies in 1938. Despite his respect for Allport's cultivated and integrated approach to psychology, he turned to the experimentalists for his research. His topic proved appropriate to the times. It was a study of the power of propaganda broadcasts to influence public opinion.

Throughout the Second World War he worked in a variety of offices concerned with the management of information, commuting between Washington DC and Princeton. Towards the end of the war he moved to a post in Europe. Returning to Cambridge, Massachusetts, and completing his doctorate in 1947, he stayed on at Harvard until he moved to Oxford in 1972.

By the early 1950s it had become clear to Bruner and his colleagues, particularly *George Miller*[1] (b. 1920), that some institutional arrangements were needed to bring together 'the distinctive human forms of ... using knowledge of all sorts ...' (Bruner, 1983b: 122). Preferably an institution should be founded for this purpose at Harvard. A grant from the Carnegie Corporation enabled the setting up of a Center for Cognitive Studies. By 1960 this had become the dominant place for such studies worldwide. However, as Miller remarked, mainstream psychologists looked askance at the revival of the use of mentalistic concepts. However, he and Jerome Bruner were happy to be with psychologists who were 'unafraid of words like *mind*, and *expectation*, and *perception*, and *meaning*' (Miller, 2003: 142).

Many of the most important members of and visitors to the Center were from outside psychology as such. Nevertheless, the Center attracted young psychologists of talent, whose influence eventually spread worldwide.

By the late 1960s Bruner began to find his vision of an eclectic but cognitively oriented research tradition under threat. It seemed to him that psychology at Harvard had become, as he says, 'centrifugal' (Bruner, 1983b: 252). Specialized groups went their own ways. He was even asked to disband the Center in the interests of 'tidiness'! Not surprisingly, by 1972 he was ready to move.

In that year he was elected to the new Watts Chair in Psychology at Oxford. This went with a fellowship at Wolfson College, a newly endowed graduate society. There he found a very congenial atmosphere. With few exceptions the loosely linked group of Oxford people interested in the human mind and our human attempts to understand ourselves was both sympathetic to Bruner's way of thinking and appreciated by Bruner himself. At that time Oxford was the pre-eminent centre for philosophy in the world and philosophy of mind, a sibling to Bruner's increasingly narratologically–oriented psychology, was congenial to him. Almost all his time at Oxford was occupied in his studies of human development and with attempts to tie such work into ideas about and programs for schooling.

In the early part of 1980 Bruner published a major article in the *Times Literary Supplement*, deploring the continuing neglect of meaning (intentionality) at the heart of psychology. In some ways it was preaching to the converted. However, even at Oxford, there were still some people mired in the old positivistic conceptions of the past. A public debate was organized between the pro and anti 'Brunerians'. Bruner's allies clearly won the debate, but the event served as an appropriate moment for his return to the United States after a very productive 10 years in Oxford. A new project opened up, the chance to pull together the work of a lifetime in an autobiography (Bruner, 1983b). A grant from the Sloan Foundation freed him from official duties to set down the developments that he had inspired and that had inspired him.

There was, of course, unfinished business. Returning to his hometown in the mid-1980s, Bruner began a new academic career at the New School for Social Research in New York, and later at New York University. It gave him a chance to set about completing the project begun in the 1950s with the classification experiment. How did narrative work in the shaping of thought and action? He continues to work on this project to this day.

What has he contributed?

In this book we explore the contributions of Bruner as a psychologist. He is equally or perhaps even better known in education circles, where he has been very influential. The insights he brought to bear in that field derive very directly from his work in psychology. I could have chosen to locate him among the developmentalists, though, from the point of view of this book, his influence on the growth of cognitive psychology has been of paramount importance. Like Vygotsky, Bruner contributed, in one way or another, to the tidal wave of new ideas that challenged the old psychology in the latter years of the 20th century.

Bruner first came to prominence as the man who helped to put an end to behaviourism and inaugurated a return to a cognitive approach to human behaviour. He re-established cognition in a central place in psychology with an elegant and decisive series of experiments. Just how to interpret the positive meaning of these experiments remains problematic to this day. What is sure is that they negated one of the fundamental principles of behaviourism, that environmental contingencies and stimuli are enough to account for the entire gamut of human psychological phenomena, either directly or through conditioning. This thesis had become closely allied with the idea that all learning was the result of conditioning. Bruner's experimental results also had relevance to another powerful idea. It had been a widely assumed but rarely explicitly formulated principle that there is a culture-free basis for all human psychology in the functions of the brain and nervous system. The experiments themselves were on perception, which might have been thought to be the branch of psychology most closely tied to neurophysiological systems common to all humanity. Yet, even there, concepts like 'meanings' and 'conventions' seem to be called for to account for the experimental results. However, whatever way his experiments are interpreted, they mark Bruner's place as one of the founders of cognitive psychology.

He nicknamed the crucial studies the 'Judas Eye' experiments. They were aimed at exploring the viability of a fundamental principle: 'that the world looked different depending on how you thought about it' (Bruner, 1983b: 65). Remember that behaviourism was based on the contrary principle, that perception was no more and could be no more than conditioned responses to sensory stimuli. Whether it was Pavlov's prior associations or Skinner's consequent contingencies of reinforcement, cognition as such had no role to play in our seeing and hearing what we see and hear, or, for that matter, in doing what we do. The metaphor of the 'Judas Eye' is drawn from the way a peephole in a door, the Judas Eye, permits one a mere glimpse of the visitor, and yet, more often than not, one recognizes the whole person. It is typical of people to go 'beyond the information given' in what they see and hear of the world around them.

How far could the recognition of what was seen be explained without recourse to bodies of knowledge people already had? Furthermore, how far could conscious apprehension of the meaning of a word be understood without prior unconscious recognition of the kind of word in question?

Bruner, with various colleagues, including Leo Postman, conceived these experiments in terms of various dogmas of psychophysics, the inheritance from the German psychologists of the 19th century, such as Gustav Fechner (1801–87). One series of experiments explored the principle that the magnitude of a sensation was proportional to the magnitude of the physical stimulus producing it. Another concerned perceptual thresholds, for example, how long would it take for the meaning of a word to be apprehended or the colour of a suite of cards to be recognized? In fact the experiments revealed something very much more general: the role played by cognitive schemata in a wide variety of common psychological phenomena, such as understanding words and recognizing things. In this Bruner was building on some aspects of **Frederic Bartlett**'s (pp. 47–54) studies of the psychology of remembering. The Harvard group effectively demonstrated the necessity of treating perception as a mode of cognition. 'Meaning' was to become an indispensable concept in psychology.

A corollary of the above principle of magnitudes requires that in a series of perceptual experiences, the larger and brighter objects will be judged smaller and less bright than their physical magnitudes would require, while the opposite should hold for the smaller and fainter objects. They should appear larger and brighter than their physical magnitudes would lead us to expect. Using two groups of children, one from poor families and one from the better off, Bruner found that higher denomination coins were matched to a larger elliptical image than would be expected, and those of a lower value to a smaller image than would have been expected. The effect was more marked with the children from the poorer background. Clearly the relative value of the coins to the children was implicated in the perception of shape.

The 'words' experiment required a tachistoscope. This device was required to control the time a person was exposed to a word, at a constant intensity of light. One hundred words were selected, some of which were likely to be disturbing to the undergraduate participants. The times to write down the first word that came to mind on hearing the 'stimulus' word were recorded. Some time later, each participant was shown the six words with his or her slowest reaction times, six words with the fastest reaction times, and six average words. The tachistoscope allowed the experimenters to measure the length of time it took a participant to recognize this or that word. Not surprisingly, most often the time taken to recognize a word was predictable from the time taken to write down a free association. However, the really important finding was this: some participants very quickly recognized words that they had taken a long time to free-associate, and some 'quick-to-associate words' were seen only after a 'preternaturally long exposure' (Bruner, 1983b: 79). Not only shocking words, but words likely to have strong valuation significance for the undergraduates were used in subsequent experiments. Karl Pribram has told me of an earlier version of this experiment by Jung.

Allowing the participants to guess what a word was before they were sure of it extended the scope of the experiment. High value words were often guessed wrongly but the guesses were of words with appropriate cognitive associations. The meaning of the words was being grasped before the word was consciously recognized. Otherwise how could one account for the quicker and slower than normal recognition times? The physical properties of the words-as-signs were the same whatever their meanings.

A later experiment with anomalous playing cards fitted in well with the results of the earlier Judas Eye studies. The experiment was based on a pack of cards in which the colours had been reversed, so that some clubs and spades were red and some diamonds and hearts black, intermingled with normal cards. The tachistoscope was used to present the cards for increasing periods of time. At first, anything red was declared to be a heart or a diamond. Eventually, and it took some time, the trick cards were recognized to be anomalous. Once the participants realized there were trick cards in the pack, the recognition time for real cards increased. Recognition, as Ferdinand de Saussure had realized long since, was not just a matter of seeing or interpreting what was there, but also ruling out alternative possibilities.

These experiments no doubt showed that bodies of knowledge were involved in what had seemed the most biological of psychological phenomena, perceiving. But what processes were involved? In 1955 Bruner turned to studies in another style, how people went about reasoning in tasks defined in simplified 'model' worlds. The reasoning involved in classifying things into groups, depending on some choice of criterial characteristics, became the target of the research. Cards bearing different shapes and colours were provided to participants, whose task was to work out the classification system used by the experimenters, by asking whether or not two cards with certain patterns did or did not belong in the same group. The results turned out to have far reaching significance. The first phase of the programme was based on reasoning that would reveal non-natural type-concepts behind the cognitive problems. However, Bruner moved on to naturalistic material, such as an adult, a child and a gift. In these cases a narrative was implicit in the material. The subjects stayed with the narrative as their interpretative device in the face of other conflicting items. Not until 15 years later did the significance of this finding strike him. More important at the time was his publication of *A Study of Thinking*. It can rightly be identified as the inaugural work in the first cognitive revolution.

Later in life Bruner ruefully admitted that the cognitive revolution of the 1950s was quickly hi-jacked by the computationalists. Be that as it may, the idea of studying cognition in following what people do when confronted with problems in model worlds has become a major technique in the attempt to realize **Alan Turing**'s (pp. 82–86) project of a computational psychology. The most advanced attempt at the use of this technique was, no doubt, the study reported by **Allen Newell** and **Herbert Simon** (pp. 86–93) in 1975.

Bruner's response was to turn to developmental psychology, the 'origins of mind', as he had now come to conceive it. In 1956, after visiting **Jean Piaget** (pp. 34–43), and making his first acquaintance with the work of **Lev Vygotsky** (pp. 26–34), Bruner began systematic work in developmental cognitive psychology, particularly, as time went by, with the investigation of the development of language as a set of cognitive skills.

Bruner's studies of the acquisition of linguistic skills in the course of symbiotic language games serve to illustrate the Vygotskian methodology particularly well. Bruner is not the only heir to the mantle of Vygotsky, but among those he influenced, his work comes closest to the Vygotskian 'spirit'. Bruner was not alone in looking to the immediate socio-cultural environment for the sources of higher order cognitive skills. However, he has been the most influential.

Bruner followed up a Vygotsky-inspired programme of developmental research. He introduced the term 'scaffolding' to describe the contributions of the more competent practitioner in psychological symbiosis. The focus of his psycholinguistic studies turned on attempts to answer a series of basic questions. How do the linguistic practices of talking about a common object of concern, and the related practice of asking for or demanding something, become established? What are their prelinguistic precursors? What goes on in the zone of proximal development of the capacity to maintain a focus on a common topic?

Bruner began his investigation with an analysis of the four conditions for the success of the act by which one person draws the attention of another to a common object, by means of words. There must be a signaling of a referential intent, a shared attention to a common object. There must be some minimal overlapping of understanding of the nature of the object of shared attention, but it can remain vague. There must be a social practice for the management of joint attention. And finally, there must be a goal structure in relation to acts of referring, so that success or failure of such an act can be assessed and made manifest.

The zone of proximal development includes object highlighting, when the mother moves an object into the child's line of sight, with an appropriate and emphatic vocalization. This presupposes a natural endowment, shared by the great apes, by which a very young baby can follow the direction of another's line of regard. At about four months a child will search for an object along what it perceives as an adult's line of sight. From this comes the linguistic management of joint attention, in which a particular sound pattern is established as a 'place holder' for later language, as the search for an attended object is successful. The next step involves the development of the practice of pointing at the object of joint attention, eventually being used as a device to draw the attention of someone else to it. Bruner notes that pointing is a distinct gesture from that by which an infant indicates something it wants to hold. It is a device 'for singling out the noteworthy' (Bruner, 1983a: 75). It appears first of all when a familiar object appears in a new context. The beginning of the use of demonstratives, particular sounds uttered consistently with acts of pointing, is followed by the appearance of words for types of objects to which attention might be drawn including, Bruner suggests from one of his studies, a word for 'something-of-interest-but-we-do-not-know-what'. At the same time, at least in Western culture, pointing to pictures in books and saying the appropriate words plays a large part in establishing linguistic reference.

Summing up his studies, Bruner (1983a: 88) says: 'discourse and dialogue are ... the sources of reference. If they were not, each speaker would be locked in a web of isolated reference triangles each of his own making – if indeed he could construct such a web on his own.'

An infant has a natural tendency to reach for something attractive, to try to grasp it. In doing so it stretches its hand towards the wanted thing, for example, a red ball. A bystander, realizing the infant wants the object, or at least interpreting the infant's gesture as an expression of a want or an intention, completes the task by picking up the red ball and giving it to the child. Bruner distinguished deictic pointing, an act of reference, from request formats, though each develops from a basic biologically grounded movement. Shortly thereafter, the child moves to a second phase, by throwing the ball away, and waiting for the obliging bystander to get it. In reaching and stretching, the infant emits a grunt of effort. Soon it simply produces the grunt without a full stretch attempt to get the ball. At that moment, the practice of vocalizing to express a want or make a demand is initiated. The vocalization is subsequently shaped by further symbiotic activity on the part of the bystander into verbal requests, such as 'Diddy ball', and so on until we get to 'Please, would you be kind enough to pass the ball', if we are lucky. Somewhere along this trajectory, the 'scaffolding' is gradually dismantled until the whole of the cognitive procedure of expressing wants as requests is in place, that is a body of knowledge has been acquired.

Bruner's Judas Eye experiments established the place of cognitive schemata, sets of rules, bodies of knowledge, and so on at the heart of most of the phenomena we pick out as psychological. **Noam Chomsky**'s (pp. 68–77) 'transformational grammar' shared the cognitivist conviction that psychology could not proceed in the absence of concepts that referred to cognitive processes. But *where* is thinking to be found?

Bruner's first proposal was implicitly Cartesian, that is we must reintroduce 'the mind' as an arena in which mental processes occur, the processes that later came to be called 'informational'. Thus, forgetting the admirable advice of William of Ockham, entities were multiplied without necessity. These were taken up in the computational psychology which sprang from the first cognitive revolution. It was Bruner himself who began the transformation of cognitivism into something a good deal more subtle. The mind exists not only in individual thinking but also in the human conversation, in people manipulating symbols in a collective process. It exists in both public intercourse and private reflection. This led him to return to explore the role of narrative in shaping thought and action. The storylines characteristic of a culture become organizing principles of personal cognition. This, we recall, was one of **Frederic Bartlett**'s (pp. 47–54) key findings in the study of remembering.

In *Acts of Meaning* (Bruner, 1990: 42–3), Bruner sets out the principles of a psychology which accords with the insight that 'folk psychology' must be at the core of any future human science. It will be the study of the actual organizing principles in use in everyday life among some group of people. It concerns 'human agents doing things on the basis of their beliefs and desires, striving for goals, meeting obstacles which they best or which best-them, all of this extended over time'. It is narrative in nature, that is has 'inherent sequentiality' or plot. This feature determines 'the mode of mental organization in terms of which it is grasped' (Bruner, 1990: 44). Bruner suggests that human beings have a 'readiness for narrative', an inclination to think in storied terms, to order experience as a story. Finally, narrative links what is ordinary with what is remarkable. It allows both for the maintenance of the routine and for the accommodation of the exceptional within the same storyline. In the last two or three decades of the 20th century narratological studies proliferated, in such new lines of development as 'positioning theory' (Harré & Van Langenhove, 1999). Perhaps Bruner's latest contribution will prove the most important of all.

Further Reading

Primary Sources

Bruner, J. S. (1983a) *Child's Talk*. New York: W. W. Norton.
Bruner, J. S. (1990) *Acts of Meaning*. Cambridge, MA: Harvard University Press.

Secondary Sources

Harré, R. & Van Langenhove, L. (1999) *Positioning Theory*. Oxford: Blackwell.
Miller, G. A. (2003) The cognitive revolution: a historical perspective. *Trends in Cognitive Science,* **7/3**, 141–4.

Autobiography

Bruner, J. S. (1983b) *In Search of Mind*. New York: Harper and Row.

George Alexander Kelly (1905–67)

At several points in this story we have encountered people whose declared aim was to bring a 'new psychology' to life. **Lev Vygotsky** (pp. 26–34) and **Wolfgang Köhler** (pp. 136–142), **Ivan Pavlov** (pp. 8–15) and **B. F. Skinner** (pp. 15–24), all declared this to be their aim. Kelly too set about creating a new psychology. In each case we need to attend to the kind of psychology this or that self-declared innovator took be 'old'. For Vygotsky and Köhler it was a strictly experimental psychology based on the methods of the German experimentalists. For Pavlov and Skinner it was a psychology that took its domain to be the mind or consciousness. Kelly saw himself in opposition not only to Freud's psychodynamics but also to the way that the psychology of individuals had been deleted from the project of a scientific psychology. He came to favour idiographic enquiries over nomothetic methods. He tried to restore the study of individual people against the prevalent focus on the extraction of general trends from statistical data. He had strong interests in psychotherapy. It was this, perhaps more than anything else, which drew him to attempt to find a way of extracting and analysing the moment-by-moment systems of concepts that individual people were actually using in their thinking and in the management of their actions.

Kelly was almost brutally sidelined from the mainstream of American psychology. *The Psychology of Personal Constructs* must be one of the most important 'unread' books in the history of the subject. It is a treasure house of sophisticated observations on the philosophy of science, as well as a subtle and carefully delineated presentation of a 'new psychology of the person'. However, like many innovators ignored by the establishment of their own country, he found a ready following abroad, particularly in England. Led by Fay Fransella and Don Bannister, psychologists in the UK took up his methodology for the exploration of the cognitive repertoires of individual persons. They benefited from the publication of a very fine manual (Fransella & Bannister, 1977) and various computer programmes with the help of which Kelly-style work can easily be carried out.

Recently he has been rediscovered in his own land.

Who was George Alexander Kelly?

He was born on 28 April 1905 on a small farm in Kansas. His father, Theodore, had been a clergyman, but had taken up farming for health reasons. George's mother, Elfleda, had been a schoolteacher. In George Kelly's origins we have a repetition of a pattern we see often in the lives of the characters in this book. A disproportionate number have sprung from the bourgeosie, the worthy and aspiring middle classes, though more often from the professions than from trade.

However, this would give little insight into his upbringing. As Neimeyer and Jackson (1997: 364) emphasize, the simplicity and isolation of the small farming community of Perth, Kansas, would have been tolerable only for one who could create for himself some meaning for a style of life that offered little of significance in itself. Even for an era in which the 'frontier' still had some meaning, his upbringing was extraordinary. While he was still a child he accompanied his father on a trek all the way to Colorado, by covered wagon, to stake a land claim, in the hope of becoming the last of the true homesteaders. The land they chose was not well supplied with water and a permanent move to Colorado never eventuated. According to one biographer (Boeree, 2004: 2) George's early education was in 'one room country schools' supplemented by tuition from his parents. As an only child he evidently benefited from their undivided attention.

At the age of 13 he was sent to boarding school in Wichita. After high school he entered the Friends' University, completing his undergraduate studies in mathematics and physics at Park College in 1926. In the course of his undergraduate career he excelled as a public speaker. Still searching for a niche, he took a master's degree in sociology from the University of Kansas.

His early career seems to have been as peripatetic as his childhood and as directionless as his higher education. He had a part-time post in a workers' college in Minneapolis, teaching 'public speech'. He also instructed future citizens in the American way, in classes in citizenship. He is said to have worked for a while as an aeronautical engineer. Rootless still, he moved to a job in a junior college in Sheldon, Iowa, teaching drama. There he met and married Gladys Thompson.

Suddenly we see a huge change in his fortunes and the beginning of a focus on psychology in practice. In 1929 he received a fellowship for study abroad, and made the best possible use of it. He went to Edinburgh where he took the B Ed with a thesis on the assessment of the future success of teachers. By 1930 he was back in the Middle West, at the University of Iowa, getting his PhD in 1931 on a topic in educational psychology, on speech and reading disabilities.

At the age of 26, married with a good academic qualification he looked around for a job. This was the time of the Great Depression, and he was fortunate perhaps to find a position at Fort Hays State College in Kansas.

It was here that he initiated a remarkable project that bore fruit as the root of his general approach to psychology, and the source of his most enduring contribution to methodology. In the 10 years he spent at Fort Hayes his major preoccupation was the provision of clinical services in the rural areas of the state. He set up a traveling clinic with his students. They visited every community in the western part of the state. In this way he came into close contact with the farming people of whom he already had an intimate knowledge from his childhood. He realized that these people and their children were mainly concerned with making sense of their lives, and were very far from being the victims of Freudian 'hang-ups' or poor conditioning as the behaviourists would have it. This directed his clinical work towards studies of how such people made sense or failed to make sense of their situations. It was at this juncture that he came up with the idea of people as scientists, proposing and testing hypotheses. The most effective means of making sense of things came from the lives of the people themselves rather than from the traditional clinical repertoire. Kelly called this approach 'Constructive Alternativism', emphasizing that the world is perceived in the light of a specific and personal construction which may need to be revised to create alternative construals.

During the Second World War he worked as an aviation psychologist, joining the Bureau of Medicine in Washington. In 1945 he took a job at the University of Maryland, followed almost immediately by an appointment as Director of Clinical Psychology at Ohio State University. At last he seemed to have found a place to stay, and there he spent the next 20 years. His efforts were partly devoted to developing the clinical psychology programme, at which he seems to have been notably successful. Partly they were devoted to the presentation of his psychology of personal constructs. The two volume exposition of that theory was published in 1955. He made numerous forays abroad and visits to universities within the United States. For most people he was taken to be above all a clinical psychologist, and indeed he had considerable influence on the development of clinical testing, particularly in the context of schooling.

By the early 1960s he had become very well known and highly respected as a clinical psychologist, and more particularly for his capacity to organize very successful clinical training programmes. He was appointed to an important chair in clinical psychology at Brandeis University in 1965. There he died, in 1967, with many writing plans uncompleted.

What did he contribute?

For most psychologists Kelly's name is associated with Personal Construct Theory. The basic idea is quite radical. Instead of thinking of a person as having a fixed set of schemata with which to make his or her world meaningful, a common presumption in cognitive psychology, Kelly began to work with the idea that people constructed conceptual resources to cope with the problem in hand, and even to identify what that problem might be. So not only were cognitive resources idiographic, but the form they took was contextual. Each person at each problematic juncture in his or her life constructed a conceptual repertoire to deal with it.

In the preface to *A Theory of Personality* (Kelly, 1963) he warns the reader that most of the familiar concepts of mainstream psychology, like 'learning', 'motivation', 'stimulus' and the like, will not be found in what follows. He was far ahead of his times in suggesting that it might be illuminating to credit ordinary people with the same cognitive powers to be exercised in the representation, prediction and control of the world as those made use of by scientists. It was wrong, he argued, to allow psychologists to claim something like scientific method as their exclusive domain, while their subjects were 'propelled by inexorable drives' (Kelly, 1963: 5). Here Kelly introduces his metaphor of 'man-as-scientist', forming and testing hypotheses both to make sense of the world as his cognitive resources make it available to him, and to attempt to control the situations that he encounters.[2]

By labelling his approach 'constructive alternativism', Kelly pointed to two features of human efforts to cope with life. 'Man looks at his world through transparent patterns or templates which he creates and then attempts to fit over the realities of which the world is composed. The fit is not always very good' (Kelly, 1963: 9). Such patterns consist of *constructs*. Constructs are ways of viewing the world.

People are also capable of constructing alternative patterns of thought, though sometime they have to be encouraged to do so. It is this aspect of constructive alternativism that ties Kelly's theoretical approach to the practicalities of dealing with clinical problems. Generally people are engaged in improving their systems of personal constructs in the face of the difficulties of life.

Kelly's studies convinced him that constructs consisted of pairs of elements giving each construct a positive and a negative pole. A 'construct' could be represented as a polarized pair of elements, one of a 'finite number of dichotomous constructs that make up a construct system' (Kelly, 1963: 61). The term 'construct' has crept into psychology-speak but it has been deprived of much of its original meaning. Nowadays it is usually used as a synonym for 'concept'. Kelly wanted to resist this as a generic interpretation in that it focused on the abstract aspect of thinking about the world, excluding the practical. For the same reason he was wary of giving 'constructs' an exclusively linguistic construal.

One of the most powerful aspects of Kelly's approach is the idea of a 'range of convenience'. A construct, say 'light-dark', has a domain of application that could roughly be defined as 'visual appearances'. Numbers are not within its range of convenience. However, when we talk of a winter evening as 'dark', the use of that term brings with it the whole construct, so 'light' is implicated too. Psychological systems have limited ranges of convenience. Kelly uses these ideas to deal with the fact that both psychological and physiological constructs seem to be required in the study of human beings' ways of coping with life. They have different ranges of convenience, yet, sometimes, there may be material events which can be construed in several construct systems. There is not as yet, nor, he thought, will there ever be, a universal construct system.

The task of psychology was to bring out the construct system a person was using at a specific time to deal with a specific situation. Every psychological construct system has a limited range of convenience. Kelly modestly remarks that his own construct system is appropriate for personality and interpersonal relationships. However, it does seem to have a greater range of convenience than that.

How and why do people create personal construct systems? They do so to antici-pate what is likely to come and to plan their actions. All cognitive and other processes are shaped by such anticipations. We anticipate events by 'construing their replica-tions' (Kelly, 1963: 50). By that he means making use of past experience. Of course things never go exactly as they did before. Here we come to another aspect of the way that psychology must be personal. 'A person's construction system varies as he successively construes the replication of events' (Kelly, 1963: 52).

Within a construct system, there are various internal relations. For example, there are hierarchical relationships, as in taxonomy. Sometimes the relation between con-structs is 'tight', that is when one of a pair of constructs is consistently used in the same way as the other. For example, 'steep–sloping' and 'dangerous–safe' might be used in very similar ways, to make very similar discriminations, in an architectural discussion or in skiing talk. There are loose relationships between constructs too (Kelly, 1963: 56–9).

Looking at the open set of construct systems in use by an individual, we should not be surprised to find that some are inconsistent with others. Kelly remarks that a person may successively employ a variety of construct subsystems which are inferentially incompatible with one another (Kelly, 1963: 83).

Since a person is forever modifying, extending and developing his or her con-struct system, Kelly has no place for an independent study of learning, as a separate department of psychology. 'Learning is not a special class of psychological processes. It is synonymous with any and all psychological processes' (Kelly, 1963: 75).

The growth of construct systems under the pressure of experience requires a distinction between constructs which can readily grow and those which cannot. This distinction is captured by his concept of 'permeability'. A construct is per-meable if it allows new items to be incorporated within its range of convenience. For example the permeability of 'heavy–light' is illustrated in the way its range of convenience expanded to cover chemical isotopes, such as 'heavy water'.

It comes as a surprise to find that Kelly did not care to be called a cognitive psychologist. What could be more cognitive than personal construct systems? He seems to have meant that other aspects of a person's life, not only thinking but also emotions, can be explained by reference to personal construct systems. For example, he thought that the source of many emotional experiences is some kind of transition. For instance, the realization that one's construct system is inade-quate for some task or situation leads to anxiety. This is not an analysis of what an emotion is, rather an analysis of the situation that elicits an emotion.

In summing up his point of view Kelly remarks that one of the ways his system is at odds with mainstream psychology in his time is its insistence on anticipation of events rather than reaction to events. Life is a matter of construing and reconstruing events in readiness for what is to come. Constructs not only are ways of making sense of the world, but this activity is in the interests of predicting and so, to an extent, being able to control the future. His point of view also focuses on the construct systems of individuals, taking account of their subjective experiences.

The application to clinical problems is very clear. People are troubled by the meaninglessness of their experience and their inability to manage their lives. Kelly's response was to suggest that the prime source of the trouble is an inadequate construct system. Encouraging the growth and modulation of the system, the tool for reconstructing events and so of managing them better is placed in the hands of the individual person. Clinical problems are problems for individuals, and their evolution must be at the level of individuals as well. Though he did not explicitly refer to the role of the social dimension in construct formation, the place of the local culture in providing sources for construct formation is implicit in every aspect of his 'new psychology'.

Kelly's work made very much more impact in the United Kingdom than in his own home country. This was particularly true of the methodology he developed to enable an investigation to display the system of personal constructs that a person was using at a particular moment to construe some aspect of life and action at that moment. The method was wholly idiographic, that is the research target was always the construct system of an individual person. The method has been called the 'Repertory Grid' technique. The most important manual for investigating the construct system was published in Britain in 1977, by Fay Fransella and Don Bannister. Others have followed.

Again, as in Kelly's other innovations, the basic idea is very simple. Consider any three items: A, B and C. There will surely be some way in which A and B are alike and some way in which C differs from them. In accordance with the theory of personal constructs, this pattern of similarity and difference must be the result of the construal of the threesome according to a dichotomy. The positive pole of the construct is the attribute or respect in which A and B are alike and the negative pole is whatever it is that differentiates C from A and B. An answer to the question 'In what respect are A and B alike and how do they both differ from C?' is the verbal expression of the construct with which this bit of construing was accomplished. Suppose our triad is 'spaghetti', 'vermicelli' and 'lasagne'. The first two are cylindrical and the third item is flat. So a possible construct for thinking about and managing pasta is 'cylindrical–flat'.

The idea of a repertory grid is simply a systematization of this kind of analysis. A group of *elements*, A, B, C and so on, are selected, relative to the problem in hand. The person whose construct system we are eliciting is asked to consider the elements in triads, and answer the 'similarity and difference' question for each triad. The list of answers is an expression of some fragment of that person's construct system, relative to the range of convenience tapped by the choice of elements. One can make the list of elements as long as one likes and so elicit more and more complex construct systems.

In the next step, the constructs so elicited can themselves be posed as a set of elements and a repertory grid of superordinate constructs elicited for construing them. In this way a richer and richer systematic expression of a person's cognitive resources can be displayed.

The recent revival of interest in idiographic studies, the psychology of individuals (for example see the recent work of **James Lamiell** (pp. 179–183), 2004), has led to a recovery of the work of George Kelly, sidelined for too long. Kelly's insistence on the personal nature of personal constructs raises a very fundamental question for cognitive psychology. Where is anything approximating to a general, pan-human law of cognition to be found? Such examples as Thorndyke's Law of Effect are of such abstractness and generality that citing them seems to have very little concrete explanatory force.

Further Reading

Primary Source

Kelly, G. A. (1963) *A Theory of Personality: The Psychology of Personal Constructs*. New York: Norton.

Secondary Source

Fransella, F. & Bannister, D. (1977) *A Manual for Repertory Grid Technique*. London: Academic Press.

Biographies

Boesee, C. G. (2004) George Kelly. *Internet Encyclopedia of Psychology.*
Neimeyer, R. A. & Jackson, T. T. (1997) George A. Kelly and the development of Personal Construct Theory. In W. G. Bringmann, H. E. Luck, R. Miller & C. E. Early (Eds), *A Pictorial History of Psychology* (pp. 364–72). Chicago: Quintessence Publishing Co.

Avram Noam Chomsky (1928–)

The abandonment of behaviourism in the second half of the 20th century was due in no small part to the vigor of the criticisms of the theories and methods of this school of psychology by Noam Chomsky. The most visible focus of his attack was a very thorough criticism of **B. F. Skinner**'s (pp. 15–24) book on language

(Chomsky, 1959), to which we will return. More importantly for the longer term history of psychology in the last century was his espousal and defence of a version of cognitivism. He shifted the focus of linguistics from the question of how instances of speech and writing were produced to the deeper question of the nature of linguistic knowledge. People do not store a huge repertoire of sentences to be produced on appropriate occasions, nor is language a matter of conditioned responses. Linguistic knowledge must consist of a capacity to create new sentences as they are called for. Chomsky's most influential theory of linguistic knowledge was based on the idea of rules for constructing such sentences. In his later revisions of his initial theory of linguistic competence he moved away from rule systems to a scheme of 'principles and parameters'. However, from the point of view of his influence on cognitive psychology, only his conception of linguistic competence as knowledge of rule systems is important.

Allied to this was a return to mentalism, the thesis that there exist mental states and processes, distinct both from public performances and from the brain processes that might support them. He went further in insisting not only that many of the principles of cognition were innate, but that at least those involved in the apprehension and production of the deep structures of language were universal, to be revealed by analysis in all cultures and languages.

Despite the fact that Chomskian linguistics no longer commands the same enthusiasm as it once did among linguists, some, at least, of his leading ideas and principles have become a part of our taken-for-granted ways of thinking about human beings.

Who is Noam Chomsky?

He was born on 7 December 1928 in Philadelphia. His father, William Chomsky, was a noted Hebrew scholar, author of several books on the Hebrew language. His mother, Elsie Simonofsky, like her husband had emigrated from Russia.

Robert Barsky's (1997) biography of Chomsky lays great emphasis on the influence of the Chomsky family on their elder son. He grew up in the closely knit world of immigrant Jews. His father, arriving penniless from Russia, managed to build a distinguished career in the Jewish schools of Philadelphia. He put himself through Johns Hopkins University to achieve the qualifications necessary to become eventually the head of Mikveh Israel school. At the same time he was building a career as a scholar of the Hebrew language. Evidently a gentle and good natured man, we can certainly see a source for his son's linguistic interests, but not for his political radicalism. That seems to have come from his mother Elsie. She was a teacher of Hebrew, but also one of the generation of Jewish radicals that emerged from the Great Depression. She inspired her son to a broader radicalism than simply discontent with such local matters as the place of the Jews in the city of Philadelphia. Where the often publicly reticent Noam Chomsky got his sense of self-righteousness, evident as much in his resistance to academic criticism as in his unremitting attacks on the villainy of the well-meaning, can hardly have been from his amiable father. His competitiveness as a child has been remarked upon.

Young Noam entered the University of Philadelphia in 1945, to study philosophy and linguistics. An important influence on his subsequent career was the prominent linguist Zelig Harris, then teaching at Philadelphia. Chomsky majored in linguistics and went on to a master's degree in 1951. By then he had married another linguist, Carol Schatz.

The pattern of his childhood and youth echoes that of many of those from excluded communities in different places who have contributed to the 20th-century developments in our conceptions of what it is to be a human being. In the parental generation all kinds of oppressive restrictions were dissolved or escaped from, whether by revolution in the case of **Lev Vygtosky** (pp. 26–34) and **Alexander Luria** (pp. 105–13), or by prior family emigration in the case of Chomsky and **Stanley Milgram** (pp. 207–11). Above all, though not exclusively, it was the Jewish community that benefited most from these profound social changes.

Chomsky spent four very productive years as a Fellow of the Harvard Society of Fellows. During this time he developed most of the leading ideas that figure in the work for which he is best known. His PhD dissertation of 1955 was already concerned with the transformational analysis of syntactic structures as a route to the representation of linguistic knowledge.

In 1955 he joined the faculty at MIT, where he has remained for the whole of his academic career. During his time there the departments of linguistics and philosophy were merged, creating a department well suited to the breadth of his interests.

However, he has had another career, very different in its impact on the world outside the academic subject of linguistics. It seems that it was the war in Viet Nam that first drew him into radical politics. His publicly expressed position has often been described as 'left wing', but that characterization seems to be seriously misleading. He has been a critic of authoritarian institutions of all kinds. Instead of the traditional left-wing presumption that the care of the populace and the moral standing of the community should be handed over to the government, his political stance has been anarchist, close to that of Kropotkin. Governments give rise to bureaucracies which become impervious to outside influences, pursing policies that serve their own interests. His most famous political publication, *American Power and the New Mandarins* (1969), was addressed to the role of the government bureaucracy in the mismanagement of the Vietnam war.

Not surprisingly he has been a critic of the policies of the US government that have led to many foreign interventions, from the ill-starred operations in South East Asia to the most recent actions in Central America and the Middle East. The root of his criticisms is to be found in a rejection of capitalism as a means of production of the necessities of life, since he believes that these incursions are motivated by the need to protect and perhaps even expand the influence of US business and its ideology. It seems that this rejection is rooted in something yet deeper, a distaste for hierarchical systems of control, of which bureaucracies and capitalist business enterprises are prime examples. He has worked out these critical ideas in a variety of books and articles, notably *What Uncle Sam Really Wants* (1992).

Chomsky's visits to university campuses are usually welcomed with great enthusiasm. However, his standing among the student community has little to do with his work in linguistics and its implications for cognitive psychology. It can be put down almost wholly to the excitement of his political speeches: the man who is willing to say the unsayable, to find the worm in the apple.

Throughout the years of his absorption in political causes he has continued to develop his linguistic theories. His most recent work shifts away somewhat from the doctrines that made him famous and which had such an impact in the revolution that led to cognitive psychology. It is hard to find any direct Chomskian influence in contemporary thinking at the cutting edge of psychology. The shift of attention to the interpersonal locus of psychological phenomena has left his deep-seated individualism behind, at least for the moment.

What has he contributed?

Chomsky's contributions to our conception of human nature arise indirectly from the concepts and theories he pioneered in developing a new turn in linguistics. However, his thought grew and changed in such a way that it is necessary to distinguish a classical Chomskian period from his later positions.

The classical Chomsky is the author of *Aspects of the Theory of Syntax* (1965) and *Cartesian Linguistics* (1966). In these two books, the same ideas are presented from somewhat different points of view. The former is an analytical presentation of a way of understanding our knowledge of language. The latter is a historical survey of linguistic theories in which Chomsky finds prefigurements of his own lines of argument.

Four main ideas or principles are evident and explicitly defended in his work.

There is the distinction between a theory of *performance* and a theory of *competence*, between explaining what someone does and explaining how it is that the person can do it. These are not theories in the sense that one encounters theories in physics and chemistry, that is descriptions of actual or possible generative mechanisms. They are formal systems representing their subject matters at high levels of abstraction. A theory of competence is a formal representation of a body of linguistic knowledge.

There is the distinction between the *surface structure* of linguistic utterances and the *deep structure*, the base form from which the surface structure is derived. Generative, transformational rules are the formal means by which the forms of deep structures are transformed appropriately to be produced as meaningful utterances displaying the surface structure of a natural language.

Chomsky has been insistent throughout his writing on the *innateness* of the basic cognitive resources on which language as a human practice depends. He dismisses the role of the social matrix of childhood just as much as the demands of the practical uses of words as sources of the forms of language per se. The basic cognitive requirements for language are inherited, in the form of a Language Acquisition Device, with which the auditory environment of infants is searched for linguistic forms.

The fourth major thesis is the *universality* of deep grammatical forms throughout the human race. Only human beings have the language capability. Language is species specific. Only human beings have the capacity for both semantics and syntax (and perhaps phonology as well), the key components of language as such.

All four 'principles' are to be understood in the context of a strong return to mentalism. Cognitive linguistics is a theory of mental states and processes. Occasionally Chomsky made a half-hearted attempt to suggest neural mechanisms by means of which the cognitive tasks of language acquisition and management are carried on, but they played no role in the theory, except as sites for the universality that is the result of the genetic origins of the language capacity.

Though he seems the archetype of a theoretician, Chomsky claims empirical support for at least some of the above principles. The highly contentious claim that the basic cognitive requirements for language are innate is supposedly supported by the rate at which children pick up their mother tongues. It is far too fast for any kind of conditioning theory to be plausible. Nor could it be the result of a kind of proto-scientific inductive extraction of grammatical generalizations from the data of the speech with which an infant is surrounded. The linguistic performances from which they would have to be extracted are too messy and variable. Chomsky also claims to have evidence that in all linguistic cultures the stages of acquisition and the errors to which children are prone are the same. If these features of language acquisition are universal then surely they must be rooted in something innate, part of what it is to be human.

Both the strength of his commitment to innateness and the vagueness of exactly what the thesis comprises are evident in his *Rules and Representations* (1980: 91), where he claims that 'certain factors that govern or enter into the adult system of rules, representations and principles belong to universal grammar; that is, they are somehow represented in the genotype. ... Among the elements of the genotype ... are ... certain basic properties of the mental representations and the rule systems that generate and relate them.'

An alternative proposal, based on evidence assembled by **Jerome Bruner** (pp. 54–62) and others, suggests that there are certain linguistic games played by mothers and children everywhere in which one can discern the means by which certain linguistic universals are acquired. Bruner's studies of the role of the 'peek-a-boo' game could be seen as challenging Chomsky's innateness principle.

One of the most telling insights that has tended to support at least part of Chomsky's linguistics is the remarkable fact that people can and do produce an endless stream of novel sentences with a finite set of resources. Indeed most sentences with which people make statements, ask for directions, upbraid a malefactor and so on have never been heard before, and with rare exceptions will never be heard again. Yet their intent is perfectly clear and they are usually understood immediately. One might remark that musicians do the same with even more restricted resources. The idea of base structure and transformations existed in music theory long before it emerged in linguistics.

Let us now turn to each of these main theses to show them in Chomskian form.

What is a generative grammar? Chomsky is quite clear that it is not a psychology of language use. 'It attempts to characterize in the most neutral possible terms the knowledge of the language that provides the basis for the actual use of language by speaker-hearer' (Chomsky, 1965: 9). Such a grammar simply assigns structural descriptions to sentences. It is not a model of speech production. The application of this notion to cognitive psychology should go no further than designing a means of representation for various bodies of knowledge, such as knowledge of the past, knowledge of tennis, knowledge of social conventions and so on. In so far as one might mount a general criticism of the Chomskian project his use of formal devices for expressing these bodies of knowledge is surely problematic. Furthermore, it is concerned with knowledge belonging to individuals, setting aside the question of bodies of knowledge that exist only in the public domain of common practices. It can be compared with **Serge Moscovici**'s (pp. 216–221) concept of a *représentation sociale*, as a body of social knowledge.

There are three components in a generative grammar. There is a phonological component, a semantic component and a syntactical component. 'The base of the syntactical component is a system of rules that generate a ... set of basic strings, each with an associated structural description called a base phrase-marker' (Chomsky, 1965: 17). These are the elementary components of deep structures. The rules for construction of these ordered sequences of phrase markers, noun phrase etc., comprise the phrase-structure grammar. There is also a set of transformation rules, which convert phrase markers into more complex phrase markers. These generate the surface structure of sentences that appear in overt speech acts, from deep structural bases. For example, the linguistic knowledge implicit in a host of well formed sentences can be expressed as follows:

Base structure: S(sentence) → NP (noun phrase) VP (verb phrase)

Transformations:

VP → V (verb) NP
NP → DET (definite article) N (noun)
NP → N

So we have a representation of the knowledge of a certain syntactic form, exemplified in 'Jill stroked the cat', and innumerable sentences like it, such as 'Henry crashed the car', 'James wanted the money' and so on.

Language in use is surely a flow of meaningful signs – how then is semantics incorporated into the scheme? Chomsky tackles this question in reflecting on what informs subcategorizations, such as the subcategories of Noun into Abstract, Common, Human and so on. This is linguistic information of prime importance. Can it be presented formally? He offers the idea of rewrite rules to be applied to the basic items in the deep structural analysis. He lists the following rules: 'N → Proper', 'N → Common', 'Proper → Pr-Human', and so on. Using them allows these categorial distinctions to be incorporated formally in the syntactic representations of sentences.

Are these rules language-specific or are they universals? Chomsky notes several sorts of possible universals. There might be certain fixed syntactic categories to be found in the syntactic representations of sentences in all languages. There might be semantic universals, for example that every language will have devices for referring to persons. This suggestion has been developed by Wierzbicka (1992). There may also be formal syntactic universals 'that involve the character of the rules that appear in grammars' (Chomsky, 1965: 29).

How do we know whether a hypothetical grammatical form is correct? Chomsky notes the necessity of relying on the intuitions of the native speaker in the absence of some more objective method of assessment, though he is rightly cautious about suggesting any concrete possibilities. He is right too in dismissing any suggestion that this methodology might render the linguistics based on it 'unscientific'.

There have been attempts to apply this idea to other ordered structures in human life, such as menus. Each cuisine can be expressed in terms of a generative transformational grammar, the result of the application of which is an acceptable menu. The idea of representing bodies of knowledge in rules and schemata rather than repertoires of representations of individual action sequences has also been influential in social psychology. For example the idea of knowledge of appropriate situated public performances as 'scripts' has been used by Schank and Abelson (1977) and is the basis of the role-rule model of social action proposed by Harré and Secord (1972). The recent development of 'narratology' is based on the idea that people manage their lives in accord with certain general storylines. It has strong echoes of the Chomskian conception of the roots of competence (Shafer, 1992).

From his earliest writings Chomsky was concerned to expound and defend a strong innateness thesis over and against the empiricism of most linguists and philosophers. In broad terms, he argued that human beings were so constituted that they were only able to acquire a body of linguistic knowledge that incorporated certain grammatical principles. His argument is presented in the form of a discussion of what sort of language acquisition devices a human being might possess innately.

His critical account of the empiricist point of view is notable for its strong individualism. He envisages a child being born with some very rudimentary capacities, for example, to perform 'a preliminary analysis of experience' and that 'one's concepts and knowledge, beyond this, are acquired by application of the available inductive principles to this initially analyzed experience' (Chomsky, 1965: 48). Since this is surely implausible, the only alternative he envisages is the theory of innate ideas. The idea that language is acquired socially in symbiotic joint activities with others is not even mentioned. His one-phrase account of Wittgenstein's 'language game' of language acquisition is inaccurate. Vygotsky does not get even a passing mention.

Given the individualism of his overall approach, Chomsky finds allies in 17th- and 18th-century authors. Using such sources he presented a much more detailed account of the innateness theory in his *Cartesian Linguistics* (1966). Chomsky notes with approval the strong connection between the powers of language and creative and original thinking of many authors in the period. However, it is difficult to know what to make of his declaration that 'human language, in its normal use, is free from the control of independently identifiable external stimuli or internal states and is not restricted to any practical communicative function' (Chomsky, 1966: 19). It seems obvious that its normal use is to describe things, to express feelings and to give orders, apologize and so on. Of course, the tropes of metaphor and simile provide a powerful means of outreach to what has never been thought before. However, that does not mean to say that humdrum linguistic practices of everyday are not the normal uses of language.

Chomsky's influence was hugely amplified by his famous and widely disseminated review of B. F. Skinner's book on language (Chomsky, 1959). Skinner had attempted a comprehensive theory of language acquisition and subsequent language use exclusively in terms of operant conditioning. Chomsky mounted a powerful argument to show the impossibility of learning language by any process of conditioning, classical or operant.

Of greater interest to psychologists was his approving presentation of the linguistic observations of William von Humboldt. Creative speech production and speech perception must make use of the same generative system, since it is in terms of this system that the elements of language are defined. This may very well be true, without it being the case that the generative system is, in any interesting way, innate in individuals.

The thesis of innateness of syntactic categories is tied up with the principle of universality. As we saw above there are many possibilities for the existence of universals in the domain of human language. A claim for universality is obviously greatly strengthened by evidence of innateness. The best attitude to adopt for the use of this pair of concepts to categorize the foundations of linguistics or of cognitive psychology in general is particularly difficult to know. This is because even if one were to push most of the influences that bring language into being in the individual into the social world and the close personal interaction of the family circle, some innate capacities must still reside in the individual. **Ludwig Wittgenstein** (pp. 240–246) emphasized the 'human form of life' and 'natural expressions', in reference to what we would now call 'human ethology'. Chomsky's efforts to formulate a theory of language acquisition in isolation from developmental psychology makes his contributions difficult to evaluate.

Innateness and universality of the language skill are linked to another strong thesis. Chomsky has been insistent that language is species-specific – only human beings have it. The way this thesis has worked itself out in debates with ethologists who have attempted to establish human-like language skills in chimpanzees and gorillas has been to highlight a clear distinction between semantics, the study of the intentional use of meaningful signs, and syntax, the systematic ordering of meaningful signs into sentence-like structures. There is no doubt that apes make use of meaningful signs in the course of social life and in the management of practical activities. It is also clear that there is little positive evidence to support the idea that they are capable of ordering signs in a syntax-like way. Chimps and gorillas do not have such a level of cognitive capacity that would enable a generative transformational grammar. Their language-like activities do not display the kind of consistent surface structures that would suggest any kind of deep structures shaping the forms of cognition.

Taking the Chomskian theory seriously as an account of language skills and their implementation in speaking, writing and reading prompts the question of the reality of the structures and processes that it seems to presuppose. He argues that: 'There is no reason for a linguist to refrain from imputing existence to ... [an] initial apparatus of mind' (Chomsky, 1980: 187) by analogy with a physicist taking seriously the hypothesis that there are thermonuclear reactions in the sun. But this begs the question. Thermonuclear reactions are known and have been observed elsewhere than in the interior of the sun, so like all good realist models they already possess ontological plausibility. The problem with Chomsky's 'grammars' is that there are no sources for his model of cognition other than grammar itself, the very 'what-is-it' that is in question.

Taking thinking seriously raises a deep and longstanding metaphysical conundrum. *How* does thinking exist? In what *realm of being* should thoughts be located? Must a return to cognitivism be paralleled by a return to the Cartesian vision of human beings as composed of two kinds of stuff, material bodies and immaterial minds? In Chapter 4 we turn to the work of the computationalists, and the problem of how best to make working models of cognitive processes that do not lead inexorably to the Cartesian mind. If computation is an abstract model of thinking, perhaps computers might be concrete models of active brains.

Further Reading

Primary Sources

Chomsky, N. (1959) Review of B. F. Skinner's *Verbal Behavior Language,* **35**, 26–58.
Chomsky, N. (1965) *Aspects of the Theory of Syntax*. Cambridge, MA: MIT Press.
Chomsky, N. (1966) *Cartesian Linguistics*. New York: Harper and Row.
Chomsky, N. (1969) *American Power and the New Mandarins*. London: Chatto & Windus.
Chomsky, N. (1980) *Rules and Representations*. New York: Columbia University Press.
Chomsky, N. (1992) *What Uncle Sam Really Wants*. Berkeley: Odonian Press.

Secondary Sources

Harré, R. & Secord, P. F. (1972) *The Explanation of Social Behaviour*. Oxford: Blackwell.
Schank, R. C. & Abelson, R. B. (1977) *Scripts, Plans, Goals and Understanding*. Hillsdale, NJ: Erlbaum.

Shafer, R. (1992) *Retelling a Life*. New York: Basic Books.
Wierzbicka, A. (1992) *Semantics, Culture and Cognition*. Oxford: Oxford University Press.

Biography

Barsky, R. F. (1997) *Noam Chomsky: A Life of Dissent*. Cambridge, MA: MIT Press.

Reflections

Frederic Bartlett's (pp. 47–54) work faded from sight for decades after his death. It was based on detailed empirical studies, involving long-running and painstaking research. He made no use at all of the key components of the methods of enquiry practised by most psychologists, that is he did not use the independent/dependent variable design of experiments, nor did he subject his results to statistical analysis. **Jerome Bruner**'s (pp. 54–62) challenge to behaviourism came from another critical perspective. He did not hesitate to develop hypotheses about unobservable cognitive processes, the existence of which would *explain* the results of his experiment. Coming forward with hypotheses referring to schemata and rules, he led the way to a cognitive psychology that takes mental processes seriously. On the question of just what ontological status such processes should be assigned he remained agnostic.

Far from the Harvard–Oxford axis **George Kelly** (pp. 62–68) hammered out a kind of home grown 'cognitivism' of his own. His writings make clear that he was well aware of the need to recover a methodology of scientific realism for psychology. He added two ingredients of importance. The first was the firm insistence that cognition is idiographic, unique in kind to each individual. His second contribution was a method for tracking real people thinking about real issues in real time, the method of Repertory Grids. The structure of an individual's cognitive resources appears in the internal analysis of each person's grid. Here is the method of correlations properly applied.

Cognition is subject to norms of correctness. There are rules for thinking, speaking, reasoning, remembering and the like *correctly*. Are such rules no more psychologically significant than reports of the norms evident in a practice? **Noam Chomsky**'s (pp. 68–77) revival of a kind of mentalism in linguistics soon spilled over into psychology. Though in his original theory the notion of 'rule' was a device for representing linguistic knowledge, it was natural to go on to suppose that something rule-like was at work in the genesis of orderly behaviour. People are very sensitive to violations of the linguistic standards and, so it turned out, to violations of social norms as well.

The question of the status of rule hypotheses in a realist psychology is still controversial. There is no doubt that people frequently follow rules as instructions for what to do. Are other kinds of orderly behaviour the result of unconscious processes that are similar in character to overt rule-following? Or is rule talk a metaphor for information processing realized in the brain as a computational device? These questions remain to be answered.

Notes

1 George Miller has been a staunch supporter of cognitive psychology. He is well known for his observation that the number of symbols one can conveniently hold on to is 7 +/– 2.

2 This text was written in 1955. At that time, the convention of referring to 'men and women' by the generic 'he' was standard grammatical practice. The species was usually referred to as 'Man'.

4

The Computationalists

The advent of cognitive psychology in the mid 20th century opened up the question of the best models with which to represent the cognitive processes that were presumed to underlie overt cognitive performances. It was all very well to have fashioned a representation of a body of knowledge, but how was it implemented in action? A model of something is a representation based on an analogy between the model and its subject. Scientific models are often used to represent mechanisms and processes that are at the time unobservable. Trying to extend our powers of observation to test the verisimilitude or truth-like qualities of our models is one of the most important and fruitful ways that the natural sciences grow. Scientific models are also used to abstract the salient features of something complicated or of something which is in some way indeterminate or ill-defined. For example, weather maps present simplified models of the complex flux of pressure and humidity in regions of the atmosphere. Here the subject and source of the model are the same, namely the processes occurring in the atmosphere. When models are used to represent processes which are currently beyond the reach of observation, necessarily the source and the subject of the model are different. Darwin's theory of evolution by natural selection was the expression of a model or representation of the process that he imagined had occurred in nature over vast stretches of time. He based it on what he knew of the methods of selective breeding used by farmers and gardeners to transform existing strains of animals and plants. The natural sciences are rich in this kind of model. Here the subject (whatever happened in the remote past) and the source of the model (what we know about selective breeding) are different. The plausibility of the model depends in part on whether the source, in this case selective breeding on the farm, can be identified in some way with a possible process in nature. Both kinds of models appear in the work of the computationalists.

As long ago as the 16th century the project of building a machine that would simulate human and animal behaviour was taken seriously. Various automata were constructed that mimicked some relatively simple actions of people and animals. These models, including models of full-sized orchestras, were mostly driven hydraulically. Some of these can be seen in a curious museum near the town of Eau Clair, Wisconsin, in the United States. A hydraulic model of the nervous system was popular at the time. Some philosophers conjectured that animals were just fleshly hydraulic machines.

The idea that an actual machine could simulate human cognitive powers was not pursued seriously until the 19th century. The title of La Mettrie's book, *L'Homme Machine*, published in 1749, was more a metaphor for a materialist explanation of cognition than a serious attempt to propose a thinking machine to reproduce at least some of the cognitive powers of a person. In the 1840s, Thomas Babbage (1791–1871) made a machine which, at least in principle, could perform arithmetical calculations mechanically. By now the source of mental models had moved on to mechanisms. In the 20th century electrical systems, including the telephone network, began to be used as a source for models of various aspects of human psychology.

It is one thing to construct a machine that simulates a human being performing a cognitive or practical task. It is quite another to play with the idea that a machine could think as a human being thinks, and thus would be conscious. This possibility was still far fetched at the beginning of the 20th century. However, during the Second World War, the idea of making a serious comparison between a machine's capacity to perform human tasks and a human being's cognitive capacities took a huge step forward with **Alan Turing**'s (pp. 82–86) theoretical and practical inventions in computation. His ideas were very quickly taken up by many others, including the idea that machines should, in certain circumstances, be said to think. If machines could properly be said to be think, at least in principle, perhaps people were, in their own way, thinking machines, working in a similar way. This startling conjecture was the foundation for a new turn in psychology, the computational model of mind. Computing machines and their internal processes became a fertile source for models to represent cognitive processes.

When asked what had been his aim in life **Marvin Minsky** (pp. 93–98), one of those whose work is to be discussed in this chapter, replied 'To construct intelligent machines'. This answer prompts the question that has bedeviled the project of building a computationalist psychology: 'Is an *intelligent* machine a device that can only *do* what people can do, or is it one that can also *think* like people think?' Behaviourists would not make any distinction between these alternatives. For them only overt behaviour is relevant to a scientific psychology. However, for cognitive psychologists this is a real question. Perhaps people are machines, though not in the same way as locomotives or grenade launchers. For an admirably clear and well-written introduction to the contested relation between cognition and computation Minsky's *The Society of Mind* (1987) has not been bettered.

George Miller (1920–) was one of the leading founder members of the Center for Cognitive Studies, set up at Harvard in 1967. With **Jerome Bruner** (pp. 54–62) he threw himself into a vigorous programme of research and writing to bring to fruition the insights that had led to the flight from positivistic behaviourism to a psychology that fulfilled the tenets of scientific realism. Miller was responsible for one of the most pervasive and influential models that shaped cognitive psychology, the < Test, Operate, Test, Exit > or 'TOTE' machine. This device continued to perform a task until a certain desired state had been reached, and then it stopped. Such a machine could be looked at in three ways. It could be a plan for an actual machine with the links between parts conduits for energy. It could be a flow chart for the processing of information through a series of boxes. It could be a computer running a programme drawn from a memory store. Miller and others not only adopted models like the TOTE machine, but attempted to develop mathematical descriptions of the phenomena and of the schemata that were employed by people in creating them. The actual results of this kind of work were disappointing. However, Miller's enthusiasm and his faith in formal modelling of cognitive processes provided some of the impetus to keep the computationalist programme running.

The 20th century saw a great many advances in the mathematical analysis of computation and the design of more and more powerful and successful computing machines. The use of this technology as the groundwork for a new science of mind was enthusiastically promoted and just as strongly contested. The era began and ended with the publication and intense discussion of two famous thought experiments. The Turing Test strongly suggested an identity between computation and thought. However **John Searle**'s (pp. 98–101) thought experiment of the 'Chinese Room' seemed to undercut the idea, even in principle. These imaginary experiments will be described and their significance explained as we go along. At this point, we need to understand the importance of thought experiments in the sciences. The history of the computational model of mind is very largely a history of theoretical debates and thought experiments.

The development of physics has depended on the judicious invention of imaginary experiments. Newton's Laws describe situations in which there is neither a driving force, nor any resisting friction to interfere with the pure motion of material things. Einstein's images of moving trains and falling elevators were not just illustrations of the special and general theories of relativity, but it seems they were integral to the thinking that produced them. Computational psychology is very much in the same mould as Newtonian and post-Newtonian physics and Darwinian biology, heavily dependent on 'thought' experiments.

Alan Mathison Turing (1912–54)

This remarkable man must be credited with three innovations that bore on the programme of research that linked computing machines to human cognition. The first was the discovery of a set of rules and procedures by the use of which any computable function could be evaluated in a finite number of steps. The second was the invention of an abstract machine that could perform these operations in a purely mechanical way (Turing, 1936). The third was his contribution to the design of a practical version of his abstract machine, the electronic computing machine. After the Second World War Turing was responsible for the basic plan of the first computing machine that incorporated its own programmes, the ACE machine developed at Manchester University.

Within a decade practical computing machines were being used for the performance of all sorts of routine jobs. They were not just sophisticated adding machines. They were capable of simulations of the performance of many of the everyday cognitive and manual tasks on which our way of life depends. Information technology (IT) as a branch of engineering has been a huge success.

The suggestion of a strong link between this branch of engineering and psychology was first clearly articulated in a paper Turing wrote in 1950. He proposed a test which would justify us in saying that any machine which could pass it should properly be said to be thinking. The obverse of this idea was the principle that opened up the possibility of computational psychology, that any being which can think must be a kind of computing machine.

Who was Alan Mathison Turing?

Alan Turing was born in London on 25 June 1912. His father was an administrator in India, while his mother came from an Anglo-Irish family who were also long involved in the subcontinent. He was brought up, as were many of the children of the British Raj, by various foster parents. He entered Sherborne School in 1924, going up to Kings College, Cambridge in 1930. His biographer, Andrew Hodges (1983), emphasizes Turing's intellectual isolation during his school days. As an enthusiast for science and mathematics in a school which aimed to place its best pupils in Oxford and Cambridge to study classics, he was something of an outsider.

All this changed at Cambridge. His academic successes were crowned by a Fellowship at Kings in 1935. His personal life matured around his realization of his homosexuality, unstigmatized in the college of such men as J. M. Keynes. His mathematical studies turned increasingly to fundamental questions of the logic underlying mathematical enquiries. The German mathematician David Hilbert had posed the issue clearly – could there be a method by which the provability of any mathematical assertion whatever could be decided? To answer this question Turing began his famous analysis of what a purely mechanical process of reasoning would require. The result was his description of an abstract machine and the rules for its use that would represent all possible formal mathematical procedures. The Turing machine became the theoretical foundation of all real computing machines. He was able to use the specification of the Universal Turing Machine, a machine that would itself specify the rules for specific calculations, to show that there were necessarily unsolvable problems in mathematics.

In 1936, Turing enrolled as a graduate student at Princeton, completing his work on Hilbert's problem, to some extent in isolation. The leading mathematician at Princeton at that time was Alonzo Church, who published his solution to the Hilbert problem just before the publication of Turing's solution, which had been mysteriously delayed. There is little doubt of Turing's priority. He returned to Cambridge in 1938, somewhat disillusioned with academic life.

At the outbreak of war, he officially took up work as a cryptographer or code breaker at the newly established centre at Bletchley Park, though he had been secretly at work for the government already. The organization at Bletchley grew very rapidly, each group specializing in one of the cryptographic problems posed by the German codes. Turing himself set to work on breaking the code generated by a German coding device, the Enigma machine. His success in discovering the working of the first version of the machine was short-lived. A new and more complex version of Enigma was developed. Eventually the workings of this machine too were mastered, using the same methodology that Turing had developed for the original 'Enigma problem'. However, he had already become interested in using digital electronic devices for performing large numbers of calculations very quickly, whatever the problem to which they were relevant. He led the engineering group that produced a machine to decode the latest Enigma encryptions. Even before the war ended Turing was thinking of how to use these advances to build a real electronic version of his Universal Turing Machine, a mechanism that would perform all possible computations.

He realized that the key to the advancement of electronic computing was to input the programme into the machine, as well the data on which it was to operate, rather than laboriously reprogramming it for every new type of computation. The necessary hardware was slow to materialize, until the Americans announced their plan to develop an advanced electronic computer, EDVAC. It was still primitive relative to Turing's proposed machine, since it did not store its own programmes. Eventually the British effort did get underway with ACE, the Advanced Computing Engine. The Manchester machine was designed to store its own programmes, giving it the capability to switch from one task to another, without any additional electronic components. Here we have the first hint of a parallel with the way human beings think. We do not have to learn a new technique every time we encounter a slightly different problem. The ACE machine was never built. The implementation of Turing's idea of the stored programme was pushed forward by others at Manchester, and in 1948 the first such machine was switched on. Deeply disillusioned by what he regarded as inexcusable 'messing about', Turing did not even attempt to publish any of his papers or lectures of this time. It has only recently been realized how far he had already moved beyond the then state of the art.

From the late 1940s, Turing's interests moved away from computation and programming towards mathematical chemistry, and the problem of the genesis of chemical structures. In 1951 he published a paper that was to prove seminal in this field too.

Throughout the period, he had been continuing to work for the government intelligence services on code breaking. The Cold War had begun and a new array of encryption systems made their appearance. To his dismay, his security clearance was revoked. Though always discrete, he had never concealed his sexual orientation. In Britain at that time homosexuality was not only a statutory crime, but in the atmosphere of suspicion, the threats of espionage and the possibility of blackmail it had come to be perceived as a threat to the security of the nation. As a homosexual, Turing was vulnerable. However, worse was to come. In 1952, he was arrested in connection with an alleged relationship with a young man who had burgled his house. The details of this extraordinary story can be found in Hodges's (1983) biography. Turing escaped prison by submitting to the humiliating alternative of a course of hormone treatment. The episode, a shameful disgrace to Britain, ended with his suicide. He killed himself by eating an apple into which he had injected strychnine.

What sort of man was this, that he could be at the forefront of so many innovations and yet, in his lifetime, receive not only so little recognition, but also so little support when the exigencies of wartime had passed? Personal reticence and dislike of the limelight is one strand in the story. The isolation inevitable in those days of those whose sexuality did not fit the official paradigm is probably another.

What did he contribute?

A certain amount of detail will be necessary to appreciate the relation between the Turing Machine, actual computers and the project of computational psychology. Turing's imaginary machine consists of an endless tape which runs through a read and write head. The head can erase whatever symbol is already printed there and print a 0 or 1 instead. Turing proved that all possible computations could be performed by the machine, if its operations were controlled by following a finite set of rules in a finite number of steps. For example, a step in a calculation might require that the tape be moved three places through the head; if a 1 is found there it is erased and replaced by a 0; if a 0, no action is to be taken. Numbers are represented in the binary code as strings of 0s and 1s. Thus, we have the natural numbers written as the sequence 0, 1, 10, 11, 100, and so on instead of the familiar base 10 representation as 0, 1, 2, 3, 4 and so on. However, binary strings need not stand for numbers. *They can be assigned other kinds of meanings.* In the ASCII code each letter of the alphabet is assigned a binary number. If we can find computable functions to represent relations among whatever non-numerical objects the strings represent, for example the spelling conventions of English, we can use the power of the computer to simulate any cognitive process for which such a function can be found. We could construct a programme that would check the spelling of English words. Classifying is a cognitive procedure of profound psychological importance. If a way of classifying could be expressed as a set of computable functions we would have the basis for simulating the cognitive process of ordering things into kinds. We would need to define a relation 'is a' linking a description of an individual with a description of a kind or species to express 'Tweetie is a bird' formally. It might be based on the requirement that the attributes of the species be among the attributes of the individual. Thus classifying Tweetie as a bird could be accomplished if among Tweetie's attributes were the defining properties of the kind 'bird'. The relevant groups of attributes could be represented by strings of binary digits ('bits') and a computational rule for comparing them worked out.

By 1950, Turing believed he had put in train everything needed to build a thinking machine, a kind of artificial brain. This encouraged him to try to bring out the link between psychology and computation in a thought experiment. Here was the famous Turing Test. A human being, let us call this person 'the operator', sits at a console with a keyboard and VDU. Screened from the operator is another human being, the 'responder', similarly equipped, and a computer. Each can be linked to the operator's screen. The operator can key in whatever question he or she likes. Turing argued that if the operator could not tell whether the responder was the person or the computer, then we would be obliged to say that the computer was thinking when it replied to the operator's questions in a human-like way. Giving human-like answers was enough, Turing thought, to conclude that the machine was thinking like a human being.

The original Turing Test explored the question of whether we should say that a machine can think. The complementary question, of course, is whether the human responder in the test should be described as an organic computer.

The pattern of relationships implicit in the Turing Test is something like this:

Brain is to Thinking as Computer is to Computing

This scheme can be decomposed into two comparisons: that between thinking and computing; and that between brains and computing machines. As far as Turing was concerned, the pattern represented a thought experiment, since he had no empirical research to rely upon. The next step in this progression would be to define two psychological research programmes, exploring each of the comparisons.

Further developments did indeed follow each of these two lines. At the Carnegie Institute of Technology in Pittsburgh, **Herbert Simon** and **Allen Newell** (pp. 86–93) pursued the possibility of writing programmes that would faithfully simulate human cognitive processes, some of which they had studied in detail. For 30 years they pursued Turing's first comparison. Elsewhere, in particular at MIT, led by **Marvin Minsky** (pp. 93–98), others tried to create electronic devices that could serve as analogues of the nets of neurons of which the human brain was made. In this way they hoped to explore the viability of Turing's second implicit comparison, the brain as a computing device, a Universal Turing Machine.

It is important to realize that once a word, rule, concept, melody or whatever has been represented in the machine, everything that follows is a matter of physics. The strings of 1s and 0s are represented in the machine by the electrical states of registers, something like rows of switches. '1' is represented by a switch being on, '0' by a switch being off. Running a programme is a physical process, sending electrical impulses in a certain pattern, a pattern that changes the states of registers. Is there a corresponding physical system in the human brain, and are there physico-chemical processes that are comparable to the running of a programme?

Just as the psychologists of the 17th and 18th centuries shifted from hydraulic models to mechanical, so in the 20th century computational modellers took up successively two very different conceptions of computing machines. The original model was based on a type of machine in which a central processing module drew 'data' and 'programmes' from ancillary 'memory stores'. In such a machine processing was sequential. Simulation of the output of human cognitive processes was made possible by the extraordinary speed with which such machines eventually accomplished huge numbers of computations. The brain to machine comparison prompted a different device, the 'neural net', in which there were many simultaneous computations being performed in the nodes of an interconnected net. By the 1960s it had been shown that a properly set up net could be used to instantiate a Turing Machine, and so do whatever the other type of machine could do (McCulloch & Pitts, 1943). It turned out it could do very much more, in some cases coming close to the realistic simulation of the performance of a person on a similar task (Bechtel & Abrahamsen, 1991). Furthermore, since the ultimate source of the model was the layout of cells in the various organs of the brain, the plausibility of the model seemed to be assured. It now seems certain that Turing himself had anticipated these developments.

Further Reading

Primary Sources

Turing, A. M. (1936) On computable numbers. *Proceedings of the London Mathematical Society,* Series 2, **42**, 230–265.
Turing, A. M. (1950) Computing machinery and intelligence. *Mind,* New Series 59, 433–450.

Secondary Sources

Bechtel, W. & Abrahamsen, A. (1991) *Connectionism and the Mind.* Oxford: Blackwell.
Copeland, J. (1998) *Artificial Intelligence.* Oxford: Blackwell.
McCulloch, W. S. & Pitts, W. H. (1943) A logical calculus of the ideas immanent in nervous activity. *Bulletin of Mathematical Biophysics,* **5**,115–133.

Biography

Hodges, A. (1983) *Alan Turing: The Enigma of Intelligence.* London: Burnett Books.

Herbert Simon (1916–2002) and Allen Newell (1927–92)

Parallel to the work of **Marvin Minsky** (pp. 93–98) and his colleagues at MIT to be described in the next section, another approach to the project of a computationalist psychology was under way in Pittsburgh at what became Carnegie-Mellon University. This was the collaboration between Herbert Simon, an economist with a deep interest in understanding how people solved problems, and Allen Newell, a mathematician and engineer with an equally deep interest in devising computer programmes that would perform the same (in some sense) problem-solving procedures as those used by people.

Who was Herbert Simon?

He was born in Milwaukee on 15 June 1916. He grew up in a family where vigorous political and literary discussion accompanied every meal. His father was an engineer with keen intellectual interests. The local schools offered an excellent basic education. By the time he went to high school, young Herbert had already developed an interest in natural science and mathematics. At the same time, the intense political discussions in the family circle continued to focus his attention on social issues. When he went up to the University of Chicago in 1933 he had already determined that his life would be spent as a 'mathematical social scientist'. He would bring the methods of mathematical physics to the understanding of social processes. Moreover, this is more or less what he did.

From 1939 to 1942 he directed a research group at the University of California at Berkeley, looking into municipal administration. Effectively, as he himself has said, he was doing operations research. At the same time he continued to work for his doctorate at Chicago, largely by mail. He returned to Chicago as a professor in political science in the Illinois Institute of Technology, but he began to take an interest in economics, attending a high level seminar in the University of Chicago. He turned to studying the patterns of thinking involved in decision-making in economic matters. One could say that by the mid 1950s Simon had become a psychologist interested in problem solving in general, rather than an economist with psychological interests.

In 1949 he moved to Pittsburgh to take part in the setting up of a new Graduate School in Industrial Administration at the Carnegie Institute of Technology. His ambition to be a mathematical social scientist was as strong as ever, but he still lacked the means to achieve it. However, by then he had met Allen Newell, a man dedicated to setting up a project to create mathematical models of human thought processes, formal models that went beyond the limits of logic. Like Simon, he had been drawn to the psychology of human problem solving. His aim was to develop computer simulations of problem-solving techniques, based on empirical studies of real people solving real problems. Simon realized that Newell's project was the basis upon which his own research programme could be built.

Their collaboration on the project of the computational formalizing of human cognitive processes was at its most fruitful in the 1970s, but their intellectual interactions endured until Newell's premature death at the age of 65, and in the full flower of his talents. In 1978 Simon won the Nobel Prize for economics, largely for his work on decision-making.

He continued to take an active part in the furtherance of these researches, by the encouragement of many younger people who had been attracted to the project. He died on 9 February 2002.

Who was Allen Newell?

He was born on 19 March 1927 in San Francisco, the son of a professor of radiology at Stanford University. He attended the Lowell High School which, at that time, was highly regarded academically. However, Allen was more interested in the great outdoors. He was not very bookish, and his school record was moderate at best. He was keen on football, mountaineering and sailing. In a memoir later in life, he spoke warmly of the influence of his father, who was as accomplished in practical skills as he was in intellectual matters. Instead of going on to university, on graduating from high school Newell almost immediately enlisted in the navy. After completing his service, he entered Stanford University to study physics.

In 1949, he began work in the Rand Corporation studying decision-making in organizations such as the Air Force. This work led him to the idea that at the heart of all forms of cognition, be they in organizations or in individual minds, was information processing. The possibility of using computing machines to manipulate symbols other than for the purpose of arithmetical calculations had by then become a reality. Putting the two insights together determined his life work – the simulation and eventually modeling of human cognitive processes.

It is important to bear in mind that Newell brought to his collaboration with Simon the intention to model thought processes rather than the thinking brain. The Newell–Simon collaboration explored only one of the relationships between computers and human beings that were implicit in Turing's original conjecture. Moreover, it involved an intensive investigation of how people actually went about solving problems, as a vital preliminary to simulating these processes on a computer, and hence, via the necessary programmes, finding a mathematical theory of problem-solving.

After nearly 40 years of intensive work along these lines at Carnegie-Mellon University, in close contact and in intensive collaboration with Herbert Simon for much of the time, Newell died of cancer in 1992. It has to be said that while the efforts to carry through the project led to a deeper understanding of how people solved problems, the efforts by Newell and his collaborators to transfer this understanding to the programming of thinking machines was ultimately a failure. Neither side of Turing's 'equation' could be satisfactorily realized at that time and with the tools available.

What did they contribute?

The collaboration between Newell and Simon had something of the character of the famous teaming up of Albert Michelson and Edward Morley in physics. Like Michelson, Newell had been in the US Navy and was a driving and ebullient character, while Simon, the sober Midwesterner, was not unlike the steady and meticulous Morley.

Though each published influential work independently, they were in almost daily personal contact. Their collaboration required some give and take. Simon ruefully reports his dismay at Newell's erratic working hours.

The project demanded a detailed analysis of human cognition, particularly methods of problem-solving, which would then guide the writing of programmes which would get the same results as human thinking by using a mathematical model of the very same means. The key to their collaboration was the computer and computation. Turing's speculations were to be tested in a number of technically sophisticated attempts to write programmes which would simulate the processes of problem-solving that had been revealed by their empirical research, their studies of real people at work solving problems.

The influence of the thinking behind the Turing Test is obvious in the working out of the project. However, they were bothered by the fact that the steps in human cognitive processes were unobservable, passing too swiftly to be recorded. They tried to fill this gap in the research programme by having their participants talk through the problem-solving work as they were doing it, reporting their thinking step by step. The upshot of the work was twofold. On the one hand, they were able to produce detailed step-by-step descriptions of the procedures used by real people in trying to solve real problems. On the other hand, they made heroic efforts to use the results of these studies to develop programmes that would indeed model human cognition. The results of some very fine-grained research studies appeared in their classic *Human Problem Solving* (1972).

The Newell–Simon project simply bypassed the philosophical problem of the relation between mind and body. They were intent on constructing an abstract model of cognition. How this model could be realized other than in a computation and in what medium other than a computer they did not attempt to answer.

Their procedure involved four steps. First, various parts and processes of computing machines were labeled anthropomorphically, with words from the vocabulary ordinarily in use for human thinking. Second, they made an empirical study of people solving problems in real time, recording moment-by-moment commentaries. In the third step they abstracted the rules that the problem solvers reported as guiding their moves. Finally, the fourth step involved writing a programme based on the abstracted rules, and running it on a computer, to simulate the problem solving procedure.

The first round in this cycle is the project of artificial intelligence to devise systems that perform the same tasks as those performed by human beings. 'Sameness' is defined in terms of the comparability of the input and output of a person performing a task with the input and output of a machine performing an analogue of the task.

The second round is the project of a new kind of cognitive science, to devise a plausible formal model of actual cognition. At this moment in the 21st century, the term 'cognitive science' has acquired another related meaning. It is sometimes used to mean research into the neural mechanisms that could realize the hardware necessary to run the real 'programmes' with which human beings actually solve problems and perform other cognitive tasks. Newell and Simon did not venture so far.

Newell and Simon's terminological bridge between machine and human being is based on a simple thought experiment. We are to imagine a machine in interaction with the world. There is a relation between the internal states of the machine and various relevant states of the world. The necessary vocabulary is built up as follows (Newell, 1990):

Representation: There is an external state, X, and an external transformation, T(X), for example X causes some subsequent state to occur. X is encoded as an internal state, X', of the machine. If there is an internal transformation T'(X') that can be run in the machine, which decodes as T(X), then the internal states of the machine *represent* the causal relation between the relevant external states of the world (Newell, 1990: 59).

Symbol: A symbol token is a physical object representing something, and a *symbol* is the set of all similar symbol tokens. Moreover, that a certain physical state of a machine is a symbol token allows states of the machine to be taken to be cognitively significant.

Knowledge: An abstraction from the content of internal representations and internal processes, and the goals for which they are used. One can look on the symbol token 'New York is north of Washington' as expressing an item of *geographical knowledge*, if people use these marks to plan a journey, for example. Since symbol tokens are material things, the complex mark 'New York is north of Washington' is also a material thing. It could be a state of a machine that was picking out the best travel plan for a customer.

Symbol system: A symbol system consists of a memory, containing structures which contain symbols, and symbols, patterns providing access to other structures.

Operations: These are processes that take symbol structures as input and provide symbol structures as output (Newell, 1990: 77). It is important to grasp that Newell intended the whole of such a system to be a material structure, and to be just the structure which made human cognition possible. *Architecture* is a fixed structure which realizes a symbol system.

Search: A symbol system must generate a procedure for finding some object that will count as a solution to a problem. There must also be a test for the successful outcome of a search. A system is 'intelligent' in so far as it uses all the knowledge it has in realizing its goals.

A computer is a device which could realize a symbol system. Artificial intelligence is a branch of engineering, devoted to creating symbol systems that will perform tasks ordinarily accomplished by human beings, *defined in terms of input and output*. There need be no presumption that a person will perform the same task in the same way as the machine performs it. However, the project undertaken by Newell and Simon involved going further in finding a way to simulate the thought *processes* of people solving problems. It was intended to be a contribution to cognitive psychology.

What of the attempts to carry through the empirical side of the project? Before the effective research collaboration between Newell and Simon petered out in the early 1970s, the group from Carnegie and Rand had tried to construct a General Problem Solver based on the principle of hierarchical means/end pairs, a project also underway in Eastern Europe. The empirical research began with an analysis of the commentary with which a subject reported how he was going about trying to solve a 'cryptarithmetical' puzzle. For example, 'DAVID + GERALD = ROBERT' can be interpreted as an arithmetical sum. The problem is to work out what numbers should be assigned to the other letters, given that D = 5. The analysis is set out in detail in Newell and Simon (1972: 260 ff.).

A 'problem space', an assignment of letters to digits, includes symbol structures as knowledge states. There are operations that produce new states of knowledge. A final state is to be reached by applying operations to successive knowledge states. Such an operation might be 'addition'. Or it might be the conditional 'delete assignment', applied if a particular assignment of numerals to letters leads to a contradiction.

Among several attempts to follow through with this methodology, the chess programme, NSS, though easily defeated by a moderate chess player, did serve to demonstrate that some measure of successful searching for a goal could be programmed by including 'heuristic strategies' in the programme. The attempt to model analogical thinking with a programme called Merlin, however, was acknowledged to be a failure.

The main achievement of the group was the development of a 'language' for the SOAR system, upon which Newell pinned his hopes of a breakthrough into computational cognitive psychology.

Here is a description, part paraphrase, of the SOAR system from Michen and Akyürek (1992: 10). Note well the use of a variety of metaphors drawn from the vernacular vocabulary for describing people thinking.

> The SOAR system formulates an internal goal, and then searches its memory for data structures that determine a problem space. If found it searches for a data structure within the problem space that matches the current problem states … it attempts to find operations that allow it to modify the current state in such a way that the distance from the goal [state] … is reduced. If 'stuck' it seeks a new sub goal to solve the impasse … going through the search process again. It continues until the problem is solved or its knowledge is exhausted.

Transposing this way of specifying cognition to the analysis of human thought runs into a major snag. Despite the anthropomorphic language the SOAR system remains problematic. In order to qualify as psychology, the abstractly defined symbol system must resemble or model the relevant mode of human cognition. Newell argued for the psychological relevance of the computer-modeling project from the evident fact that human beings 'build a huge number of response functions' (Newell, 1990: 114–15), that is, in 'computer speak', that they manage the tasks of everyday life in a huge variety of ways. He concluded that human beings must be symbol systems. Why? To complete the Turing parallels Newell (1990: 116) pointed out that: 'To compute any computable function a computer must have the structure of a symbol system.' How do we pin down which one of the infinitely many possible response functions a computer could employ in reaching a certain output from a given input? Which ones are plausible models of at least some human thought processes, each of which must have the same pattern of input and output to be a candidate? Newell and Simon built their psychological project on the assumption that this problem could eventually be solved.

The SOAR project has not been a success. As Michen and Akyürek (1992) admit, the system is 'unstable'– in short, it does not work.

Human beings do not flail around trying out this or that transformation function, or problem-solving strategy. They make use of specific, culturally validated schemata. The development of this side of the project involved the independent work of **Marvin Minsky** (pp. 93–98) with his concept of a 'frame'.

To make a reasoned judgement as to the success or failure of the computational models that emerged from the collaboration between the Carnegie Institute and the Rand Corporation, and Minsky's ingenious combinations of mathematical insights and engineering intuitions, we need to bear in mind a distinction between the development of information processing devices as engineering, and those devices as contributions to psychology. Both Newell and Simon were perfectly clear that their project was to understand human thinking in sufficient depth and detail to write programmes that simulated thought processes. The test was pragmatic: did the programme do what a person did? Along with this went the question: did the programme running in the computing machine do what the person did in the same way? Did it display how the person reached a decision, solved a problem and so on?

One can hardly deny that information processing as engineering has been an outstanding success. 'IT' dominates our way of life, after barely three decades of vigorous development in the marketplace. Has the science of psychology been advanced in the same measure? Or at all? It seems fair to say that the work of the Carnegie-Rand group was a failure. Despite the success of their naturalistic studies of human beings solving problems in bringing out the strategies used in actual cases, they were unable to effect the transposition of the rules they observed people using into computational concepts and processes to illuminate the mechanisms of cognitive processing in the way that both Simon and Newell had hoped. Simon's dream of becoming a 'mathematical social scientist [psychologist]' was never realized. Was the project of computational psychology doomed from the beginning? Was it conceptually flawed?

Theoretical criticisms of artificial intelligence *as psychology* have been voiced from the very beginning of the developments described in this chapter. Winograd and Flores (1986) pointed out that the 'languages' of computational systems lacked several of the most important features of actual human languages, for instance the way meanings are dependent on the here-and-now context in which words and other symbols are used. Among a number of telling philosophical arguments the most prominent by far has been the thought experiment proposed by **John Searle** (pp. 98–101) to test the pattern of analogies implicit in the rationale of the Turing Test.

Further Reading

Primary Sources

Newell, A. (1990) *Unified Theory of Cognition*. Cambridge, MA: Harvard University Press.

Newell, A. & Simon, H. A. (1972) *Human Problem Solving*. Englewood Cliffs, NJ: Prentice Hall.

Secondary Sources

Michen, J. A. & Akyürek, A. (1992) SOAR: *A Cognitive Architecture in Perspective*. Dordrecht: Kluwer.

Winograd, T. & Flores, C. F. (1986) *Understanding Computation and Cognition*. New York: Ablex.

Autobiography

Simon, H. A. (1991) *Models of My Life*. New York: Basic Books.

Marvin Minsky (1927–)

In the years that followed the introduction of computing machines into commerce, library cataloging, banking, the military and so on, literally thousands of mathematicians, physicists, engineers, philosophers and many others were involved in the rise of the computer. More and more tasks, traditionally handled by human beings, were performed by computers. At the same time, more and more people took up the project of computational psychology, that is the attempt to read back from the simulation of human tasks by computers to computational hypotheses as to the way human beings perform human tasks.

Marvin Minsky made two essential contributions to the working out of the implications of the Turing Test. Following up the analogy between brains and computers, in 1951 he designed the first working model of a neural net, a structure resembling the fine structure of the brain. It rejoiced in the acronym SNARC.

The practical project of designing programmes that could be used to simulate cognition required a way of simplifying the huge amount of data and the multiple rules involved in any actual cognitive task. Could a practical means be found of constraining the procedures to handle this embarrassment of riches? Was there any way of selecting from among the infinitely many ways that a computer could be programmed to perform the task that seemed human-like? Minsky's answer to these problems was the concept of the 'frame', which went some way towards answering these questions, at least in principle.

Who is Marvin Minsky?

Marvin Minsky was born in New York on 9 August 1927. His schooling included the highly regarded Bronx High School of Science and the Phillips Academy in Massachusetts. He went directly from Phillips into the US Navy until just after the end of the Second World War. He studied mathematics as an undergraduate at Harvard, and completed his doctorate in 1954 at Princeton. After a short spell at Harvard, he joined MIT, where he held a number of posts.

Wisely, American universities do not now cast out their best at the whim of an arbitrary retiring age, and Minsky is currently Toshiba Professor of Media Arts and Sciences at MIT. In cast of mind, Minsky shared Turing's mix of skills in creating abstract systems and coming up with powerful insights into the practical devices that could be built to realize them.

What has he contributed?

Minsky explored some of the mathematical issues that arose from the fact that the Universal Turing Machine did not restrict the infinitely many programmes which any actual Turing Machine could use to produce any given input and output. Without some such restriction, the project of simulating human thinking with a plausible model of actual cognition is doomed to failure, however successful it might be as artificial intelligence (AI), knowledge engineering.

He realized that there must be certain local schemata or 'frames', with which human beings actually work. A frame must include a manageable and finite set of data and rules, abstracted from an indefinitely large range of theoretical possibilities. The most accessible account of frames is to be found in Minsky (1987: Ch. 24), from which this exposition is taken. Here is how he defines a 'frame':

> A frame is a data structure for representing a stereotype situation, like being in a certain kind of living room or going to a child's birthday party. Attached to each frame are several kinds of information. Some of this information is about how to use the frame. Some is about what one can expect to happen next. Some is about what to do if these expectations are not confirmed.
>
> We can think of a frame as a network of nodes and relations. The 'top levels' of a frame are fixed, and represent things that are always true about the supposed situation. The lower levels have many *terminals* – 'slots' that must be filled by specific instances of data.

Minsky made several suggestions about the fine structure of his frames, for instance that the requirements for filling slots may themselves require subframes, and the requirements for completing subframes yet more detailed subsubframes. There may also be requirements that have to be met for filling more than one slot at once.

A frame-array is a set of frames with the same terminals. This idea captures the commonsense observation that the same people, things, events and so on may be thought about in a huge variety of ways.

A fragment of a frame for the relatives present at a child's birthday party might look like this:

Sally's Birthday Party

Frame

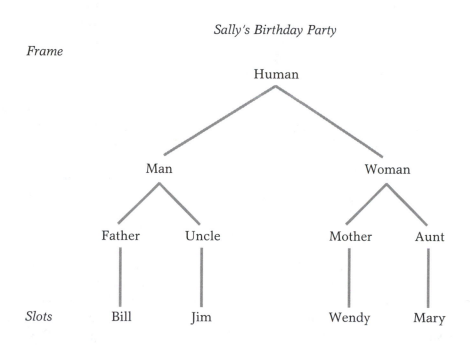

Slots   Bill   Jim   Wendy   Mary

For thinking about little Sally's birthday party, the items above are not distributed atomistically throughout an indefinitely extensive knowledge system but related very tightly within this frame. For example, in this frame 'father' and 'mother' are internally related concepts, since they are the parents of little Sally.

Minsky allows for the instability of a frame during an episode in which a person is carrying out some cognitive task. A frame may need updating moment-by-moment, modifying the frame 'axioms'. Wendy falls ill on the morning of the birthday party. How will we now celebrate the anniversary? There may be several ways in which the existing frame could be updated. It could be cancelled. It could be postponed until next Saturday and so on.

Minsky's main technical contribution to the computational model was the demonstration of the viability of the idea of a network model of artificial nodes connected in complex ways. The idea goes back long before his work, but Minky's was the first workable simulation of such a net.

Turing's implicit analogy between thinking and computing included an unspoken assumption that the thinking organ, the brain, must resemble the computing machine in various fundamental ways. The principle of multiple realizability declares that all sorts of material set-ups could be used as physical realizations of Turing machines. However, Newell had committed himself and the Carnegie-Rand group to a certain kind of computing machine, defined by a certain kind of 'architecture'. It contained a symbol system and consisted of a central processor and a memory. This is the basic architecture proposed by Von Neumann.

Studies of the fine structure of the brain have revealed a net-like structure of neurons, linked by dendrites and axons and connected by synapses. Could a machine be built that would be a model of a neural net? If such a machine could be built would it function like a brain functions, in particular could it perform as a Turing machine carrying out routine cognitive tasks? In a mathematical *tour de force*, Minsky demonstrated a working model of such a machine which could be set up on an ordinary computer. This led to the development of a new branch of cognitive science, *connectionism,* or parallel distributed processing, *PDP.* Could it do more? Could it perform operations that a Von Neumann machine could not?

Who was ultimately responsible for this innovation? It seems clear that the first inkling of such a project can be found in some remarks by Turing in 1947. The history of the development of the rudimentary idea can be followed in McClelland and Rumelhart (1986). Would one have to build a network of inter-linked mini-computers to simulate a neural net? The key to all subsequent developments was Minky's (1951) demonstration that it is possible to create a simulation of a neural net that is itself a simulation of a net of real neurons. The simulation could be run on a computing machine that is based on the Von Neumann architecture of memory stores and a central processing unit, thus bypassing the hardware problem of making a material analogue of the net of neurons. Subsequent research on neural nets and connectionist models has been based on Minsky's innovation, and its further developments (Minsky & Papert, 1988).

Here is how a PDP machine works. Imagine an array of nodes, representing neurons. They are connected in all possible ways (see Figure 4.1). Each node receives inputs and emits outputs via the connections it has with other nodes. The input switches on a certain pattern of nodes (artificial neurons) at edge A. Suppose that edge A receives inputs from the environment, switching on some input nodes (giving them the binary value 1) while others are off (giving them the binary value 0). In this way the state of the input edge represents a binary number. The outputs from these nodes flow through the net to edge B. In the end, the neurons at edge B will display a certain on/off pattern of 1s and 0s, also expressing a binary number. By adjusting the strengths of the connections, a net can be 'trained' to emit any desired output relative to some given input. For example, we might input a binary pattern representing 'sparrow'. The net could be trained to output a binary pattern of activated neurons representing 'bird'. Such a net could be

Input surface

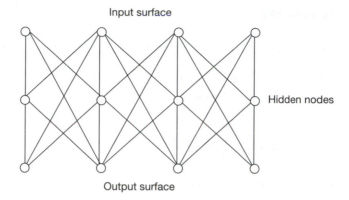

Hidden nodes

Output surface

FIGURE 4.1 A SIMPLE FEED-FORWARD NEURAL NET

thought of as a classifying subsystem of an imaginary brain. It would be one among a huge number of very extensive nets trained to perform other cognitive tasks. It has been shown that a net trained to perform one task could be trained, in some circumstances, to perform other tasks, without interfering with the requirements for the original task.

In a PDP or connectionist device there is no memory store and no central processing module. The whole net incorporates the data it has learned. There is no specific location for an item of knowledge. A computational model based on this principle looks to the brain as the source from which its design is derived by abstraction from the complexity of an actual brain organ. The test of the adequacy of the model is whether it can be trained to perform a cognitive task in good conformity with the way a person performs the task. This is a stronger requirement than just achieving a match between patterns of input and output. A striking example of a successful connectionist model of the hippocampus and its memory functions can be found in McLean, Plunkett and Rolls (1998).

Minsky's proposals seem to be bearing fruit, albeit slowly, in ways that the original efforts to follow up Turing's conjecture have not.

Further Reading

Primary Sources

Minsky, M. (1987) *The Society of Mind*. New York: Simon and Schuster.
Minsky, M. & Papert, S. A. (1988) *Perceptrons*. Cambridge, MA: MIT Press.

Secondary Sources

McClelland, J. & Rumelhart, D. (1986) *Parallel Distributed Processing*. Cambridge, MA: MIT Press.

McLeod, P., Plunkett, K. & Rolls, E. T. (1998) *Introduction to Connectionist Modelling of Cognitive Processes*. Oxford: Oxford University Press.

John Rogers Searle (1932–)

Since the whole project of computational psychology has turned out to be a vast thought experiment, touching reality only here and there, it is only fitting that the most telling criticisms of the Turing double analogy between brains and computers, thinking and computing, should have been formulated as a thought experiment. This was John Searle's Chinese Room.

Who is John Rogers Searle?

John Searle was born in Denver, Colorado in December 1932. He did undergraduate work at the University of Wisconsin. In 1955 he went up to Oxford as a Rhodes Scholar. After taking his BA he went on to the then most prestigious Oxford graduate degree in philosophy, the oddly named 'B Phil'. His supervisor was J. L. Austin, well know for his development of the insight that words are frequently used to accomplish social and practical acts rather than for true or false descriptions of matters of fact. Searle took his D Phil in 1957. He was a lecturer at Christchurch, Oxford from 1957–1959. He returned to the United States to the philosophy department at the University of California at Berkeley, where he has remained for the rest of his career. Searle's early work was devoted to developing Austin's speech-act theory along a number of dimensions. His interest in language led to his devising the now famous thought experiment, the Chinese Room, to test the plausibility of all computational models of cognition. This thought experiment and others he has devised turn on the concept of 'intentionality' or meaningfulness as a defining feature of thought. In his later work he has used this concept in several studies of the nature of human cognition in relation to the organic basis of human existence.

What has he contributed?

In 1972 he published the first of several versions of a thought experiment, designed to show that the project of computational psychology was based on a conceptual mistake, so deep as to render the project worthless.

To understand the force of Searle's thought experiment, usually referred to as the 'Chinese Room', we must remind ourselves of a principle fundamental to the Newell–Simon project, the symbol system hypothesis.

A symbol is a set of similar symbol tokens, material states of information-processing machines. Each symbol token is a material state of the machine, 'representing' something in the machine's environment. A symbol token can have no meaning, in the ordinary sense. It is subject to causal processes in the machine, which do not have any meaning either. All the meaning is in what a human being can make of it.

Do human beings actually think by means of the causal transformations of strings of meaningless symbol tokens? If we are inclined to answer in the negative then the project of transposing insights from AI to cognitive science is severely compromised, if not rendered empty. Perhaps a machine can mimic the results of human beings trying to solve problems, but that is of no interest to psychologists unless it can be shown that how the machine solves problems is sufficiently similar to the way people do it to throw light on human cognition.

The distinction between syntax, the rules for manipulating symbols, and semantics, the conventions for the interpretation of symbols, plays an important part in the argument. The key concept around which Searle's thought experiment was built is that of intentionality, the meaningfulness of a symbol. A symbol, or more generally, a sign, has physical properties, such as size, colour, location, shape and so on. Consider a triangular piece of wood nailed to a tree in the forest, with the apex in a certain direction. As a signpost, it has an additional property over and above all and any of its physical properties. It has a meaning for a human being out for a hike – 'Go this way!' To see the piece of wood as having this meaning the hiker must understand a convention. This property is the intentionality of the sign. Searle's thought experiment was aimed at showing that the computationalist conception of the mind as a symbol system failed to preserve the crucial feature of the means or media of cognition, intentionality.

The Turing Test would oblige us to say that a computer understands Chinese if it could be programmed to output correct answers in Chinese to questions posed in Chinese. To upset this inference, Searle asks us to imagine a person, let us call him 'Jim', confined to a room but with input and output slots for messages to be received and replies to be sent out. The room is equipped with lists of Chinese ideographs, and rules for manipulating them. Jim is completely ignorant of Chinese; indeed, he does not even know that the ideographs he receives have a meaning. Outside the room are some Chinese who write out questions on slips of paper in Chinese, and push them through the in-slot. Jim applies the rules for manipulating the signs, meaningless to him, and returns the results through the out-slot. The Chinese read the results of Jim's work as answers to questions.

Jim has passed the Turing Test, but he is not thinking out answers to questions. He is mindlessly following rules of association among meaningless signs.

However, this is how the Newell–Simon symbol system hypothesis defines computation. The point of the thought experiment is twofold. Jim could have been thinking, but the symbol system hypothesis does not require him to do so in order to provide answers to the questions put by the Chinese. From their point of view, the behavioural pattern is 'Question/Answer'. However, Jim is not, as Newell would have it, using 'knowledge' and 'displaying intelligence' in the ordinary sense of those words. Neither is a computer that performs the same task. At best a machine can manage the syntax of a cognitive procedure, but there is no place for semantics. Only the Chinese persons who write the questions and read the answers have a grasp of the semantics of the ideographs.

One might go further and deny that the 'rules' of machine computation are in any way comparable to syntax. The rules of syntax govern the possible combinations of symbols, according to their word classes, not according to their material properties. But the instructions in a programme are realized in the machine as causal processes, acting on the electrical properties of registers. There is nothing of language in the machine. Searle's thought experiment questions the implicit suggestion that a machine can literally understand questions and answers. It also throws doubt on the complementary idea that what the machine and the programme can do throws any light on what people actually do.

Searle's thought experiment generated a vast literature, with contributions from both critics and admirers. He has responded to these discussions over the years. However, the basic form of the argument has remained unchanged. The appearance of connectionist models might seem to change the nature of the Turing proposal, since there are no internal processes purporting to map the alleged processes of human cognition in that model of brain activity. Of course, to complete the Turing analogy it would be necessary to make the same claim about human thinking, namely that it is not a process in which meaningless symbols are manipulated according to rule. Indeed that is just what enthusiasts for PDP models will say. Searle offered another thought experiment to the same end for such models. However, his Chinese gymnasium, in which messages are passed from person to person along connectionist links, has not seemed anything like as forceful as the original parable.

The last word has not yet been said on the joint project of artificial intelligence and its complement, computational psychology. Whatever is happening in people's *brains* when they think, it is evidently not computation in the sense of Newell and Simon. Ironically, what Newell and Simon found out about what was happening in people's *minds* when they were thinking, that is their conscious states and processes, was not a kind of computation either. The success of some of the connectionist models of brain processes in simulating the overt pattern of conscious cognition does suggest that there may be a new era of cognitive psychology around the corner. Naturalistic analyses of how people reason can perhaps be linked to the brain processes that underlie our reasoning powers, by developing connectionist models of real neural nets in the various organs of the brain. This development will be followed up in Chapter 5, in which the lives and works of some of the 20th century's biopsychologists are presented.

Further Reading

Primary Source

Searle, J. R. (1980) Minds, brains and programmes. *Behavioral and Brain Sciences,* **3**, 417–424.

Secondary Source

Preston, J. & Bishop, M. (2002) (Eds) *Views into the Chinese Room.* Oxford: Clarendon Press.

Biography

Hirstin, W. (2001) *On Searle.* London: Wadsworth.

Reflections

In several of the natural sciences scientific realism has required the provision of a formal explanatory level between observable phenomena and the ultimate level of generative mechanisms. In biology the algebra of genes and chromosomes was worked out and used very effectively while the chemical mechanisms of meiosis and mitosis were unknown. In chemistry the familiar formulae were developed long before anyone had any real idea of the nature of chemical atoms and their bonds. The power of the computationalist models comes from their occupying this intermediate status. On the one hand they represent a formal system, the running of which would produce the known phenomena if it were successful. On the other hand they represent, schematically, a possible neural mechanism which would implement the abstract formal system and its workings. This was already clear to **Alan Turing** (pp. 82–86). The pattern 'Thinking : Brain :: Computing : Computer' underlies the entire programme of artificial intelligence and cognitive science.

Not surprisingly, the working out of Turing's insights has been a much more formidable task than it once seemed. **Allen Newell** and **Herbert Simon** (pp. 86–93) realized that the research programme must start with a micro-analysis of real people really solving real problems. Unfortunately, their efforts to find the relevant computational model were unsuccessful. The possibility that the use of the wrong kind of computational model had blocked their progress became clear from the work of **Marvin Minsky** (pp. 93–98). Brains are neuronal nets, so surely any model which is designed to simulate not only the human patterns of input and output but cognitive processes themselves should also conform to net-like architecture. The full exploitation of his work is yet to be achieved. However, it looks ever more promising. Furthermore, it brings psychology firmly back into the scientific realist camp from the point of view of scientific method, allying it with such sciences as chemistry and biology.

Whatever the future holds, **John Searle**'s (pp. 98–101) thought experiment has to be dealt with. It certainly shows that Turing's Test proves very little about human beings. It also shows that the symbol system of Newell and Simon is unsatisfactory. The problem of how to preserve intentionality in the workings of a material mechanism like a neural net is still unsolved.

5

The Biopsychologists

Since Pierre Jean Georges Cabanis (1757–1808) first clearly enunciated the thesis that the brain is the one and only organ of thought, the project of grounding the psychology of human beings in states and processes in the brain has been pursued with more or less success. The project is formidable. Until recently it was impossible to study the living brain of a person going about a cognitive or practical task, or experiencing an emotion or seeing, hearing or touching something. At the same time, a succession of conceptions of the way that the human brain worked drew on whatever happened to be the latest technology of the era. In the 17th century it was hydraulics, in the late 19th century it was the telephone system and in the latter part of the 20th century the computing machine. There are 10^{11} neurons linked in a dense network of synapses, producing much the most complex thing in the universe as we know it. The difficulty of carrying out studies of the workings of living brains and the speculative character of models of brains in action add up to a formidable scientific problem indeed, if we are bent on finding out what is happening in the brain when a person is thinking, acting, feeling and perceiving.

The influence of biology on psychology has led to two long-running debates of deep significance. How far can psychology be reduced to neuroscience? Or to put the matter more dramatically, how far can mental concepts be replaced by neurophysiological concepts in describing and explaining human social and cognitive activity? This debate revives a centuries-old debate in philosophy on the alleged dualism of mind and body. The second debate turns on the question of the relative importance of inherited tendencies (human nature) and cultural factors (human nurture) in building a scientific psychology. Is psychology more a natural than a cultural science? How far should psychology be reduced to genetics?

We can divide the 20th century into two eras: before scanning techniques for studying the living brain were invented, and after their introduction. In the first period, brain function and cognition were related indirectly by inferences from the observations of the loss of some specific function when there was damage to a certain region of the brain. The method had an obvious weakness, in that the part that had been damaged may have been playing only a minor role in the total relevant brain activity. The relatively fine grain of **Alexander Luria**'s (pp. 105–113) functional analysis of the brain can be put down to the huge variety of brain injuries that came his way during the Second World War with a consequential variety of functional deficits.

The first 'scanning' technique to be introduced was the ECG recording of the electrical activity of the brain as a whole, which displayed several different frequencies characteristic of sleeping and waking states: the alpha, beta, theta and delta rhythms. The method has been revived in recent years by Suppes and Han (2000). In 1975 a new technique for studying the living brain was invented. It depended on detecting the products of the radioactive decay of fluorine atoms which had been attached to an analogue of glucose. This substance is taken up by different parts of the brain at different rates, depending on the current activity of a region. This is the technique of positron emission tomography or PET scanning. At about the same time the use of strong magnetic fields to produce detectable resonance effects in the water molecules in the internal organs made possible direct observations of soft tissues including anatomically distinct parts of the brain. This is the technique of magnetic resonance imaging, or MIR.

These techniques have been extraordinarily important in detecting and mapping tumours and haematomas in the brain itself, facilitating surgical and other treatments. It has also made possible a second avenue of access for neuropsychologists, enabling the differentiation of active brain regions while a participant is performing particular cognitive and perceptual activities. Another very different avenue of access to the living brain is opened by taking advantage of the opportunity provided by the exposed brains of conscious patients undergoing surgical treatment for epilepsy. **Wilder Penfield** (pp. 113–118) was able to use delicate electrical probes to map the locality of cognitive and other functions of the cerebral cortex.

Supplementing these methods with the systematic invasive production of lesions in the brains of monkeys, serving as models for the study of human neuropsychology, and correlating these with observable behavioural effects, **Karl Pribram** (pp. 118–125) and others have extended and improved the characterization of functionally distinct brain regions. However, none of this would have been possible without the insight of Charles Sherrington (1857–1952) that the brain was not just a device for linking sensory input with muscle-activating output. There is an intimate and continuous interplay between afferent and efferent nervous fibres even to the surface of the skin. Sherrington is also remembered for the invention of the useful word 'synapse', to describe the point of intersection of dendrites and axons, as they form into neural nets.

The integration of these techniques with the formal models developed by computer scientists to simulate human cognitive performances has only just begun. It seems likely that this marriage will help to bridge the gap between the relatively coarse-grained distinctions revealed by scanning methods and the exceedingly delicate and complex neural structures that are to be found in the living brain.

These researches suggest a biological rather than a spiritual basis for the human mind. Ethology, the study of animal behaviour in naturalistic settings, bears on this large question from another direction. The 20th century saw a rapid growth in such studies, inspired by the pioneering work of **Konrad Lorenz** (pp. 125–133), Nikolaas Tinbergen (1969) and many others. Their researches have shown that there is a complex matrix of inherited routines and acquired skills involved in the reproductive lives of animals and birds. These include the marking out of territories, the struggles to establish and maintain a place in the local social hierarchy, the rituals of the mating season, and many more. Natural selection clearly plays a part in the establishment of inherited routines and also in the background organismic conditions that make the learning of cultural practices, such as the songs of some species of birds, possible. At the same time this development, when generalized to human beings, has posed the age-old 'nature or nurture?' question more sharply, and in a very much more complicated way than here-to-fore.

The work of Lorenz and others seemed to show the importance of natural selection in accounting for many complex behavioural patterns exhibited in the lives of mammals, fish, birds and even insects. Hypotheses about the natural selection of human psychological and social tendencies have inspired a generation of geneticists to look for corresponding genetic sources of human social behaviour and psychological traits. In practice, research results announced by the popular press have come mostly from generalizations of studies of the behavioural genetics of mice to human kind. One must, therefore, regard some of the more startling announcements with a certain degree of skepticism (Badcock, 2000).

By the end of the 20th century there were literally thousands of neuroanatomists, neurophysiologists, neurochemists, neuropsychologists and others in even more recondite specialities, working on the functional aspects of the human brain. Apart from these, the medical side of brain studies cut across these professional divisions. Many of those who worked as neuroscientists were also directly involved in clinical work on the diagnosis and treatment of people with psychological problems that appeared to be related to defects in the brain.

Further Reading

Badcock, C. (2000) *Evolutionary Psychology.* Cambridge: Polity.
Suppes, P. & Han, B. (2000) Brain-wave representation of words by superposition of a few sine waves. *Proceedings of the National Academy of Sciences of the USA*, **97**, 873–843.
Tinbergen, N. (1969) Ethology. In R. Harré (Ed.), *Scientific Thought: 1900–1960* (pp. 238–268). Oxford: Clarendon Press.

Alexander Romanovich Luria (1902–77)

The idea that the brain is the organ of thought and the only organ of thought remained largely schematic until the middle of the 20th century. Various areas and regions of the brain had been mapped during the 19th century, for example Paul Broca (1842–80) had shown that an area in the lower part of the left frontal lobe was the seat of one aspect of language capacities, the ability to use words in intelligible speech. In 1908, Carl Wernicke (1848–1905) had located an adjacent region of the brain which seemed to be the seat of the capacity to organize language according to local syntactical rules. However, the understanding of the brain as a living organ and the tracking of the processes by which cognition was accomplished were scarcely begun. Coming quite late in life to this issue, Luria adapted some of the techniques he had developed to deal with war casualties to a study of the neurology of cognition, more systematic in the retelling than in the execution of the work itself.

Who was Alexander Romanovich Luria?

Alexander Luria was born on 3 July 1902, in the ancient town of Kazan, which lies about 1000 km east of Moscow. Despite its remoteness and its population of only 140,000, it possessed a university of some antiquity. Alexander's father, Roman Albertovich Luria, was a doctor and, after the revolution, taught at the Kazan Medical School. Father and son did not always get on, since Roman Luria very much wanted his son to follow him into medicine. Not long after the revolution, Roman Luria moved to Moscow as Vice-Director of the Central Institute for Advanced Medical Studies. He soon became one of the most influential medical men in the whole of the Soviet Union, particularly in the training of doctors. Alexander Romanovich remarks in his autobiography that his family was indifferent to religion, and sympathetic to the revolution, though not themselves active revolutionaries.

The Lurias were of Jewish origin, and had suffered from the Imperial restrictions on the lives and educational possibilities that **Lev Vygotsky** (pp. 26–34) too had endured. The revolution opened up higher education to everyone, regardless of social class and religious affiliations. Alexander Romanovich describes how extraordinary was the sense of freedom and social and human possibility that followed the opening of the colleges and universities to people of all classes and faiths. By way of contrast with the situation before the revolution, he cites a 19th-century Imperial edict denying higher education to the children of people in manual occupations. It makes extraordinary reading in the 21st century.

Swept up in the enthusiasms of the day, young Alexander Romanovich rushed through his secondary studies at the gymnasium, graduating in 1918. He describes the chaos that greeted him as he entered the university. Thousands of students were exercising their right to a higher education, demanding it of institutions which lacked the resources to cope. As a result, young Luria more or less educated himself, following a wide reading programme particularly oriented to German experimental psychology, that seemed up-to-the-minute in that remote place. However, he was struck by the way that the experimental psychology of the German tradition had ignored the relation between psychology and social life. He also realized how paradoxical traditional associationist psychology had turned out to be. The person who took note of his/her own mind could not be a cluster of ideas in that mind. He wanted to find a 'realistic psychology' that took account of how people actually thought and how they really lived. Most of all he found inspiration in the 'idiographic/nomothetic' distinction of Windelband (1898 [1998]). Every human being is unique, though all human beings are, in certain ways, alike.

During this spate of reading, he came across the writings of **Sigmund Freud** (pp. 270–280). He was, at least for a while, an enthusiastic convert. With some of his young friends, he founded the Kazan Freud Society. He wrote to Freud and was delighted to receive a reply agreeing to act as patron of the society. However, his belief that the psychology of an individual has a social origin turned him away from Freud. 'I finally concluded', says (Luria, 1979: 24), 'that it was an error to assume that one can deduce human behavior from the biological "depths" of mind, excluding its social "heights".'

He graduated in 1921, and began medical studies. Among his many extra-curricular activities was the founding of a journal for the study of psychological aspects of manual labour. He was particularly interested in the relation between language and labour, as well as the effects of fatigue on manual skills. He invited V. M. Bekterev, an influential member of the Moscow Institute of Psychology, to be a member of the editorial board of the journal. This led to an invitation from K. N. Kornilov to come to Moscow. Kornilov had been busily revamping the Institute of Psychology. As an enthusiastic Pavlovian, he went so far as to include 'reflexology' in the title of the Institute. This was the first intimation of the influence of Pavlovian materialism that affected the whole of Soviet psychology for the next 30 years. Bright young men were needed to staff the reformed Institute, and Luria was among those recruited.

Luria's enthusiasm for a 'new psychology' was intense. He began to work with Alexei Leont'ev, focusing on the interplay between verbal/practical activities and emotion. Already at this time, he had formed a very definite idea about the unity of psychological phenomena in the individual. Here was a sharp distinction from American psychology of the era, which was based on the principle that cognitive activity can be analysed into distinct units, each of which can be studied separately, almost independently of the person. Working with Alexei Leont'ev, he developed the 'combined motor method' in which a simple physical movement was required in response to a verbal instruction or cue, and the reaction times and dynamics of the movement measured. In this way, he hoped to develop a public objective indication of something private and subjective. True to the principles of 'realistic' psychology, Luria built up a research programme on real life emotions, using the combined motor method in studies of the emotional states of criminals, during and after arrest, while on trial and after sentencing. These studies, true to the principle of psychology of real people in real situations, were face to face.

In 1924, his life changed again. In that year, he met **Lev Semionovich Vygotsky** (pp. 26–34), whose conception of the psychology chimed with his own ideas. However, Vygotsky's conception of the cultural/historical/instrumental nature of an ideal psychology went much further than Luria's more modest studies of the role of language in the management of labour. Like many others, he fell under Vygotsky's spell, an influence which lasted for the rest of his life.

With Alexei Leont'ev, Luria and Vygotsky became inseparable. They were soon to be called 'the Troika'. They studied the new generation of German psychologists, including Lewin, Stern and the Gestaltists, **Wolfgang Köhler** (pp. 136–142) and Koffka. They took up the idea of emergent processes, dynamic attributes of a person that could not be deduced from knowledge of the relevant Pavlovian reflexes, even though these reflexes were essential to the higher order process. The Troika met weekly to plan experimental studies to be undertaken with their students. They were inspired by the Vygotskian concept of the cultural/historical/instrumental method, the only way they believed that psychology could make progress towards a truly scientific discipline.

Luria became the Director of the Laboratory of Psychology in the Krupskaya Institute of Communist Education, where he developed another experimental programme, particularly directed at understanding the regulatory role of speech in practical action. He began to take an interest in neuropsychology, drawing his inspiration once again from **Vygotsky**. Lev Semionovich had begun medical studies to pursue the neurological side of this conception of psychology as a unitary science, in which the cultural/historical aspects of human life were bound into a system with the biological basis of all human action, the instrumental component.

Inspired again by Vygotsky, Luria organized two expeditions to Uzbekistan, to study the effect of literacy programmes on the cognitive powers of people who had hitherto been largely illiterate. Once again he aimed at a realistic psychology, and, in a striking anticipation of 21st-century methodological ideas, assembled a large collection of records of actual conversations in which Uzbeks were encouraged to perform various cognitive operations. The upshot was very clear. There were distinctive cognitive styles and patterns of thought among illiterate Uzbeks, unlike anything found among literate Russians. As we saw with **Vygotsky**'s involvement in this project, the finding was unacceptable to the authorities and the work was not published or even referred to until very recently.

In the 1930s, the influence of the Pavlovians was sufficient to prevent the Troika and their students setting up an independent psychology institute in Moscow. Kharkov in the Ukraine seemed far enough away to allow them independence. Pushed by Vygotsky, Luria and Leont'ev left Moscow to set up a new Institute of Psychology, under the wing of the local Psychoneurological Institute. Vygotsky 'dropped in' from time to time in the course of his endless journeyings. After Vygtosky's death, Luria and Leont'ev quickly returned to Moscow.

In 1936, Luria changed direction again. His own account of the events of that year implies that his decision to take up medical studies was linked to the development of his research interests, and directly influenced by Vygotsky's taking up medical studies himself. Whether Luria's decision to enter medical school was a free choice or not, his leaving the Institute was in keeping with the trends of the time. The years of the purges tore Soviet life apart. Many of the leading figures in all walks of life were executed, exiled or dismissed. Returning to medical school, whatever may have been the reason, Luria acquired the necessary training to begin clinical practice as a neurologist. He began work in the Neurosurgical Institute. He describes those two years as the most satisfying of his whole life.

The Second World War offered him another, though grim, opportunity to go forward with his studies in neuropsychology. He began the 'study of dissolution and restoration of higher psychological functions in terms of the brain mechanisms that control them' (Luria, 1973: 56). Shortly after the German attack in 1941, Luria was commissioned to open a hospital in the Urals for the treatment of soldiers with brain injuries. Three years of intensive work followed, involving new ways of diagnosing local brain damage and developing well-grounded methods of treatment.

After the war, he returned to Moscow and continued to work there during the period of *perestroika* and the opening up of the Soviet Union. True to Vygotsky's vision, he began to undertake a mapping of the many cognitively significant regions of the brain through the integrated activities from which the higher cognitive functions emerged. His method of research was still based on the injury/deficit/ function pattern of reasoning that had been used in the 19th century by neurologists like Paul Broca. His unique contribution was partly the result of a huge number of clinical cases, and a finely honed intuition in the use of the threefold formula linking deficits to functions.

During his last years he put together the results of his 30-year study of a man of exceptional powers of memory, the 'little book' as he called it, which set the seal on his fame (Luria, 1987). The message of the book was the extraordinary degree to which exceptional powers of memory were integrated into and influenced every aspect of the subject's life, both personal and social.

In the last decade of his life Luria published extensive records of his many research programmes, including the work on the comparative cognitive development of twins. He also put together a massive collection of the results of his studies of various kinds of cognitive impairments. This work displayed in detail the use he had made of these results to work out the functional organization of the brain (Luria, 1973).

Alexander Romanovich Luria died on 14 August 1977, faithful to his friend and mentor, Lev Vygotsky.

What did he contribute?

Alexander Romanovich Luria contributed to a wide variety of developments in psychology. His work was both innovatory and insightful. Luria finds a place in this book as a major influence on 20th-century neuropsychology, within the framework of medicine, rather than for his independent scientific studies. However, before I turn to describe this aspect of his work, his other contributions should at least be noted.

In the long term, the most important aspect of his work, it seems to me, was his taking up Vygotsky's principle of the necessary integration of higher cognitive functions, and their origin in the social and historical situation of each and every human being. His first six years in the Moscow Institute were devoted to furthering Vygotsky's conviction that higher mental functions come about through 'an intricate interaction' between biological aspects of *Homo sapiens* and cultural factors that have also evolved over millennia.

The programme of the Troika can be divided into three lines of research, in each of which Luria took a major role. The extensive ethnographic study of the people of Uzbekistan concerned the problem of how higher cognitive functions differed in different cultural environments. In this way, the historical/cultural aspects of cognition could be differentiated from the biological aspects. The second study involved comparisons between monozygotic and fraternal twins. The former group necessarily shared an identical genetic makeup. The project involved longitudinal studies to follow differences in how twins of each category developed. Finally, the group began comparisons between the development of normal and retarded children. This project had both a scientific and a practical side. The work not only helped to lay bare some of the biological factors in cognitive development, but also led to the establishment of educational curricula to try to make good some of the defects in cognitive function that had resulted from biological abnormalities. Tied in with this, the Troika and their students maintained a continuing interest in the verbal management of behaviour, a theme again coming directly from Vygotsky's insights into developmental psychology, and his critical response to **Jean Piaget**'s (pp. 34–43) characterization of children's psychology as 'egocentric'. 'Egocentric speech' was not a sign of self-regard, but a device for the verbal management of action by self-instruction.

Luria's method of research took its start from the established principle that a study of localized brain damage could be a method for investigating the cerebral structures and processes that underlay higher cognitive functions. Vygotsky had pointed out that the principle fell short in its neglect of the question of the integration of functions. However, empirical research into the integration of higher order functions at the neural level that it suggested was impossible until a clearer idea of the local functioning of the brain had emerged.

In his account of the way that his own views of the role of the brain in cognition developed, Luria emphasized the influence of Henry Head's work on aphasia, published in 1926. Head argued that disturbances in language function underlay disturbances in cognitive functions. This fitted well with the Vygotskian principle of the *symbolic* mediation of all higher cognitive functions, the main mediating system in human beings being language. Furthermore, it pointed to the indirect method of brain research that became Luria's trademark. When some part of the brain is damaged or destroyed, that is there is a 'lesion' at that location, and there is a correlated distortion of some psychological function, it is proper to infer that the undistorted psychological function is due, in part, to the role that the intact part plays in the functional system with which the higher order cognitive process is performed. Luria's studies of the neural mechanisms of cognition were not only indirect, using the injury/deficit/function pattern of reasoning, but they were also unsystematic. They depended on the kinds of brain injuries and cognitive and motor deficits that were presented by the patients who came his way in his medical practice, both during and after the Second World War.

In the Neurosurgical Institute he was faced with clinical problems very unlike those that are tackled in pure scientific research. Research becomes diagnosis and the testing of diagnostic hypotheses is carried out in curative regimes and procedures. The result of this work was the realization that such higher order activities as speaking involve not one region of the brain but a complex and individually differentiated pattern of functions: 'It should be apparent that if the operation of intellectual processes is thought of in terms of functional systems instead of discrete abilities, we have to reorient our ideas about the possibility of localizing intellectual functions [in the brain]' (Luria, 1979: 141).

Luria laid great emphasis on a clue to the complexity of the functional systems that came from N. A. Bernshtein's studies of motor activities. These had shown not only that different muscle groups were involved at different stages in the same overall activity, but that both afferent and efferent neural pathways were involved. The changing position of the limbs had to be fed into the system in order for the appropriate 'instructions' to be sent to the muscles.

Luria's methodology is simple to describe but it required a large measure of personal intuition to make it effective as a research tool. In diagnosing the sources of some disruption to a higher order cognitive or complex motor function, one has first to find out which 'links in the normal system of the working constellation of brain zones' are disrupted. Once that is achieved, the work of finding alternative linkages can begin. Underlying this methodology is a deeper principle. The relevant 'constellation of brain zones' can be discovered step by step, by identifying the *various* regions where damage disrupts a *specific* cognitive function. It is worth remarking that Luria's highly personal methodology, depending as much on insight as on logical inference, gives results not all that different from those achieved by 21st-century techniques such as PET scans and functional MRI. Typically, a 'constellation of brain zones' is revealed. Neither the links that create a functional system nor much of the fine structures of the various zones are revealed by either scanning technology as yet. Nor, of course, could they have been revealed by Luria's methods.

In defining the project of neuropsychology that grew out of his wartime work, Luria made the important point that this science necessarily involved two quite different lines of research. 'On the one hand,' he said (Luria, 1979: 157), 'I had to move from brain structures to a deeper understanding of the neurophysiological mechanisms that were operating in these structures. On the other hand, our psychological analysis of higher cortical functions was by no means complete, and we needed improved psychological analyses as well.'[1] He cites **Wilder Penfield** (pp. 113–118) as one of the post-war neuroscientists who began to reveal the deeper structure of the brain. An important insight emerged from this research: that rather than a one-way flow of neural impulses from the lower to the higher structures, there were neural pathways in both directions. This was particularly important in the anatomy of the reticular formation, presumed to be the key to the activation of the brain in general. For the systematic development of this work we must turn to the experimental programme of **Karl Pribram** (pp. 118–125), whose studies were based on the use of rhesus monkeys and macaques as models of *Homo sapiens*.

The remarkable power of the joint method of linguistic, psychological and neurological research can be illustrated by the successful research attack on understanding the neurological basis of the fundamental linguistic distinction between the paradigmatic dimension of word use and the syntagmatic dimension. This distinction was introduced by Ferdinand de Saussure. The paradigmatic dimension of the use of a word is the category of beings referred to. Thus the paradigmatic dimension of 'bread' includes 'cake', 'biscuit' and so on; that is, it belongs in the category of farinacious foodstuffs. The syntagmatic dimension of the word is its sequential relations with others in an endless variety of sentences, such as 'Fetch me some bread', 'If there is no bread let them eat cake', and so on – uses that involve fulfilling our intentions. Our ability to use the word 'bread' to mediate thought and action requires mastery of both dimensions of meaning.

Luria and his team found that lesions in the forward part of the left hemisphere impair fluent syntagmatically-organized speech, leaving categorization relatively intact. Patients could name single objects but could not construct complex fluent sentences. However, patients who had lesions in the rear of the head, though speaking fluently, could not manage semantic relationships between individual words (Luria, 1979: 169–170). Of course, Luria recognized very well, that an undamaged left hemisphere is a necessary but not a sufficient condition for mastery of the syntagmatic dimension of word use. Some of the aphasias and speech defects studied by Broca and Wernicke anticipated these results.

To round off this brief account of a life extraordinarily rich in psychological research, let us look into the 'little book', the report on his decades-long study of the man with a remarkable memory. Luria was interested in two distinct questions: how did S. perform these feats, that is by what technique? And what effect did the possession of this unusual talent have on the whole of his mental and social life? It turned out that his memorial method was more or less identical with that developed as a specific 'art' in classical times and greatly developed in the renaissance (Yates, 1966). It was based on eidetic imagery. S. imagined himself going for a walk through a part of Moscow and 'attaching' the items he wanted to remember to items along the walk. Any difficulties he had in remembering something were the result of ill-chosen things and situations along his path. Along with the eidetic imagery went pronounced synaethesias. He described how he experienced the colours of sounds and the hues of days of the week.

The effect on the rest of his mental life was most marked by the fact that since he forgot nothing, the whole of his life from infancy was there for immediate recall. In addition to the memorial imagery employed in his memory feats, Luria reports that S. had other image-related powers. He was able to regulate his heart rate and body temperature at will, through the management of images, such as 'running after a train'. The intensity of his 'inner life' militated against a career in the world of other people. He found it easier to slip into daydreams than to apply himself to practical tasks.

For Luria, the *Mind of a Mnemonist* (1987) expressed two of his deeply held principles. The higher order cognitive functions, such as those displayed by S., were an integrated system. The case of S. showed, too, how deeply idiographic psychology became when a researcher entered into the details of someone's mental life.

Luria did not undertake a systematic experimental programme of research into the neurological basis of higher order cognitive functions. Yet, by the exercise of an intuition honed by many years of clinical experience, he was able to make significant contributions to our understanding of the brain as the organ of thought.

Further Reading

Primary Sources

Luria, A. R. (1973) *The Working Brain*. Harmondsworth: Penguin.
Luria, A. R. (1987) *The Mind of a Mnemonist*. Cambridge, MA: Harvard University Press.

Secondary Sources

Windelband, W. (1898 [1998]) History and natural science (trans. J. T. Lamiell). *Theory and Psychology*, **8**, 5–22.
Yates, F. A. (1966) *The Art of Memory*. London: Routledge and Kegan Paul.

Autobiography

Luria, A. R. (1979) *The Making of a Psychologist*. Cambridge, MA: Harvard University Press.

Wilder Penfield (1891–1976)

The differences between those neuropsychologists who believed that higher cognitive function were strictly localized and those who held to a more global image of the relevant aspects of brain activity were made less radical by the experiments conducted by Wilder Penfield. He showed that there were some places in the living brain where an electrical stimulus elicited recollections of very complex experiences, sometimes including the auditory illusion that music was actually being played. At the same time he was able to demonstrate the spread of neural excitations across several brain regions.

All four of our neuropsychologists were, at one time or another in their careers, medically trained and even practising medicine. Penfield's discoveries came about in the course of medical work with people suffering from brain tumours. The remarkable fact that the brain has no sensitivity to touch, or even to massive injuries and the excision of substantial parts, was known to Aristotle. Nevertheless, it is the site of thought and feeling. Penfield's investigations of the living brain during surgery made the relation between the states of the brain and human experience even more puzzling than it had been heretofore. Later in life he reflected deeply on the significance of his 'brain maps', pinpointing localized areas of psychological sensitivity.

Who was Wilder Penfield?

He was born in Spokane, Washington on 26 January 1891. His father had a medical practice that had effectively failed by the time young Wilder was eight. His mother was evidently a woman of character and tenacity of purpose, a cast of mind he later claimed to be his own most important trait. She took her three children to live with her parents in Hudson, Wisconsin. In this remote provincial town she not only founded a first rate school, the Galahad, which her younger son attended, but also fostered in the boy a burning ambition to win a Rhodes Scholarship to Oxford. The Rhodes has particularly demanding standards, requiring not only pre-eminence in academic matters but evidence of more than average sporting prowess. Imbued with the Rhodes as his goal, Wilder entered Princeton in 1909.

He describes his freshman self as plodding of mind and gangling of body. His first efforts to find a place on the football squad were unavailing until a friend advised him to take up wrestling. The results were dramatic. Not only did he develop a powerful physique, but he won the wrestling title for his year. In the end, thus re-equipped so to say, he found a place on the university football team.

His academic career also followed a jagged path. At first determined to take up some other profession than that at which his father had failed, nevertheless half way through his undergraduate studies he opted for medicine. He put this down to some excellent lectures in biology and the influence of his mother, with her strong sense of service to one's fellow humans.

After one abortive attempt, he did eventually win a Rhodes' scholarship and took up a place at Merton College, Oxford, in 1914. At this time Oxford had the benefit of two men of great distinction. Sir Charles Sherrington held the chair of Physiology and Sir William Osler was Regius Professor of Medicine. From the former he picked up a taste for meticulous research into the mechanisms of the brain and nervous system that supported behaviour of many kinds. From the latter he gained a further impetus to devote his skills to the amelioration of suffering rather than to pure research. It turned out that by following the path of the latter he found his way into pursuing the former.

The United States had not then entered the First World War, but Penfield volunteered to serve in a Red Cross Hospital in France. He never reached the front. His cross channel ship was torpedoed. Shortly after recovering from the effects of this mishap he returned to the US and entered the Johns Hopkins Medical School, taking his MD in 1918. After a short spell in Boston, he returned to Oxford to work with Sherrington, and later held a research fellowship in London.

His subsequent career turned on the balance he tried to strike between practising neurosurgery for the relief of suffering and furthering research into the intriguing realm of neuropsychology, an interest which he owed above all to

Sherrington. For several years he pursued this double life at Columbia University, aiming to be 'a neurologist-in-action'.

During his New York period, he began to think of the desirability of working with a group of people, specialists in different aspects of neurology and the nascent field of neuropsychology. The cooperative effort of the group would, he thought, greatly advance an integrated knowledge of the brain and the relation between brain activity and cognition, feeling and action. The opportunity came in 1928, when he joined McGill University medical faculty and took up posts in neurosurgery at two of the leading Montreal hospitals.

At the beginning of the 1930s, Wilder set about realizing his project for a neurological institute. A successful application to the Rockefeller Foundation led to the opening of the Montreal Institute of Neurology in 1934. Within a very short time, under his leadership and inspired by his example, it had become one of the premier institutions for brain research in the world. Here he continued combining useful neurosurgery with deeply insightful experimentation into the nature and location of psychologically relevant brain functions.

During his lifetime, he was the recipient of an extraordinary number of honours and awards, in the United States, Canada and Britain, and yet the ultimate honour, the Nobel Laureate, eluded him.

He retired in 1960, and immediately took up another career, as historical novelist and biographer. Late in life, he completed a highly readable account of his lifelong study of the brain (Penfield, 1975). Just before he died in 1976, he finished an autobiography based on the letters he had written to his mother over many decades.

What did he contribute?

Penfield's professional life was devoted very largely to the relief of epilepsy by neurosurgery. Epilepsy falls into two main categories. There are automotisms, in which the sufferers lose consciousness but continues to perform the routine activities in which they were engaged prior to the attack. For example, a person may continue walking through the streets along the route originally planned or one that was part of a daily routine. Much better known and much more alarming are convulsive seizures in which the entire system of bodily musculature is involved, except the mechanism of breathing. The cause of both kinds of epilepsy is electrical. A discharge at one place in the brain becomes amplified and spreads to other regions, where the normal afferent neural impulses are triggered but without the usual coordination patterns of inhibition and excitation that control orderly behaviour. Depending on which regions of the brain the rogue excitation spreads to, the outcome will be an automism or a seizure. In many cases, the sufferer reports a special feeling or 'aura' preceding an attack.

If the location of the damaged region where the initiating excitation originates can be found and that part of the brain excised, in many cases the epilepsy is cured, and the patient suffers no further attacks. The clinical practice just described turned out to be the basis of a series of discoveries that enabled Penfield to map the locations of many cognitive functions, as recognized in the conscious experiences of his patients. This was possible because the surgery required that the patient be conscious. The surgeon needs to know when the boundary between the tumour and the active healthy brain region has been reached. This can only be done by asking the patient to perform simple cognitive tasks. The skull is opened under local anaesthetic but the brain itself is not sensitive. It can be touched, parts excised and so on without the patient feeling any discomfort. However, the patient does have striking experiences under electrical stimulation of specific regions of the cerebral cortex and can report on them then and there.

No better account could be found than Penfield's own summing up of the methodology of his researches (Penfield, 1975: 13):

> Since a gentle electric current interferes with the patient's use of a convolution of the brain and sometimes produces involuntary expression of its function, a stimulating electrode could be used to map out the cortex and to identify the convolutions as the patient described his sensations and thoughts. Also, the electrode, if used with discretion, would sometimes produce the beginning of the patient's epileptic seizure and, thus, disclose the site of the brain irritation. By talking to the patient and by listening to what came into his mind each time the electrode was applied to the cortex, we stumbled upon new knowledge. If we removed convolutions as treatment for the fits, we learned about brain function in another way as soon as the nature of the patient's loss was determined after the operation.

Penfield makes it perfectly clear that he and his colleagues did not perform these procedures in the interests of science, but always in the interests of the patient. However, at the same time, they provided an unrivalled opportunity to map the functional properties of the cortex in the course of the thousand and more such operations that were performed in the Montreal Neurological Institute during his tenure as Director.

Penfield drew a distinction between the 'mind's mechanisms', subserving higher cognitive functions, and the 'computer's mechanisms', subserving habitual motor processes. This working or identifying distinction was based on the fact that when a discharge in the prefrontal or temporal areas of the cortex spreads to higher brain mechanisms it produces automatisms, while a discharge in the secondary and motor convolutions of the cortex bombards the sensory-motor mechanisms in the brain stem, producing a seizure. There is a neurological hypothesis to be derived from these facts, namely that the highest brain mechanism is directly connected to the temporal and prefrontal areas while it is connected indirectly with the motor and sensory areas. Penfield emphasizes the existence of two mechanisms, that which is essential to consciousness and that which ensures sensori-motor coordination. He saw these as acting together to form a central integrating system. Sensory input comes to this integrated system and its action gives expression to thought and intentional behaviour. The difference in the effects of epileptic discharges in these two areas enables the relevant regions of the brain to be clearly identified.

On the question of the relation of mind as the content of conscious experience and the neural processes in the brain that accompany all thought and action, Penfield became convinced that they were of quite different orders of existence. He pointed out that when he was stimulating an area of the brain of a conscious patient two streams of consciousness were flowing. One is 'driven by output from the environment' (Penfield, 1975: 55). The other is the result of the stimulation exerted by the current from the electric probe. If the highest brain mechanism is the source of the mind, then these experiments should result in mental confusion, but they do not. They are simultaneous but fully ordered and independent.

Behind these observations lies a deeper insight. Penfield became convinced that the cerebral cortex was not the seat of consciousness. The architecture of the brain suggested to him that its role was the elaboration of neural impulses. The frontal and temporal lobes of the cerebral cortex are not fixed functionally in the infant. The temporal lobe on one side or the other of the brain becomes the seat of the capacity for speech. Evolutionarily new, these areas of the cortex are involved in the interpretation of experience and the utilization of those interpretations in the management of action.

Why consciousness? Penfield's answer is to emphasize the role of the fine tuned management of attention in human cognition. For example, when the electrical stimulation of some location in the cerebral cortex elicits a very vivid and complex experience, the original of the experience is re-presented in far more detail than if it is remembered in the ordinary way. However, what is in the elicited experience is exclusively what was attended to at the time. Unattended aspects are not recovered. Sleep differs from wakefulness in the capacity of the conscious person to selectively attend to what is of interest in the environment, be it external or internal to the body.

Here are two examples from his own overview of his work (Penfield, 1975: 25–27): Stimulating the temporal lobe of an exposed brain with a 3-volt electrical current, his patient said, 'Yes, Sir, I think I heard a mother calling her little boy somewhere ... It was somebody in the neighbourhood where I live'. With similar stimulus to the fissure of Sylvius, also a region of the temporal lobe, another patient reported, 'I had a little memory – a scene in a play – they were talking and I could see it – I was just seeing it in my memory'.

The functions of mind are largely carried out by the utilization of brain mechanisms. Yet, the mind, as Penfield substantializes it, seems to be independent of those mechanisms, in much the same way that a programmer is not part of the computer he or she programmes. In response to the objection that 'the activities of the higher centers and of mental states are one and the same thing', Penfield argued that he could not find brain mechanisms that accounted for 'mind-action', even though the brain mechanisms 'awaken the mind' and 'give it energy' (Penfield, 1975: 104).

Penfield's demonstration of localization of function leaves us with the problem posed to **Alexander Luria** (pp. 105–113) by **Lev Vygotsky** (pp. 26–34) and still unsolved. How are the higher cognitive functions integrated into a coherent system? The development of scanning techniques in the years since Penfield carried out his pioneering 'probing' have left the situation almost as obscure as it was in Vygotsky's time. Just as Penfield found multiple locations for various higher functions, or at least locations for processes involved in such functions, the scanning techniques show up scattered regions of the brain implicated in such processes as reasoning, remembering and so on. Penfield's tentative step towards a solution was to point out the way in which the higher brain stem is a kind of terminus for neural connections both to and from the cerebral cortex. Epileptic discharges that terminate in that region of the brain lead to immediate unconsciousness.

Further Reading

Primary Sources

Penfield, W. (1958) *The Excitable Cortex in Conscious Man*. Springfield IL: Charles Thomas.
Penfield, W. (1975) *The Mystery of the Mind*. Princeton, NJ: Princeton University Press.

Secondary Source

Bear, M. F., Connors, B. W. & Paradiso, M. A. (2001) *Neuroscience* (Chs 12, 14, pp. 751–2). Baltimore, MD: Lippincott, Williams and Williams.

Autobiography

Penfield, W. (1977) *No Man Alone: A Neurosurgeon's Life*. Boston: Little Brown.

Karl Harry Pribram (1919–)

By mid century the pioneering work of **Wilder Penfield** (pp. 113–118) and **Alexander Luria** (pp. 105–113) and many others had established the outlines of a mapping between sensory, cognitive and motor functions of a human being and anatomical features of the brain. However, these 'maps' were far from complete, and in some cases needed drastic revision. In most cases, the discovery of significant correlations had been made in the course of medical treatments for pathological conditions, either spontaneous or due to injury. A systematic exploration of the psychologically relevant anatomy of the human brain by deliberate interference with normal functioning was clearly ruled out on moral grounds.

A great deal of scientific research makes use of convenient models or analogues of the real system under investigation. Using the monkey as a model for the human being enabled Karl Pribram to carry out a systematic research programme to extend the basic outlines of neuropsychology into a maze of significant detail. Monkeys served as models for working out the neuropsychology of certain social relations as well as certain perceptual/cognitive functions such as attention. For the most part Pribram's conclusions made use of a long-standing pattern of reasoning – the injury/deficit/function inference. If we find a deficiency in some cognitive or motor function well correlated with injury to a certain part of the brain, we may infer that the same part, when intact, serves some role in the brain processes by which the original function is performed. By systematically inducing lesions in various parts of the brains of his monkey subjects, and comparing pre- and post-operative performances and capacities, he was able to enlarge the scope of the correlations between brain anatomy and psychology.

In later life, he turned more and more to theoretical analyses of the phenomena he had been studying empirically. He followed up his contribution to *Plans and the Structure of Behavior* (Miller, Galanter & Pribram, 1967) with further theoretical reflections, inspired in part by the development of PDP or connectionist computational systems.

Who is Karl Harry Pribram?

He was born on 25 February 1919 in Vienna, where his father, Ernest August Pribram, was a bacteriologist and immunologist. His mother was Dutch, and the way he tells it, he owes his existence to a swimming party by the Danube in the summer of 1918, when both his parents were serving in the medical services of the Austrian army. In 1923 he was sent to a children's home in Switzerland, seemingly due to troubles between his parents, since shortly afterwards his father emigrated to the United States to join the faculty of medicine at the University of Chicago. Karl returned from Switzerland to Vienna when he was seven. A year later he and his mother left Austria to rejoin his father in Chicago.

The Chicago school system was poorly funded, but the Catholic schools to which he eventually went were problematic for him in another way. He incurred the wrath of the nuns by his skepticism on religious matters. Religious instruction turned him into a lifelong atheist. In the fall of 1932, after some unsatisfactory years in local schools, young Karl was sent to Culver Military Academy in Indiana. This, it seems, was his heart's desire as well as his father's wish, since the place specialized in the training of cavalry and horse drawn artillery. In his autobiography he confesses to a mild attack of 'hippomania'. An introduction to physics and chemistry in his final year at Culver allowed him to leave high school with a broad educational background including some science as well as history and literature.

He entered Chicago University in 1936, to study biology and medicine. He met regularly with his father, which seemed to broaden his mind still further. From his pre-clinical courses he picked up a long-standing interest in the integration of the functions of the whole human being. However, the clinical course both intrigued and disappointed him. Working with patients was rewarding, but the authoritarianism of the medical establishment appalled him. By attaching himself as a willing assistant to some of the professors he was able to take his first steps in research. The most important influence came from Frank Gerard in neurophysiology, from whom he picked up the principle of inference from damage to the brain to correlated cognitive or motor deficit to intact function. He took his MD in 1941.

For the next seven years he practised neurosurgery. Most of his work involved the removal of brain tumours, with as little damage to the surrounding tissue as possible. He learned how to localize brain tumours from Paul Bucy, using a technique pioneered by **Wilder Penfield** (pp. 113–118). This stimulated an abiding interest in the general question of the localization of cognitive and motor functions in different regions of the brain. Looking to widen his experience Pribram moved to Jacksonville, Florida. The Yerkes Primate Laboratories, later relocated in Atlanta, were nearby. He divided his time between his practice and the study of primates. Already he was beginning to think of primate models of human neuropsychology.

In 1948 he moved again, this time to Yale, into a research post. Here he continued his studies in neuropsychology. His work turned on the relation between brain processes and psychological functions. However, these experiments were performed on monkeys, so that, for the most part, the psychology was confined to overt motor behaviour. However, the studies of pre- and post-operative social interactions and of the ability to resist distractions clearly implicated cognition, and opened up a bridge for the inference to the human case. The proximity to Harvard led to some short debates with **B. F. Skinner** (pp. 15–24) and a long-term collaboration with George Miller and **Jerome Bruner** (pp. 54–62). In 1967, at the Stanford Center of Advanced Studies, he joined with Miller and E. Galanter in writing the influential *Plans and the Structure of Behavior*. By that time, Pribram had already moved to a faculty position at Stanford. He spent the next 10 years there continuing the programme of research into the functional structure of the monkey brain and its relation to behaviour.

It is worth remarking that he lost a finger to a mishap with Washoe, the signing chimpanzee. The revenge of the primates perhaps?

Moving back east, Pribram settled first at Radford, Virginia, and more recently joined Georgetown University in Washington DC as Distinguished Research Professor.

What has he contributed?

Karl Pribram added to our understanding of the way the primate brain functions in supporting social relations and carrying on cognitive activities. From his studies of the organization of the components of the limbic system he clarified its role in the integration of brain function. Moreover, his deep theoretical reflections threw light of another kind on how brain, thought and action are integrated.

Apart from some serendipitous observations during his time as a neurosurgeon, Pribram's studies were almost exclusively devoted to unraveling the functional architecture of the sub-human primate brain, particularly the brains of monkeys. Some 1500 animals were operated on during the course of his research programme. His methodology was a generalization of the reasoning by which earlier investigators had used accidental brain damage to identify the regions of the location of functions of the undamaged brain. By deliberately excising parts of the brain in a systematic programme he was able to unravel the location-to-function relation in greater detail than had been achieved before. The question of how to link these studies to the problems of human cognition and brain function has preoccupied him in later years.

After the removal of parts of the brain and the severing of various nerve tracts and fibres, the monkeys were tested in various ways, including the use of an updated version of Skinner's 'box' with its levers and rewards. Defects in and variations from the behaviour of the intact animals were noted. If there was no change in a capacity as it had been displayed in a test before the operation to remove a part of the brain, then the part excised or the pathway severed did not play a major role in the function under investigation, if it played any part at all. If the performance was disrupted then the region that had been removed or rendered inoperative in the brain was functionally significant. To make the results of the experiments with monkey brains significant for the human case, the reasoning becomes more elaborate. Superimposed on the basic injury/deficit/function argument is a hierarchy of analogies between the brains of monkeys and those of people, as well as analogies between the cognitive and social behaviours of both species of primate, the rhesus monkey and *Homo sapiens*.

The formal weakness of the logic of this argument is obvious. Removing the seats leaves the motive function of a car unaffected, while severing the ignition leads immobilizes it. It does not follow that the ignition leads play a major role in locomotion. Pribram was well aware of this reservation. Many experiments, in which adjacent parts of the cerebral cortex are dissected one by one, can be added up to give a convincing overall picture of function and location. Pribram called this the 'intersection of sums' technique. Only by a comprehensive programme of excisions and dissections can a full picture of the function/location relation be built up. The strength of the monkey to human neuropsychological analogy has proven very difficult to assess, since it involves both anatomical and psychological comparisons.

Pribram's first research programme was aimed at settling the question of whether certain deficits in human behaviour correlated with damage to the brain depended on cortical injuries or were explicable by reference to damage to the sensory-motor systems alone. He noted that in no instance did the invasion of the adjacent primary sensory-motor systems produce the deficit, thus confirming the independence of the systems.

In subsequent investigations Pribram made major revisions in our understanding of the brain region/cognitive-motor function relation. For example, he showed that the temporal lobes played some role in vision as well as their well-established role in hearing. His most important revisions concerned the extent of the limbic system, the main coordinating organ of the brain as a whole. The limbic forebrain should include, he argued, the amygdala and other adjacent regions. All could be shown to be connected to the hypothalamus, the 'top' of the old brain, identified by Penfield as the seat of consciousness, and the lynch pin of the relation between cognition/intentional aspects of mind and motor performances.

The research procedure involved some very invasive tactics. It will be helpful for the reader to appreciate the nature of neuropsychological research using animals as models for the human brain to follow a pair of representative studies in detail. Whereas Luria and Penfield took advantage of accidental damage to the some part of the brain to explore the relation between brain regions and psychological and motor functions, Pribram and his colleagues actively induced lesions in the brains of their subjects.

With colleagues Rosvold and Mirsky, Pribram undertook a study of the role of the amygdala in social behaviour. Six rhesus monkeys were caged together for nine months so that a social order would grow up among them, including patterns of dominance. At the end of this period, each was operated on. 'An 18 gauge sucker was inserted into the amygdala [through an opening in the skull], and the entire formation removed' (Rosvold, Mirsky & Pribram, 1954: 174). When they had recovered, the monkeys were reunited and their behaviour monitored. This study turned out to be somewhat inconclusive. 'The pattern of social interaction within the group to which it is reunited ... [is determined] more by the length of time that the relationship had existed ...'; [this] may be 'as important as the lesion and the extent of the lesion in determining the effect of a brain operation on the social behavior of a monkey' (p. 177). The project was completed in this way: 'When the behavioral observations had been completed, the operated animals were sacrificed and their brains prepared for histological examination' (p. 174).

The question of the extent of the limbic formation in the brain is an important aspect of the search for the means by which brain activity is unified. A comparative study of the role of the amygdala and the hippocampus in the organization of a complex cognitive-motor task was carried out in a similar way with J. H. Douglas (Douglas & Pribram, 1969). Six immature Rhesus monkeys were subject to bilateral removal of the amygdala by aspiration. Three more were subjected to removal of the hippocampus. The skulls of a further small group were damaged as if in preparation for the removal of the brain region, but without the operation. The question was whether the removal of the amygdala or the hippocampus had any specific effect on the ability of the monkeys to resist distraction in performing a task in which they had been trained. The monkeys learned to press on a screen only when a 0 rather than a 5 appeared. Pressing when the 0 was 'up' led to a rewarding food pellet. Once the pattern of behaviour had been established distractions were introduced, with other numbers displayed at other locations. Sometimes a monkey merely glanced at the distractor and went on with the task. Sometimes the distraction was enough to lead it to press the distractor display. The group from which the hippocampi had been removed tended to make the distraction response markedly more often than the others. There was no difference however on the distraction trials in the speed with which a pressing was made. The results contradicted a previous hypothesis that the hippocampus has a response-inhibiting function. The 'hippocampal' monkeys inhibited the trained response to try the new stimulus. In fact, the 'amygdala' monkeys were more easily distracted. The experiment not only disconfirmed one hypothesis, but tended to show that the amygdala is 'concerned with increasing attentiveness as a function of reinforcement'. This seemed to be lacking in the monkeys from which the amygdala had been removed.

In both experiments the results do display a correlation between brain structure and cognitive processes. However, they have a certain haziness from a neuropsychological point of view. In the study of the role of the amygdala in social behaviour the social environment seems to play a major role as the source of interactions. It should also be noticed that the experimental technique 'questioned' the brain in a quite large scale way. For instance, the hippocampus contains 3 million cells in the human being, arranged in a complex triple layered net.

Later, Pribram turned to explore the functional role of the posterior cortical convexity, a region that displayed the central Sherringtonian control principle, that afferent and efferent neural connections were necessary to adequate performance. Inhibitory and excitatory neural impulses were both required for a complex motor function to be realized.

All of this work was interpreted using the injury/deficit/function inference rule. So much for monkeys, but how should the results be applied to human beings? The human to monkey analogy is more complex than a simple similarity and difference equation, since there must not only be a structural analogy between the organs, but there must be a corresponding analogy between the functions, and that depends on an analogy between the behavioural patterns.

In his later theoretical writings Pribram proposed a more direct empirical programme for the human case. There are at least three possibilities for linking brain processes and structures to psychological and motor functioning to assess the adequacy of the basic analogical reasoning from monkey brain to human brain. The living brain has an associated electric field with marked periodicity, giving the alpha, beta, theta and delta waves. EEG devices using electrodes taped to the scalp can be used to record these rhythms. The development of computerized analysis can be used to pick up very small scale variations in wave forms that seem to be associated with different cognitive tasks.

The advent of PET scans and fMRI imaging allows the location of activated areas to be mapped in real time. This technique can be used to confirm and enlarge the results of the injury/deficit/function inferences as to the areas engaged in this or that task. Finally Pribram (1971) suggests that the adoption of connectionist computational models of brain activity may lead more or less directly to strong hypotheses as to the fine structure of the relevant sub-brain organs and regions, such as the hippocampus and the amygdala.

All of these ideas have been realized to some extent. Suppes and Han (2000) have carried through EEG studies that have proven sensitive to linguistic differences at the order of single words. fMRI and PET scanning have confirmed at least some of the functional hypotheses based on the injury/deficit/function principle. The work of McCleod, Plunkett and Rolls (1998) has shown that a successful connectionist model of the hippocampus can be constructed and run, emulating the memorial functions of the brain organ itself.

It is a striking fact that those who have actually worked in the experimental probing of real brains in real people and other primates have eschewed simplistic materialist reductions of cognition to brain function alone. **Penfield** (pp. 113–118) and Pribram alike have written extensive critiques of reductionism. Reading Pribram's publications from the 1970s one is struck by how many of the insights expressed therein have become leading principles of the way the integration of psychology with neuroscience seems to be developing in the first years of the 21st century, though his priority has rarely been acknowledged.

Adopting the favoured image of the third millennium, the brain as computer, Pribram's analysis of the conundrum of the relationship between psychological phenomena and brain processes (the 'mind-brain connection' as he calls it) reworks the computational metaphor.

> … the language describing the operations of the neural wetware, the connection web [in the brain] seem(s) far removed from the language used by behavioral scientists to describe psychological processes. But the distance which separates these languages is no greater than that which distinguishes word processing from machine language. (Pribram, 1971: 341)

One is inclined to respond 'What distance could be greater?' That a mark on a screen is seen as a word means that it is meaningful for a person of a certain culture, in addition to any physical properties it may have. Behavioural scientists' language must remain true to the vernacular, however far it is developed. If not, it has nothing to do with psychology, that is with the description and understanding of patterns of thought, feeling and action. Even if we allow that the brain processes by which a person carries out some procedure are self-organizing at the neural level, the gap between intentionality of signs and their material properties, the only properties which can be represented in a symbol system, one for one in a computer, is enormous. The situation, as Pribram notes, is quite different with a connectionist model of the brain. That which is presented to a person as a meaningful sign exists only as a structure in a net, not as an entity in a register.

In an insightful sketch of the methodology that links reports of personal experience with our knowledge of the brain as a mediator between 'environmental' and 'organismic' attributes and influences, Pribram (1971: 100–101) showed how by realizing that reports of private experience are dependent on a public medium of description, the domain of subjectivity can be incorporated in a scientific psychology. What do descriptions of private experiences describe? They must of course be emergent properties of the material system of the organism. Emergent properties come into being as a result of the complexity of the structure of a system, such as a net of neural nets. Spurred by **Jerome Bruner**'s (pp. 54–62) *Acts of Meaning*, the cutting edge of psychology has used Pribram's insights on the relation between neuroscience and psychology to link up with the analytical philosophy of **Ludwig Wittgenstein** (pp. 240–246), in which the priority of the vernacular in the expression of subjective experiences is worked out in detail.

Karl Pribram has been influential at least as much through his theoretical insights as through his empirical studies. It is amusing to read him declaring that his theoretical writings are strictly based on empirical facts. Of course, absent theory there are no facts. He is not alone in adopting this self-deprecating rhetoric – Isaac Newton, the arch theoretician of physics, also declared that he based his hypotheses on 'experiments concluding positively'. It is remarkable how many of the advances of the last decade are prefigured in Pribram's writings from the 1970s.

Further Reading

Primary Sources

Douglas, R. J. & Pribram, K. H. (1969) Distraction and habituation in monkeys with limbic lesions. *Journal of Comparative and Physiological Psychology,* **69/3**, 473–480.
Miller, G. A., Galanter, G. & Pribram, K. H. (1967) *Plans and the Structure of Behavior.* New York: Holt, Rinehart, Winston.
Pribram, K. H. (1971) *Languages of the Brain.* Englewood Cliffs, NJ: Prentice Hall.
Rosvold, H. E., Mirsky, A. F. & Pribram, K. H. (1954) Influence of amygdalectomy on social behavior in monkeys. *Journal of Comparative and Physiological Psychology,* **47**, 173–178.

Secondary Sources

McLeod, P., Plunkett, K. & Rolls, E. T. (1998) *Introduction to Connectionist Modelling of Cognitive Processes.* Oxford: Oxford University Press.
Suppes, P. & Han, B. (2000) Brain wave representation of words by superposition of a few sine waves. *Proceedings of the National Academy of Sciences of the USA,* **97**, 8738–43.

Autobiography

Pribram, K. (1996) Karl Pribram. In L. R. Squires (Ed.), *The History of Neuroscience in Autobiography,* Vol. 2 (pp. 307–349). Washington, DC: Society for Neuroscience.

Konrad Lorenz (1903–89)

Animals have been used in moral tales at least since Aesop collected his fables. In those stories their behaviour reflected their natural dispositions to some extent. However, their main role was as illustrations of human vices and virtues. The industrious ant is contrasted morally with the feckless grasshopper.

The Cartesian analysis of human beings into an immortal soul and perishable material body reflected a traditional and absolute distinction between man and beast. Animals were nothing but material mechanisms lacking the divine spark. The material and brutish body we shared with the animals was the source of a mass of temptations for the immaterial soul to overcome.

The advent of ethology changed all that. Darwinian evolutionary theory closed the gap between animals and humanity with a smooth though hypothetical continuum of anatomical transitions. This has been largely filled in with empirical discoveries. Was there also a smooth continuum between the social and cognitive aspects of the lives of animals and corresponding aspects of human life? Darwin himself inaugurated scientific ethology and emphasized the existence of a behavioural continuum with his wonderful study of the display of emotions in animals and man (Darwin, 1872).

While Pavlovian approaches to the study of animal psychology were dominant, the further exploration of Darwin's insights hung fire. **Ivan Pavlov** (pp. 8–15) was much more interested in conditioned than in natural reflexes. However, in the 1930s a revival of Darwin's project sprang up, particularly in Europe, though it also had sources in the United States. Oscar Heinroth began systematic observational studies of the lives of animals and birds in their natural environments. How differently the psychology of animal life appeared when released from the bondage of the laboratory cage and the 'experimental method'.

In 1974 Konrad Lorenz, Nikolaas Tinbergen and Otto von Frisch shared the Nobel Prize for their revelations of how animals, birds and insects lived in natural surroundings. This work was firmly grounded in Darwinian evolutionary theory. Whatever routines could be shown to be inherited must have an explanation in terms of their contribution to reproductive success.

Not long afterwards the idea that human beings too might display some of these patterns of thought and action began to be suggested in popular literature (Morris, 1967). The tradition of Aesop was reversed. Now human beings were to be exemplars of at least some of the behaviour patterns observed in animals, suitably remodeled for the world of *Homo sapiens*. Though Lorenz contributed to this development, he was always careful to emphasize how different human beings were from even their nearest animal relatives.

Who was Konrad Lorenz?

He was born in Vienna on 7 November 1903, the second son of Adolf Lorenz. Konrad's father had developed a treatment for congenital hip dislocation that brought him international fame and a considerable fortune. He was able to build a huge house outside the city in the village of Altenberg, close by the river Danube. Here young Konrad spent a good deal of his childhood, commuting to school in the city. He attended the Schottengymnasium from the age of 11. However, the advent of the First World War forced the family to move into an apartment in the city, as daily travel to and from Altenberg became more and more difficult.

In his Nobel autobiography Lorenz gives a very detailed and lively account of his childhood obsessions with all sorts of animals and birds. His family indulged his hobby and encouraged his projects. He was fortunate in having a like-minded friend, Bernard Hellman, with whom he conducted many of his early experiments with fish and crustacea. Among his teachers was a Benedictine monk, Phillip Heberdey, who taught the Darwinian theory of natural selection. Another and remarkable influence on young Konrad was his nurse, Resi Führinger, who helped him in his first experimental task, the rearing of a brood of salamander larvae. Living by the river, Konrad became greatly interested in waterfowl, particularly ducks and geese.

'Obsessed with evolution', as he describes himself as he finished high school, nevertheless instead of studying paleontology he followed his father's wishes and enrolled in medical school. His first encounter with medicine was a stint at Columbia University in New York, where he began the pre-medical course. He soon returned home, to enter the medical faculty of the University of Vienna. There he came under the influence of Ferdinand Hochstetter, a distinguished embryologist and comparative anatomist.

Lorenz realized, even at that time, that the comparative method was as applicable to patterns of behaviour as it was to anatomy. He became an instructor in Hochstetter's department before graduation. Karl Bühler proved to be another important influence, bringing him into contact with the work of **William McDougall** (pp. 191–194) on instincts and vitalism. He also read Watson the behaviourist. As he himself says his disillusionment was profound. None of these people knew animals, that is had any inkling of how they lived in their natural surroundings.

During his time as an assistant in Hochstetter's laboratory Lorenz continued his comparative studies of the behaviour of animals and birds. He had encouraged jackdaws to establish a colony in the attics of his father's house at Altenberg, and there some of his most illuminating work was done. At this time too he came across the writings of Oskar Heinroth. Here, for the first time, Lorenz found a mentor, whose influence on his own ideas was fundamental. The second most potent influence on Lorenz was Wallace Craig, with whom he came into contact in the 1930s. Craig managed to persuade Lorenz to give up the idea of patterns of behaviour as 'chain reflexes', in favour of the theory of Von Holst, that the origin of behavioural routines was the disinhibiting of pre-existing neural activity.

In 1936 Lorenz met Nikolaas Tinbergen, with whom he later shared the Nobel Prize. In discussions with Tinbergen the key ideas of ethology, namely innate releasing mechanisms and fixed action patterns, were clearly formulated. Shortly thereafter Lorenz published a paper on the dangers of domestication, which he believed tended to enfeeble a species. However, he expressed his ideas in the racist terminology of the Nazis, the 'new rulers' as he called them later. He recalled this incident with regret in his later years.

In 1939 he took up the chair of psychology at Königsberg through a curious series of chances which included von Holt's playing the viola in a quartet one of the other members where recommended Lorenz for the post. During his time there he had the opportunity for vigorous discussion on philosophical matters with his idealist colleagues in philosophy. This led to his attempts to bring the Kantian conception of the a priori element in human life into relation with Darwinian biology.

The Second World War had begun in 1939. Lorenz joined the military as a doctor in 1941, and by 1942 was working on the Eastern Front, where the German attack on Russia had stalled. He was taken prisoner by the Russians almost immediately, and thereafter spent three years in various hospitals in Russia and Armenia. Like **Ludwig Wittgenstein** (pp. 240–246) in Italy, Lorenz began to write a study of epistemology while in captivity. When he was eventually repatriated the Russians allowed him to take his manuscript with him, as well as his tame starling.

At first Lorenz was able only to set up a small research station at Altenberg financed by the English author J. B. Priestley. The conservative stance of the Austrian Ministry of Education precluded any hope of a job in Austria for so dedicated a Darwinian as he. However, he was soon in the happy position of choosing between two attractive jobs, one in Bristol, England, and the other in Germany. The chance to take his assistants with him led to his accepting the German position which very soon transformed itself into the Max Planck Institute, at Seewiesen. Here he remained for the rest of his academic career.

The culmination of his life work was surely the award of the Nobel Prize, shared with his colleagues and friends, Nikolaas Tinbergen and Eric von Frisch, in 1974. He continued active work, particularly in developing the application of ethological principles to human behaviour. He died on 27 February 1989.

In accordance with the customs of the Nobel Laureate, Lorenz wrote an autobiography (Lorenz, 1973). It is worth remarking on the way in which he gave so much credit to his friends and mentors in the origin of the ideas that animated his work. He even found a good word for his Russian captors who encouraged him to work on his philosophical studies while a prisoner of war. He emerges as a man of outstanding modesty and generosity of spirit.

What did he contribute?

In answering this question the focus must be on the influence that the development of ethology has had on the psychology of the latter part of the 20th century. There were direct influences on social psychology, particularly to be seen in the rise of sociobiology. Perhaps more important in the long run was the legitimating of evolutionary psychology. This has led to innumerable studies of the alleged relationship between genetic endowment and psychological and social attributes of the mature human being.

Lorenz's own innovations included the discovery and experimental verification of the phenomenon of 'imprinting'. He began an intensive study of inherited fixed action patterns, complex routines that played important roles in reproduction, the ultimate descendent of the ideas of von Holst. This also required attention to innate releasing mechanisms, factors that contrasted with the role of imprinting as a source of stable patterns of behaviour. Above all, it was the work of Lorenz that brought the Darwinian conception of development to the fore in a wide range of human studies through its evident success in the domain of animal behaviour.

If Darwin was right about the extension of natural selection from anatomical and physiological aspects of organic beings to behavioural routines, these patterns should display certain characteristics. They should be activated without having been learned, and, integrated with other routines, they should be able to be shown to be adaptive to successful breeding. For example, one of Lorenz's most striking studies, with Tinbergen, concerned the phenomenon of the removal of eggshells from the nest after the young birds are hatched. An eggshell is bright white within, even though it may have camouflage colours on the outside. Shell fragments will attract the notice of predators. Shell removal routines occur among birds that nest in places open to predators, but do not occur among species that nest in places safe from predation. Selection pressure is an obvious explanation for the distribution of this routine.

However, there is more to activating a routine than merely inheriting the neurological machinery that operates the sequence of actions that are conducive to more successful breeding than would otherwise occur. The routine must be triggered by the right kind of stimulus. Following von Holt's insight he reasoned that there must be a releasing mechanism which opens the way for the potential activity to be manifested. Some releasing mechanisms are certainly innate. For example, godwit chicks display appropriate behaviour in the presence of adult godwits immediately on hatching. Experiments enabled the most important adult characteristics required for this recognition to be identified. However, it turns out that the young of many species do not recognize members of their own species unless they have been introduced to them at a certain definite period after they have been hatched or born. This phenomenon has come to be called 'imprinting'.

Throughout his career, Lorenz returned again and again to the question of the balance between the innateness of a routine, ultimately grounded in Darwinian selection via the genetic code, and learned patterns of behaviour. The English ethologist, W. H. Thorpe, had shown that while some bird song was innate, in some species the melodies were learned. It was in the phenomenon of 'imprinting' that a kind of intermediate process of acquisition of a routine appeared. Even as a child Lorenz had noticed that a duckling he had acquired straight from the egg would follow him about rather than go with its biological mother.

The phenomenon is displayed in particularly striking form by geese, as Oskar Heinroth first observed. Whichever being a gosling sees first, that being attracts the behavioural routines appropriate to conspecifics. Lorenz's contribution was a careful experimental study of the phenomenon. His first experiments were aimed at determining the temporal limits on the possibility of imprinting. Too early or too late imprinting does not occur. His work with jackdaws showed that the releasing condition for each innate routine was imprinted separately. To test this he successfully imprinted a jackdaw with crows as flying companions and with jackdaws as reproductive partners. It also turned out that nurturance routines towards young jackdaws involved innate releasing mechanisms, since they were initiated without independent imprinting.

How far does the Darwinian account of complex behavioural routines go? The first thing to observe is how sharply it contrasts with the conditioning theories of **B. F. Skinner** (pp. 15–24) and **Ivan Pavlov** (pp. 8–15). The animal is not a *tabula rasa*. It is a highly organized organism, with a well structured nervous system. A great deal of the behaviour of animals and birds is not learned. Even much of that which is learned is tied in to biological conditions, in the phenomenon of imprinting. The obvious question concerns the degree to which all of this applies to human beings.

Lorenz himself turned to careful and detailed philosophical analyses of the situation of the scientist who proposes to undertake studies of human life. His reflections crystallized into three major principles or prescriptions for such a science. It was clear to him that the whole range of relevant phenomena had to be comprehended. A fully developed human science must be a hybrid enterprise involving the study of the human organism and the subjective experiences of which such a being is capable. Nevertheless, these higher order features of humanity are grounded in physiological mechanisms, not Cartesian mental substances. It was also clear to him that all such studies must be historical, in the sense that Darwinian biology is historical. 'For, if we ask why a particular organism is structured in one way rather than another, the most important answers will be found in the history of the species concerned' (Lorenz, 1977: 34). Finally, Lorenz expresses a strongly 'emergentist' standpoint in declaring that 'the whole is its parts … even if … it acquires a number of system characteristics in its evolution' (Lorenz, 1977: 33). Life, for him, was 'an eminently active enterprise aimed at acquiring both a fund of energy and a stock of knowledge, the possession of the one being instrumental to the acquisition of the other' (Lorenz, 1977: 27). Here we note a link to cognitive psychology and a further move away from behaviourism.

Lorenz was also insistent on the folly of premature experimentation, a lesson that could be learned by many academic psychologists. Comprehensive naturalistic description must come before any attempt to probe further by active experimentation.

However, the impact of his work on the general public came about first through the writings of popularizers, particularly Desmond Morris (1967) and Robert Ardrey (1967). Ardrey's use of ethology is particularly interesting in that it was based on analogies between certain human practices, such as the spacing of houses in suburbia, and the behaviour of animals and birds, in defining territories. The biological, Darwinian basis for a genetic explanation for the howling of monkeys, the urinary marking of places by dogs and the dawn chorus of birds is the establishment of an area sufficient to maintain an adequate food supply. This imperative has long since disappeared from the human world, but the genetic source of a drive towards territoriality has survived, so Ardrey argues. Morris makes similar analogies and inferences. These and other writings have certainly created an atmosphere favourable to biological and evolutionary explanations of human patterns of thought, feeling and action.

Lorenz's generalizations from the adaptive behaviour of animals to the complex patterns of human society and psychology were somewhat programmatic (Lorenz, 1967). *Edward O. Wilson* (b. 1929) has been one of the leading proponents of Lorenz's style of generalization from the animal to the human world with quite detailed speculations about the genetic basis of many aspects of human thinking. In later writings he has tried to strike a balance between cultural and natural sources of characteristic human patterns of thought and action. He remarks that genetic evolution of human traits occurred 'over the five million years prior to civilization ... by far the greater part of cultural evolution has occurred ... [in the last] 10,000 years. ... The behavior [explained genetically] should be the most general and least rational of the human repertoire ...' (Wilson, 1978: 34–35). This of course leaves a great deal of human psychology to be accounted for by cultural factors, evolving symbolic systems that have developed over thousands of years.

However, his work has been taken as an inspiration by many genetic psychologists who have tried to find evidence for the influence of genes on everything from mothering skills to schizophrenia. While psychological phenomena are constituted of meanings which are ordered according to rules and norms, biological phenomena are constituted of organisms and their unfolding states ordered according to causal laws, some of very great complexity. It seems that humans live in disjointed worlds, the relationships between which are still not well understood.

A wide range of cognitive, temperamental and other features of individuals have been ascribed to genetic sources, in that an inherited neurological structure or an inherited pattern of endocrine secretions predisposes people who have this ancestral history to display them. Many of these studies make use of twins, looking for common patterns in the lives, the behaviour and the intellect that survive separation and different conditions of upbringing. However, more have come from generalizing from animal studies to human psychology, particularly from studies of mice. Here are some recent examples of claims for a genetic basis for human psychological traits. I take these two examples from many in my file that have recently appeared as science reports in *The Times* of London.

A gene that may explain why some people are more likely to suffer depression has been discovered by scientists, paving the way for improved treatment for a mental illness that strikes one in five people. Research in the United States has revealed that a variation in a single gene significantly affects the brain's production of serotonin, a chemical messenger that plays a crucial role in depression. Though the mutation has so far been identified only in mice, the findings have excited mental health researchers. ... This offers further evidence that depression is a genetic condition, to which your genes make you particularly vulnerable [commented Ms Wallace of SANE] ... if people accept that there is a genetic vulnerability, then it helps to erase the stigma of mental illness. People are less likely to being blamed for being sufferers. (*The Times*, 9 July 2004: 6).

However, vulnerability is only one of the conditions that are involved in the development of mental disorders. Depression is not itself a 'genetic condition'.

The second example illustrates the dangers of popular generalizations. After a brief introduction referring to the recent film of the siege of Troy, the article goes on:

> US scientists claim to have found a 'warrior gene' in the chromosomes of our primate cousins which is 25 million years old. If the same gene drives us to take up the sword then, as the author Thomas Fuller noted, anger may indeed be 'one of the pillars of the soul'. Scientists became interested in a gene called MAOA when they discovered in 1995 that [male] mice that lacked it had serious anger-management problems ... affected male mice ... were quick to attack an intruder and failed to establish the dominant-submissive relationships that normally result in fewer scraps overall. The same gene had been implicated in human aggression when it was found that a Dutch family whose men had excessive bouts of aggression carried a rare MAOA gene mutation. ... Tim Newman ... has discovered that forms of the gene, linked to aggressive behaviour in macaque monkeys, have been in primates for at least 25 million years. (*The Times*, 10 July 2004: Body and Soul Section, pp. 10–11)

The inheritance not only of fixed action patterns but also of various tendencies and vulnerabilities, via the transmission of genes in normal and variant forms, can hardly be denied. The generalization of very limited data from distant biological relatives must be undertaken with caution. Matt Ridley's recent discussion of the balance between biological sources and cultural origins of personal characteristics is a welcome respite from the speculations of journalists (Ridley, 2003).

Further Reading

Primary Sources

Lorenz, K. (1952) *King Solomon's Ring*. (trans. M. K. Wilson). London: Methuen.

Lorenz, K. (1967) *On Aggression*. London: Methuen.

Lorenz, K. (1970) *Studies in Animal and Human Behaviour* (trans. R. Martin). London: Methuen.

Lorenz, K. (1977) *Behind the Mirror*. New York: Harcourt Brace Jovanovich.

Secondary Sources

Ardrey, R. (1967) *The Territorial Imperative*. New York: Dell.

Darwin, C. (1872 [1979]) *The Expression of Emotion in Man and Animals*. London and New York: St. Martin's Press.

Morris, D. (1967) *The Naked Ape*. New York: McGraw-Hill.

Ridley, M. (2003) *Nature and Nurture: Genes, Experience and What Makes Us Human*. London: Fourth Estate.

Wilson, E. O. (1978) *Human Nature*. Cambridge, MA: Harvard University Press.

Biographies and Autobiographies

Lorenz, K. (1973) *Autobiography*. Nobel e-Museum (Medicine).
Nisbett, A. (1976) *Konrad Lorenz*. London: Dent.

Reflections

The outstanding conclusion that emerges from our discussions of the lives and works of the neuroscientists in this chapter is the inescapable role of reports of private experiences by the people who take part in these very varied studies. The art of neuroscience, as practised by **Wilder Penfield** (pp. 113–118), consisted in finding correlations between locations in the brain which, when stimulated, were accompanied by reportable private experiences. Complementary to this methodology **Alexander Luria**'s (pp. 105–113) use of the injury/deficit//function pattern of reasoning led to a very similar pattern of correlations of localized brain activity with cognitive, affective and practical activities. Luria and Penfield were surgeons. The opportunities for scientific research into the key correlations were limited to what came their way. Serendipity can take one only so far. **Karl Pribram** (pp. 118–125) set about a systematic exploration of the same correlations, working with monkeys as a model for all primate cognition. None of these distinguished neuroscientists drew materialist reductive conclusions from their research. Indeed, their interpretations tended in the other direction, emphasizing the necessity and the unanalysability of the relation between experience and neural activity. Perhaps it is the one brute fact on which the nature of humanity rests.

Biology was greatly enriched in the 20th century by advances in our understanding of the role of Darwinian selection in the dynamics of the nervous systems of invertebrates and vertebrates alike. The general layout of the structures of brain and nervous system is inherited like every other aspect of animal and insect bodies. We now know that this pattern of inheritance is not sufficient to account for the full range of competences and capacities that are displayed by mature organic beings in general. **Konrad Lorenz**'s (pp. 125–133) insights into the complex interplay between inherited, imprinted and cultural factors in the expression of relevant bodies of knowledge should make us very cautious indeed in interpreting the reports of genetic research into the sources of cognition and behaviour. The picture that emerges is a kind of confirmation of Vygotsky's historical/cultural/instrumental approach to the creation of a truly scientific psychology.

Note

1 This project was greatly refined in the last decade of the century. Computational models of brain systems have begun to reveal how specific regions function, while the growth of discursive psychology has opened up the details of patterns of cognition.

6

The Psychologists of Perception

When a human being is awake there is a colourful and ever changing field of related things experienced by each person (and higher animal) centred on the bodily location of the perceiver. Colours, sounds, tastes, sensations of touch and so on are there to be observed by almost everyone, though some people may lack sensitivity to certain colour differences, to pitch relations and so on. There are permanent things to be seen and touched, melodies to be heard, tastes to linger over and so on. What is the relationship between the sensory properties of things and the ordered and structured entities we perceive? It seems that conscious experience is private and personal, while the world in which we live and which we unreflectingly claim to know is public and available to almost everyone. How can this seemingly impassable gulf be bridged?

Attempts to understand how people perceive the world around them, and the states and configurations of their own bodies, go back at least as far as Aristotle. In the 17th century, the philosopher-psychologists of the era took for granted that sensations were mental entities impressed on the mind as the effects of emanations from material things reaching the sense organs. According to the 'official' doctrine of the era one group of sensations, such as shape and motion, were primary, resembling the real qualities of material things, while another group of qualities, such as taste and colour, were secondary and did not resemble the states of material things that caused a person to experience them. This basic distinction was challenged in the 18th century by George Berkeley and by Thomas Reid. They made the first systematic attempts to use the geometrical configuration of the movements of the eyes to analyse the source of our ability to see objects as three-dimensional things. These pioneering studies secured the dominance of the sense of sight in the research programmes of psychologists and philosophers, to the neglect of touch, hearing, taste, smell and the sense of movement and the way we know the positions of the parts of our bodies.

In the early 20th century the psychology of perception was still oriented to vision. The starting point was the work of the German psychophysicists. Their research was concerned with the relation between physical stimuli, including neural impulses, and the corresponding sensations experienced by individuals. Gustav Fechner (1801–87), professor of physics at Leipzig, enunciated the law that the intensity of a sensation was proportional to the logarithm of the intensity of the stimulus.

Johannes Müller (1801–58), who worked in Berlin, proposed the 'law of specific energies', that each sensory nerve produces its own specific sensation. Hermann von Helmholtz (1821–94), something of a universal genius, contributed a principle or general hypothesis to the psychology of perception, that perceiving was an active process. It was not the passive reception of stimuli at the sense organs.

The psychophysicists had unraveled some of the relationships between physical stimuli and sensations of which a person is consciously aware, but we do not perceive just sensations. We are aware of coloured patches no doubt, but we see a three-dimensional world of things. We are aware of sounds but we hear articulate speech, rhythms and melodies. We are aware of pressures on the skin, but we feel shapes and textures. What is the relation between bodily sensations and perceptions? The brain and the neural components of the perceptual systems must play a crucial part, but it cannot be exhaustive of the conditions of perception.

In the 20th century the first attempt at a comprehensive account of perception came from a group of psychologists originating in Germany, the most prominent of whom was **Wolfgang Köhler** (pp. 136–142). The 'Gestalt' school, as they are usually called, emphasized the role of pattern or structure in what we perceive. They believed that perceived structures had analogues in the physical organization of the brain in the act of perceiving. This approach faded from view as a general theory of perception. Shortly after the end of the Second World War two major general explanations of the basis of our powers of perception were on offer.

James Jerome Gibson (pp. 142–148) built his account on the neuropsychological hypothesis that perceptual systems of vision, audition and so on were mechanisms which automatically extracted higher order invariants from sensory stimuli. These were the things we saw, heard, touched and so on. Perceptual systems were active. A built-in tendency to active exploration was supplemented by deliberate exploratory activity as the person or animal interacted with its environment.

Richard Gregory's (pp. 148–154) equally comprehensive theory was based on the principle that perception was a mode of thought. According to his basic thesis perceptions were literally non-verbal hypotheses as to the things and events in the material environment which were affecting the various sensory organs. The brain activity which was evident as a person was perceiving something in the environment was to be understood as a kind of implicit reasoning from the sensory data, taken as premises, to the perception, interpreted as a hypothetical conclusion. Like his German predecessors, particularly Helmholtz, Gregory's studies were focused almost exclusively on vision. Gibson was a supremely competent experimenter, and his theory owes a great deal to his empirical investigations. Gregory is a supremely competent expositor, and his theory owes a great deal to his interpretations of such phenomena as ambiguous figures and illusions.

Psychology in general in the 20th century has followed the same two paths. Is it the study of causal processes, eventually located in the brain and nervous system? Or is it a study of the construction of meanings and the uses of rules of which language is the supreme example? In the split between the theories of

Gibson and Gregory we have yet another example of this divergence. Could it be that they are both right? **David Marr**'s (pp. 154–156) attempt to construct a formal, computational model of aspects of perception opened up one path for further research. The famous serendipitous discovery by **David Hubel** and **Torsten Wiesel** (pp. 156–158) of the specific receptivity of single cells opened up another.

Wolfgang Felix Ulrich Köhler (1887–1967)

The extraordinary sophistication of the Gestalt movement in psychology of which Wolfgang Köhler, with Max Wertheimer (1880–1943) and Kurt Koffka (1886–1941), was the progenitor, stands in startling contrast to the rather naive psychology current elsewhere at the time at which it was developed. Köhler was a first class mathematician. He was among the first to point out exactly where the American mainstream had deviated from good scientific practice, in the wholesale adoption of the methodology of dependent and independent variables in shaping empirical studies. His deep knowledge of the natural sciences enabled him to maintain a dialogue with the methodology of physics and chemistry as these sciences are actually practised, throwing a great deal of light on how a scientific psychology ought to develop.

The basic ideas of Gestalt psychology were almost all to be credited to Max Wertheimer. However, in the context of this series of life stories, it is Köhler whose work merits our attention. Wertheimer seems to have been a man who was unwilling to pursue an insight in the kind of single minded way that would bring a project to a satisfactory completion.

The concept of structure or 'Gestalt', with which Köhler and his collaborators have been associated, was just one among many key concepts that they introduced in what was fated to be a vain attempt to reconstruct psychology as a science along the lines of physics and chemistry. Almost all of Köhler's methodological points concerning the scientific fallacies that come from the dissection of wholes have been more or less ignored.

Who was Wolfgang Köhler?

He was born in Reval, now Tallinn, the capital of Estonia, then a part of the Russian Empire, on 21 January 1887. There had been a strong German presence in the Baltic states for many years. For example, **Emile Kraepelin** (pp. 263–270) spent some important years as a professor at what is now the University of Tartu. Köhler's father was headmaster of a school for the children of the German community in Tallinn. In 1893 the Köhler family returned to Germany. In the way of German middle class families, young Wolfgang and his brother and sisters were broadly educated and well trained for professional careers.

In 1905 he began his university studies with brief sojourns at the University of Bonn and then at the University of Tübingen, moving from one university to another, as was the custom in Germany. He eventually settled in the University of Berlin. Throughout this phase of his education Köhler studied the natural sciences and mathematics intensively. He was fortunate to be able to attend the lectures of the great physicist Max Planck in Berlin.

In 1909 he was awarded the PhD for work in the psychology of audition, with particular reference to music. His mentor in this work was Carl Stumpf (1848–1936), well known for his work in the psychology of hearing. Like many cultivated Germans Köhler was an accomplished musician and played the piano more than competently. In later life he expressed considerable satisfaction that his early work in psychology fitted so well with his deep cultural interests.

His first academic post was at Frankfurt University. Here he came into contact with Max Wertheimer (1880–1943) and Kurt Koffka (1886–1941). Köhler seems to have had a special knack for foregrounding whatever scientific research had attracted his interest, giving it priority over any personal matters. This made him an ideal collaborator. With Wertheimer and Koffka, he began to lay out the principles of a new kind of psychology, one that would be developed along lines that had already proved so successful in physics and chemistry, in which he and his colla-borators were very well trained. The study of structures and their transformations is the distinguishing feature of the natural sciences in the modern era. The paradigm to which they directed their efforts has come to be called 'Gestalt psychology', the study of the role of patterns and structures in psychology. The work at Frankfurt was largely concerned with developing an adequate psychology of perception, one which did away completely with the idea that percepts were additive summations of elementary sensations, in favour of the idea that every percept was a structure or whole. The character of the elements of such wholes was largely determined by the role they played in the structure. The Gestaltists deliberately exploited the parallel of their structural thinking with molecular chemistry and field physics.

In 1914 Köhler took up an invitation from the Prussian Academy of Sciences to direct the work of a primate research centre to be established on the island of Tenerife in the Spanish Canaries. There he remained during the next six years. Among the many important discoveries he reported in his classic work, *The Mentality of Apes* (1921), was the ability of chimpanzees to solve problems by making use of available material resources in the environment. For many people Köhler's name is linked with the transformation of our conceptions of our fellow primates that emerged from his studies.

It seems fairly certain that Köhler did not confine himself to primatology while in Tenerife. The island was very well placed for the observation of the shipping that was playing a vital role in the war between Germany and the Western allies. The British, who had occupied the islands, certainly thought he was spying on Allied convoys and tried to persuade the Spanish authorities to search Köhler's house. It emerged later that he had indeed established a radio transmitter and receiver in a part of his house forbidden even to his family.

The studies of apes had established his reputation as one of the leading psy-chologists of the day and so it was not surprising that he returned to Germany to become Director of the Psychology Institute at the University of Berlin. He continued to work there until his exile to the United States in 1935. Among his co-workers at the Institute were his one time mentor Max Wertheimer and Kurt Lewin, the man who carried through some of Köhler's mathematical insights.

The way in which he drew together the detailed results of fine-grained psychological research with fundamental problems in epistemology gave his work a very broad appeal at the time. In the years just before the Nazi takeover of Germany he traveled extensively in the United States, South America and Europe. There remains the question as to why this did not lead to a more substantial and permanent influence of Gestalt psychology in the United States. This puzzle is the more tantalizing when we bear in mind that he was later elected to the presidency of the American Psychological Association for 1958–9.

Köhler should be remembered as one of the few prominent Gentile academics to openly confront the Nazis with their programme for racial 'purity'. His growing outrage came to a head with the forced resignation of James Franck, Nobel Prize Winner. Köhler wrote an article of protest that appeared in the newspapers on 28 April 1933. The support he received from some Germans and from many people abroad practically assured that he would be a target himself, even if only indirectly. A growing tempo of interference in his own institute led to his finally leaving in 1935 for what seemed likely to be permanent exile in the United States.

He quickly found a position at Swarthmore College in Philadelphia. Though he had adequate research facilities for himself there, the lack of a graduate programme meant that the momentum of the Berlin years was lost. After his retirement from Swarthmore in 1958 he joined MIT where he inaugurated the graduate programme in psychology, working there from 1960 until 1968.

From about 1950 Köhler began to teach again in Germany on an occasional basis. He established an enduring relationship with the Free University of Berlin during the next few years. However, it has to be said that for the most part his sage advice on the methodology of research, and his efforts to bring psychology into line with the way physics and chemistry had actually developed, fell on deaf ears. The fallacies he pointed out in the 1920s, particularly the 'destructive decomposition of structures', continue to be visible in academic psychology even today.

He married twice. In his later years he retired to a farm in New Hampshire, dying there on 11 June 1967.

What did he contribute?

Köhler first became widely known through his work on animal cognition, particularly the problem-solving capacities of primates. Having first shown that hens responded not to individual shades of colour but to pairs of shades, that is to a pattern or Gestalt, he began to experiment with chimpanzees. He was interested in two questions: would chimpanzees use tools to solve problems? And, would they arrive at solutions more by an insight into the situation as a whole than by random trial and error? His work established that these animals were able to think in a sophisticated way, seeing a problem situation as a whole. For example, he allowed some chimps to see him hide a stick in the roof of their cage. Next day he put some bananas outside the cage but within reach if the animals used a stick to pull them in. These chimps had previously solved the problem by using a stick prominently placed in the enclosure. In the experiment one of the animals remembered where the stick was hidden, recovered it and used it to get the bananas. Building 'ladders' with boxes was another innovatory problem-solving strategy that they soon developed (Köhler, 1921 [1927]).

Köhler was very well aware that the ideas of the Berlin Institute of Psychology to which he had returned in 1921 were in sharp contrast to the metaphysical principles that dominated American experimental psychology. The Americans presumed that it would be possible to separate atomic elements from the complex patterns of environmental situations and human experience, in order to apply the simple dependent/independent variable methodology. Wertheimer, Köhler and Koffka realized that abstracting one feature from the structure of which it is a component changes that feature. In some cases it renders worthless the experimental study that presumes its identity in isolation. At the same time it destroys the structure within which the isolated feature had significance.

The experimental programme of the Gestaltists began with the study of perception. It seemed clear that it was impossible for meaningful and structured perceptions to be synthesized from meaningless, atomic constituents. The two key requirements for a theory of perception were to account for the *meaning* and the *organization* of what is seen or heard or touched.

Wertheimer made the point forcibly: 'When we are presented with a number of stimuli we do not as a rule experience "a number" of individual things, this one and that. Instead larger wholes separated from and related to one another are given in experience' (Wertheimer, 1938: 78). It must be emphasized that the Gestaltists maintained that the structure or pattern of a whole is an objective property of that whole, not imposed a priori by the mind. Various rules of structure were discovered in the Berlin Institute, such as the law that similar things will be grouped together. Other laws included the law of completeness, that incomplete but symmetrical figures will be seen as complete. Köhler argued that these could all be seen as consequences of a general law, his Law of Pragnanz, that experiences will take on the 'best' form that is possible in the context. Köhler was insistent that there was overwhelming experimental evidence that the structural properties of organized wholes were not insertions by the mind, but objective attributes of the wholes in question. 'Up to the present time there has been a tendency', says Köhler (1928: 216), 'to regard the remarkable properties of wholes, especially the possibility of transposing their translocal properties [such as the sameness of a melody in different keys] as the achievement of "higher" processes. From the view point of *Gestalt* theory sensory organization is as natural and primitive a fact as any other side of sensory dynamics'.

Perhaps even more important were the experimental demonstrations of the way that perception of such matters as shape and motion were dependent on context.

There are some basic experimental displays of the distinction between perceived speed, relative to context and physical speed, independent of context, which are summed up in Köhler's lectures of 1938 (Köhler, 1939: 8–15). One of the experiments that was most influential on Gestaltist thinking was the way in which two black bars, separated by a small distance, were seen depending on the sequential times at which they were presented. If there was only a small difference between the times at which each was shown, they were seen to appear simultaneously. If the interval was lengthened, an observer would see a single bar moving across the screen. To avoid any predisposition to explain the phenomenon as 'apparent motion', Wertheimer and his colleagues called it the 'phi phenomenon'. They insisted that the motion was not an illusion but an observable fact. 'Illusory contours', such as the completion of an incomplete figure, were treated in the same way. The seeing of completed figures was not an illusion. Structure is as much an objective feature of what is seen as colours and other sensory items.

Studies of the differences in visual speed when objects moving with the same physical velocity are presented in differently structured contexts were also used to demonstrate Gestalt principles. For example, large circles moving across a large aperture in a screen are seen to be moving more slowly than small circles of the same velocity, moving across a small aperture. This is not an illusion, but the perception of a structural property of the set-up, namely certain relations of proportionality between the circles and the apertures.

Köhler cited the figure/ground distinction, as identified by Edgar Rubin, as another example of the role of Gestalt patterns in perception. The shape that is seen as the figure usually stands out from the ground in a third dimension. The familiar fact that objects are more or less easy to identify depending on their surroundings was another phenomenon for which Gestaltists provided careful empirical tests. For instance, Köhler investigated the conditions that facilitated identifying the expression of a face presented upside down. The gravitational field becomes part of the conditions of perception. In a wide variety of studies, including working with animals and birds, the principle that organisms react to structures, that is to relations between individual stimuli rather than the stimuli considered independently of one another, was well established.

Köhler in particular was determined to tie Gestalt analysis of perceptual and cognitive processes to the brain. In his Page-Barbour Lectures of 1938 (Köhler, 1939: Ch. 2), he describes the development of Gestaltist *field theory* in detail. The fact of the internal relation between elements and patterns suggests a field concept, that is that we should view each perceptual element as having an influence at places distant from it, thus contributing to an organized or structured perception. This is the basic principle of field physics. Indeed Köhler explicitly cites Michael Faraday (1791–1867) as a source of field concepts (Köhler, 1939: 65). How could there be fields of influence displayed in perception unless there were processes in the brain that had a field-like character? It was a short step to hypotheses as to the actual existence of such fields, and suggestions as to the neural mechanisms by which they might be realized. In this way not only would there be structured groups of entities in experience, but there would be corresponding or *isomorphic* structures of neural representations in the brain, the influence of each element spreading throughout the structure. This idea, though promising, did not seem to be in accordance with developments in neuroscience in the mid-20th century. One sometimes sees the isomorphism hypothesis cited in explanation of why Gestalt psychology made little mark, except for the rules that are exemplified in the perception of groups of objects as wholes. However, with the advent of connectionist models of cognition, requiring nets of artificial neurons which store or process information as wholes, the Gestaltist ideas seem to be coming back. This is perhaps most strikingly exemplified in the hologram theory of **Karl Pribram** (pp. 118–125). He has suggested that perceptual information is distributed over a field of neural nodes, and recovered in the same way as the information encoded in the cells of a hologram is recovered by incident light.

The second main mathematical idea that Köhler introduced was the *vector*, a representation of an influence that had both magnitude and direction. Vector interactions follow very definite laws in mathematics. This approach was picked up by Kurt Lewin (1890–1974), one of Köhler's students, who had also come to the US as a refugee from Nazi persecution. He developed a comprehensive theory of the human personality that eschewed statistical methods. Instead he proposed using vectors to represent an individual's cognitive resources and life course. Lewin presented the dynamic field of an individual in terms of potentialities for movement in certain directions. For example, he developed this theory as a way of analysing the behaviour of soldiers in relation to a *krieglandschaft* or 'war landscape', and their perception of the texture of threat in a dangerous environment.

The structural or interactionist view of human cognition and the insight that perception is not a matter of sensory bricks and associationist, conditioned or even cognitive mortar, have once again become dominant in psychology. The recovery of the work of **Lev Vygotsky** (pp. 26–34), the spread of **Jerome Bruner**'s (pp. 54–62) ideas of meanings and storylines, the growing evidence for something like fields of electrical- neuronal activity in the brain, all suggest a re-examination of the Gestaltist point of view.

Köhler's writings are very accessible. They present his views in a limpid and systematic fashion, lavishly illustrated with experiments and observations.

Further Reading

Primary Sources

Köhler, W. (1921 [1927]) *The Mentality of Apes*. New York: Liveright.
Köhler, W. (1928 [1938]) *Gestalt Psychology*. New York: Mentes.
Köhler, W. (1939) *Dynamics in Psychology*. New York: Liveright.

Secondary Sources

Lewin, K. (1951) *Field Theory in Social Science*. New York: Harper and Row.

Wertheimer, M. (1938) Laws of Organization in perceptual forms. In W. Ellis (Ed.), *A Source Book of Gestalt Psychology*. London: Routledge and Kegan Paul.

Biography

Jaeger, S. (1997) Wolfgang Köhler. In W. G. Bringmann, H. E. Luck, R. Miller & C. E. Early (Eds), *A Pictorial History of Psychology* (pp. 277–281). Chicago: Quintessence Publishing Co.

James Jerome Gibson (1904–79)

As a person moves through a material environment the substantial things that fill it continue to be perceived as three-dimensional objects, even though the stimuli that reach the brain via the retina are continually changing, and the retina itself is two-dimensional. The basic idea of perception as the experience of invariance under transformation is at the root of Gibson's understanding of the psychology of perception. Rather than conceive of the perceiver as passive and the mind as a blank slate on which sensations are impressed and somehow organized into shapes and arrangements of things, some of which are in relative motion, Gibson thought of perception as the upshot of active exploration of the streams of energy that fill the environment and impinge on the sense organs. The perceptual systems such as lens, iris, retina, optic nerve, visual cortex, or pinna, eardrum, basilar membrane, hair cells, primary and secondary auditory cortex, skin and finger and wrist joints, explore the energy flux in search of invariant relations. 'The animal and the environment,' he said (Gibson, 1966: 8), 'make an inseparable pair'.

Who was James Jerome Gibson?

He was born on 27 January 1904 in the small town of McConnelsville, Ohio. The family were strict Presbyterians, and James was brought up in the religious atmosphere of the times. Like many Midwesterners who made their lives elsewhere, he became an agnostic in later life. After attending the local high school he began his university education at Northwestern University, later transferring to Princeton. He completed his PhD in 1928, working on the relation between learning and memory.

In 1928, immediately after receiving his PhD, he joined the faculty of Smith College, one of the highly regarded all-women colleges, sister to such places as Radcliff in Cambridge, Massachusetts and Vassar in Poughkeepsie, New York. His meeting with the well known Gestalt psychologist, K. Koffka, at Smith, had a profound influence on his way of looking at the phenomena of perception. The

Gestalists had emphasized the supreme importance of structure in perception, and this idea infused all of Gibson's later work. In 1932 he married Eleanor Jack, who had come to teach at Smith in 1931. When the Gibsons moved to Cornell in 1949, the statutes of the university precluded her taking up a post in the psychology department. However she continued to work in psychology as a research assistant. There is no doubt that she was involved in most of James Gibson's subsequent work on the psychology of perception, though one must say she received less credit than perhaps was her due. Her own publications concerned aspects of development in high level perceptual skills, in particular reading.

The American involvement in the Second World War from 1941 saw Gibson bringing his considerable expertise to tackle various psychological problems that arose in the training of pilots. He became director of the USAF unit in Aviation Psychology. How the pilot experiences the world became for him a working model for visual perception in general. 'The world with a ground under it – the visual world of surfaces and edges – is not only the kind of world in which the pilot flies; it is the prototype of the world in which we all live' (Gibson, 1979: 60). In studying the pilot's perception during the 'landing glide' with an eye to how to train a pilot to identify the point at which the aircraft will reach the ground, he realized that the key was an invariant property of the ever changing image on the retina. As one moves through a landscape the relations between the elements in the visual field expand, giving gradients of deformation. Where the expansion is least is the point at which the plane will touch down (see Figure 6.1). He brought this experience back to Smith College, where, encouraged by his conversations with Koffka, he wrote his classic text, *The Perception of the Visual World*, published just after he left Smith for Cornell.

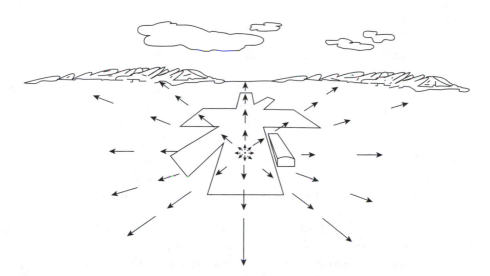

FIGURE 6.1   THE OUTFLOW OF THE OPTIC ARRAY IN A LANDING GLIDE

Source: Gibson, J. J. (1986) *The Ecological Approach to Visual Perception*. Hillsdale, NJ: Lawrence Erlbaum.

With the publication of *The Senses Considered as Perceptual Systems* in 1966, Gibson's ecological theory of perception with its array of brilliant supporting experiments became widely known, but perhaps it has been less fully appreciated than it should have been. Despite the clarity of the exposition, the reader needed to grasp some new and powerful concepts which were required to express the radical insights on which the ecological account of perception rested. The shift from conceiving of the perceiver as a passive receptor of stimuli to an active explorer of the energy flux emanating from the material environment required the abandonment of deeply entrenched presuppositions. Gibson's experimental programme focused on the sense of sight and the sense of touch. Work on an ecological theory of auditory perception is still underdeveloped.

The Gibsons made several extended visits abroad, but their connection with Cornell continued after James Gibson's retirement in 1972 until his death in December 1979. He remained active in his later years, publishing his last book in the year in which he died.

What did he contribute?

'When the senses are considered as channels of sensation', Gibson (1962: 3) remarked, 'one is thinking of the passive receptors and the energies that stimulate them ... it does not explain how animals and men accomplish sense perception', that is, see a world of permanent things, hear sounds as melodies or speech, discern the shapes of things by touch. What is missing from the passive receptor theory? The stimuli that affect the sense organs are changing continually as the animal moves about an environment. It follows that whatever it is that is the source of the experience of permanent properties of things must be something in the flow of stimulus energy other than the causes of sensations. There are geometrical features of the material environment which are present as higher order invariants in that flow. The key idea is that these invariants do not change as the patterns of stimulus on the retina or on the hair cells of the cochlea change. 'These invariants correspond to permanent properties of the environment' (Gibson, 1962: 3).

Gibson's radically new theory, already well articulated in his first book of 1950, written while he was still at Smith, was based on the hypothesis of an active organism. 'The active observer gets invariant perceptions despite varying sensations'. How does this come about? The answer to this question was fundamental: the organism explores the energy flux. 'The movements of the eyes, mouth, and the hands ... seem to keep on changing ... the input of sensation, just so as to isolate over time the invariants of the input at the level of the perceptual system' (Gibson, 1966: 4). Somehow as perceivers we 'pick up' the invariants in relations between changing sensations, and these form the basis of the experience of permanent structures in the environment. The agency of active exploration of retinal, auditory and tactile images can be a property of the perceptual system itself, as in the saccadic movements of the eyes (rapid shifts of point of attention of which we are unaware), or the exploratory movements of the hand in perceiving a shape, or a movement of the whole organism, such as the pilot bringing a plane in to land. The key point is the idea of an activity in the course of which, for the case of vision, while the sensory image on the retina is changing, the perceptual system is abstracting higher order invariants from the changing point of view such as the point of touch-down on an airfield.

A new theory requires new terminology to express the new insights on which it is based. Part of the explanation for the slow acceptance of Gibson's ecological theory of perception was the way he expressed his radically different point of view. He used the word 'pickup' for the process by which invariants in the stimulus energy were taken in by the active organism. His choice of a term for the process as a whole, 'direct perception', was unfortunate, suggesting, as it did, that the passage from stimulus to conscious experience was not mediated by anything. The point was that what an organism perceived was neither the result of the imposition of order on fleeting sensations, nor was it the result of inferences drawn from sensory data. It was neither sensory nor cognitive. The passage from sensory image to perceived object was not mediated by sensations, particularly not by sensations somehow being cobbled together into perceived things. The invariants were fundamental, sensations clothing them in colour, texture and so on. Information pickup was not information processing.

The other important Gibson terminological innovation was the word 'affordance'. To emphasize the priority of the uptake of invariants, Gibson asked his readers to think of the environment as a rich resource of possibilities of action. In perceiving a knife as something sharp one *saw* that it afforded cutting. In hearing a sound as a tone above the tonic one *heard* that it afforded resolution. The environment is the source not only of sensations, but affords the experience of permanent things and in a general kind of way what can be done with them. The relation between environmental states and conditions and the two components of perception, sensations like colour and pitch, and visual invariants such as shape and auditory invariants such as tonic and dominant, the first and fifth notes of a scale, are radically different. Sensations are caused via stimulus of the retina, hair cells of the cochlea, and so on, but invariants are abstracted from the energy flux by active exploration, for what it will afford to an organism with its specific organs of sense.

The phenomenon that is at the heart of the Gibsonian view of perception is easily replicated. When one moves one's head from side to side the sensations one is experiencing related to the pattern of stimulus on the retina are changing, while the world continues to be experienced as stationary, for example a book on the table. However, when something passes by a stationary head, the book is moved for example, the visual sensations are very similar to those one experiences when one moves one's head. Yet, the book is seen to move and the head becomes the stationary frame against which the motion is perceived. There must be another ingredient in the process of perception, part of which is an unattended awareness of the movement of one's own head. One is aware of the book, stationary or moving. In the ordinary course of events, as one walks around the desk, one is not aware of the state of motion of one's own head.

Gibson once remarked that he hoped that his new concepts would never shackle thought as the old terms and concepts had. On the old sensationalist view it had to be presumed that one learned how to organize sensations into perceived things or imposed a prior schema that existed independently of visual, auditory or tactile sensations.

We can follow Gibson's brilliant programme of experimental tests and elaborations of the theory best by starting with one of the great experiments in the history of psychology, the experimental study of the perception of shape by touch (Gibson, 1962). Gibson needed to show that sensations produced by touching the skin with objects of different shapes did not result in accurate perceptions of those shapes if there was no movement between the test object and the surface of the body. If this were so, then there must be more to tactile perception of shape than sensations of touch on the surface of the skin. The second step would be to show that if the hand could be used in active exploration of the shape by moving it over the object, then accurate perception of shape did occur. The stimulus objects were common kitchen cookie cutters.

Using a simple device to make sure the pressure with which the cookie cutters touched the hand was the same in all the experimental conditions, Gibson carried out three studies. In the first, the stimulus objects were pressed on a stationary hand. The shapes were correctly identified in only 29% of the trials. However, when the shape was actively explored by moving the hand over the stimulus object, the wrist, fingers, palm and so on changing their relative orientations to the shapes, they were correctly identified in 95% of the trials. In a third experiment the hand was stationary and the cookie cutters were moved over the surface of the palm. In this condition, the shapes were correctly identified in 72% of the trials. The exploratory movements allow for the identification of shapes as invariants in the relations between the edges, angles and corners of the objects. The role of the finger and wrist joints in the perceptual process is remarkable. It showed that it was not only the tactile sensations that yielded invariants, but also kinesthetic neural impulses that were not registered in consciousness as such, but only indirectly in the awareness of shape.

Summing up his discoveries, Gibson (1962: 160) remarks: 'Tactual perception corresponds well to the form of the object when the stimulus is almost formless, and less well when the stimulus is a stable representation of the form of the object. ... the role of the exploratory finger movements in active touch would then be to isolate the invariants ... in the flux of sensation.'

Among a plethora of observations and experiments on visual perception the 'stake in the field' experiment has the beauty of simplicity. If perception is based on the retinal image, then a distant object should appear smaller than it is, because the image in the retina will be smaller. Choosing a very long flat field, Gibson planted a stake at increasing distances, at each distance asking one of his participants to estimate its height. He reports that 'the judgements of the size of the stake did *not* decrease, even when it was ten minutes walk away and becoming difficult to make out. The judgements became more *variable* with distance but not smaller. Size constancy did not break down.' The implication was that 'certain invariant ratios were picked up unawares by the observers and that the size of the retinal image went unnoticed ... no matter how far away the object intercepted or occluded the same number of texture elements in the ground. This is an invariant ratio' (Gibson, 1962: 160).

Gibson lists the main invariants in visual perception as 'optical structure under changing illumination' and 'under change of point of observation', invariance of structure 'across sampling of the optical array', and 'local invariants of the ambient array under the local disturbance of its structure' (Gibson, 1962: 310–311). The retinal image is explored for invariants, for example the ratios of the lengths of sides of a cube as its image on the retina changes during the rotation of the object in real space. These are what we see.

Instead of thinking of the image changing and moving relative to the retina, we must think of the retina moving with respect to the image, and thus *exploring* its geometrical features.

By making another shift in our way of thinking about the psychology of perception Gibson's discoveries and his interpretation of them become clearer. Thinking in terms of 'information' rather than in terms of the contents of states of conscious awareness enables us to think of perception in terms of the information that eventuates in a conscious experience, but may not itself be wholly conscious. Some of the information that is implicit in perception is not given as sensation, but is the result of a process of geometrical analysis performed by the perceptual system as it is used to explore the environment. Some of this information flows to the brain from proprioceptors, nerve endings in the joints and muscles, information that is almost never represented directly in states of conscious awareness. This information is directly represented in what is perceived, mediated neither by hidden cognitive processes nor past experience.

Getting the conceptual tools in order is one of the most important aspects of scientific research. The puzzle about the perception of motion and rest, the fact that the pattern of stimulus on the retina may be the same when the head moves past an object and when that same object moves past the head, is readily resolved if one gets one's concepts right. Gibson argues that motion *of* the retinal image is a misconception. Motion *in* the retinal image, change of pattern, is not displacement with reference to the retina. In perceiving visually the retina is displaced *over* its image, exploring it for invariances in the relations between the sensory elements as their disposition on the retina changes. The eye is constantly in motion, the point of attention changing with great rapidity. These are referred to as the 'saccadic' eye movements, rapid jumps or saccades from one point of fixation to another. The perceiver is not aware of these movements. According to the thesis of ecological optics it is the invariants in retinal image that are maintained as the image is constantly changing and are 'picked up' by the brain. They are what we see.

How does it come about that the perceptual systems behave in this way? It is not learned, nor is the structure of percepts inherited. The perceptual apparatus of an animal species evolves with the environment. This view has been called the thesis of the 'reciprocity of animal perceptual capacities and the key features of the environment in which it is evolving'.

Further Reading

Primary Sources

Gibson, J. J. (1950) *The Perception of the Visual World*. Boston: Houghton Miflin.
Gibson, J. J. (1962) Observations on active touch. *Psychological Review*, **69**, 477–491.
Gibson, J. J. (1966) *The Senses Considered as Perceptual Systems*. Boston: Houghton Miflin.
Gibson, J. J. (1986) *The Ecological Approach to Visual Perception*. Hillsdale, NJ: Lawrence Erlbaum.

Secondary Source

Michaels, C. F. & Corello, C. (1981) *Direct Perception*. Englewood Cliffs, NJ: Prentice Hall.

Biography

Reed, E. (1988) *James J. Gibson and the Psychology of Perception*. New Haven, CT: Yale University Press.

Richard Langton Gregory (1923–)

Richard Gregory has been the leading proponent of the cognitive account of perception. Like Gibson he rejected the sensationalism of the tradition that had been established in the 17th century by the British empiricists. Perception is not just the putting together of elementary sensations. What one perceives is a great deal richer in information about the environment than its simple sensory content.

Gregory's earliest book, *Eye and Brain* (1966), has been immensely influential as a textbook, shaping the beliefs of generations of psychology students. It was re-issued in rewritten form in 1998. The clarity of the exposition, the richness of the illustrations, as much as the intellectualist doctrine, have played key roles in its perennial popularity.

Who is Richard Langton Gregory?

He was born on 24 July 1923, the son of C. C. L. Gregory, the leading astronomer at London University. He went to King Alfred School, Hampstead, and in 1941 into the RAF, serving in the signals until 1947. He then went up to Cambridge to read Philosophy and Experimental Psychology. From 1950 to 1953 he worked in the Medical Research Council Unit in Cambridge, spending part of the time seconded to the navy to improve the methods of escaping from submarines. From the MRC unit he went on to a Lectureship in Cambridge and to a Fellowship at Corpus Christi College.

From 1970 until his retirement in 1988 he held a professorship in the Medical School at the University of Bristol. In his retirement he has been, as always, intensively active, publishing substantial and highly original work on and around the problems of mind and consciousness. One would not give an adequate picture of the man without mentioning his extraordinary facility in the invention of instruments, mainly for research into the problems of perception, and his legendary brilliance as a lecturer. He has also been instrumental in the development of the public understanding of science.

What has he contributed?

Gregory's cognitivism starts from the same intuition as does the direct perception theory of Gibson. 'In ideal conditions,' says Gregory (1998: 2), 'object perception is far richer than any possible images in the eyes.' However, from this point on his account of perception diverges further and further from that of **James Gibson** (pp. 142–148). While agreeing that 'the added value must come from dynamic brain processes', Gregory eschews a biological or even a mathematical explanation, since he claims that the process of perception involves 'employing knowledge stored from the past, to see the present and predict the immediate future' (Gregory: 1998: 2).

For Gregory the prime historical source for his way of conceiving of perception was the work of Hermann von Helmholtz. According to Helmholtz perception is a species of unconscious inference, from sensory data as premises to hypotheses as to what there might be in the environment. Unlike inferences proper, from propositions to propositions, the conclusions of these inferences manifest themselves to us as something essentially pictorial. At first sight this conception of what is seen, heard, touched and so on seems to run counter to common experience. We perceive things rather than representations of things. Propositional expressions of the natures of the things that are in the environment seem to be quite different from perceptions. However, it is clear that the electro-chemical signals which enter the visual cortex from the complex neural structures of the retina are digital rather than analogue. There is nothing in the least pictorial about what enters the visual cortex. Yet, what we see can be physically matched and compared to representations which are pictorial, such as photographs, diagrams, models, sculpture and paintings, all of which are extended in space.

Just as Gibson developed a special vocabulary appropriate to the intuitions and insights he wanted to share with his readers, so too have Gregory and the cognitivists. 'We now think of the brain as representing, rather as the symbols of language represent characteristics of things ...' (Gregory, 1998: 5). He goes on to say that the typical cognitivist concepts of meanings and rules '... seem necessary for processes of vision; though its syntax and semantics are implicit, to be discovered by experiment' (ibid.). This approach can soon come to seem very puzzling. The objects of perception, those things, events and so on which we perceive, do not seem to be the least like symbols, nor does it make sense to suggest that what one perceives is a representation of something in the environment. It *is* something in the environment. The cognitivists face a problem that the advocates of the direct pickup view do not face, namely if the relevant states and processes in the brain are symbolic transformations according to rule, how is it that the person in whose brain these processes are going on sees trees, hears bells, touches fur and so on? We will not get an answer to our question, from either Helmholtz or Gregory. Does this matter?

We must now follow Gregory in working out his conviction that the fallibility of vision is such that 'knowledge and assumptions add so much that vision is not directly related to the eye's images or limited by them – so quite often it produces fictions' (Gregory, 1998: 6). Illusions, visual fictions, play an important part in Gregory's supportive arguments for the Helmholtzian position, that is for the claim that the processes of perception are knowledge-based.

Gregory makes much of a parallel he sees between perceptions and the predictive hypotheses of the sciences. In the sciences hypotheses not only refer to what is to be expected in the future, but also to hidden or unobservable properties of material systems. Visual images, like experimental data, are of little use in practical activities, 'until they are read in terms of significant properties of objects' (Gregory, 1998: 10). Any pattern of visual stimuli can be interpreted in infinitely many ways. What we do depends on the interpretation we have given to the pattern. 'Seeing objects involves general rules, and knowledge of objects from previous experience, derived largely from hands-on exploration' (Gregory, 1998: 11). What is the basis for this powerful claim?

When we turn to the content of Gregory's famous book, *Eye and Brain* (1998), we find a brilliant exposition of the *neurophysiology* of vision. The amazing techniques of PET scanning and fMRI show very clearly that large areas of the brain are active when someone is perceiving something. But what is the brain doing? The rather coarse-grained images of brain activity do not answer that question. Is the brain automatically performing complex mathematical analyses in search of invariants, as Gibson would have it? Or is it performing logical and conceptual operations, below the level at which such activities are experienced by a conscious being? Is it analyzing physical properties of the sensory flux, or is it reasoning, applying past knowledge to a problem of interpretation? The neurophysiology does not permit a resolution. Indeed the ambiguity of brain anatomy extends into such details as the fact that the key areas of the brain that receive fibres from the optic nerves receive more fibres from the higher centres than from the eyes themselves. Clearly seeing involves higher level brain activity. Is it cognitive or is it analytical?

Gregory has supported his Helmholtzian theory of perceptions as knowledge-based hypotheses by a wide variety of observations and experiments investigating or inducing visual abnormalities (Gregory, 1998: Ch. 8). People blind from birth have usually accumulated a considerable body of knowledge about how things would look, from what they know about how things feel, as extended in space. Having sight newly made possible as adults, people seem to be ready to identify things visually only in so far as they have plausible conjectures as to how things would appear visually, a kind of hypothetical knowledge. Though babies can see objects of special interest from birth, such important visual perceptions as the permanency of objects during times in which they have been hidden from the infant have to be acquired. This still leaves open a Gibsonian interpretation, but the phenomenon of visual agnosias, not knowing what it is one sees, seems to indicate the role of knowledge based on past experience of the uses and meanings of things in the acts of perceiving them.

Another source of support for the Helmholtzian theory comes from the problem of accounting for illusions. The size–weight illusion is easily reproduced. If two material things of the same weight differ markedly in size, the smaller feels heavier than the larger. Gregory claims that this is a *cognitive* illusion. 'The muscles are set for *expected* weights. As larger objects are usually heavier than smaller objects, the smaller weight calls for less muscle force – so it seems surprisingly heavier than the larger weight' (Gregory, 1998: 198). The illusion, so Gregory affirms, depends on one's *knowledge* of objects. To make clear the force of the Helmholtzian thesis, Gregory uses the distinction between 'top-down knowledge' and 'bottom-up signals' to separate out the components that go into such illusions as ambiguous figures, for example Boring's 'two women' illusion (see Figure 6.2).

In reviewing a great many ambiguities, distortions and illusions of perspective Gregory makes use of hypotheses from both 'directions' as it were. The key experiments that he believes establish the priority of the top-down component are based on the phenomenon of the Necker cube (see Figure 6.3). Focusing our visual attention on one vertex or another, we can see it as if looking down on the top surface or as if looking upwards into the under surface of the top. Let us call the change of perspective 'flipping'. The physical components of the drawing or the wire frame do not change. Yet, in flipping from seeing one face at the front becoming the back, the cube can even be seen to change from a regular right-angled cube to a truncated pyramid, if there is sufficient 'depth' in the cube. In some cases there are no bottom-up depth cues in the way the retinal image would look, so sometimes scaling relations between a quadrangle seen as the smaller top of a truncated pyramid or the perspectively reduced back of a regular cube must be 'downwards' from knowledge assumptions, how we are accustomed to expect things to look. The top surface of a truncated pyramid is smaller than the base, just as the back side of a cube is seen as smaller than the front by reason of perspective.

FIGURE 6.2   WHAT IS THE AGE OF THE LADY?

A final argument for 'top-down' knowledge involvement in perception is the phenomenon whereby we see a certain figure as a completion of an incomplete figure. Every one is familiar with the three-dimensional appearance of shadow letters. Kanizsa's triangle is another example cited by Gregory (see Figure 6.4) drawn from the work of the Gestalt psychologists.

Gregory has never shirked the issue of the evident disparity between material states of the brain and the experiences a person has somehow 'on the basis' of the existence of those brain states. He admits that we have not the faintest idea how to provide an explanation of the fact that, as such pioneers as La Mettrie pointed out in the 18th century, the flow of brain activity is accompanied by a stream of thoughts and feelings which bear no resemblance whatever to the neurophysiological processes now observable in the brain itself.

Gregory's proposals for what the brain does as we perceive things and processes in our material environment leave open the question of how the brain transforms the language-like cognitive acts into seen, touched, heard and felt objects. We need another analogy to try to answer this question, an analogy that will supplement that between perceptions and hypotheses.

Gregory says explicitly that sensory signals are not adequate for direct or certain perceptions; so, he argues, 'intelligent guesswork is needed for seeing objects'. By contrast, Gibson would agree that sensory signals are not adequate. Therefore, he argues, the active organism must explore retinal images for higher order properties, invariant relations, for example geometrical structures preserved under transformation. The brain of higher organisms carries through these explorations

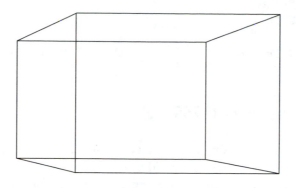

Necker cube

FIGURE 6.3   THE NECKER CUBE

FIGURE 6.4   THE KANIZA TRIANGLE

automatically, because it is built to do just that. For Gregory the brain is actively involved in the process of perception, but as an inference machine, drawing conclusions from premises. The retinal image is the source of the premises of the inferences, but it is the conclusions of these inferences that we see.

Further Reading

Primary Sources

Gregory, R. L. (1997) *Mirrors in Mind*. London: Penguin.
Gregory, R. L. (1998) *Eye and Brain*. Oxford: Oxford University Press.

Secondary Source

Gordon, I. E. (1997) *Theories of Visual Perception* (Chs 6, 7, 8). Chichester: Wiley.

David Courtney Marr (1945–80)

What is happening in the optical, auditory or tactile systems as the analysis of the structure of images proceeds? David Marr, following the Gibsonian line, and realizing the complexity of the processing broadly sketched by **James Gibson** (pp. 142–148), began to think in computational terms as if the brain was a computing machine. According to Marr, the next step along these lines must be to go further into the question of how the extraction of invariants is accomplished – that is, 'an information processing problem', invoking the 'computational model of mind' (Marr, 1982: 30). In Chapter 4 we saw how much contemporary psychology owes to **Alan Turing** (pp. 82–86). According to Turing, the form of any and every higher order process ought to be expressible in a computable function, and 'run' on a computer. It was indifferent whether the hard ware was a pattern printed on a silicon chip or a pattern of neural networks among the 10^{11} cells of the human brain. According to this principle it makes perfect sense for Marr to try to devise a computational model that would replicate whatever it is that the brain does, be it Gibsonian analysis or Gregorian inference.

Who was David Courtney Marr?

He was born on 19 January 1945 in Essex. He was educated at Rugby School, going on to Trinity College, Cambridge. He completed his undergraduate studies in mathematics in 1966. He then began work on a doctoral project in theoretical neuroscience, under the supervision of Giles Brindley. The project was both rigorous and highly general, providing a formal theory of the function of the brain. The theory allowed for empirical testing, and it has been borne out to some extent. This study led on to the work for which he is best known, his formal theory of visual perception developed in Cambridge in the early 1970s.

In 1973 he took up an invitation from **Marvin Minsky** (pp. 93–98) to join the Artificial Intelligence Laboratory at MIT. After four years as a 'visiting scientist', he joined the faculty and became a full professor in 1980. For the greater part of his time at MIT he worked on his computational model of visual perception.

In 1978 he developed leukemia, from which he never recovered. He died on 17 November 1980. The book from which the material in this chapter is mainly taken (Marr, 1982) was published posthumously.

What did he contribute?

Marr's project is based upon the AI or artificial intelligence reading of **Alan Turing**'s (pp. 82–86) analogy between brain and computing machine. By creating a programme that would simulate certain aspects of perception when run on the input from a video camera into a computing machine, Marr hoped to model what was happening when a brain dealt with the input from an eye. An underlying and now contested presumption of Marr's project is that the brain processes inputs in the same or at least in a very similar way to the processing of binary representations in the registers of a traditional computer, in which there is a memory store and a central processing device. This has now been replaced by the more sophisticated notion of a neural net. It seems possible that Marr's project might still be happily realized by a connectionist model.

However, a preliminary stage of Marr's project was to develop a set of geometrical figures which might be necessary and perhaps sufficient as the constituents of all possible three-dimensional figures as perceived. Even if the computational aspects of the project fall victim to a better understanding of the brain/computer analogy, the analytical parts of the project might be recovered.

Here is how Marr's model of the perceptual process worked. Vision, he argued, 'can be thought of as a mapping from one representation ... [as] arrays of image density values as detected by the retina' (Marr, 1982: 31) to another representation, but now in terms of items of a radically different kind. To reach a Gibsonian invariant several steps are required. 'At each level the primitives are qualitatively similar symbols – edges, bars, blobs and terminations or discontinuities – but they refer to increasingly abstract properties of the image' (p. 91). Once a computational theory for a process has been formulated, that is a proposal including basic elements and rules for their combination and manipulation, 'algorithms for implementing it may be designed, and their performance compared with that of the human visual processor' (p. 331).

The project reflects the basic principle of computational modeling in psychology: there is a mathematical description, there is a piece of the retina, and there is a silicon chip. All three are similar at the most general level of description of their function. According to the computational point of view, if the running of the programme parallels the neuropsychological process, the scientific problem of perception has been solved. In short, like **Richard Gregory** (pp. 148–154), Marr (1982: 354) summarizes his project with the thesis that 'perception is the construction of a description'. However, here, once again, the gap between neuropsychology and experience opens up. I see a tree, not a description or representation of a tree. One has to admit that the most fundamental question that is raised by the psychology of perception, namely how is visual *experience* possible, is not addressed by Marr's project.

However, it is not clear where a solution to this problem might be found. In circumstances such as these it may turn out that the puzzle will vanish when we have made a careful dissection of the question. The posing of the question may be a symptom of some deep laid philosophical confusion. It can be said, however, that the brilliance of Marr's formal analysis of the requirements that might go into a computational model of the perception of solid objects does give some indirect support to the Helmholtzian programme.

Further Reading

Primary Source

Marr, D. (1982) *Vision: A Computational Investigation into the Human Representation and Processing of Visual Information.* San Francisco: W. H. Freeman.

Secondary Source

Gordon, I. E. (1997) *Theories of Visual Perception* (Chs 7, 8, 9). Chichester: Wiley.

Biography

Edelman, S. & Vaina, L. M. (2001) David Marr. In N. J. Smelser & P. B. Baltes (Eds), *International Encyclopedia of the Social and Behavioral Sciences.* New York: Elsevier.

David Hubel (1926–) and Torsten Wiesel (1924–)

We could study the brain itself, rather than a model of it. This is just what happened in the 1950s when David Hubel and Torsten Wiesel carried through a very detailed study of the relation between an object seen and localized brain activation. Living human brains being sacrosanct, their research object was the brain of the cat.

Who are David Hubel and Torsten Wiesel?

David Hubel was born in Windsor, Ontario, on 27 February 1926. He studied at McGill University, going on to work in the Montreal Medical School. He joined Johns Hopkins medical school in 1954, leaving for Harvard in 1959. He was awarded the Nobel Prize in 1981. Torsten Wiesel was born in Uppsala in Sweden on 3 June 1924. He worked at the Karolinska Medical Institute until moving to Johns Hopkins in 1955, and on to Harvard in 1959.

What have they contributed?

Hubel and Wiesel examined the optical system of the cat brain cell by cell, trying to find the links between stimuli to the retina and the firing of cells in the inner layers of the visual cortex. They made their great discovery by accident. They tried various simple visual stimuli without succeeding in producing any activity in the cells of the visual cortex. To their surprise they detected a response to what they realized was the moving shadow cast by the edge of the glass slide that they had been using to support bright circular patches, the original visual stimuli, as they slid it into the apparatus. Restarting their research in the light of this serendipitous effect, they used bars of light on a screen as simple objects in different orientations to the horizontal. When these were presented to a cat it turned out that different cells responded differently to differently *oriented* objects. Any given cell responded strongly to a certain specific orientation, weakly to alignments on either side of the favoured angle, and not at all to markedly different orientations. The same phenomenon was found with neural responses to movement (Hubel & Wiesel, 1959). Not only that, but the brain is organized three-dimensionally. They found that all the cells in a column at right angles to the surface of the visual cortex respond to simple objects in the same orientation, while those in adjacent columns do not.

The same is true of the primary auditory cortex, though Hubel and Wiesel studied only vision. Each column of cells responds to the neural impulse from a sound of a specific pitch 'picked up' by frequency-sensitive hair cells in the cochlea. If we can generalize these findings to human perceptual systems no doubt the same would be found in the tactile systems with which we recognize shapes and textures by touch.

This discovery seems at first sight to provide strong support for **Richard Gregory**'s (pp. 148–54) approach to the psychology of perception. By fitting an egg shell into the back of the eye of an ox Johannes Kepler (1571–1630), had demonstrated that an inverted image of what was seen formed on the retina. Is this image somehow transported into the brain? If it is, then there are literally pictures of the world in the visual cortex. Hubel and Wiesel's findings dispose of this age-old misconception completely. A diagonal bar at a certain angle to the horizontal does not cause a diagonal image anywhere but on the retina. After that, the specific column of cells in the visual cortex that are sensitive to that type of extra-mental entity sends an on/off neural signal deeper into the brain. The signal symbolizes but does not picture the diagonal line, just as 20° C symbolizes but does not picture how warm it is.

These findings, important though they are for understanding how we see, nevertheless further exacerbate the deep problem for the understanding of perception: what is it that we see? The absurdity of the pictures in the brain theory, that would have required an inner eye to view them, and an inner-inner eye to view the pictures explanatory of that eye's capacities, and so on, seems to have given way to something more subtle but equally problematic. **Richard Gregory** claims that perceptions are hypotheses. It may well be that brain states symbolize things and their properties, and that a certain state of the brain can be illuminatingly likened to a hypothesis. However, that insight says nothing whatever about the nature of human perceptions. I see a tree from my window, not a symbol of a tree. I may well form a hypothesis about what I see, that it is a beech, for example. But what I see is not a hypothesis.

Somehow human experience and no doubt feline experience, too, are of an integrated, seamless world. The martial arts expert follows the changing orientations of his opponent's weapon as a smooth transition and responds to as an integrated trajectory. Yet each column of cells is sensitive to a specific orientational feature of the retinal stimulus. Ironically, as we learn more and more about the workings of the neural mechanisms with which we accomplish visual, tactile and auditory perception, the relation between the states of the brain and the details of human experience becomes still more puzzling and obscure.

Further Reading

Primary Source

Hubel, D. H & Wiesel, T. N. (1959) Receptive fields of single neurons in the cat's striate cortex. *Journal of Physiology*, **148**, 574–591.

Secondary Source

Goldstein, E. B. (2001) *Blackwell Handbook of Perception* (pp. 82–85). Oxford: Blackwell.

Further Experimental Researches

The significance of the work so far described in this section cannot be fully appreciated without some mention of two important discoveries that throw light on the wider context of perception. **James Gibson** (pp. 142–148) had emphasized the importance of active exploration in the processes of perception. Did this hold true of the development of perceptual capacities too? It almost goes without saying that perception presupposes conscious awareness in the perceiver. In the mid 20th century a simple but telling experiment was carried out by *Robert Held* and *Alan Hein*. The idea that an organism actively explores the material world, building a sense of its place in an appropriate environment, goes back to the biologist Jakob von Uxküll (1909). Each species of organism, equipped with a specific set of perceptual systems, lives in its own world, its *umwelt*. In studying the surviving perceptual capacities of a man with a damaged brain, *Lawrence Weiskrantz* (b. 1926) came across striking evidence that a person could come to know something about the environment without being conscious of the experience. He labelled this 'blind sight'.

Robert Held and Alan Hein (1963) carried out an experimental programme to examine the relation between active exploration and the development of perceptual systems in the young organism relative to such an *umwelt*. Baskets were attached to the ends of a beam free to rotate about its central point. A kitten was placed in one of a pair of baskets in such a way that the animal could not use its limbs. The other basket had holes for the second kitten to put its feet on the ground and actively move itself around. The set-up ensured that the kittens were both in the same environment. While the perceptual system of the passive kitten failed to develop, that of the active kitten followed the usual pattern of progressive maturation.

This experiment brings to the fore a second major theme of 20th-century psychology, the contrast between conceiving of the organism, and particularly the person, as a passive being, the behaviour of which is the product of causal processes, be they cognitive or neural, and thinking of the organism as actively engaged in projects, many of its own devising. It seems evident that the experiment carried out by Held and Hein gives a further boost to the activity theme that we have found in the writings of both **James Gibson** and **Richard Gregory** (pp. 148–154). The person is not a *tabula rasa*, a clean slate, on which the senses inscribe sensations. The organism's perceptual systems are instruments or tools with which a person (or a cat) explores and masters the material environment.

People are not conscious of Gibsonian explorations of the image on the retina. The fact that people are not aware of such important phenomena in the visual system as the saccadic movements of the eyes suggests that there might be other aspects of the visual system that are action-guiding but of which the actor is not conscious. Beginning in the 1960s Weiskrantz set about a long-running study of the practical skills of a man, 'D. B.', who had had a small tumour removed from the right visual cortex. This had the effect of partial blindness, in that he could not see anything presented in his left visual field. In a series of experiments Weiskrantz and his assistants presented D. B. with various objects in the 'empty' part of his visual field. He was asked to identify each object, though he was not consciously aware of it. Among the objects presented were lines in different orientations, line gratings and so on. 'For each type of psychophysical determination [that is for each type of object presented] D. B. was required to choose among a fixed set of alternatives' (Weiskrantz, 1986: 32). He was right, even when he declared he was only guessing, very much more often than chance.

What does this remarkable phenomenon show? The thesis common to both Gibson and Gregory, that perception does not depend only on the sensations of which we are consciously aware is supported again, but this time from a very different source of evidence. The visual system as a whole was sufficiently intact to perform the analytical operations on the retinal images in D. B.'s eyes, picking out invariants. Since there were no sensations to be integrated the empiricist account of perception is undermined even further by the phenomenon of blind sight.

Further Reading

Held, R. & Hein, A. (1963) Movement produced stimulation in the development of visually guided behavior. *Journal of Comparative and Physiological Psychology,* **56**, 872–876.
Von Uxküll, J. (1909) *Umwelt und Innenweldt de Tiere.* Berlin: Springer.
Weiskrantz, L. (1986) *Blindsight.* Oxford: The Clarendon Press.

Reflections

As we have explored the work of our leading characters it has become clear that nothing learned so far about the neurology of the perceptual systems settles the question of what the brain does in bridging the evident gap between the paucity of visual, auditory and tactile stimuli and the complex, multi-dimensional world of perceptions. Were we to follow **James Gibson** (pp. 142–148) in supposing that the brain serves as an analytical device abstracting higher order invariants from the transitory and ever changing sensory stimuli, we would be hard put to explain how someone sees a telephone or a Chinese ideogram or a piece of soap. Whatever these things afford is a matter of post-natal cultural experience. Surely **Richard Gregory** (pp. 148–154) is right about the indispensable role of local knowledge in the processes by which we come to see, hear, touch and so on what we are experiencing. Sensory inputs are 'greatly enriched by stored knowledge and general rules'. There is top-down input into what is perceived. Yet, it seems perverse to assert that what is seen is literally a hypothesis, even if pictorially expressed, to be tested by subsequent experience. Gregory's analogy between the role of hypotheses in scientific research and the role of perceptions in how we live our everyday lives seems forced. What we see, touch, hear and so on are not representations of things and events and processes in the environment. They are the furnishings of the world. While it is no doubt illuminating to suggest that the activities of the brain of a perceiver are language like, it is evident that perceptions are not symbolic, however much their meaning depends on local bodies of knowledge.

The earlier work of the Gestalt psychologists led away from the old empiricist conception of a percept as a collection of sensations. By the mid-1930s they were emphasizing the reality of structure as a property of percepts. Perceived wholes were not something we synthesized from sensory fragments but were as real as colours, sounds, tastes and smells. **Wolfgang Köhler**'s (pp. 136–142) role as spokesman and presenter of the insights of his colleagues in Berlin and later in the United States made sure that the Gestaltist point of view was widely known.

There seems to have been a revival of these ideas recently. Conventional wisdom has it that Köhler's speculations about electrical fields in the brain mapping structural properties or fields in what was observed were shown to be erroneous and this contaminated, one might say, the reception of the whole programme. **Karl Pribram** (pp. 118–125), though not directly influenced by the Gestaltists, nevertheless has begun the development of an account of perception modelled on the idea of a hologram, information as to shapes and so on distributed over the relevant nodes in the brain. Reading what Köhler himself had to say about brain fields gives one a very different impression from the occasional asides in textbooks.

PART TWO

From Individuals to Groups

PART TWO

7

The Personologists

Human beings appear to differ from one another along many dimensions. Some people are gloomy and pessimistic. Others are cheerful and optimistic. There are shy people and there are ebullient people. There are submissive people and aggressive people. Attributes like these are the marks of differences in personality. Are they permanent traits of people, or do they come and go with the situations people find themselves in? How are we to explain the differences between presentations of self of different people in the same situations and the same person in different situations? Is a 'scientific' personology possible, in the sense of the possibility of the discovery of lawful relations between personality traits and the types of situations in which they are displayed? Are personality traits, if they exist, explanatory of human behaviour? The authors whose lives and works are to be discussed in this chapter had very different views on these questions. Some believed in the existence of traits, others thought the very idea incoherent.

The 'humours' theory of human types, originating in antiquity, had held sway in Europe for at least a millennium. According to this classification, there were four basic human personality types: choleric, phlegmatic, melancholic and sanguine. The terminology is still in use today in the vernacular. The four temperaments were grounded in the physiology of the four humours. These were believed to be constituents of the human body, which varied in proportions from person to person and from time to time. A person in whom the hot and dry humours predominated was choleric, the cold and dry person was melancholic and so on. With the demise of the physiology of humours, theoretical support for the ancient quadruple personology collapsed, though it has survived as a commonsense classification.

The 20th century saw a revival of interest in the psychology of personality, led by **Gordon Allport** (pp. 167–172). In the first chapter of his (1961) book, he frames the study of personality in a general conceptual scheme. There he distinguishes personality from character, and both from temperament. He introduced the concept of 'trait' as the main analytical tool, though with subtlety and appropriate reservations against its misuse. Allport's books were amongst the earliest to address the question of a scientific personology. They are still of outstanding intellectual quality. Reading his *Pattern and Growth in Personality* (1961), one has to remind oneself how long ago it was published, so relevant is it to the 21st century. Most of the work published after the Second World War has used methods presupposing positivistic philosophy of science and relying on dubious statistical inferences. Anticipations of most of the current criticisms of these attempts at a 'scientific' study of personality are already to be found in Allport's writings.

Allport's work straddles the rise and decline of the trait theory of personality. He was largely responsible for introducing the concept in the 1930s and in the 1960s provided the most telling criticisms of the misuses of the concept by people like his erstwhile colleague, **Raymond Cattell** (pp. 172–175). **Hans Eysenck** (pp. 175–179) was surely the most widely read British psychologist in the 20th century. However, as we shall see, he was among those whose work has proved most vulnerable to the kind of criticisms made by Allport and others. While 'personality' was the main topic of research for both Cattell and Eysenck, each undertook studies of other major dimensions or groups of dimensions along which they presumed people differed intrinsically, for example 'intelligence'. Here we are concerned mainly with their contributions to personality research.

Allport's emphasis on the complexity of the explanatory 'packages' required to understand people's behaviour has been echoed by many later writers. For example Walter Mischel argues that 'one must take account of interaction between various qualities in the person and in the situation'. It follows that the most important research question is to ask 'when are situations more important for explaining behaviour … when are personal variables likely to be most influential?' (Mischel, 1986: 496). However, the main research thrust in personology has been animated by a rather simple version of the concept of a 'trait'. Trait theorists have been accused not only of logical errors in their use of the concept of a trait, but also of misunderstandings of statistical methods. The most recent and telling of these criticisms can be found in the work of **James Lamiell** (pp. 179–183).

Some of those who contest the presuppositions of trait theory, that is the alleged permanence, stability and universality of traits, have tried to develop another style of personality psychology, the dramaturgical theory. According to this theory, personalities are displays, performances suited to the immediate situation and to the people therein. Personality types are like roles in a play. In accordance with the dramaturgical theory the opening paragraph should be written: When and in what circumstances is this person likely to appear gloomy and pessimistic, playing some homespun version of Hamlet? When and in what circumstances is this very same person likely to appear ebullient and optimistic, in performing some more heroic role? There is no X which any given person *is*. Each of us has mastered the local repertoire of personality types to some degree, and is a more or less skilful performer.

Dramaturgical theorists observe and sometimes record actual human interactions. They analyse what they have seen or heard, looking for the conventions by which appropriate personality attributes are displayed, drawn from a working repertoire, finding who makes use of them and in what circumstances. **Erving Goffman** (pp. 183–186) made outstanding contributions to the study of personality as a dramatic performance.

The trait theory and the dramaturgical approach are not irreconcilable. A person who is in command of a repertoire of personality types, to be displayed in the appropriate circumstances, must be ascribed certain capacities and skills. Like traits, the form in which capacities and skills are ascribed is conditional. '*If* such and such a situation occurs including this or that type of person, X will probably display such and such a personality attribute'. X's repertoire could be expressed in a hierarchically arranged set of capacities.

Gordon Willard Allport (1897–1967)

The contested concept of 'personality trait' has been the focus of both practical studies and theoretical debates for half a century or more. It appears in commonsense psychology and there are plenty of trait words in the vernacular. Its appearance in academic psychology has been linked with the use of a certain range of methods of enquiry, involving questionnaires and statistical searches for general 'factors', to play the role of 'source traits'. Gordon Allport was not only responsible for the introduction of the trait concept into psychology of personality, but also for a vigorous attack in the way it had been taken up and, he believed, abused by others.

Who was Gordon Willard Allport?

He was born in the small town of Montezuma in Indiana, on 11 November 1897, the youngest of four boys. His mother had been a teacher, and managed a strongly religiously oriented family life. Before he went to school, the family moved to Glenville, near Cleveland. His father was a physician, with a clinic attached to the family home, though Allport Senior dabbled in other enterprises as well. As they grew up his four sons assisted in the practice, washing bottles and helping patients. Gordon was educated locally at Glenville High School. In 1915 he entered Harvard, where his elder brother, Floyd, had studied psychology. Like many young men of his era he was inducted into the armed services during the First World War, but it ended before he could take part in the fighting. He took his BA in 1919 in philosophy and economics.

Unsure of his life course, he spent a year at Robert College in Istanbul, where he found himself comfortable with teaching. He returned to Harvard to begin preparations for a doctoral study in psychology with Hugo Münsterberg. He took his master's degree in 1921 and his PhD in 1922, with a study of personality traits.

Benefiting from a traveling scholarship he moved abroad again for two years, to Germany, where he became particularly close to William Stern and Franz Koffka. He moved on to Cambridge, England, to work with **Frederic Bartlett** (pp. 47–54). He returned to an instructorship at Harvard in 'social ethics' for the years 1924–1926, and in 1925 he married Ada Gould. Still not settled, the Allports spent four years at Dartmouth College, finally returning to Harvard where Gordon worked for the rest of his life.

On his return he found a kindred spirit in Henry Murray, who had already begun to reflect on how the psychology of personality might be developed (Murray, 1938). Between 1922 and 1961 Allport moved away from an exclusive concentration on a psychology of traits to a much more sophisticated and eclectic view of human nature, emphasizing more and more the contingencies of the situations in which people act, and the idiosyncracy of individuals. A nomothetic conception of personality studies as a search for general laws was displaced by one in which more attention was paid to idiographic methods and conceptions, the characteristics of each person as an individual.

He continued to work on refinements of his conception of what it was to be a person throughout his life. His most important publication on personality psychology was his *Pattern and Growth in Personality* (1961), a thorough revision of his pioneering *Personality: A Psychological Interpretation* (1937). He remarks ruefully that towards the end of his academic career his writing was dominated by requests for chapters for the books of others and for write-ups of papers delivered at all sorts of meetings around the world.

Perhaps he will be best remembered for a small but brilliantly written book on the roots of human psychology, *Becoming*, published in 1955.

He held fast to a profoundly important moral principle throughout his life. 'Arrogance in psychological theorizing,' he said (Allport, 1965: 7), 'has always antagonized me; I believe it is better to be tentative, eclectic and humble.' Indeed that trio of rare virtues defined the leit motif of his life and work. He died on 9 October 1967.

What did he contribute?

Rather apologetically, Allport offered a 'definition' of personality so general as to cover both the 'trait' theory taken up by **Raymond Cattell** (pp. 172–175) and **Hans Eysenck** (pp. 175–179), and the dramaturgical analysis of personalities as presentations, developed by **Erving Goffman** (pp. 183–186). 'Personality', he says (Allport, 1937: 28), 'is the dynamic organization within the individual of those psychological systems that determine his [her] characteristic behaviour and thought.' While acknowledging that attribution of personality characteristics to someone is 'in the eye of the beholder' and highly variable with the situation as it is understood both by the actor and the observer, nevertheless he thought that there was good reason to hold that people had some relatively stable psychological characteristics. It made sense to look for idiosyncratic aspects of the thoughts and habits of individuals in trying to explain differences in what people did in more or less the same situation. It remained an open question whether there were attributes that everyone shared in some measure.

With the assistance of H. S. Odbert, Allport undertook the preparation of a catalogue of *all* the words in English that were available to describe people with respect to the characteristics that they did, could, or might display. The list was huge, including some 18,000 words. He classified them into four groups, noting that this vocabulary was used to pigeonhole people and their behaviour rather than to explain it. For example, in the first group were psychologically 'neutral' terms such as 'excitable', having no particular evaluative significance. Then there were words for more ephemeral characteristics, such as moods, emotions, and styles of talk; for example, 'angry' and 'mocking'. The third group included words used to express social judgements and/or personal character, such as 'louche', 'hated' and so on. The final group included words used to refer to physique and their metaphorical employment for psychological personal qualities, such as 'strong'. Allport's plan was to separate the morally neutral words from those with an evaluative element. Almost all of the 18,000 words for personal characteristics have a wide range of uses, and most could be used evaluatively.

However, Allport's major contribution to the theory of personality was the concept of a personality *trait*. Traits are permanent dispositions to behave in certain ways. Different traits are revealed in different situations. The concept of a disposition is fundamental to the physical sciences. For example, solubility describes the permanent tendency for a substance to dissolve in some solute, usually water. Conductivity describes the capacity of a substance to allow the passage of heat or electricity. All instances of sugar have the same solubility, and all instances of copper have the same conductivity.

Though Allport does not draw on the analogy between personality traits and physical dispositions, it is certainly the same idea from a logical point of view. Setting aside his natural caution in coming up with definitions, he offers a tentative account of the concept of a trait as: 'a neuropsychological structure having the capacity to render many stimuli functionally equivalent and guide equivalent (meaningfully consistent) forms of adaptive and expressive behavior' (Allport, 1961: 347). This definition grounded personal dispositions in permanent attributes of the human organism. Vague and unsatisfactory as this 'definition' may be, it did allow him to distinguish between common and personal traits. 'Common traits are, then, those aspects of personality in respect to which most people within a given culture can be compared' (ibid.). Common traits are generalized over a *population*, such as New Yorkers. Personal traits are aspects of the personality of an individual and they are generalized over the *situations* in which a person finds him or herself. Similarities of response to similar situations by a human *individual* (and an animal too) are displays of personal traits.

However, what is the status of traits, from a scientific point of view? The language of the above definition suggests that Allport took them to be the causes of people's behaviour. For example, the words 'render' and 'guide' are active verbs. The human being as active producer of his or her actions seems to be deleted. Allport certainly did not intend this consequence, but he seems to have found it difficult to shed the language of causality in describing the role of psychological traits. In his autobiography (Allport, 1967: 13) he remarks that while rejecting both the environment as the direct or indirect cause of behaviour, and the hidden forces of the Freudian picture, he was still reluctant to adopt the voluntarism of the agent-self. Since he wanted to emphasize the role of conscious states in explanations of behaviour, this reluctance is all the more puzzling.

As I have observed from time to time, the failure of some research programmes in 20th-century psychology to achieve the status of a model science, such as physics or chemistry, must be put down to the adoption of a seriously defective philosophy of science, positivism. According to this philosophy only correlates between types of observable phenomena are admissible into science. Positivism was nowhere more damaging than in personology. One of Allport's strengths was his realization that positivism was a bad guide to building a science. It allowed him to make a distinction between nominal and veridical traits. The former are wholly displayed in what people are interpreted as doing. The latter are attributable to individual people as real psychological structures. Just as solubility is taken to be grounded in the molecular structure of a material substance, so veridical traits are grounded in certain psychological or perhaps neural structures of human beings. Positivism can recognize only nominal traits, because they make no reference to unobservable psychological or even molecular structures in the individual, forbidden by the positivist ukase on any theorizing other than generalization.

Common traits are more nominal and less veridical than personal traits. Common traits are revealed by the analysis of data from a population and are artifacts of the method. Personal traits are revealed in the actual behaviour of a real person. They reflect a person's consistency in how he or she behaves in roughly similar situations. If someone does much the same thing almost every time he or she is faced by criticism, for example attacking the credentials of the critic, it is not unreasonable to ascribe a permanent psychological structure to that person, a structure which is activated in this and similar circumstances.

This brings us to Allport's powerful criticism of the use of population statistics as a support for an explanatory theory of human behaviour in terms of *source traits*. **Raymond Cattell** (pp. 172–175) joined the Harvard psychology department in 1944. He brought with him a highly sophisticated statistical method for revealing commonalities in large bodies of data: factor analysis. In the context of personology, it allowed a psychologist to associate a large number of lower level psychological attributes into groups, the most general of which were to be 'source traits'. The possession of a source trait was supposed to explain why an individual displayed this or that surface trait.

Allport evidently did not care for this proposal by his new colleague. He remarks (Allport, 1961: 329–330): 'Is it reasonable to presume that all people do in fact possess the same basic constitution of personality, differing only in the degree to which they possess this or that source trait?' The answer is surely 'No'. Any theory of personality, whether based on 'traits' or not, must allow for and account for variability in a person's conduct, and even in his or her character over time.

Allport pointed out three main difficulties with the very idea of a source trait, as it might be revealed by statistical analysis of large bodies of data. First, there is no proof in the statistical method that factorial units, statistically arrived at as groupings of traits, correspond to source traits, that is to features of human beings that would explain their behaviour in this or that situation. Secondly, the naming of traits with seemingly psychologically relevant words is largely arbitrary. Examples reveal an incoherent mix of diverse aspects of personhood. He asks his readers to consider whether the answers to the following four questions (slightly simplified), allegedly indicative of the source trait 'Guilt-proneness Confidence', make sense: 'Do you avoid exciting situations because they are too fatiguing?' 'Yes'; 'Do you think progressive educational methods are less sound than the traditional?' 'Yes'; 'Do you enjoy people more than books?' 'Yes'; 'Are you uncontrollably afraid of some particular animal?' 'Yes'. The only reason for putting these items together is the correlations between them. Correlations no more establish semantic commonality than they do common causality! Allport also notes that factor analysis reproduces the weaknesses of the methods of data gathering upon which it relies, for example that answers to questions are at least partly determined by the form in which they are asked and by who is thought to be posing them.

At the end of the day Allport confesses that he is 'lukewarm towards models that render personality in terms of mathematical and statistical constructs' (Allport, 1961: xi). He points out the need for an idiographic approach in these words: 'the more we search out ... what is uniform in human nature the more urgent it becomes to account for uniqueness in the form and pattern of the whole' (Allport, 1961: x). More and more considerations of this sort appear as he builds up the necessary qualifications that might begin to make trait theory acceptable scientifically.

Parallel to his investigations of personality went a development of an analysis of the concept of the person itself. Hostile both to depth psychology, with its insistence on the long-term effects of past experiences, and to behaviourism, with its insistence on independent and shallow habits, he offered an account of personhood that emphasized the autonomy of maturity. This led him to a study of the sorts of values that people espouse.

From time to time he undertook other kinds of studies. For example, in the course of the Second World War he investigated the passing on of rumours, in an experimental programme very like that done some years before by **Frederic Bartlett** (pp. 47–54), with whom he had studied at Cambridge.

Further Reading

Primary Sources

Allport G. W. (1937) *Personality: A Psychological Interpretation.* New York: Holt, Rinehart and Winston.
Allport, G. W. (1955) *Becoming.* New Haven, CT: Yale University Press.
Allport, G. W. (1961) *Pattern and Growth in Personality.* New York: Holt, Rinehart and Winston.

Secondary Sources

Mischel, W. (1986) *Introduction to Personality.* New York: Holt, Rinehart and Winston.
Murray, H. A. et al. (1938) *Explorations in Personality.* New York: Oxford University Press.

Autobiography

Allport, G. W. (1965) Gordon Allport. In E. G. Boring & G. Lindzey (Eds), *A History of Psychology in Autobiography* (pp. 3–25), New York: Appleton-Century-Crofts.

Raymond Bernard Cattell (1905–98)

People do not display their 'personalities' all the time and in every encounter. It follows that attributions of personality traits must take the form of conditionals, such as 'If criticized, he smiles and thanks the critic'. Logically, traits are dispositions. However, even if one were to subscribe to the principle that each person has a fixed and permanent personality as a bundle of traits, the question of the organization of these conditional attributes can be raised. Is there any reason to think that there are superordinate and subordinate traits? Should the psychology of personality work towards a 'Linnaean' catalogue of behavioural dispositions? Cattell seems to have taken for granted that there was a limited range of generic traits of which everyday traits were species. He called them 'source traits'. They would be revealed by the mathematical technique of factor analysis applied to reveal higher and higher order correlations among subordinate traits at the level of 'species'. This would be a 'theory of personality'. Cattell went further and proposed a genetic or biological explanation of personality and other distinguishing attributes of human beings.

Who was Raymond Bernard Cattell?

He was born in Plymouth, England, in 1903. His father was an engineer, working mainly on developments of various kinds of motors for the military. He did very well in school, and took up a county scholarship at Kings College, London, where he read chemistry. In those years London was alive with projects for new ways of living, new educational theories, new views of the place of women in society, and so on. Cattell developed an interest in using scientific research in the interests of social reform. After some practical experience in the progressive school at Dartington Hall, he took up a formal academic training in psychology, taking his PhD at University College, London, in 1929. His supervisor was Charles Spearman, one of the leading statisticians of the era. Young Cattell worked with Spearman on the development of the method of 'factor analysis' which was to dominate his research for good or ill for the next 70 years.

In those days, a doctorate was not a necessary condition for appointment to a university lectureship. Cattell had already begun to teach at Exeter University in 1926 before he had completed his PhD. In 1932, he moved to Leicester to the child guidance programme. In 1937, he began his long career in the United States, at first as a research associate with Edward Thorndyke at Columbia, and then at

Clark University, where he remained until 1941. In 1944 he joined the Harvard psychology department at the invitation of **Gordon Allport** (pp. 167–172). Cattell's first marriage, to Monica Rogers, was dissolved about this time, some blaming his tigerish devotion to work that took precedence over family life. Cattell's conceptual subtlety, though at odds with his statistical methodology, sets him off against the over-simplifications of other trait theorists, such as **Hans Eysenck** (pp. 175–179), and seems to reflect the influence of Allport's wide-ranging mind. However, left to himself, he slipped back into a theoretical stance at variance with Allport's point of view, in particular in his adherence to the concept of a source trait.

In 1946, Cattell moved to the University of Illinois at Champagne-Urbana. In the same year he married Alberta Schuetter. The mandatory retirement rules still in force in those days deprived the university of his services in 1973. For the next 25 years he continued to work with the same demonic energy, at first in Colorado. In 1978 he moved to Hawaii, where he taught at the Hawaian School of Professional Psychology.

His last years were marred by a bitter controversy concerning the racist implications of his insistence on a genetic basis for personality. He had been nominated for the award of the Gold Medal of the American Psychological Association in 1997. When this became known, a group of people raised objections to the award, accusing Cattell of expressing racist views in his writings. The controversy became a matter of public concern, and the award was postponed. In the end Cattell himself declined the medal. Whether the bitterness of the dispute and Cattell's sense of being wronged and traduced had effects on his health we will never know. He died on 2 February 1998, very soon after these events.

What did he contribute?

Cattell's researches were driven by method much more than by a theory. His reliance on statistical analyses was absolute. His work is heavily marked by the influence of Spearman, the inventor of one of the most important measures of correlation, and the associated technique of factor analysis.

Cattell published widely, but the book most germane to his work in personality psychology was *The Scientific Analysis of Personality* (1965). Though, perhaps under the influence of Allport, he included both situations and roles in his conception of the total 'package' within which personality played a major part, his main theoretical concept was the 'trait'. How he interpreted the concept deserves careful examination. He distinguishes three kinds of traits: 'abilities', 'temperamental attributes', which covered a wide variety of specific responses, and 'dynamic traits', involving matters like 'motives'. Roughly speaking, Cattell's 'traits' seem to be tendencies to respond to situations and other people. Dynamic traits come and go with people's shifting motives. For Cattell a psychological type was no more than a collection of relatively permanent traits. He insisted that clarity could only be achieved by paying attention to the details, that is traits that are summed up in 'type' talk.

Surface traits are to be explained by 'source traits' that 'operate as an underlying source of observable behaviour' (Cattell, 1965: 67). They should be distinguished from surface traits which are defined in terms of overt behaviour. For example, Eysenck's extravert/introvert dimension is a distinction in surface traits. This suggestion raises some fundamental issues in methodology. As we will see, Cattell arrives at his catalogue of source traits by a mathematical analysis of the distribution of behavioural descriptions. Source traits are mathematically created groupings of surface traits. Logically they seem to be higher order classificatory categories, like genera in biology. How then could they be the *sources* of anything? This ontological problem of the nature and standing in psychological reality of source traits was never resolved in Cattell's writings. Had he been an old fashioned positivist this question could never have arisen. According to that account of science, scientific concepts were nothing but ways of referring to clusters of observable behaviours. A source trait, interpreted positivistically, just collected up more specific kinds of behaviour. Cattell wanted such traits to be the sources of specific behaviours. This presumes that they must have some more robust mode of existence in the human being than as mere mathematical artifacts. The most telling criticism of the very idea of source traits came from Cattell's erstwhile colleague, **Gordon Allport** (pp. 167–172), as we have seen.

Instead of trying to reduce complex patterns of behaviour to simple relationships between a dependent and an independent variable, Spearman had provided his protégé with a method for analysing the contributions to a certain outcome of a great many variables: multivariate analysis. The principles of this kind of analysis are quite simple. The first step is to correlate every variable with every other. Those which are highly correlated are taken as compound second order variables. Correlations are sought between these to create compound third order variables. The process is repeated until there are no more good correlations, and we have arrived at independent super variables. Each group of second or third order variables is renamed as a 'factor', presumed to be 'responsible' for the coming into being of manifestations of instances of the lower order members in each group in the appropriate conditions. The analysis does not settle any question as to the psychological or physiological reality of the 'factors' since they are merely names for groupings of lower order entities, generated by the mathematical procedure.

Here are some of the surface traits underlying the source trait 'neuroticism' (Cattell, 1965: 211), which is itself a name for a cluster of behavioural traits or tendencies, drawn from 'intelligence', 'ego-strength', 'dominance', 'surgency (extraversion)', 'tender-mindedness', 'non-conformity' and so on. 'Neuroticism' is the name for the group comprising low ego-strength, high tender-mindedness and high non-conformity. Now identified as a source trait, it begins to play the role of a hypothetical underlying cause of local manifestations of its component traits. Remember that none of these terms describes any actual behavioural tendency or disposition, but a lower order compound variable extracted by analysis of answers to questionnaires. Some of these expressions have made their way into the vernacular.

However, armed with Allport's criticisms, we can easily see that though the names that appear in the list above seem to be psychologically meaningful, they are mere labels. To test this, simply look up the list of actual, observable behavioural dispositions each of these statistical clusters encompasses, and the incoherence becomes evident.

How could someone of Cattell's obvious sharpness of mind fail to realize that the source trait concept had little if any psychological authenticity? If we compare his life experience with that of Allport, a certain narrowness is evident. After he left Harvard he was surrounded by colleagues and students who were very much under his personal influence. At the same time his headlong rush of activities, writing faster than most people can read it was said, precluded the reflective leisure that is one of the conditions for fruitful self-criticism. There is something tragic about a life work built upon sand.

Further Reading

Primary Sources

Cattell, R. B. (1965) *The Scientific Analysis of Personality*. Harmondsworth: Penguin.
Cattell, R. B. (1979) *The Scientific Use of Factor Analysis in Behavioral and Life Sciences*. New York: Plenum Books.

Secondary Source

Pervin, L. A., Cervone, D. & John, O. P. (2005) *Personality: Theory and Research* (Ch. 7). New York and Chichester: Wiley.

Biography

Sills, D. L. (1989) R. B. Cattell. In *International Encyclopedia of the Social Sciences: Biographical Supplement* (Vol. 18). New York: Macmillan.

Hans Jürgen Eysenck (1916–97)

The popularity of trait theories of personality owes a good deal to Hans Eysenck's enthusiastic endorsement of the theory and to his use of statistical analyses of answers to questionnaires to identify the most general traits in personality. He published the results of his method-driven researches in a series of popular books. His views have become very well known, and some of his terminology has become part of the vernacular, albeit somewhat differing in meaning from the original. His work stands at the opposite pole from the dramaturgical theory of context dependent personality repertoires. In particular, he has made considerable efforts to link the traits revealed by his analysis of the answers people give to the Eysenck Personality Register to distinctive brain states and processes.

Who was Hans Eysenck?

He was born in Berlin on 4 March 1916 into a theatrical family. His parents divorced when he was only two. Thereafter he was brought up by his grandparents. The family was Jewish and, like many from that community, he left Germany at the age of 18 just as Hitler and the Nazi party took over the government. He came to England, where he remained for the rest of his life.

He entered the University of London as an undergraduate and took his PhD there in 1940, under the supervision of Sir Cyril Burt, about whose researches there has been a good deal of controversy. During the Second World War Eysenck held the post of Chief Psychologist at Mill Hill Emergency Hospital. This milieu provided him with his first major research opportunity to test the reliability of psychiatric diagnoses. The issue of the best treatment for the mentally disturbed continued to interest him, particularly as he had come to develop a hostile attitude to standard psychiatric practice, and to Freudian psychotherapy in particular. Many years later, he published an influential and controversial attack on the efficacy of the 'talking cure' (Eysenck, 1973).

After a spell at the Maudesley Hospital, for the rest of his working life his home ground was the Institute of Psychiatry in the University of London. He took up a post there in 1946. Shortly thereafter, he founded the first course in clinical psychology in any British institution of higher learning. There, too, he conducted the stream of statistical studies from which he drew the material for a prolific output of books and articles. He retired in 1983, but continued to work until his death on 4 September 1997.

What of the man? He was a curious mixture of the amiable and the dogmatic. It would have been difficult to fit him into the slots of his own theory of personality. His relaxed manner concealed a demonic energy, exercised in the service of theories of personality and of intelligence that did not arise so much from the studies he carried out, but seemed to have preceded them. He was not afraid of controversy. His publications that purported to demonstrate the lack of efficacy of psychotherapy led to a fierce public debate. He claimed to have shown that people who had not received psychoanalytic treatment for mental disturbances recovered at the same rate as those who had. His adherence to a neurological and ultimately biological explanation of personal attributes led him to espouse the strongly contested idea that intelligence was largely inherited. Again this led to him into controversy, in that this doctrine rather easily slips over into racism. Late in life he published a statistically based study which seemed to support the principles of astrology, which again was vigorously contested. How could he sail so unperturbedly through these rough waters? The answer, I believe, lay in his faith in his methodology, the statistical analysis of answers to questionnaires, supplemented here and there by excursions into neuropsychology.

What did he contribute?

The idea that scientific research was aimed at falsifying hypotheses played almost no role in his conception of scientific method. Whatever came out at the end of a statistical analysis must be a truth, even if it tended to support planting seeds according to the phases of the moon. In this chapter, it is his theories of personality that will interest us, and the methods by which he sought to establish them.

Eysenck was convinced that personality arose primarily from the neurophysiology of the individual. Differences in temperament must, therefore, be due to differences in the neurophysiology of individual human beings. These differences, in turn, were built in as individual genetic endowments. However, though the direction of causality was from neurophysiology to personality, the order of discovery was the reverse. This called for a method for investigating personality traits in search of the most fundamental dimensions on which people differed. Instead of making careful observations of human displays of personality characteristics, Eysenck chose to analyse what people *said* about themselves.

The people involved in his studies were provided with questionnaires of various kinds, essentially lists of words that are ordinarily used for describing personality, character, and temperament. Each individual rates him or herself on the degree to which they exhibit the attribute in question. So one might describe oneself as cheerful rather than gloomy, fond of company rather than happier alone, and so on. The answers can be correlated into groups, so that 'cheerful' is highly correlated with 'fond of company', and anti-correlated with 'gloomy' and 'happier alone'. Now we have the makings of a dimension along which personalities vary. Using this method, Eysenck came up with two prime dimensions, *neuroticism* and *extraversion/ introversion*.

The dimension of neuroticism picks out people who are calm and collected in their life events from those who are anxious and inclined to panic under stress. Eysenck believed that his data showed that people 'high on neuroticism' were more likely to suffer from nervous disorders. According to his general theory, the differences between people on this dimension of behaviour must have an explanation in differences in the way their brains function. The sympathetic nervous system reacts to immediate situations with a variety of responses that ready the body for action. Typical emotions associated with arousal of the sympathetic nervous system are fear and anger. Those people who are high in neuroticism must, therefore, have more responsive sympathetic nervous systems than those who are calm under pressure. In turn, this difference must be put down to different genetic endowments. From the point of view of philosophy of science this strongly realist approach cannot be faulted.

The dimension of extraversion/introversion has become part of our everyday vocabulary for describing differences between people. Extraverts are cheerful, out-going, and unself-conscious, while introverts are shy, self-conscious, and self-critical. People high on extraversion, that is extraverts, are more likely to commit violent crimes than introverts, so he declared. Notice how the poles of the dimension have shifted from attributes to types – 'extraversion' has become 'extravert' – what one is rather than what one does. The mandatory neurophysiological explanation is based on the balance between the supposed processes of excitation and inhibition. In a state of excitation a person is very aware of what is happening and, unless brain activity is inhibited, likely to remember what has happened, and so to have material on hand to agonize over. Keeping out of the limelight is an obvious life enhancing strategy for the introvert.

Eysenck always had in mind the use that might be made of his researches in clinical psychology. He set about linking his dimensions to mental troubles. His studies tended to show that people high on both neuroticism and introversion will be more likely to develop phobias than people of other temperaments. This led him to expand the scope of his researches to include people diagnosed as mentally ill, and confined in mental hospitals. Once again, the analysis of answers to his questionnaires revealed another dimension, *psychoticism*.

This method of research seems at first sight to be nothing but a study of the semantics of a certain everyday vocabulary. What are these dimensions but rules for the use of words – what **Ludwig Wittgenstein** (pp. 240–246) called a 'grammar'? One cannot say that one is both cheerful and gloomy because the rules for the use of English preclude that combination. To counter this difficulty, a problem which reappears in many research projects in psychology, Eysenck looked for other ways in which his dimensions could be manifested in such a way that he could draw on them as data for his correlational studies.

He tried to devise experiments in which personality variables rooted in neuro-physiology would be displayed directly. Here is his experiment to 'measure' degree of suggestibility, the 'sway test'. A person is given a heavily loaded tray and told to close his eyes and recite 'I am falling, I am falling …'. Everyone starts swaying, but the degree of sway is, so Eysenck (1952: 106) tells us, a measure of 'suggestibility'.

Both **Raymond Cattell** (pp. 172–175) and Hans Eysenck placed considerable reliance on correlational methods to arrive at their 'dimensions' or 'source traits'. However, Cattell was much less willing than Eysenck to bind his personalities to a three-dimensional bed of Procrustes. He finished up with a score or so of source traits, compared with Eysenck's three dimensions of personality. Moreover, both presumed that there are sufficient commonalities, at a sufficiently low level of abstraction, to make the research methodology worthwhile. If all that is in com-mon between a coral reef and a banana is that both are found in the tropics, we are not really much further forward in biological science. Eysenck was well aware of Windelband's famous distinction between idiographic studies, one person at a time in depth, and nomothetic studies, abstracting commonalities from a population (Windelband, 1898). Some have argued that personality, character and perhaps temperament are so widely differentiated between human beings that the results of nomothetic studies are useless in criminology and psychiatry, and close to worthless as science. The statistical process, particularly multivariate analysis, wipes out the very thing we would like to know: How likely is it that this wife-beater will offend again? How impervious will this worry-wart be to a course of training in looking on the bright side?

Eysenck's methods have nothing to offer us on these important questions. Furthermore, they are unable to chart the life course of someone who is extravert with some people and introvert with others. Such a person would have to be a kind of chimera, in Eysenck's view, incorporating two different physiologies, as a centaur is both man and horse.

Further Reading

Primary Sources

Eysenck, H. J. (1952) *The Scientific Study of Personality*. London: Routledge and Kegan Paul.
Eysenck, H. J. (1973) *The Experimental Study of Freudian Theories*. London: Methuen.

Secondary Sources

Pervin, L. A., Cervone, D. & John, O. P. (2005) *Personality: Theory and Research* (Ch. 7). New York and Chichester: Wiley.
Windelband, W. (1898 [1998]) History and natural science (trans. J. T. Lamiell). *Theory and Psychology*, **8**, 5–22.

Autobiography

Eysenck, H. J. (1990) *Rebel with a Cause*. London: W. H. Allen.

James Thomas Lamiell (1950–)

The style of psychology of personality that we have been following has been dominated by the to-and-fro between two main ways of looking at the attributes of human beings. On the one hand there have been those who have tried to find universal traits that in more or less degree can be used to characterize individual people, and by extension the differences between them. 'Jean is more charming than June', 'Ekaterina is more charming than Natasha', 'Moonflower is more charming than Virtuous Rose' and so on. 'Charming' is taken to be a universal trait, and to be present in differing degrees. On the other hand there have been many who find this attempt at universalization not only artificial but implausible. Personalities are individual. Ekaterina's charm is of a quite different order from Jean's. The issue has been muddied by the fact that there have been serious logical errors in the reasoning that have led to the postulation of common traits and to treating individual differences as causal factors in behaviour.

In the 1980s James Lamiell had already brought some of these fallacies to the attention of psychologists of personality. His warnings fell on deaf ears. It is astounding to see the very same fallacies rife in the field even in the 21st century. Lamiell appears in this book as a psychologist whose ways of thinking *should* by now have been adopted by everyone interested in the scientific study of personality. Perhaps the reader who turns back to look at the logical slippages in the writings of **Raymond Cattell** (pp. 172–175) and of **Hans Eysenck** (pp. 175–179) will be able to get a sense of how extraordinary it is that the 'Lamiell lessons' have not yet been learned.

Who is James Thomas Lamiell?

James Lamiell was born on 8 February 1950 in Canton, Ohio. His father, Thomas Joseph Lamiell, worked for most of his life in customer relations jobs. His mother, Rita, married Thomas in April 1941. The marriage was short lived. After the premature death of Thomas at 53, Rita Lamiell supported her family single-handed. Young James seems to have inherited some of the independence and strength of character of his mother.

Growing up in Canton, Lamiell graduated from St. Thomas Aquinas High School in 1968. He matriculated at Bowling Green State University in Ohio in September 1968, graduating in 1972 with a dual concentration in psychology and philosophy. He began his graduate studies at Kansas State University in the fall of 1972. Concentrating on the field of personality psychology, Lamiell completed his Master of Science degree in 1974, going on to a doctorate under Leon Rappoport.

Lamiell's first post-PhD academic position was at the University of Illinois at Urbana-Champaign. It was here that he began to interest himself in the issues pertaining to the distinction between 'nomothetic' and 'idiographic' approaches to the study of personality. In the early 1980s, he began to publish elegantly wrought articles laying out the logical foundations for coherent reasoning in personality psychology, and in particular for a proper understanding of the nature of the knowledge generated through the statistical procedures that had become foundational within the field.

After six years at Illinois, Lamiell moved to Georgetown University, into a department which was at that time encouraging the new wave in psychology that was beginning to emerge from under the long shadow of an implicit positivism. By the early 1990s, Lamiell was beginning to investigate the pioneering works of the German philosopher and psychologist William Stern (1871–1938), whose comprehensive system of thought, critical personalism, seemed to Lamiell to complement the ideas that he had been trying to develop.

What has he contributed?

Discussion as to the shape and methods of a psychology of personality seemed at first sight to centre round the question of whether there are personality concepts that can be applied systematically and reliably to individuals, but which at the same time can be used properly of any human being anywhere. Tied in with this is the question of whether the personalities of individuals are sufficiently distinct to make the nomothetic level of research mostly irrelevant. Lamiell's contribution to the foundations of personality psychology has been to reveal the conceptual confusions and logical fallacies in the way these issues were resolved by mainstream psychologists in the 20th century.

The distinction underlying much of the debate derives from Windelband, who, in 1898, first drew the distinction between idiographic and nomothetic styles in research. In a nomothetic approach we seek general laws applicable to all the members of a domain. Of necessity, this requires the use of general concepts. In the idiographic approach we seek adequate descriptions of individuals in all their particularity. It is important to realize that though we may make use only of concepts applicable to all people, they may be present in unique degree or form in each person.

The confusions to which Lamiell draws attention begin with muddling up two kinds of generality. Allport's 'common attributes' are observed in everyone, such as having a certain height. The concept of 'height' expresses a common attribute, and the measure 1.62 m expresses the unique degree to which this person exemplifies the common attribute. This has been routinely confused with another kind of generality, the average property. A group of people has an average height, arrived at by the simplest of all statistical procedures. However, no member of the group is that height, nor could the height of any member be recovered from the average.

The use of statistical methods in personality psychology to arrive at 'general' concepts of aspects of personality can reach only as far as average attributes. It cannot reach 'common' attributes. So it makes no sense at all to try to describe a human individual in terms of the traits put forward by mainstream psychologists, such as 'nurturance' or 'neuroticism' (Lamiell, 2004: 183). To find genuinely 'common' traits would require a quite different methodology, a case by case study of individual human beings looking for commonalities, and an induction over the population of tentative hypotheses derived therefrom.

To illustrate how persistent the logical errors have been in this field we can glance at the work of McCrae and Costa (1987). They have come forward with a scheme they call 'The Big Five'. These are Eysenck-like dimensions along which all the subtle and culturally distinctive ways that people manifest themselves are to be represented by 'measures'. The Big Five are arrived at by the same problematic methodology as Cattell's loosely bounded group of personality defining attributes, and suffer the same defects. The five factors are 'neuroticism, extraversion, openness to experience, agreeableness-antagonism, conscientiousness-undirectedness'. The component constructs under each of these are as diverse as those criticized by Allport. Any theory that arrives at 'traits' by factor analysis is almost certain to lack psychological authenticity, as well as slipping across the boundary between common and 'average' traits.

A typical experiment in the traditional paradigm does not involve the close examination of individual cases but instead the evaluation, via tests of significance, of differences in treatment group means. However, group means are not properties of anything real, so they can be neither psychological causes nor effects at the level of individuals.

Resort to probabilities does not allow us to escape the distributive fallacy. It is impossible to deduce an individual's propensities from aggregate data. The probability that a particular person will be neurotic can only mean that in the population to which that person belongs such and such a proportion are neurotic, in the absence of an idiographic study of that individual as he or she displays personal characteristics in various life situations. This point was made more than a century ago by John Venn, but its frequent repetition by logicians since then seems to have been ignored. Even when we give a personalist interpretation to probabilities as measures of degrees of belief, they become expressions of the degree of belief the *psychologist* has in his or her aggregative assertion. They say nothing about any actual person in the population covered by the study.

Treating differences between people as if these were the causes of differences in behaviour is another common fallacy. If person α does A in a situation S, and person β does B in a very similar situation S', the difference between α and β cannot be used to explain the difference between behaviour A and behaviour B. Both differences are logical artifacts, and so have no psychological reality. Lamiell's thorough examination of the statistical fallacies embedded in trait theories and in reifying individual differences may perhaps eventually lead to a more sophisticated methodology than is evident in most statistical studies of personality, temperament and character.

To illustrate the shape that a logically coherent psychology of personality would take, Lamiell has emphasized the work of William Stern. His critical personalism was the fruit of working out the consequences of careful attention to the conceptual basis of studies of human beings as people actively engaged in life projects, both large and small, rather than a way of creating more mathematical abstractions (Lamiell, 2004).

Further Reading

Primary Source

Lamiell, J. T. (2004) *Beyond Individual and Group Differences*. London and Thousand Oaks, CA: Sage.

Secondary Sources

McCrae, R. R. & Costa, P. T. (1987) Validation of the five-factor model of personality across instruments and observers. *Journal of Personality and Social Psychology*, **52**, 81–90.

Windelband, W. (1898 [1998]) History and natural science (trans. J. T. Lamiell). *Theory and Psychology*, **8**, 5–22.

Goffman, Erving (1922–82)

How does it come about that people are perceived to be the sort of people they wish to be seen to be? By what means are 'selves' publicly presented? According to the dramaturgical approach, life is in many ways like performances of stage plays. Personality is something like the style that characterizes a certain role in an everyday drama. Lawrence Olivier can play a feckless entertainer in one play, and a gloomy Scandinavian prince in another. Life is not identical to the stage. One must recognize a distinction between a deliberate and well-planned display of personal traits at one pole and habits of self-presentation that can easily be mistaken for permanent traits at the other. The role of smiles, frowns, nods, gestures, accent, skilful management of social rituals and so on, and the unfolding dramas in which they play a part as they contribute to impression management was the research focus for Goffman and others who have adopted the dramaturgical model of social action. Goffman expressed the main principle of the presentational conception of personality and character in the statement: Not men and their moments, but moments and their men.

Closely allied to this principle is **Michael Argyle**'s (pp. 212–216) idea of social skills. This need not be given a Machiavellian interpretation. It simply means that there is always the question of how to be seen or heard as a certain kind of person and the possibility of succeeding or failing at it. Argyle's research focus turned to extracting explicit and teachable rules of self-management from close observations of how what people do leads to their being seen as belonging to this or that type of person. Goffman was more concerned with the skills of self-presentation that people had picked up along the way, so to speak, though he was also interested in deliberate management of personality displays.

Who was Erving Goffman?

He was born on 11 June 1922 in Manville, Alberta. His family moved to Toronto while he was still a child. He used to explain his fascination with the presentational aspects of personality as due to his youthful predicament, shyness coupled with poverty. At the local dance hall, as a young man, he would stand in the doorway between the bar and the dance floor, too poor to buy a drink and too shy to ask one of the girls to dance. This gave him a perfect viewpoint with which to watch the change in presentational style that came over the men as they moved from the bar to the company of the girls in the dance hall.

He took a BA in sociology and anthropology at the University of Toronto in 1945. A chance meeting led to him moving to the University of Chicago for graduate work. His research project was to make a detailed study of social interactions among the people of one of the Shetland Islands off the coast of Scotland. Here he focused once again on the minute features that made up the texture of personal interactions, unnoticed for the most part by the actors themselves. The thesis was written up in Paris, resulting in a PhD in 1953. Published first as a research monograph by Edinburgh University, it very soon found a commercial publisher, and with its publication Goffman suddenly found himself famous.

However, immediately after his graduation he could not find a suitable job and worked for a year as a research assistant with Edward Shils. In 1956, supported by an NIMH grant, he undertook a detailed study of the inner workings of a large mental hospital in Washington DC. Howard Blumer brought him to the University of California at Berkeley in 1961. After a year at Harvard in 1967–8 he moved to the University of Pennsylvania, to the Benjamin Franklin chair, where he remained for the rest of his life.

Goffman's personal reticence was well known, though he had a taste for good restaurants and hotels. He enjoyed taking up an ironic stance to life, mocking his own pretensions to distinction, as well as puncturing those of others. He died of cancer in Philadelphia on 19 November 1982.

What did he contribute?

Goffman's research into the way personalities are displayed covered a wide variety of cases. Three stand out from his voluminous writings. The first in chronological order was his study of the presentational devices in use in a Scottish community on one of the smaller Shetland Islands. Then he turned to studying how people with 'spoiled' identities, possessors of social stigmata, managed to conceal discreditable identities and 'pass' as acceptable persons in this or that particular milieu. Ethnomethodologists have also contributed to our understanding of this widespread social phenomenon (Garfinkel, 1967). Indeed the very term 'ethnomethodology' refers to the methods by which normal appearances are constructed. The third strand was directed to observations of a feature of personhood that is missing entirely from the work of **Hans Eysenck** (pp. 175–179) and **Raymond Cattell** (pp. 172–175), namely the role of a certain style of presentation of self in the phenomenon of civility, the moment-by-moment construction of a reliable social order providing an unproblematic background to our everyday lives.

Before briefly describing the upshot of Goffman's research, it will be well to realize just how different is his methodology from that favoured by Eysenck and Cattell. For Goffman and the dramaturgical school, personalities are displayed in learned and habitual performances. They do not exist as such in individuals, but in the way individuals are perceived by others, and in some cases, how an actor perceives him or herself. This opens up the possibility of the social valuation of personal traits. Instead of studying the semantics of the language with which people describe personality, character and temperament, including their own, the psychologist must make a close study of how people actually behave, using lexicography only for purposes of classification. If personality is a collective product rather than a set of relatively permanent personal dispositions, the interactions between people must be recorded and analysed. A great many of the devices by which social order is continuously maintained are not consciously attended to or managed by ordinary folk going about their everyday lives. Yet, in the absence of these devices, the social order would be fragile indeed. Despite Eysenck's protestations that his methodology is truly scientific, adherents of the dramaturgical school would see his studies as lacking a proper empirical basis, compared with Goffman's close and detailed observations.

Taking the social character of the production of personality presentations, together with the possibility of a valuation of personality traits as they appear in such displays, allows for support, sabotage and collusion.

In his classic study, *The Presentation of Self in Everyday Life* (1959), Goffman spelled out the ingredients of the collusive activities by which specific personal attributes were made visible in social interactions. The dramaturgical model calls for the identification of scenes, of a cast of characters and of an audience before whom the 'drama' is played out. This led Goffman to the idea of a 'team', the people who support one another's presentations of this or that 'self' shown in displays of personality and character. Watching the transformation of personality displays as waiters passed to and from the kitchen of a hotel led Goffman to introduce a distinction between front stage and back stage as places for personality displays. In the former there are certain formal demands on the kind of personalities and characters to be displayed, demands which are relaxed backstage where other presentational conventions take over, not necessarily looser ones.

The concept of 'collusion' must be carefully qualified in describing Goffman's research. It is a metaphor highlighting the way people sustain each others' performances. It should not be interpreted as a kind of Machiavellian deception, in which members of one group get together to put something over on others. Of course, this does sometimes occur. He realized that studying how bank robbers and conmen 'do normal appearances', such as 'being trustworthy', as a deliberate technique of self-management, can throw light on how ordinary people do normal appearances by habit and custom. In a later study, 'Face work' (1969), Goffman looked at the way a group of people subtly corrects the performance of one of their members, when the actions of the delinquent could be taken to suggest shared vulgarity, ignorance or boorishness on the part of the group. A feeble joke might be supported by more laughter than it deserved, and a mispronounced French word be taken up and correctly pronounced by others in the group.

According to the dramaturgical account, every individual has a repertoire of possible coherent personality displays. For the most part custom, convention and habit, coupled with what others are doing at the time, brings out some suitable pattern of displays from the repertoire. This allows for the possibility that cultures differ in the available and acceptable personalities in the local repertoire. It also allows for individual differences in the resources people have for showing themselves to be 'of the right sort'.

In the dramaturgical paradigm there are no traits. Instead we must theorize in terms of repertoires. Statistical analysis of answers to questionnaires does not touch psychological reality. That must be tapped by intensive and detailed observation of people in situations, each of them 'doing their thing'. The question as to what narrative is being lived out is central to the interpretation of people's actions. This insight takes us back to **Jerome Bruner**'s (pp. 54–62) 'second cognitive revolution', in which the role of storylines in the organization of action is of major importance.

Further Reading

Primary Sources

Goffman, E. (1959) *The Presentation of Self in Everyday Life.* Garden City, NY: Anchor.
Goffman, E. (1968) *Stigma.* Harmondsworth: Penguin.
Goffman, E. (1969) Face work. In *Where the Action Is.* London: Allen Lane.

Secondary Source

Harré, R. (1992) *Social Being* (2nd edn.). Oxford: Blackwell.

Biography

Manning, P. (1992) *Erving Goffman.* Cambridge: Polity Press.

Reflections

The history of personality psychology in the 20th century is surely the history of the ups and downs of the trait theory. **Gordon Allport** (pp. 167–172) rejected his own brainchild in favour of something more subtle. His criticisms of the use of factor analysis to identify source traits are very powerful. If we ally his critical analyses with **James Lamiell**'s (pp. 179–183) demonstrations of logical and mathematical fallacies in the work of the leading trait theorists we have good reason to be cautious about continuing to think of personalities in terms of traits. It seems that actual people have a repertoire of personality displays dependent on the type of situations each encounters and the other people who are there at that time. **Raymond Cattell** (pp. 172–175) and **Hans Eysenck** (pp. 175–179) certainly elicited *something*. Looked at from the critical perspective of Allport and Lamiell it seems that their researches, taking the form of answering questions, accessed one among many possible clusters of personal dispositions, that which comes to the fore when questions are to be answered. Both Cattell and Eysenck fell into the trap of making ungrounded inductions from a special case, as well as neglecting the idiographic dimension.

Owing almost nothing to the trait tradition, **Erving Goffman**'s (pp. 183–186) 'repertoire' treatment of personal displays focused on the actual, moment-by-moment presentations of personal types and the largely symbolic means by which such presentations were successfully achieved. His theory allows for the important fact known to every self-reflective person, that which part of the repertoire one makes use of is dependent on the situation.

Is there anything to be rescued from the trait theory? The fact that it still has a place in the psychology journals suggests that there are psychologists who find it useful, even convincing. However, I doubt whether in the form in which it was used by Cattell and Eysenck it has much future. Their methodology is a major part of the problem. The use of questionnaires and other forms of self-report are, from a logical point of view, conversations, at one remove at least from what people do. Furthermore, the use of statistical analysis to extract the core of the material violates other methodological desiderata. As to the future of personality psychology, only time will tell!

8

The Social Psychologists

The social psychology of the 20th century developed from several sources. One was surely Norman Triplett's studies of social facilitation, the effect of onlookers and pacemakers on individual performances (Triplett, 1898). **William McDougall**'s (pp. 191–194) concept of the so-called 'group mind', the crystallized history of a culture, forming the background to how people interact with one another, was influential in the beginning of the era, though abandoned by a later generation of social psychologists. However, something like it was revived late in the century with the rise of cultural psychology and associated developments (Shweder, 1993) in which the idea of bodies of knowledge of social conventions and meanings was revived. Whatever our historical judgements, there is no doubt that by the second half of the 20th century two distinctive schools of social psychology had been established. There were those who looked for universal laws of social interaction, and there were those who believed that the patterns of social life were predominantly a matter of local cultural conventions and customs. Interwoven with both were increasingly subtle discoveries about those aspects of the biology of primates that were involved in social interactions.

In the United States **Fritz Heider** (pp. 194–199), emigrating from Europe, influenced several generations of psychologists, even though, paradoxically, his most important ideas were ignored by many who saw him as their mentor. However, his conception of social psychology as a study of the ways *individuals* think and feel about each other did more or less define the field for many years. He believed that if a person's thoughts, feelings and actions towards another were 'out of balance', they tended to be reconfigured in such a way as to restore the balance. **Solomon Asch** (pp. 199–202), who came to the United States from Poland as a child, experimented on the conditions under which the expressed opinions of individuals were influenced by the views expressed by the members of the group to which the individual belonged.

Soon a generation of American-born psychologists turned to social psychology. Almost without exception they took for granted that social psychology was to be a study of the effect of the opinions and actions of individuals on individuals. For example, 'interpersonal aggression' was studied by correlating the effect of watching a film clip of a savage boxing bout on the willingness of laboratory subjects to give electric shocks to a supposed victim (Berkowitz, 1991). Similarly, many very active investigators tried to study the conditions for the formation and change of attitudes by setting up tensions between the beliefs and actions of laboratory subjects, to see under what conditions attitudes would tend to change (Festinger, 1957).

The experimental method was largely taken for granted. But, critics pointed out that some psychological phenomena can be studied in real life. This was Darwin's method in evolutionary biology. However, this is often difficult to manage. Sometimes it is possible to construct a model world in which people act as they think fit. The use of colonies of *drosphila melangaster* to study genetics is an example of the use of this methodology in biology. **Muzafer Sherif**'s (pp. 202–207) study of the formation of hostile groups at a children's summer camp is an example of the model world methodology in social psychology.

Occasionally it is possible to abstract independent and dependent 'variables', and by manipulating the former to bring about changes in the latter. This method depends on meeting a very demanding condition, namely that the properties represented by variables retain their original significance when abstracted from the complex systems of which they form a part. The failure to satisfy this condition was one of the long-standing criticisms of the kind of social psychology that was largely practised in the 20th century.

American social psychology moved further and further away from Heider's emphasis on the priority of the concepts of ordinary language in identifying social psychological phenomena. The leit motif of American social psychology was the idea of an individual response to some environmental contingency brought about by other people, both of which were abstracted as 'variables'. The organizing concept was causality. The preferred method of research was the experiment, in contrived and simplified conditions, usually a laboratory, exemplified by **Solomon Asch**'s famous experiment on the influence of other people on people's willingness to express their opinions. Many social psychologists adopted a causal framework for explaining the results of experiments. Though **Stanley Milgram**'s (pp. 207–211) studies of 'obedience' involved the setting up of model worlds in which people would act naturally but in well defined conditions, he still took for granted that social psychology is the study of individual attitudes and actions as they are influenced by others.

In Britain, **Michael Argyle** (pp. 212–216) established a vigorous research centre at Oxford, notable for the variety of research projects undertaken and for the different methodologies that were employed. The Oxford school was particularly concerned with the dynamics of social behaviour, highlighting the unfolding of social episodes in accordance with local rules and conventions. The organizing concept was the idea of a 'social skill' and the correlative concept of a social rule. However, Argyle himself never quite made the transition to the 'cognitive' point of view. The most succinct and revealing presentation of his work (Argyle et al., 1981) shows a markedly eclectic coverage of all that goes into social competence. However, the idea of bodies of knowledge, such as **Serge Moscovici**'s (pp. 216–221) social representations, is tantalizingly not quite in focus in any of his work. *Henri Tajfel* (first in Oxford and later at Bristol University) initiated a vigorous research programme into the sources of prejudice and intergroup conflict, basing his work on studies of the formation of social identities (Tajfel, 1978). His work was very influential in the 1970s and 1980s. It made use of a conception of the social dimension very similar to the idea of social representation, but was limited by Tajfel's adherence to an experimental research paradigm.

A second British centre developed at Loughborough in England (Billig, 1987; Edwards & Potter, 1992). Here, studies of social interaction were based on the realization of the key role played by language, both in what people did and in what psychologists said about what people did. The preferred method of research for the Loughborough group was the close observation and analysis of people acting and reacting in real-life situations or episodes. In this way they followed the means by which social reality was discursively constituted. The writings of John Shotter (1984) emphasized the priority of interpersonal and social processes in the coming to be of socially competent individuals.

In Europe, a different tradition was established, particularly in Paris, with the work of **Serge Moscovici** (pp. 216–221). He drew on and transformed a fundamental idea of the sociologist Emile Durkheim, the idea of a social representation, a shared body of knowledge that shaped the way the members of a community interacted with one another. According to this approach active agents used social representations as a resource to accomplish their projects and to manage the affairs of everyday life. This approach injected a strong cultural element into psychology.

Many of those who took up social psychology in the 20th century were, in one way or another, outsiders – people for whom the culture in which they found themselves was not second nature. This gave them a certain distance from the taken-for-granted practices of real communities. At the same time it blinded them to the ways that ordinary people who are actively engaged in social projects use the resources of their taken-for-granted knowledge of their own social worlds.

Instead of looking for causal relations between variables, in the way that marked the work of most American social psychologists, British and French social psychologists paid more attention to the identification of meanings and the rules according to which they were managed in the affairs of everyday life. Bodies of knowledge became a focus for research, particularly in France and to some extent in Britain as well.

References

Argyle, M., Furnham, A. & Graham, J. A. (1981) *Social Situations*. Cambridge: Cambridge University Press.
Berkowitz, L. (1991) *Aggression: Its Causes, Consequences and Control*. New York: McGraw-Hill.
Billig, M. (1987) *Arguing and Thinking*. Cambridge: Cambridge University Press.
Edwards, D. & Potter, J. (1992) *Discursive Psychology*. London: Sage.
Festinger, L. (1957) *A Theory of Cognitive Dissonance*. Evanston, IL: Row & Peterson.
Shotter, J. (1984) *Social Accountability and Selfhood*. Oxford: Blackwell.
Shweder, R. A. (1993) *Thinking Through Cultures*. Cambridge, MA: Harvard University Press.
Tajfel, H. (1978) *Differentiation between Social Groups*. London and New York: Academic Press.
Triplett, N. (1898) The dynamogenic factors in pacemaking and competition. *American Journal of Psychology*, **9**, 507–533.

William McDougall (1871–1938)

Social psychology has always had uneasy alliances with biology on the one hand and with anthropology on the other. While there can be no debate about the heritability of many physical characteristics of the human organism, the question of the genetic component in higher order cognitive functions and in social practices has continued to be argued over. William McDougall began his work in social psychology more as an anthropologist than a biologist, but he was strongly influenced by the prevailing biological emphases of the time.

Who was William McDougall?

He was born on 22 June 1871 into a prosperous Lancashire family. His father, Isaac, made a considerable fortune from a successful chemical manufacturing business in Oldham. His mother, Rebekah Smalley, came from the same social background of well-off, pious industrial families. William was educated at a private school, and at the age of 14 was sent to the Realgymnasium in Weimar, Germany. On his return he entered Owen's College in Manchester. From there he went up to St John's College, Cambridge, achieving a First Class in both parts of the natural sciences tripos. He began medical studies directly afterwards. In 1898 he started his clinical studies at St Thomas Hospital in London, working with Charles Sherrington. However, later in the same year he took up a lectureship at St John's College, Cambridge, rather than go on into medical practice.

In 1898 he was a member of a Cambridge University expedition to the Torres Straits in the East Indies. The leader of the programme of psychological research was W. H. Rivers, who, as we have seen, was also influential on the work of **Frederic Bartlett** (pp. 47–54). Though McDougall's work was concerned with studying the sensory skills of the local people, he evidently found the insights offered by social anthropology into the cognitive psychology of the native inhabitants of great interest.

He moved to Oxford in 1904. From that year until 1920, interrupted only by his service in the First World War, he held the Wilde Readership in Psychology at Corpus Christi College. The terms of his appointment forbade him to engage in experimental work of any kind. He had been elected to a Fellowship of the Royal Society in 1912, a rare and singular honour for a psychologist, though it has to be said that his knowledge and interests were so broad that it is perhaps misleading to pigeonhole him in so narrow a slot.

He first became well known through his anthropological writings, based on his experience during the year-long Cambridge University expedition to Borneo and the Torres Straits. His first major psychological work from his Oxford period was his *Introduction to Social Psychology*, which became a kind of defining text for the first half of the 20th century.

He held the chair of psychology at Harvard from 1920 until 1928. He published *The Group Mind* just after he came to Harvard. In that book he argued for the importance of a shared culture in psychological functioning, anticipating much that was emphasized in the developments in the last decades of the 20th century. While at Harvard, he began his experimental researches into the 'active powers of the mind' as the source of human action, in flat opposition to the conditioning theories of the behaviourists. His theoretical foundations were biological. The purposes that underlay most of human life were, he thought, instinctual, and so biological in nature and origin. He called his approach 'evolutionary psychology'. His experimental programme was a vigorous and wholly unsuccessful effort to prove that, at least in psychological matters, there was an inheritance of acquired characteristics. This work could be written off as a failure. However it was so thoroughly carried out that it gained an ironic significance in conclusively establishing that the inheritance of acquired psychological characteristics was a myth. The implication of this failure was surely that there must be cultural evolution complementing biological evolution.

Though returning more and more frequently to England in the 1920s and 1930s, he took up a post at Duke University to continue his bio-psychological studies. There he became involved in the parapsychological research that Duke was to host for many years. This proved to be another instructive failure. Nevertheless, he encouraged talented students more as protégés than disciples, amongst whom was the influential **Jerome Bruner** (pp. 54–62). McDougall died on 28 November 1938, still active at Duke University.

What did he contribute?

Throughout his life he shared the view of many British psychologists of the era as to the pre-eminence of biological factors in the explanation of psychological phenomena. In that era the biological basis of mentation was expressed in the concept of 'instinct'. This had some similarities to the more recent concept of the genetic basis of inherited tendencies to perform certain patterns of behaviour, for example the 'fixed action patterns' described by ethologists such as **Konrad Lorenz** (pp. 125–133).

However, his social psychology was not reductionist. It allowed an important role for culture and tradition. He pointed to striking differences in national characteristics among European nations, particularly the French and the English. The French were characterized by the 'spirit of dependence', that is favouring centralized authority and a 'collectivist' way of life in their personal attitudes and social arrangements. The English displayed the 'spirit of independence', favouring local political structures over national institutions. However, he believed that these national social tendencies were inherited, established by natural selection. No doubt McDougall personally preferred individualism to collectivism, but in his social psychology he made no value judgements. The same was not true of his use of biological thinking in the personal domain.

Behaviourists believed in the exclusive role of learning and training in the acquisition of adult characteristics, tendencies and skills. McDougall was deeply opposed to the idea of a psychological *tabula rasa*. He believed that there was good reason to think than there were marked differences in heritable psychological characteristics, among which he gave a prominent place to intelligence. This led him to advocate a eugenic attitude to human reproduction. I do not think that he advocated state-sponsored mate selection, the kind of eugenics that was later associated with fascism in Europe. However, he did insist that mate choice should take account of hereditability. He was not averse to giving marriage guidance to the young in his 1927 book, *Character and the Conduct of Life.*

Looked at from the standpoint of the 21st century there is no doubt that McDougall's biologism encompassed a firm belief in the existence and persistence of heritable differences between people of different 'races'. However, he was equally convinced of the power of the environment to determine psychological characteristics. 'Both of these extremes [the idea of native superiority, and] popular humanitarianism ... are false; the truth lies somewhere in the midst of them ... [there is] the enormous power of heredity in determining individual character and the great persistence of innate qualities through numberless generations ...' [which interacts with the crystallized history of cultures, the 'group mind'] (McDougall, 1920: 254).

Unlike the generations of social psychologists who succeeded him, McDougall paid great attention to history and anthropology as sources of evidence for social psychological theories. His early anthropological studies had brought him into close contact with people of widely different cultures. The history of Europe and of the European migration to North America provided him with material to support his blend of hereditarianism and environmentalism. His evident enthusiasm for reconciling these seeming extremes into a coherent psychological theory emerged in the persistence of his attempts to find experimental proof of the inheritance of acquired characteristics. Living a certain kind of life in a well-defined environment ought, he thought, to predispose future generations towards that way of life. If social adaptations could be inherited then the generally neat relationship between people's dispositions and their cultures could be explained in an essentially biological way. Citing the decline of Spain after the reign of Phillip II, McDougall declared that this was due to the fact that men of enterprise and intellect were no longer produced in Spain. 'During some centuries intellectual power, enterprise and energy were steadily weeded out by a rigorous process of negative selection' (McDougall, 1920: 255).

McDougall summed up his point of view in the phrase 'hormic psychology'. By this he meant a psychology that emphasized that our actions are largely determined by ends and purposes of which we may have no conscious awareness. At the same time, the actuality of social behaviour was shaped by a body of local knowledge as to how people should behave with others. This was the 'group mind'. The instinctual forces are the result of selection, but, as he hoped to show, the selection works on acquired characteristics, acquired as each human being strives to realize the demands of the local culture. Perhaps we might say that his biologism betrayed him and hid from view the possibility that there were processes of social selection and transmission of cultural 'instincts' that were indeed Lamarckian but were not based on biological modes of inheritance.

Further Reading

Primary Sources

McDougall, W. (1920) *The Group Mind*. Cambridge: Cambridge University Press.
McDougall, W. (1948) *An Introduction to Social Psychology* (29th edn). London: Methuen.

Biographies

Alic, M. (2001) William McDougall. In *Gale Encyclopedia of Psychology*.
Brand, C. (1997) William McDougall. In *Cycad Web Works*.

Fritz Heider (1896–1988)

Fritz Heider seems to have been the author of one of the great 'unread' books of the 20th century. If Heider had truly been the father of social psychology, then in several important respects the offspring ignored much that the parent had stood for, except the individualism and the idea of a striving for psychic balance. His major work, *The Psychology of Interpersonal Relations* (1958), was a sustained attempt at the analysis of the 'commonsense' or vernacular concepts with which real people manage their lives. The method is very close to the analytical tradition in philosophy. Heider's analyses fit easily into the framework of philosophical psychology, the study of concepts embedded in the vernacular.

The concept of 'balance' dominated Heider's theorizing. It was this concept that proved to be influential in the work of those who cited Heider as their guide. Cognitive 'forces' within an individual would tend towards equilibrium. Attitudes could be positive or negative, and that determined how people acted towards one another. Heider combined the principle of 'balance' with the thesis that the concepts embodied in ordinary language were the means through which people managed their social lives. There was room in Heider's psychology for conventions, rules, customs and the like, though he tended to lay out his conclusions in causal terms.

Heider's point of view was misunderstood by most of his contemporaries. Reading his major work closely shows how much it pointed forward to the discursive psychology of the late 20th century. However, the concept of balance was central to the social psychology of the mid century.

Who was Fritz Heider?

He was born in Vienna in 19 February 1896, into a prosperous upper middle class family of part Hungarian origin. His family moved to Graz when he was a child.

According to his own account, he enjoyed an idyllic childhood. His father was an architect, with several absorbing hobbies, including archaeology. His mother had been a talented amateur actress, and was evidently of a lively disposition. His early education was with a tutor at home. He finally entered the local primary school when he was nine. Two incidents seem to have made a huge impression on him. First, he damaged an eye when playing with a cap pistol. Moreover, a minor infraction of the social code of his first secondary school was so upsetting to him that his parents removed him to a new school where the emphasis was on the classics rather than science. The injury to his eye kept him out of the First World War. Dissatisfied with the local school, he transferred himself to the Gymnasium. In his autobiography he records in some detail his adolescent musings, particularly his reflections on the way people behaved.

After an abortive effort at architecture, he entered the Law School at the University of Graz in 1914. Like many students in the German-speaking world he took courses at several universities, eventually concentrating on philosophy. At the same time he began to study some psychology with Vittorio Benussi, later professor at Padua. His mother's death in the influenza epidemic of 1919 brought him into close contact with his father. Their frequent quarrelling set him to wondering about the sources of human emotions. However, his final years at the university were spent under the guidance of Alexius Meinong (1853–1920), culminating in 1920 with a dissertation on the problems of perception.

He set off for Berlin, staying with relatives, and living by slowly selling the rare books his father had at one time accumulated, supplemented by private tutoring. Freed from the immediate necessity of earning a living, he studied where his interests took him, particularly at the Psychology Institute. He was fortunate that at that time both Max Wertheimer and **Wolfgang Köhler** (pp. 136–142) were teaching in the Institute. There he met and worked with Kurt Lewin, evidently a more approachable person that the patrician Dr Köhler. He lived a rather aimless life, spending time on the estate of a relative in Czechoslovakia. He made several visits to Italy, though still quite uncertain of the course his life might take.

However, in 1926 he retuned to Berlin to work with Kurt Lewin, whose innovatory use of topological concepts in psychology has still not been fully appreciated. Shortly thereafter job offers began to come. He chose to go to Hamburg, to the department headed by William Stern. Here he encountered one of the major intellectual schisms in psychology between the monists of the Gestalt school and the non-Cartesian dualism of Stern. Mutual respect existed between these points of view. On occasional visits to Vienna Heider attended meetings of the psychoanalysts, and by way of a change, he also went to meetings of the positivists of the Vienna Circle.

By 1930 the peripatetic life was ceasing to satisfy him. Thanks to William Stern, who had been asked by Koffka to find him an assistant, Heider was offered a post at Smith College, with the opportunity to do research at the Clarke School for the Deaf in Massachusetts. This trans-Atlantic move proved to be permanent. With remarkable alacrity he found a wife, marrying Grace Moore in December 1930. She too was a psychologist, and played an influential part in Heider's intellectual development.

By then with a family of boys, the Heiders moved to jobs at the University of Kansas in 1947. They continued to live there for the next 41 years. Younger psychologists were often astounded to learn that Fritz was still alive and active, and some made the pilgrimage to Lawrence, Kansas, to visit him. He died in Kansas at the age of 92 on 2 January 1988.

What did he contribute?

Heider's ultimate aim was to create a theory according to which puzzling patterns of behaviour might make sense. At the same time, rightly, he emphasized the existence of commonsense concepts and practices with which people managed their interpersonal relations. Psychological phenomena were shaped by the vernacular, but an explanatory theory can be built from abstractions, such as his preferred concept of 'balance'.

Heider was not a prolific author, but his 1958 book, *The Psychology of Interpersonal Relations*, proved to be influential, though it is now clear its main message was ignored by most of his contemporaries. He made a point of restricting his inquiry to 'how a person thinks and feels about another person ... how he reacts to the actions of others ... a person reacts to what he thinks the other person is thinking ...' (Heider, 1958: 2). Social psychology becomes the psychology of individuals in small-scale social situations. Furthermore, he disclaimed any interest in unconscious mental processes, which he identified with the theories of **Sigmund Freud** (pp. 270–280).

He believed that one must build a scientific social psychology on the psychological concepts ordinary people use to manage their lives and to understand what other people are doing: '... the ordinary person has a great and profound understanding of himself and of other people which, though unformulated or only vaguely conceived, enables him to interact with others in more or less adaptive ways' (Heider, 1958: 2). He goes on to argue that 'scientific psychology has a good deal to learn from commonsense psychology. In interpersonal relations fruitful concepts and hunches for hypotheses lie dormant and unformulated in what we know intuitively' (Heider, 1958: 5-6). Insights concerning interpersonal relations can be found in profusion in literary works such as plays and novels. However, the most important idea, one that looks ahead to the end of the century, concerns ordinary language. It 'serves us well, for it has an infinite flexibility and contains a great number of general concepts that symbolize experience ... [however] it lacks a systematic representation' (Heider, 1958: 7).

What place is there for social psychology? According to Heider the job of the psychologist is to construct a language that will represent the interpersonal relations discriminated by the conventions of ordinary language and to display their place in a general system. 'Though the words of conventional language do not reveal their interrelations, it does not mean that there are none. It will be our task to make them manifest through a conceptual analysis' (Heider, 1958: 9). Among the most important tools will be the analysis of the uses of words to clarify these implicit relations. Quoting widely, including Gilbert Ryle's *Concept of Mind* (1949), and various works of **Gordon Allport** (pp. 167–172), Heider remarks that novelists 'are able to give descriptions of human behaviour that are often more complete and concrete that those of a psychologist' (Heider, 1958: 7).

A similar style of analysis will be required to clarify descriptions of social situations narrated in plays and novels. The result of the analytical work will be a list of 'cultural primes', basic concepts out of which the concepts of everyday language are constructed. He lists 'life space, perceiving, causing, can, trying, wanting, suffering, sentiments, belonging, [and] ought' (Heider, 1958: 18). The rest of the book consists largely of analysing these concepts in detail. Such a project has been realized in recent years in the work of Anna Wierzbicka (1992). She has extracted a small number of transcultural components of locally distinctive psychological concepts in much the same manner as Heider recommended.

Heider himself vacillates between the two leading paradigms. His adoption of a causal framework for explaining how people viewed each other was at first confined to the uncontroversial observation that when people interact with one another they are embedded in a matrix of causal influences, their material environment. Implicit too is the principle that how people behave toward one another will be causally dependent on how they view one another. This is clearly contrary to the principle that social behaviour as identified with the help of vernacular concepts is shaped by adherence to local rules and conventions, regardless of one's personal likes and dislikes. Heider contrived to live with this inconsistency.

After systematizing the conceptual resources available in the vernacular, social psychologists have a second task: the formulation of a theory. Heider framed his basic theory of social action again in causal concepts. People were impelled to try to achieve various kinds of 'balance' between cognitive items and actions. The human actor as a knowledgeable social agent dropped out of his account of the cognitive processes underlying social activity.

Heider expressed his 'balance' theory quite formally. 'By a balanced state is meant a situation in which the relations among the entities [thoughts, attitudes, actions etc.] fit together harmoniously; there is no stress towards change' (Heider, 1958: 201). The basic algebra is defined by the following: 'L' means 'likes', 'DL' means 'dislikes'. Presuming that an actor has a positive attitude to anything he or she undertakes, so we have 'U' and 'not U'. For example (Heider, 1958: 203) here is a formal representation of an unbalanced state:

'p is dissatisfied with the lecture' (pDLx) is a negative relation. 'p delivered the lecture' (pUx) is a positive relation. Conclusion: The dyad has one positive and one negative relation and is therefore unbalanced.

Presumably our professor will be dissatisfied and perhaps try to do better next time to restore balance. Heider went on to analyse more complex patterns of 'items', setting out the rules for determining which patterns of positive and negative attitudes were balanced and which unbalanced.

As a colleague of Lewin, it comes as no surprise to find that Heider had a predilection for expressing himself in little formulas. For instance, throughout his book and elsewhere, he writes 'pLo' for 'p likes o' and 'p~Lo' for 'p does not like o'. In discussing 'benefit' and 'harm' he defines things thus: 'when o benefits p, he causes something, x, that is positive for p, and ... when o harms p, he causes a negative x' (Heider, 1958: 252). Unfortunately these formulas do not lead to any algebraic theorems and proofs. They are hopelessly vague and general. The concept of causation seems singularly ill-chosen to express the relations abstracted in the formulae. Is the 'x' something p feels, say a warm glow of appreciation, or is it the box of chocolates which she has received? These little bits of algebra seem now not much more than a self-conscious attempt to emulate the style of the physical sciences, obscuring his shrewd insights into the minutiae of human behaviour.

Heider claimed that his analysis served to reveal formal connections underlying commonsense concepts. For example, he cites the conceptual triad, 'can', 'try' and 'success'. The relations between these concepts can be expressed in analytic statements, a kind of 'grammar' of concepts through which we conceive and manage interpersonal relations. **Ludwig Wittgenstein**'s (pp. 240–246) later philosophy comes to mind, as well as the 'psychologic' of Jan Smedslund (1988). The job of social psychologists is not confined to revealing conceptual relations of this kind, but also lies in separating 'factors located in persons and those that have their source in the environment of those persons' (Heider, 1958: 297). We presume a strong consistency in the environment, both material and human. Over all, Heider throws a mantle of 'causal-belonging-together' which forms the content of the 'cognitive matrix that underlies our interpretations of other people's behaviour' (Heider, 1958: 297), in a way that is also reminiscent of the *représentations sociales* of **Serge Moscovici** (pp. 216–221) and his colleagues.

It is not easy to assess Heider's influence, even though the years after the publication of his book were notable for studies in attitude change and widespread use of the concept of 'balance'. An influential book by Leon Festinger, *A Theory of Cognitive Dissonance* (1957), makes no mention of Heider or his earlier publications concerning the balance theory. However, it is customary to cite his distinction between attributing the cause of someone's behaviour to the person and attributing it to the environment as the source of the long-running research paradigm of 'attribution theory'. Working from his 'commonsense' basis, Heider offered a number of reasons for holding a person responsible for some outcome rather than the environment in which the action occurred. Further studies have tended to support his conjectures. Perhaps fortunately, Hieder's rather quaint 'algebra' has not caught on.

Further Reading

Primary Source

Heider, F. (1958) *The Psychology of Interpersonal Relations*. Lawrence, KS: University of Kansas Press; New York: John Wiley & Sons.

Secondary Sources

Festinger, L. (1957) *A Theory of Cognitive Dissonance*. Evanston, IL: Row & Peterson.

Ryle, G. (1949) *Concept of Mind*. Chicago: University of Chicago Press.

Smedslund, J. (1988) *Psychologic*. Berlin: Springer-Verlag.

Wierzbicka, A. (1992) *Semantics, Culture and Cognition*. Oxford: Oxford University Press.

Autobiography

Heider, F. (1983) *The Life of a Psychologist*. Lawrence, KS: University of Kansas Press.

Solomon Elliot Asch (1907–96)

How far are people ready to adjust their views to those of the local majority in order to conform? In many situations there is little to be gained from being difficult, particularly in matters where there are wide differences of opinion. However, common experience suggests people do, quite frequently, dig in their toes, so to speak, and stick to their guns. Asch carried out an experiment, one of the best known in the whole of psychology, that seemed to show that agreement was most readily achieved if there was a strong consensus, and only one person initially of a different opinion. Asch's work inspired a great many studies of the conditions under which people would change their opinions to conform to those of the majority.

Who was Solomon Elliot Asch?

He was born in Warsaw in Poland on 14 September 1907, one of a large family. At that time Poland was a province of the Russian Empire. Asch's family were Jewish and were no doubt well aware of the sporadic outbreaks of anti-Semitism in Eastern Europe. In addition to these occasional threats to the Jews there were the long-running practices of social and professional exclusion that prevented them from entering most of the professions. The Russian Revolution of 1917 took Russia out of the First World War, and made Polish independence possible. It also made emigration much easier. The Asch family left Poland almost immediately after the end of the war in Western Europe. Young Asch arrived in America at the age of 13, ready to start high school in his new land. Like many immigrants at that time, after the ordeal of Ellis Island, the Aschs found a home in New York.

Solomon attended the College of the City of New York, taking his BSc in 1928. He then joined Columbia University where he began advanced studies in psychology, taking his MA in 1930, followed by a PhD in 1932. He worked under Max Wertheimer, one of the pioneers of Gestalt psychology, who had arrived from Europe in 1933, driven out by the anti-Semitism of the Nazis.

After a short period at Brooklyn College he found a permanent post at Swarthmore College in Philadelphia. Swarthmore is one of a group of outstanding undergraduate institutions in the area. By the mid 20th century it had attracted a first-rate faculty, as indeed it still does. **Wolfgang Köhler** (pp. 136–142), the best known of the Gestalt school who had come from Berlin in the 1930s, was among the psychologists present. From 1966 to 1972 Asch was Director of the Center for Cognitive Studies at Rutgers University in New Jersey. He moved to the University of Pennsylvania in 1972. He remained there, apart from a year at the Center for the Advanced Study of the Behavioural Sciences in Stanford, for the rest of his career. After retirement he seems to have settled into a comfortable old age. He died on 20 September 1996, survived by his wife, Florence.

What did he contribute?

In his experimental studies Asch found some support for three basic principles concerning the relations between the expressed opinions of individuals in situations in which their beliefs are at odds with those expressed by a majority. Here we have an extension of **Fritz Heider**'s (pp. 194–199) idea of imbalance from an individual's psyche to the pattern of relations among the members of a group. However, it is important to understand that Asch's experiments were not about beliefs, but about the *expression* of beliefs. In debriefing his 'subjects' he found that though several told him that they did not believe the majority view, nevertheless each was disinclined to express his dissent.

The first principle that emerged from his studies was the strong tendency to link personality traits with one another, to synthesize an overall picture of a person. He was not concerned with real-life episodes in which personality impressions were matters of moment, but with the inferences that people made from one *assertion* to another. For example, from the assertion that someone was shy and inarticulate people tended to make further inferences about other personality traits that person would be likely to possess.

The second principle concerned conformity to the expressed opinions of others. The 'prestige effect' is the tendency we have to express our agreement with an opinion if we believe it has been offered by someone we admire or who is thought to be authoritative on some matter.

The third principle reflected the way people conceal their true opinions and are willing to express similar beliefs to those expressed by the majority. This phenomenon was the focus of Asch's most famous experiment.

He was sceptical about the significance of experiments in which student volunteers shifted their expressed opinions towards what they were told were the opinions of the majority of people or of experts. It seemed far too easy to shift opinions in these studies. Social pressure is no doubt effective in some circumstances, but this does not 'imply uncritical submission', as Asch himself remarked. The conditions for genuine attitude change need to be more carefully dissected. Here is his procedure.

Though eight or nine people were involved, only one was really being tested – the others were confederates of Asch, the experimenter. A card was shown to the whole group in which there was a reference line of a certain length, A, and at the other side of the card three lines, two of which were of a different length from the reference line, B and C, and one, D, of the same length. The confederates all insisted that B was the one that was the same in length as A. What opinion did the subject express?

Asch remarks that in the experiment two opposing psychological forces have been brought to bear on the subject: the evidence of his senses, and the unanimous opinion of the majority. The situation was unbalanced. Furthermore, the subject was required to give his opinion in public. Sometimes the majority gave the correct answer, so that the subject would not suspect collusion. The results are not spectacular but point in the direction of the reality of social indolence: 36.8% changed their stated opinion to conform to the majority view.

How strong was the effect? It depended on the numbers involved. If there were only two people in the experiment, the effect was negligible, but if the situation was 3 against 1, then the original result reappeared. If all the confederates agreed, about a third of the subjects overall suppressed their own opinions and gave the same answer as the majority. However, when the subjects were allowed to write down their answers in a kind of secret ballot, few conformed. When one of the confederates was instructed to declare for the right answer and so the subject had support, the degree of conformity again greatly diminished. If the 'partner' at first supported the subject, and then suddenly began supporting the majority, the subject's support for the majority's erroneous opinion increased. However, if the partner was called away, then the subject continued to resist majority opinion.

When giving accounts explaining their answers, the great majority of the solitary subjects admitted that they were sure the majority was mistaken, but did not want to appear awkward or to be ridiculed. A very few said that on hearing the majority opinion they came to see the disparate lines as of equal length. They were willing to accept the authority of a majority group that somehow they, the subjects, had got it wrong.

Has this experiment anything to do with social conformity in the real lives of ordinary people? In so far as it is concerned with the expression of opinion it cannot be faulted, that is it is concerned with certain conventions for the public expression of opinions. The problem is that the experiment violates one of the methodological principles in Asch's own textbook of *Social Psychology* (1952). He argued forcibly that most social acts have to be understood in their settings. To understand social facts one must see them in their place and notice how they function.

In the light of that principle, what shall we make of the results? The first point to notice is that the experiment is carried out in a virtual social vacuum. The subjects were told that this was an experiment in visual perception. Immediately the social rules for expressing opinions in laboratories kick in. They will be relevant in other contexts just in so far as those contexts are laboratory-like. Asked to express an opinion on a film or a book or the performance of a team, norms of politeness become salient. Many people think it is rude to disagree, though the cussed or bloody-minded glory in it. The experiment is inconclusive – is it about norms of politeness, or about fear of ridicule, or what? So long as this question is open we do not know what to make of the general idea of peer pressure and group conformity. Nor does it seem to be a genuine test of Heider's principle of balance.

Asch himself remarks that all the people who took part in the experiment declared that independence was preferable to conformity. But they would, wouldn't they? As young middle class Americans this declaration is at the root of all the social norms they have been brought up with. Would we get the same result if the subjects were Taliban?

Though this experiment is often quoted and said to be of great significance, it is not easy to see what conclusion to draw from it.

Further Reading

Primary Source

Asch, S. E. (1952) *Social Psychology*. Oxford: Oxford University Press.

Secondary Source

Moghaddam, F. M. (1998) *Social Psychology* (pp. 229–239). New York: Freeman.

Biography

Rock, I. (1990) *The Legacy of Solomon Asch*. Hillsdale, NJ: Erlbaum.

Muzafer Sherif (1906–88)

Sherif's life paralleled the life of Solomon Asch in a number of ways. Both were immigrants, brought to the United States partly as a result of political events in their home countries. Both completed their PhDs at Columbia, and both were strongly influenced by Gestalt psychology in its heyday. Both were deeply interested in the psychological roots of the conformity that made group identification and joint action possible. Sherif made his name by creating plausible model worlds in which he was able to follow the outward and visible signs of the formation and structure of cohesive social groups and to trace the development of inter-group conflicts.

Who was Muzafer Sherif Basoglu?

He was born on 29 July 1906 into a well off upper middle class family in Izmir, Turkey. At that time, before the First World War, Turkey was still the centre of a large but ramshackle empire, and still 'oriental', awaiting the broad and fundamental transformations in every aspect of life instituted by Kemal Ataturk. The American International College at Izmir was one of the foremost educational institutions in Turkey, and it was there that Muzafer Basoglu took his BA in 1927. An MA at Istanbul in 1929 prepared him for graduate study at Harvard. After completing a second master's degree there he spent some time following **Wolfgang Köhler**'s (pp. 136–142) lectures in Berlin. He returned to the United States, to Columbia University, and it was there he completed his PhD with the title *Some Social Factors in Perception* in 1935.

He returned to a teaching job at Ankara University. However, he was publicly vociferous in his condemnation of the Nazi regime in Germany. At that time the Turks had allied themselves with Germany, and Sherif, as he had then come to call himself, was arrested and put in jail. His predicament seems to have struck a chord of loyalty in his former students in the United States. Pressure was put on the US State Department to obtain his release. Turkey was wisely neutral in the Second World War and so Sherif was able to return to America in 1944. Shortly thereafter he married. His wife, Carolyn Wood, became a regular collaborator in his research.

From then on his *curriculum vitae* reads like a catalogue of research institutions and research-oriented posts at universities, including Princeton, Yale, Oklahoma, Texas, Washington, and Penn State. It is perhaps appropriate for such a footloose man that he should have died in Fairbanks, Alaska, on 16 October 1988 of a heart attack during what proved to be the last of his many travels.

What did he contribute?

His earliest work closely paralleled Asch's conformity experiments. Sherif used the autokinetic effect as the basis of his study. A spot of light in a dark room seems to move around, but in patterns that differ from person to person. He showed that when three people are together in the situation their reports of the individual patterns they experience, previously ascertained, merge into a common average.

However, the work for which Sherif is best known was his construction of a model world in an attempt to understand the internal dynamics of groups in the course of inter-group conflict. Like most of his contemporaries he thought in terms of causal relations between various aspects of the research object he was studying. His basic theory was very simple. Inter-group conflict arose from competition for scarce resources. This competition brought about not only the overt conflict, but also several important psychological phenomena, such as inter-group prejudices and stereotyping of the opposition. The uses of such expressions as 'prejudice' and 'stereotype' to describe the psychological states and dispositions he believed had been brought into being by the conflict implies that the opinions these express are false. In effect he distinguished between two groups of phenomena: inter-group relations, potentially hostile, and in-group structures, such as command hierarchies, that come into being through the demands of inter-group processes.

Sherif's fame rests on a single complex experiment, nicknamed 'The Robber's Cave'. The experimental project as a whole presupposed the basic thesis of **William McDougall**'s (pp. 191–194) hormic psychology. The children who took part arrived on the scene, so to speak, with a set of cultural presuppositions which Sherif and his assistants were able to exploit.

The setting for this event was a summer camp in Robbers' Cave State Park in Oklahoma. Twenty-two middle class, white, 11-year-old boys, all strangers to one another, were divided into two groups on arrival and quartered in different parts of the camp. The whole event is described in detail with several interesting photographs in Sherif and Sherif (1956: 301–328). In the first phase of the experiment the members of each group, who at this stage did not even know of the existence of the other group, took part in all sorts of joint activities designed to foster a sense of solidarity. Group identity was emphasized with such devices as emblems, based on a group name chosen by the boys themselves. One group became the Eagles and the other the Rattlers. Looking back 50 years later it is evident that this phase of the experiment depended heavily on American cultural conventions and stereotypes, or McDougall's 'group mind'.

The second phase was even more culturally loaded. The groups were brought together in a series of competitions, such as tug of war. There were trophies and prizes for the winners. The competitive phase was supposed to last four days, but during the first two days the rivalry between the Eagles and the Rattlers quickly got out of hand. Name-calling escalated into open warfare outside the framework of the officially approved competitions. One group broke into the quarters of the others and damaged or destroyed their group emblems. There was, of course, retaliation.

In the third phase the groups were separated for a couple of days. During this time they recorded their opinions of the character of their own group and that of their rivals. It is no surprise to learn that the members of each group expressed favourable opinions of themselves, and excoriated the members of the other. Among other expressions Sherif noted 'tough', 'brave', 'friendly' of themselves, and 'sneaky', 'smart alecks' and 'stinkers' for the opposition. Unfavourable stereotypes of the member of the opposition became standardized very quickly. However, rating and rankings were quite complex. For example, popularity ranking in terms of mutual descriptions of each other was sometimes very different from ranking with respect to their contributions to the group's competitive efforts. One boy who ranked fourth on the 'popularity' scale was ranked eighth 'in terms of effective initiative and influence'. He was evidently frightened of physical conflict and withdrew from potentially violent interactions.

Sherif and his assistants followed the patterns of response displayed by the members of each group when they were defeated in a competition. Defeat led to friction within the group. However the group leader resolved these troubles by following up suggestions for a retaliatory attack on the enemy made by some of the members. After these events, such as burning the flag of the opposition, the observers noted outbursts of bragging in both groups. The emphasis on favourable assessments of character was not only on physical prowess but also on what good 'sports' they all were. Like British football hooligans, in the aftermath of contests and raids, the stories of acts of glory were told and retold.

The only way that a more relaxed inter-group atmosphere could be achieved and the mutual hostility reduced was by getting them to work together on a common task with a common goal. When the groups were brought together for a 'cook out', Sherif and his assistants had arranged that a truck would have to be sent for the food. 'Conveniently' it would not start. The boys used their tug of war rope in a combined effort to get the truck moving. Success brought mutual congratulations and jubilation. After that, they happily shared the necessary chores to produce the meal.

During the competitive phase group leaders appeared. Sherif noted various ways in which a leader maintained authority. For example, a rival for the role of leader was told to put the group logo on his shirt before a game, even though he was team captain. Low status members tended to be even more aggressive than the others, perhaps with the leader's opinion in mind.

What are we to make of this study? The first point to note is that it was not an experiment, in the accepted sense. It did not involve tracking the changes in a dependent variable consequent on changes in an independent variable, with the background held constant. It involved the construction of a micro world. As such it falls under the logic of model making. A model has a source and a subject. In this case, the source was middle class white American cultural practices and standards, and the subject, presumably, the behaviour between and within groups of human beings in general. Sherif made some desultory attempts to access similar situations in other cultures. For example, he cited a study of changes in the vocabulary used by white Americans to describe Chinese during the second half of the 19th century. Unsurprisingly, when the Chinese began to compete with Americans for jobs, descriptions of the immigrants tended to become pejorative.

The dominance of a causal framework in interpreting the Robbers' Cave study is revealingly displayed in Sherif's summary of the results of the project.

> As a consequence of repeated interaction between the two experimentally formed groups in competitive and reciprocally frustrating situations, and of the cumulative inter-group friction thus engendered, negative attitudes toward the out-group were formed by members of each in-group. These negative attitudes towards the out-group, crystallized in unfavorable stereotypes, were manifested by name-calling, derogation of the out-group, and the explicit desire to avoid association with the out-group. (Sherif et al., 1954: Ch. 6)

Furthermore, a highly contentious concept has slipped into the story. The explanation of what the children did is grounded in the attribution of 'attitudes', presumably theoretical mental entities introduced to explain the tendency of the participants to do and say the things they did. This explanatory format, like the overall causal framework, is introduced a priori, and remained unexamined throughout the writing up of the study.

Finally, it is worth asking the chicken/egg question: most team games are of English origin and spread around the world in the period of British hegemony. Did this happen because there was a universal and latent tendency to bring into being the in-group/out-group psychology described by Sherif, or was that way of being spread on the back of the games themselves and their psychological necessities? With the spread of football to the remotest corners of the globe it is perhaps too late to look into this question by any current cross-cultural study.

Sherif's 'model world' was embedded in a rich and complex cultural context. The boys in the camp drew on it for almost every aspect of the group conflict and its ultimate resolution. *Henri Tajfel* (1919–82) explored dynamics of a natural tendency among human beings to form group or social identities. By 'social identity' is meant those aspects of one's concept of oneself that derive from one's beliefs about the groups to which one thinks one belongs. Tajfel's 'minimal identity' research programme looked at the effect of assigning people to arbitrary groups and examining the consequences in terms of minimal social identity formation.

Later developments of this research paradigm invoke the idea of 'social comparison'. This concept refers to the way that people tend to form opinions of their own social standing by comparing themselves with others, often from another group (Tajfel, 1981). The core of Tajfel's research programme was a long-running series of experiments, in which he explored the conditions under which prejudicial opinions of people belong to contrasting groups were formed. He rejected the idea that the basis of hostile stereotyping could be found in the effect of individuals on individuals. Instead he pointed to the importance of the social location of people in the formation of attitudes and opinions concerning members of other groups.

Like **Serge Moscovici** (pp. 216–221), Tajfel and his colleagues took the social dimension to be exhausted by the similarity of individual people's points of view. However, his 'minimum group' experimental programme disclosed a native and universal tendency for people to form into competing teams. Nevertheless, the way this tendency is manifested depends heavily on local cultural beliefs and conventions. By choosing a conventional experimental methodology Tajfel, so far as I know, left no room for detailed observational studies of actual group interactions, unfolding episodes of the results of conflicting social identities. The abstract conception of a 'social location' can be of psychological significance only if it is realized in specific rituals and other relevant displays. Social stereotyping may exist only in the displays, and not in the cognitive resources of the individuals who implement them. Tajfel's almost exclusive concentration on laboratory studies left this dimension more or less untouched. It was eventually followed up by Billig and others at the University of Loughborough (Billig, 1991).

Tajfel never attempted a fully cognitive version of his theory of identity formation. He did not develop a scheme for the representation of bodies of social beliefs, nor of the cognitive processes by which they were accessed and implemented.

However, despite the necessary reservations one must have to the quality of the work itself, the attempt to undertake a systematic study of all that goes into the inhumanity of man to man was a worthy undertaking. Tajfel's studies together with those of his colleagues were a serious attempt to extricate what underlay the more complex phenomena studied by Sherif and **Stanley Milgram** (pp. 207–211).

Further Reading

Primary Sources

Rohrer, J. H. & Sherif, M. (1951) *Social Psychology at the Crossroads*. New York: Harper.
Sherif, M. & Sherif, C. W. (1956) *An Outline of Social Psychology*. New York: Harper.
Sherif, M., Harvey, O. J., White, B. J., Hood, W. R. & Sherif, C. W. (1954) *Intergroup Conflict and Cooperation*. Intergroup Relations Project, University of Oklahoma.

Secondary Sources

Billig, M. (1991) *Ideology and Opinions*. London: Sage.
Hewstone, M., Stroebe, W. & Stephenson, G. M. (1996) *Introduction to Social Psychology* (pp. 536–539). Oxford: Blackwell.
Tajfel, H. (1981) *Human Groups and Social Categories*. Cambridge: Cambridge University Press.

Biography

Trotter, R. S. (1985) Muzafer Sherif: A life of conflict. *Psychology Today*, Sept.

Stanley Milgram (1933–84)

The murderous and systematic attacks on Jewish and other disfavoured communities in central Europe in the time of the Nazi regime in Germany raised a deep psychological question, and not for the first time. How could sufficient people be found to staff this horrendous enterprise? Once recruited, how could they be brought to engage in the activities required for the callous extermination of millions of people? The revival of dormant anti-Semitism cannot be the whole explanation, since the Jews were not the only victims of the 'holocaust'. These questions are as old as humanity and as fresh as yesterday. The extermination of the Cathars and the killing fields of Cambodia are a millennium apart, but the psychological puzzle remains the same. Immediately after the end of the Second World War the perennial question of man's inhumanity to man was given a fresh impetus by the revelations of the German death camps. Stanley Milgram, one might say somewhat naively, tried to solve the puzzle by a programme of experiments on what he took to be the psychology of obedience.

Who was Stanley Milgram?

He was born in New York on 15 August 1933. His parents had emigrated from Europe in the wake of the rise of the Nazis in Germany. The Milgrams had a cake shop, Stanley's father was the baker and his mother served in the shop. He attended the James Munro High School, and is remembered as excelling both in science subjects and the arts. He went on to Queens College, in Flushing, New York, graduating as a political science major.

At some time in his undergraduate studies he had become strongly attracted to the idea of research in social psychology. Joining the psychology school at Harvard, under **Gordon Allport** (pp. 167–172), became a burning ambition. His persistent efforts to get a place were finally rewarded by provisional acceptance in 1954, confirmed shortly thereafter. **Solomon Asch** (pp. 199–202) had visited Harvard in 1955, and Milgram had the good fortune to serve as his teaching assistant. This led to his getting to know the method Asch had used to study conformity, in his famous experiments on compliance to a majority opinion. Realizing that the original experiments were situated in a very local cultural milieu, Milgram undertook a cross-cultural study, developing Asch's visual material into an auditory form. His results seemed to show that Norwegians tended to conform to majority opinion more than his French participants did. His association with Asch continued when he joined him at the Institute for Advanced Study at Princeton, working with him on a book on conformity. The book makes revealing reading, since nowhere is there any reference to the normative presumptions of those societies between which there are manifest differences in the willingness of people to go along with what they perceive to be majority opinion. Asch and Milgram were in search of universally applicable laws of human nature. It is a short step from studies of conformity to raising questions about obedience.

After taking his PhD in 1960, Milgram got a job as an assistant professor at Yale. Not long afterwards, he married Alexandra Merkin.

His experiments on 'obedience' stirred up considerable controversy, particularly concerning his own moral stance toward the mental anguish suffered by some of his 'subjects'. The methodology required that the experimenter should deceive the subjects as to the true topic of the study. Were these morally dubious aspects of the experimental programme justified in the pursuit of the greater good? In the event, Milgram was refused tenure at Harvard, and in 1967 he returned to his roots in New York. He was appointed to a full professorship at the Graduate Center of the City University.

In his last years, he turned to other fields of research. He undertook several very interesting studies of the psychological foundations and necessities for life in cities. Whether as reluctant hero or naïve villain, his reputation rests on the equivocal experiments with the electric shock console in the model world of the fake experiment.

He died on 20 December 1984.

What did he contribute?

It was only after his appointment to Yale that he began the studies of what he took to be obedience. This qualified phraseology is essential to understanding the significance of his work, since, as we shall see, the right way to understand the studies he subsequently undertook has become a matter for debate. Did people do what they were told because they had been ordered to do so by an established authority? Or, did they follow instructions because of their beliefs about the nature of the institutional setting in which Milgram's 'model social world' was set up?

This difference is profound, particularly as Milgram explicitly associated his results with the puzzle of how the Nazis had managed to recruit people to run the extermination camps, as they implemented the 'final solution' to the alleged 'Jewish problem'. Milgram was deeply emotionally involved with the sufferings of the Jews of Eastern Europe. It has not been unusual for those who by good fortune had escaped the Holocaust to be driven back to it emotionally and intellectually. How could such a thing have happened? Since the 1960s the question has been asked again and again – of Stalin's massacres, of the killing fields of the Khmer Rouge, of the deaths of thousands of Kurds, and looking deeper into history, of the genocide of the Tasmanians and the ethnic cleansing that destroyed the Cathars. It seems that there was nothing special about the European Jews that singled them out for genocide. Whatever are the psychological conditions, they must, it seems, be universal.

Milgram's 'experimental' programme was set up within the causal paradigm, which had become well established in American research methodology. What were the conditions which would cause ordinary people to obey orders to perform morally problematic acts? Did the experiments reveal an underlying psychological universal, a tendency to obey authority, no matter what one was ordered to do? Could one leave aside the thoughts of those who took part, as they were apparently forced into compliance? Whatever one's attitude to the experiment, we need to know what Milgram did.

Like **Muzafer Sherif** (pp. 202–207) he constructed a model world, abstracted, at least in principle, from the complex world of everyday life, if we can so describe the world of genocides. The participants were told that they were to take part in a learning experiment. The 'subjects' were seated, one at a time, at a console with clearly labeled switches, ascending from 10 volts to 400 volts. They were shown a person in another room, a confederate of the experimenter. They were told that he was the real experimental subject. They saw him strapped into an electric chair. The fake subject was able to communicate with the person working the console by a microphone. Each time the confederate made a mistake, the participant was told to administer an electric shock, of ever increasing strength. The confederate made appropriate noises and complaints as the voltage was raised. Nearly two thirds of the people randomly selected from the telephone directory were persuaded to go up to the 400 volt maximum, even when the confederate had eventually fallen silent after calling out about his weak heart.

Whenever a participant queried the dangers, Milgram or one of his assistants reassured them with the words 'You may continue. I assure you there will be no tissue damage.'

Many of those involved became upset and wanted to leave the experiment all together. They were more or less bullied into continuing. The most remarkable feature of this whole set up is that while one third of the participants refused to continue what they believed to be torturing the confederate, neither Milgram nor his assistants refused to continue their role. They knew they were making many people suffer at least some degree of mental anguish.

Note well, that the participants had been told that what they were doing was for the general good, a programme designed to improve the techniques of teaching and learning.

Milgram tried all sorts of variants of the original 'model world', including moving the whole experiment out of the university buildings to try to eliminate the effect of the institutional setting.

Comments on Milgram's project and its results have ranged from praising it for what it seemed to reveal about human nature, to outright condemnation on both methodological and moral grounds.

What did it show about human nature? Milgram interviewed his participants after they had taken part in his experiment. Their comments are revealing. Most people trusted Milgram's reassurances as to the safety of the procedure, so though they went to the 400 volt level they did not believe that they were doing the confederate any real harm. 'I have never heard of anyone being killed in a psychology department of a university', said one of them. Milgram's model world was not sourced from the Holocaust at all. While it said nothing about obedience to authority in the face of moral revulsion, it did say a great deal about the role of trust and consequential patterns of belief in everyday life. The staff of Auschwitz knew very well what they were doing, and there was no question of obeying orders in the face of moral revulsion. The moral panic that followed the publication of the results of these studies was powered by the fallacious inference that Milgram had shown there were plenty of people in New Haven, Connecticut who could be recruited to staff an extermination camp or something like it.

In a remarkable study, published in the 1970s, Mixon (1972) replicated Milgram's result by means of a thought experiment. Using only a drawing of the console, he followed the Milgram methodology, except he divided his participants into three groups: those who were asked to pretend that they believed that the high voltages would be lethal, those who believed that whole thing was a fake, and those who were not sure what the set up actually was. All the members of the first group refused to go on to dangerous levels of shock, all the members of the second group went the whole way, but the members of the third group fell into the same one third/two thirds proportion of non-compliance and compliance as had Milgram's subjects. Mixon's thought experiment underlined the fact that the basis of the experimental results was the trust/belief pattern of cognition, and not that of obedience, that is command/compliance.

Did the experiments show that the universal basis of social order must take the form of hierarchies of authority? The assumption that it did, the basis of the management of modern institutions, was thought to be vindicated. Many examples of non-hierarchical and stable social orders, readily available in the anthropological literature, were left in limbo. Studies of compliance in other cultures show similar results to those found by Milgram, but this fits well with the results of studies of trust. People tend to trust others unless they have positive evidence of untrustworthiness. In human affairs, trust is the default position.

The first reactions to Milgram's experiments were generally enthusiastic. It seemed as if not only had he revealed the source of untold examples of human suffering in the mindless obedience of functionaries to the orders of evil masters, but revealed a universal human tendency on which all social order must be built, namely established authority. His career seemed to be set fair, when he was invited to return to Harvard as an assistant professor. However, doubts surfaced, not only as to what the results had established, but also as to the moral quality of the method Milgram had used. He had lied to the participants, and had subjected many of them to considerable mental suffering. Was this justified in the light of the greater good? Did the end justify the means? Could immoral actions of one sort be used to reveal the inwardness of a greater evil? Some people at Harvard evidently thought not.

Further Reading

Primary Source

Milgram, S. (1974) *Obedience to Authority*. New York: Harper and Row.

Secondary Source

Mixon, D. (1972) Instead of deception. *Journal for the Theory of Social Behaviour*, **2**, 145–177.

Biography

Blass, T. (2004) *The Man Who Shocked the World*. New York: Basic Books.

Michael Argyle (1925–2002)

Social psychology hardly existed in the United Kingdom before the 1960s. Anthropology had flourished in London and Oxford for a century. By and large this was an observational science, with a rich background of theory. Sociology, particularly as an auxiliary to projects of social reform, was also highly developed in Britain. The idea that experimental psychology might be extended to social relations was growing in other places. Michael Argyle was largely responsible for bringing this aspect of psychology to life in England. Ironically, his original adherence to an experimental rather than observational and cognitive social psychology sparked a backlash in his own department. This reaction led more or less directly to the establishment of Oxford as a centre for an observational, language-oriented approach to understanding how social life is brought into being, with a strong emphasis on local cultural factors. In his later work Argyle himself moved in this direction.

Who was Michael Argyle?

Michael Argyle was born on 11 August 1925 in Nottingham. A happy childhood was cut brutally short in 1937 with the death of both his parents. He was brought up by two maiden aunts, in a regime he described as strict and austere. This perhaps goes some way to explain his interest in social psychology, since he was never wholly at ease in close social encounters, though he was regarded with great affection by friends and students. He went to Nottingham High School for Boys and on to Emmanuel College, Cambridge to read mathematics. Turning 18 in 1943, during the Second World War, he joined the RAF, training as a navigator. Typically, he spent some of his leave as a firefighter in the East End of London during the air raids that had continued after the 'blitz' of 1941. After the war, he served as a radio operator in Berlin.

On his discharge he returned to Cambridge, and changed to psychology, graduating with a First in 1947. In 1949 he met and married Sonia Kemp, who was reading classics at Girton College. After holding a junior post in Cambridge, in 1952 he moved to Oxford, as University Lecturer in Social Psychology. The post of University Lecturer is something of a misnomer, since the holder was in the position of managing the teaching and examining of the subject on a university-wide basis. He chaired the psychology department at Oxford in the late 1970s. During the reforms of the 1960s he became a founding fellow of Wolfson College, the second general graduate college to be established in Oxford.

Sonia Argyle was well versed in ancient languages. She was highly regarded as a copy-editor of technical books in the area of language studies. The Argyles managed to balance a demanding family life with four children to bring up with diverse social activities. The camaraderie of the department spread into generous hospitality at home. Michael was also much involved in the Anglican Church, and remained a devout and indeed enthusiastic Christian throughout his life.

Michael Argyle was an excellent lecturer and much in demand. He and Sonia traveled widely, forging particularly strong links with Australia. In later life, Sonia became seriously ill, and Michael devoted himself to taking care of her. He himself had fallen ill in Australia, and took some time to recover. Despite these personal problems he remained resolutely cheerful. Sonia Argyle died in 1999. In 2001 he married Gillian Thompson, a fellow member of his church.

After his official retirement from Oxford University, he took up a new post at the nearby Brookes University, where he continued to teach, still actively publishing until his death. Typically he continued vigorous physical activities into his 70s. Early in 2002 he collapsed while swimming. Though he was rescued, his lungs had been irretrievably damaged, and he never completely recovered. He died on 6 September 2002, buoyed up in spirit by his religious faith. In life he was a good natured and cheery man, enjoying his evenings of Scottish dancing right up to the time of his tragic accident.

What did he contribute?

His work can be divided roughly into three overlapping phases. First were experimental studies of interpersonal interactions that depended on non-verbal factors, such as eye contact. Then he moved on to attempts to extract repertoires of social skills, using a variety of methodologies. Finally he undertook a series of survey-like studies into various aspects of everyday life, such as leisure, religion and even money (with Adrian Furnham). However, his success in building up a research group including many very talented young people was more salient for assessing his influence on social psychology at large. The Friday afternoon seminars not only attracted people from other sectors of the university but became a regular meeting place for social psychologists from all over the world. Debates were vigorous and criticisms freely voiced.

Argyle's career as a social psychologist began with some rather simple experiments on the phenomenon of gaze. He tried to bring to light the circumstances under which people would look up or down, make contact or avoid it, and for how long. Did men and women display different patterns of gaze? In the beginning Argyle shared the universalist presuppositions of his American contemporaries, that the results of experiments carried on in what he presumed to be a socially neutral place, a bare room, with a small sample of the human race, could be generalized to all people everywhere. In the final writing up of the results of a long-running research programme considerable weight is given to culturally diverse patterns of gaze (Argyle & Cook, 1976: 26–34). There is even a hint of cognitive aspects of gaze in the observation that people make less eye contact than normal when they are lying. His final conclusion recalled the ideas of **William McDougall**'s (pp. 191–194) hormic psychology. Patterns of gaze were the result of the interplay between natural tendencies and learned social customs through which interpersonal respect and personal modesty are displayed.

Argyle went on to develop the idea that social behaviour was the result of the exercise of specific repertoires of skills. With a somewhat adventitious mix of methods he explored the repertoire of social skills necessary for competent social performances. At the back of this project lay his conviction that one of the sources of human happiness was a well managed and enjoyable social life. That required the exercise of social skills. The introductory chapter to his edited collection of essays on the relation between social skills and health (Argyle, 1981) is a masterly summary of the role of nonverbal aspects of interpersonal interactions, including the sources or the opinions we form of others. He coupled this with an analysis of the role of cultural conventions and etiquette in the smooth management of daily social life. Failure in either of these domains is an important contributor to social isolation.

Out of this came a training programme for people deficient in the skills that were so much second nature to competent members of a social group that they had become habitual. Argyle's approach, like that of the French school of *répresentations sociales,* required a metaphysical basis in the person conceived as an active, responsible agent, using his or her social knowledge, with others, to try to realize various plans, aims and projects. Social skills once learned had to be used in deliberate self-management.

The social skills research programme took Argyle, and those who worked with him, a long way from the causal paradigm in vogue among those influenced by **Solomon Asch** (pp. 199–202). As Argyle's interests expanded from the biologically based fixed action patterns of primitive gaze, his work made less and less use of the experimental study of the relations between independent and dependent variables.

In his later work on happiness, religion, leisure and money, some of the staples of everyday life, he turned to the use of questionnaires, seeking statistically derived factors as the outcome of the research. This body of work came to be more like the surveys of social attitudes that have been popular in Britain than strictly psychological investigations. Argyle rarely ventured on hypotheses about unobservable cognitive processes, briefly mentioning the possibility that religious belief might serve an integrative function in the person, though he did not follow this up. He made no attempt at formal or computational models of the creation of social order.

The upshot of his happiness studies was not exactly earth shaking. A stable and fulfilling home life, an absorbing hobby or leisure activity and a manageable job were the main ingredients in a life that combined contentment with the absence of anxiety. It might strike one as a curious coincidence that a church-going enthusiast for Scottish dancing should discover that dancing and religious observances were the sources of the greatest happiness!

Argyle's conclusions as to the kinds and conditions of happiness reached a very wide audience, even the in-flight magazine of British Airways.

Noticeably absent from these presentations are any hypotheses as to the cognitive processes that might explain why people said that they were happy in the circumstances and doing the things they did. Equally prominent by its absence was any analysis of 'happiness' as a name for a state of mind, feeling, and so on. At the very least the word is at the centre of a network of uses, of the kind **Ludwig Wittgenstein** (pp. 240–246) likened to family resemblances. The questionnaire method brought to light some of the rules for the use of the word 'happiness' among a certain group of English speakers. However, without the necessary analytical groundwork the results remain equivocal. Argyle never managed to close the gap between the uses of the word 'happiness' and being happy. His choice of the questionnaire method precluded it. Questionnaires offer access to what people are willing to *say* about some aspect of their lives. In the absence of observational studies, particularly participant observation, the gap between what people say and what they do remains open.

Michael Argyle's work, considered in relation to the principles that guided his life, presents the paradox of 20th-century social psychology particularly clearly. If the ways people behave with and towards others are largely a matter of human ethology and ingrained social habits, there seems to be no place for morality, for a person agonizing over what he or she *should* do. Nevertheless, Argyle was a fervent Christian. The clash between social life as the arena of morality, par excellence, based on the four core social psychological concepts of Christianity – sin, repentance, confession and absolution – and social behaviour as the product of biological and cultural forces of which individuals are often not aware, is surely a mark of irreconcilable points of view. Michael Argyle never resolved this issue. He saw his own work as directed towards the betterment of human life, a powerful moral incentive.

His personal influence on the development of this branch of psychology lay more in his encouragement of a broadly eclectic style among his collaborators and research students than in his studies. Out of this came the 'role-rule' model of social life as a collaborative, norm-guided construction (Harré & Secord, 1972). His encouragement of all kinds of research projects and his personal amiability and openness led to the emergence of a remarkably active and influential group of younger social psychologists at Oxford. Research projects ranged from observational studies of the psychological basis of football hooliganism by Peter Marsh, to experimental work in attribution theory, the way that responsibility is distributed between actor and environment, by Jos Jaspers, to studies of the organizing principles of conversations by David Clark, to social psychological aspects of driving cars by Peter Collett and Peter Marsh, and many others.

The strength of Argyle's personal contributions lay in his capacity to forge a coherent account of the genesis and maintenance of social relationships from the very disparate materials that a realistic look at these matters presented him with. On the one hand there were non-verbal communicative acts of which most people were not aware, and on the other the cultural rules and conventions of behaviour that had become second nature to the socially skilled. The weakness of Argyle's contributions was methodological. While a mix of experimental and questionnaire methodology worked well in his studies of social skills, his neglect of observational methods and his reluctance to open up a cognitive dimension limited his more ambitious projects, such as the psychology of religion and of work and money.

Though it would not be entirely correct to say that the Oxford and Paris schools of social psychology influenced each other directly, both could be seen as different ways of realizing **William McDougall**'s (pp. 191–194) thesis that the details of social behaviour were expressions of the crystallized core of a culture, shared by all the members, interwoven with patterns of interpersonal signals to which the human organism had become adapted.

Further Reading

Primary Sources

Argyle, M. (1981) *Social Skills and Health*. London: Methuen.

Argyle, M. (1987) *The Psychology of Happiness*. London: Methuen.

Argyle, M. & Beit-Hallahm, B. (1975) *The Social Psychology of Religion*. London: Routlege and Kegan Paul.

Argyle, M. & Cook, M. (1976) *Gaze and Mutual Gaze*. Cambridge: Cambridge University Press.

Secondary Sources

Collett, P. (1977) (Ed.) *Social Rules and Social Behaviour*. Oxford: Blackwell.

Harré, R. & Secord, P. F. (1972) *The Explanation of Social Behaviour*. Oxford: Blackwell.

Biography

Robinson, P. (2002) Michael Argyle. *The Guardian* (Education Section): 3 Oct.

Serge Moscovici (1925–)

How coordinated collective activities are possible has been a perennial problem for social psychology. According to social constructionists the orderliness of interpersonal activity is accounted for by the dynamics of the patterns of interaction that come into being in the course of social life, as people make use of a local body of knowledge. No one actor has the complete body of knowledge and repertoire of skills to bring order, but each of the assembled members has a fragment of what it requires. According to the school of *représentations sociales* or social representations, each person has a version of the resources of the whole and thereby is enabled to take part competently in social encounters. Serge Moscovici and his colleagues have been the main source of the theory of social representations, ultimately derived from the sociologist Emile Durkheim (1858–1917).

Closely allied with the question of coordinated social action is the problem of crowds – how best to describe the way an individual becomes a part of a crowd, and how best to explain the absorption of a person into a mass movement. Moscovici has also been responsible for reviving the interest of psychologists in this question.

Who is Serge Moscovici?

He was born in Romania in 1925. His father was a grain dealer, who it seems changed wives as readily as he changed cities. The family were Jewish. When Romania entered the Second World War on the side of the Germans, young Serge was forced to leave school. Somehow he managed to avoid the dire fate of many of his co-religionists, and spent the war in a forced labour camp. He learned the trade of welder, and after the fall of the German Reich in 1944 he was able to use his skills in Germany and elsewhere. As the Cold War 'hotted up' he made his way to Paris. In 1948 he entered the Sorbonne to study psychology, supporting himself by factory work as a welder. In his autobiography (Moscovici, 1997) he writes of the typically Parisian way in which he combined his formal studies with time spent with the literary intelligentsia of the era. He did graduate work at Stanford and Princeton universities in the United States. Returning to France he took up a post in the École des Haute Études en Sciences Sociales, from which he has recently retired.

What has he contributed?

Though there have been a number of distinguished psychologists following the general outline of a Durkheimian social psychology, there is no doubt that the leading figure has been Moscovici. His long-term collaboration with Robert Farr has meant that many of his ideas have had a ready entry into British psychology. The psychological theory of 'social representations', proposed by Moscovici, expounded by Farr (Farr & Moscovici, 1984) and developed by Denise Jodelet (1991), derives from Durkheim's concept of *représentations sociales*. However, this work does not seem to have eventuated in a single concept of 'social representation', but rather a cluster of related concepts. They have in common an emphasis on the sharing of knowledge or belief among a group of people, not necessarily in intimate contact with one another. People share a social representation when each member of the social group in question holds a similar belief to every other member. Ironically a social representation is a special case of an individual representation, in which all the individual representations in a group are similar. As a result of sharing in this sense, a group of people displays a common pattern of belief, and a common reaction to situations and people.

To get a just view of Moscovici's concept and its applications one must resolve two problems. How should one understand the concept 'social' in the phrase 'social representations'? One might prefix 'social' to 'representation' to qualify the latter term in one of two main ways. One might want to emphasize that, though each representation is a property or attribute of one and only one person, nevertheless it is shared amongst a group, in the sense that the several individual representations of group members are so similar they can be treated as identical for all practical purposes. But one might have another sense of 'social' in mind. One may want to express the idea that the representation in question is not an attribute of any single individual, but exists in the joint actions (practices) of the people of a certain community or group. The manner of existence and mode of efficacy of a social representation, and the methodology that one should adopt in studying it, will depend on which of these meanings one assigns to the term.

For the most part Moscovici has used the term in the former sense, that is to mean a shared representation. Each member of a group has their own representation but in certain important ways it is similar to every other. In a recent book, Denise Jodelet (1991) uses the term, at least implicitly, in the other sense. Many of the representations of madness and mental troubles in the community she studied do not exist in the minds of individual people but seem to be best construed as attributes of the practices of the community, particularly their ways of talking about the people from the mental hospital, the way meals are served in the homes in which patients are billeted and so on. Both concepts are useful additions to our technical vocabulary but they are not the same, and not the same in important ways.

We can also ask about the relationship social representations bear to the human conduct to which they are relevant. For example a social representation of the norms of parenting might be made available to a psychologist in the folklore of the members of the community where it is expressed as a set of rules or sometimes as a collection of exemplary stories. But in those cases in which the representation is immanent in practices it is only the psychologist who eventually can give an independent presentation of it. Indeed it might be thought to be the job of the psychologist to do just that. In the work of Moscovici and his school we find the psychologist sometimes in the one role and sometimes in the other.

Are social representations meant to be among the causes of certain kinds of conduct or are they to be taken to be like rules, fixing what ought to be done, said or thought?

To get closer to these problems and queries we can use a presentation of the concept in Jodelet (1991: 17):

> ... when we concentrate on the positions held by social subjects (individuals or groups) towards objects whose value is socially asserted or contested, representations are treated as *structured fields*, that is to say as contents whose dimensions (information, values, beliefs, opinions, images etc.) are delimited by an organizing principle (attitude, norms, cultural schemata, cognitive structure etc.). ... when we concentrate on them [social representations] as modes of knowledge, representations are treated as *structuring nuclei*, that is to say, knowledge structures orchestrating the totality of significations relative to the known object.

It is clear, in a very general way, what Jodelet means. People are treated as thinking subjects rather than reacting objects. Social representation psychology could hardly be more different from behaviourism, and its positivistic descendants in American empiricism. However, her presentation is more difficult to understand when we focus on the details. The psychological phenomena set between parentheses above are plainly very diverse in character, and some are ambiguous.

However, one major ambiguity in Moscovici's account of social representations is resolved by Jodelet in the passage quoted above. She acknowledges that the term 'social representation' is used in two quite different ways. It is employed to refer to two quite different 'entities'. On the one hand it is used to refer to 'structured fields' of very diverse kinds of elements whose nature is still to be determined, and on the other to 'structuring nuclei', a metaphor for what it is that structures the aforesaid fields.

We can now make sense of the two main cognitive processes proposed by Moscovici and his co-workers, namely anchoring and objectivication. It seems natural to interpret 'anchoring' and 'objectivication' as discursive processes, ways of making sense of things.

In objectivication, a social representation appears as an ordered set of rules through which a complex of activities, material and symbolic, are produced as an ordered whole. The term 'objectivication' draws our attention to the way in which we take, unreflectively, such ordered wholes to be objectively real. A local way of life, the daily workings of an institution, the recurrent pattern of work on a farm, and so on, are taken as real in so far as they are talked about as real, as something which exists beyond the scope of each individual who has a part to play in them. To anchor the act 'hitching a horse to a plough', that action must be seen as belonging with other seasonal agricultural actions and so as having a meaning in relation to them. Anchoring then is the process by which new items are added to a sign system, while objectivication is the process by which the elements of that sign system are produced as an ordered whole according to the rules for their proper use, rules whose existence, be it immanent or transcendent to the action, are what constitutes this or that sign as such.

To help clarify this concept family we can turn to a nine-point schema summarizing the writings of Moscovici.

1. Social representations are partly abstract and partly pictorial.
2. They allow people to make joint sense of an unfamiliar world, and thereby fix the limits of the psychological capacities of a group.
3. People use social representations to make sense of the unfamiliar through 'anchoring' and 'objectivication'.
4. Anchoring is relating an object to the prototypical case incorporated in a social representation.
5. Objectivication occurs when an object has been anchored and an image of it 'joins' the prototype.

6. Objectivication determines how a person will see the world.
7. Through social representations past experience influences the present.
8. Reality, for us, is determined by social representations.
9. The social scientist must confine his/her analysis to the consensual not the reified universe.

Allied with the development of a psychology of social representations, Moscovici has pursued an extended interest in crowds. A crowd is a group that has a certain cohesiveness and in which an individual is absorbed or caught up. French psychology has long been interested in the phenomenon of crowds, *'les foules'*. The work of Gabriel Tarde (1843–1904) in the late 19th century is usually taken as the starting point of this interest in modern times. The classic work on crowds until Moscovici's studies was *The Crowd* (1947) by Gustave Le Bon (1841–1931), first published as *Psychologie des Foules* in 1896. Both authors connected the study of crowds with political science and the philosophy of the state.

Moscovici takes his start from a critical commentary on **Sigmund Freud**'s (pp. 270–280) privileging of the psychic dimension in all social analysis, a view he shared with Le Bon and Tarde. In his discussions of social movements, world religions and so on 'he was thinking of the various categories of crowds' (Moscovici, 1981: 230). For Freud, sociology was applied psychology. In common with Le Bon, Freud took the characteristic situation of the person transformed into a member of a crowd to be the loss of 'conscious personality, the guiding of thoughts and emotions into a single direction by means of suggestion and contagion ...' (Moscovici, 1981: 237).

This is all very well but there are some basic questions that this account raises. In particular how can a mass of people have such an effect on individuals, and what is the nature of their transformation? There seems to be a regression in the psychic life of people caught up in crowds. Moscovici's solution is to draw on two general tendencies or groups of desires, which he calls 'eros' and 'mimesis'. The former leads to associations with people one would like to possess, and the latter to associations with people one would like to be. These two concepts can, Moscovici believes, be applied to account for the characteristics of persons in crowds as sketched above. The phenomena of crowd behaviour are the result, so he argues, of conflict between two desires. While the 'erotic' desire is fixed on the leader, as if the relationship was personal, one to one, the mimetic desire soon takes precedence without eliminating the erotic. The members identify themselves as alike because of the veneration each and every one has for the leader. A glance at some of the close-ups of the crowd at Hitler's Nuremberg rallies seems to display just the transition Moscovici proposes as the explanatory process through which an individual becomes a member of a crowd.

The ideas of the French school of social psychology continue to be vigorously pursued by a new generation of psychologists, including those working in Montreal.

Further Reading

Primary Sources

Moscovici, S. (1961) *La psychoanalyse: son image et son publique.* Paris: Presses Universitaires de France.

Moscovici, S. (1981[1985]) *La Psychologie de la foule.* Paris: Presses Universitaires de France.

Secondary Sources

Farr, R. M. & Moscovici, S. (1984) (Eds) *Social representations.* Cambridge: Cambridge University Press.

Jodelet, D. (1991) *Madness and Social Representations.* Los Angeles: University of California Press.

Le Bon, G. (1947) *The Crowd.* London: Benn.

Autobiography

Moscovici, S. (1997) *Cronique des années engagées.* Paris: Presses Universitaires de France.

Reflections

The difference between the two major 20th-century paradigms for a scientific psychology comes out very clearly among the social psychologists that were prominent in the period. For **Solomon Asch** (pp. 199–202), **Muzafer Sherif** (pp. 202–207) and **Stanley Milgram** (pp. 207–211), a person is a mere location, a place where various causal processes occur, some external, some internal. For **Serge Moscovici** (pp. 216–221) and others in the tradition of social representations, a person is actively engaged in bringing various projects to fruition, making use of a body of local knowledge, including standards of correct behaviour. **Michael Argyle**'s (pp. 212–216) work manages a sometimes uneasy compromise between the two seemingly irreconcilable paradigms.

The two sides of **William McDougall**'s (pp. 191–194) psychology are represented here also. Inherited tendencies seem to be the taken-for-granted basis for such studies as the Robbers' Cave, while the 'group mind' thesis is displayed in knowledge of what is the right thing to do and how it should be done, clearly implied by the concept of social representations. **Fritz Heider**'s (pp. 194–199) work seems to straddle the great divide between the causal and the cultural points of view. His emphasis on the effectiveness of ordinary language and commonsense psychology as the means of managing social life would place him with the advocates of new paradigm psychology, a psychology that regards the social universe as a matrix of meanings and the linkages in the matrix to be rules and conventions, many of which have become habits. Sometimes causal concepts are appropriate, as when he discusses the effect something in the environment can have on someone. A loud noise surely *causes* one to jump. But it is very odd to use the same concept to explain why someone is both pleased and embarrassed to be given a prize!

Social psychology has never been wholly free of the legacy of behaviourism. The idea that by creating a laboratory setting for social psychological experiments one could eliminate culture and access primordial patterns of social behaviour was just such a legacy. However, it seems evident that people bring their cultures into the laboratory with them.

PART THREE

From Theory to Reality

9

The Philosophers

Philosophy is the critical study of the conceptual and methodological presuppositions of human practices. As such it plays an integral, intimate and essential role in all the sciences. There are two main ways philosophy enters into psychology. There is philosophical psychology, the critical discussion of the conceptual presuppositions of both vernacular and academic psychology. Then there is the philosophy of psychology, the consideration of the claim that psychology can be a science like other acknowledged sciences. In the 20th century there were a great many thinkers engaged in both enterprises. A few stand out as of special importance for the purposes of this book. I have chosen John Dewey, George Herbert Mead, Edmund Husserl, Ludwig Wittgenstein, Michel Foucault and Daniel Dennett as representative of the philosophical community and its influence on the practice of psychology as a science. There is no doubt that other choices would have been possible.

Those whose lives and work I have picked out to discuss seem to me to be particularly influential on the ways that psychology as the science of thinking, feeling, acting and perceiving changed in the course of the 20th century. The psychology which seems to be emerging in the 21st century inherits more from those I have chosen than any similar group of philosophers, I believe. The rise of cognitive psychology draws our attention to the role of bodies of knowledge in psychological functioning. These include culturally diverse local categories for identifying the fine grain of psychological phenomena within broader species-wide concepts. At the same time the means by which people think, act and perceive, though having their origins both in inherited capacities and skills acquired from the local culture, are being firmly located in the human organism using a judicious mix of computational and neurophysiological models to account for how what we know is implemented in what we think and do.

In the early part of the 20th century **John Dewey** (pp. 226–232) and **George Herbert Mead** (pp. 232–235) had already seen how important aspects of the psychology of individual human beings derived from the social relations into which they were born as members of some human community. Even so intimate a matter as the sense of self could be argued, at least in principle, to have a social origin.

Edmund Husserl (pp. 235–239), the founder of phenomenology, struggled with the problem of the relation between the personal sphere of individual awareness and the common world within which each and every one of us lives. Phenomenological psychology has had a place alongside other developments during the century.

The role of language as the medium of cognition also came to the fore in the 20th century. **Ludwig Wittgenstein** (pp. 240–246) not only thought through the ways that ordinary language picked out a complex psychology of skills and dispositions, but also showed how easy it is to fall into serious misunderstandings of the psychological phenomena of everyday life through misunderstandings of the 'grammar' of important words. The shift in his philosophy from a formalist analysis of scientific discourse to a recognition of a richer and more elaborate form of life, under more complex and shifting norms, has supported some of the revisions to the project of a psychology that are already evident in the 21st century.

The realization of instabilities and historical changes in salient features of human psychology runs strongly counter to a long-standing tradition favouring nomothetic methods and universalist claims, not only for all of humanity as it now is, but for the whole history of *Homo sapiens*. Anthropologists and historians have disputed this tradition. The strength of the opposition to an uncritical psychological universalism has been enhanced by the systematic study of the coming into being during a certain epoch of a few key concepts of psychological relevance. This was the life work of **Michel Foucault** (pp. 246–252).

The latter part of the 20th century saw the link from psychological phenomena conceived as the active management of meanings, to the biology of the human organism, through the intermediary of a formal thinking machine, become the focus of attention, both in psychology and philosophy. Old philosophical problems took on new forms. How could one account for consciousness and the possibility of free action in beings that were to be pictured as information-processing devices, though as organisms they have come into being by natural selection? **Daniel Dennett**'s (pp. 253–260) writings have thrown some light on the new forms that the old issues have taken. He has shown how what we would want to preserve of the traditional concepts, at least as they have been understood in the Western Christian tradition, can be maintained in the light of our deeper understanding of the mechanisms of the human organism.

These writings can serve as exemplars of the work of many others, who have seen it as their task to resist naïve reductionism of the whole of the science of human psychic life to a branch of neurophysiology. At the same time these authors have been among those responsible for moving psychology away from an inadequate conception of what it is to create a science. Though the influence of positivism endured in some ways even after the demise of behaviourism, the current trend is towards some form of scientific realism as the foundation of psychology as a science.

John Dewey (1859–1952)

The life and work of John Dewey would surely merit a place in any catalogue of the major influences on 20th century thought. He had much to say relevant to education, to philosophy, to psychology and to the social sciences generally.

However, one would be hard put to say exactly what it was that people took from Dewey and who it was that took the most. He has been declared to have been the father of *pragmatism*. Yet his account of practices as the root of human life is nowhere as well worked out as the treatments offered by **Lev Vygotsky** (pp. 26–34) or **Ludwig Wittgenstein** (pp. 240–246). His psychological insights are shallow compared with those of his colleague, **George Herbert Mead** (pp. 232–235). However, there is no doubt that his move towards a naturalized philosophy as something like a sketch of a general psychology fitted well with the atmosphere of the time. After idealism, what? Dewey's answer was pragmatism.

Dewey's works run into dozens of volumes. His point of view underwent major and minor changes throughout his life. Not surprisingly, commentaries occupy metres of shelf space. For the purposes of this essay much that is essential to understanding Dewey's contribution to 20th-century thought can be found in the book of the Paul Carus Lectures, which he delivered in 1925. A revised edition of the texts of these lectures was published in 1929. This volume, I believe, encapsulates the 'essential Dewey'. The only major exception to this is the seminal paper of 1896, in which he developed a subtle but critical reinterpretation of the 'reflex arc'.

Who was John Dewey?

He was the third son of Archibald Dewey and Lucinda Rich, born on 20 October in Burlington, Vermont. He attended the local schools, primary and secondary, and went on to the University of Vermont in his home town. Two of his teachers seem to have had a profound and lasting influence on his thinking. He studied evolutionary theory, especially as expounded by T. H. Huxley, with G. H. Perkins. The philosophy courses, taught by H. A. P. Torey, were dominated by 'Scottish common sense', particularly the powerful synthesis created by Thomas Reid. Later in life, Dewey expressed his debt to Torey's open-mindedness and eclectic interests which he willingly shared with young John. Despite these influences, and after a period in which he struggled to reconcile idealism in philosophy with the scientific point of view of man expressed in Darwinism, he abandoned the traditional philosophical schools, to strike out on his own.

Biographical accounts of Dewey's early life do not suggest the kind of crusading zeal that drove enthusiasts such as **B. F. Skinner** (pp. 15–24) and **Lev Vygotsky** from a very early age. One gains the impression that Dewey 'modulated' into philosophy and psychology. He spent two years as a high-school teacher after graduating from the university at Burlington. During that time he began to think of a career as a philosopher. In 1880 he sent a markedly Hegelian paper to the *Journal of Speculative Philosophy*. Its acceptance confirmed him in his growing ambition to make professional philosophy his career.

He decided to begin graduate studies at Johns Hopkins University in Baltimore. There he began to feel the same tension in systems of ideas which had troubled him at Burlington. He was attracted by the idealism of Hegel under the tutelage of G. S. Morris, a Hegelian who emphasized the organic naturalism of German idealism. At the same time he was strongly influenced by the psychologist G. S. Hall, who was engaging at that time in an extensive experimental programme, modelled on the methods of the natural sciences. Without really reconciling these two influences, Dewey took his doctorate in 1894.

His first job was at the University of Minnesota, where he remained for 10 years. During the time in Minneapolis he devoted himself to attempting to create a synthesis between Hegelian idealism and experimental science. He formed a strong working friendship with J. H. Tufts, and when Tufts moved to Chicago, Dewey followed. Here he gradually abandoned his idealism, drawn by a growing interest in a rather vaguely defined pragmatism. Working out the pragmatist point of view led him to become its most prominent exponent and clarifier. The work had a decidedly psychological slant, though it was first published in a collection with 'logic' in the title. This slant led him into a practical project. He set about applying his ideas to the teaching of real children in a real school. To this end he founded a 'laboratory school'. For many who know the name 'Dewey' it is as an educator rather than as a philosopher or psychologist that he is remembered.

University administrations were as crass then as they often are now. Dewey clashed with the bureaucrats at the University of Chicago over the management of the laboratory school. Choosing to lose the nation's most famous philosopher and educator rather than back down on an unwise organizational imperative, they persisted in taking over the school, and in 1904 Dewey left. Not surprisingly, he had a plethora of offers and decided to move to Columbia University, where he spent the remainder of his academic career.

In New York, he became increasingly involved in political issues and movements, such as women's suffrage. Not only did he serve on various commissions but he published a steady stream of political writings in the popular press. He was not averse to controversy and sat on the commission that exposed the political underside of the Moscow show trials of the 1930s. He vigorously defended Bertrand Russell against those who wished to throw him out of City College for the immorality of his teachings on marriage.

He retired in 1930 but continued to work actively until his death at the age of 92, on 2 June 1954.

What did he contribute?

Dewey's own estimate of his contributions in his mature years could be summed up in a phrase: 'the method of empirical naturalism'. Material things comprise both orderly and disorderly attributes. The task of the physical sciences is to discover what it is about such things that they should be 'capable of being used as instrumentalities'. Inner natures are eschewed by physics, he claims, in favour of those features of material beings that make them able to be used as means. Intrinsic natures are revealed to sense experience. They are not hidden beyond the realm of the observable. In just these few sentences in the preface to his 1929 book (p. xvi) he laid down the outlines of 'pragmatism'. However, there is a great deal more to Dewey's thought than these observations. Considered by themselves they could scarcely be distinguished from the positivism that had begun to supercede idealism in Europe at about the same time as Dewey's point of view was being formed in his own flight from idealism. Expelling the unobservable from a scientific picture of the world expels most of physics, chemistry and biology with it.

Dewey took there to be 'one outstanding fact: the evidence that the world of material things includes the uncertain, unpredictable, uncontrollable, and hazardous' (Dewey, 1929: 39). Existence, including human existence, is both precarious and stable. From the former come religion and the superstitions surrounding chance and luck. From the latter come practical instrumentalities, including science. The material world is not only hazardous, but it is rich in orderly and stable attributes. We can use them as the bases of those instrumentalities with which to master the instabilities which continually threaten the outbreak of disorder.

From the point of view of metaphysics we must conceive of the world in terms of events rather than substances. In this respect Dewey allied himself with David Hume and Ernst Mach. They were the architects of a kind of positivism that is based on the analysis of experience into a flux of independent events, some orderly, some disorderly. With this basic metaphysical thesis as the guiding insight, histories become significant. This led him to reflect on the nature of causality, how the orderliness of some streams in the temporal flux of events is to be accounted for.

Looking back on Dewey's writings, some of his insights into the relation between the social world and human cognition suggest a strong formative influence on **George Herbert Mead**'s (pp. 232–235) philosophical psychology. Dewey begins his treatment of instrumentalities with an analysis of the concept of a 'tool'. Though people think of tools in relation to their immediate projects, 'a tool denotes a perception and acknowledgement of sequential bonds in nature' (Dewey, 1929: 103).

The traditional problem of knowledge could be formulated as 'how [can] one order of existence [thought] refer to another [nature] in such a way as to know it' (Dewey, 1929: 113). The problem of knowledge as a product of a relation between thought and nature simply dissolves if, he argues, we abandon a certain premise: 'that science is grasp of reality in its final, self-sufficing form. If the proper object of knowledge has the character appropriate to the subject matter of the useful arts, the problem in question evaporates' (Dewey, 1929: 113). Objects of knowledge are means to determine sequential changes to realize a foreseen consequence. To know something truly is to know the uses to which it can be put.

Dewey placed great emphasis on the fact that the whole of existence displays association and individuation. Individuals are at the same time unique and locked into collectivities. Language is grounded in a natural repertoire of signs and gestures when the signs are used 'for mutual assistance and direction' (Dewey, 1929: 147). For example, a gesture of pointing comes to create a situation of common concern, in which one humanoid being can come to grasp the experience of another. However, developing the idea of symbolic tools with the 'use' metaphor, Dewey remarks that meaning is not primarily a matter of anything personal and private, but an invitation to cooperate. He extends this argument to the thesis that all other agencies and instrumentalities as we know them can only come to be in social groups made possible by language. Language is both social in nature and in its effects. The objectivity of meanings is rooted in natural reactions. Long before **Ludwig Wittgenstein** (pp. 240–246) developed this idea in his later philosophy, we find Dewey offering an explicit formulation of what one might call the ethological roots of human language.

A philosopher might well be uneasy with Dewey's attempt to blend some of the leading ideas of positivism with a profoundly social account of cognition. Machian positivism was based on a committed subjectivity. His 'elements' were units of personal experience. For Dewey, social interactions are not only aetiogically, but also logically prior to individual meanings. For him naturalism in philosophy did not mean a grounding of philosophical theses in sensory experience. It meant grounding them in interpersonal interaction.

Dewey's account of selfhood is as forward looking as his sociologism in philosophy of mind. The explicit first person is used to accept responsibility for an action declaring that 'the self' is its author. 'It signifies that the self as a centered organization of energies identifies itself (in the sense of accepting their consequences) with a belief or sentiment of independent and external origination' (Dewey, 1929: 191). In an elegant aphorism, Dewey remarks that 'Authorship and liability look two different ways, one to the past, the other to the future'. The use of the first person is an 'adoptive act'. It is not to name nor does it refer to an originating power. Yet, 'the constancy and pervasiveness of the operative presence of the self as a determining factor in all situations is the chief reason why we give so little heed to it; it is more intimate and omnipresent in experience than the air we breathe' (Dewey, 1929: 202).

Dewey's pragmatism comes to the fore in his prescient treatment of cognition, though the discussion is centred round a distinction made familiar almost a century ago by Bertrand Russell, namely knowledge by description and knowledge by acquaintance. Knowledge, however elaborate and sophisticated, was in essence an adaptive response to conditions in the environment. However, this was not a passively acquired reflex. It was an active exploration, always, as he insisted, directed towards instrumental consequences. This was a kind of philosophical version of the discoveries by Sherrington and Bekhterev of the universal combination of inward and outwardly directed neural impulses through the nervous system.

Dewey's most famous paper was 'The Reflex Arc Concept in Psychology' of 1896. In this paper he discusses the proper analysis of the process through which a child learns that some attractive things are dangerous. In discussing the child and the candle, Dewey points out that in seeing it is the looking that is primary. 'We begin not with a sensory stimulus, but with a sensori-motor coordination' (Dewey, 1896: 97). 'As long as the seeing is an unbroken act, which is as experienced no more sensation than it is mere motion ... it is in no sense the sensation which stimulates the reaching ... we have only the serial steps in a coordination of *acts'* (Dewey, 1896: 106). Whatever is analysed out of the whole complex as the sensation will depend on the function of a sensation in the whole coordination. In short, psychology should be a study of the active engagement of a person in the world in pursuit of determinate projects, rather than 'dissecting out' independent reflex arcs.

The historian must surely be astounded that Skinner's 'behaviourism' could have been taken seriously 30 years *after* the publication of Dewey's analysis, an analysis that still holds good for psychology in the 21st century.

His analysis of the structure of methods of enquiry has been of equal importance. A human being encounters a situation for which its existing resources are inadequate. The next step is to isolate the features of the problematic situation that are amenable to change. A solution, essentially reworking the problematic situation, is developed in the abstract, and finally applied concretely. If the original situation can be reconstructed to allow activity to proceed, the solution is taken up as 'knowledge'. Cognition is rooted in problem-solving. There are clear echoes of this in **George Kelly**'s (pp. 62–68) psychological metaphor of 'man the scientist'. Dewey called this 'intrumentalism', though it is not the same doctrine for which the word was later used.

Perhaps Dewey is best known among philosophers for his attempt to follow William James in developing a 'pragmatic theory of truth', but deriving it from his own conception of the nature of empirical enquiry (James, 1907). Empiricists had argued that an idea or, we should now say, a proposition, is true if and only if it corresponds with the facts. Dewey argued on the contrary that an idea is true if and only if it can be employed in a successful resolution of a problem that is standing in the way of realizing some human project. This thesis has been caricatured as 'if it works it is true'.

Read as a psychologist, Dewey seems to have anticipated many of the leading ideas of those who forged the second cognitive revolution, to which **Jerome Bruner** (pp. 54–62) was a major contributor. This is particularly evident in Dewey's emphasis on the activity of the human subject, a principle that stands in sharp contrast to much of mainstream psychology, in which the person appears as no more than the site at which cause-effect relations cluster.

Further Reading

Primary Sources

Dewey, J. (1929) *Experience and Nature*. La Salle, IL: Open Court.
Dewey, J. (1896 [1972]) *The Early Works of John Dewey*. Carbondale: Southern Illinois University Press.

Secondary Sources

Ayer, A. J. (1974) *The Origins of Pragmatism*. London: Macmillan.
James, W. (1907) *Pragmatism*. New York: Longmans Green.

Biography

Tiles, J. E. (1988) *Dewey*. London: Routledge.

George Herbert Mead (1863–1931)

The psychologists of ideas, in the tradition of John Locke (1632–1704), not only made it a virtue to study only one person at a time, namely the author himself,[1] but also focused on the individual mind as the arena in which the processes of human understanding took place. The centredness of the 'sphere of consciousness' no less than the agency an individual exercised on him or herself and on the surrounding world led to long and intensive efforts to identify and understand the psychological source of personal identity, the self. The results of these efforts ranged from Descartes' immaterial mind to the mere memory-bound sequential order of conscious states proposed by David Hume. Wilhelm Wundt (1832–1920) had instituted a *volkerpsychologie*, a study of the social nature of mind as a complement to his studies of 'psychophysics', the relations between physical stimuli and sensory experiences. Perhaps Mead drew some inspiration from Wundt's project, given his sojourn in Wundt's laboratory. Whatever might have been his inspiration, he vigorously pursued the investigation of the hypothesis that the individual self is a social product.

Who was G. H. Mead?

George Herbert Mead was born on 27 February 1863, the second child of Hiram and Elizabeth Mead. At that time, Hiram Mead was a Congregationalist Minister at South Hadley Congregational Church in Massachusetts. When George Herbert was seven his father took up a professorship at Oberlin Theological Seminary. After Hiram Mead's death in 1881, his widow taught at Oberlin for a short while, before returning to South Hadley as the President of Mount Holyoke College.

However, in 1879, George Herbert had entered Oberlin College, and remained there to take his BA degree in 1883, displaying strong interests in literature and history. Like **Ludwig Wittgenstein** (pp. 240–246), he tried school teaching with a marked lack of success, and like Wittgenstein he went on to a four-year career in engineering, railroads in his case.

He entered Harvard in 1887, taking his master's degree the following year, specializing in philosophy and psychology. His mentor was the philosopher

Josiah Royce, long neglected but revived again recently. Oddly, considering his later career, young George Mead was a resident tutor to the children of the father of American pragmatism, and arguably the greatest psychologist the United States has ever produced, William James. But Mead did not study with him.

During the latter part of the 19th century there was a fashion for young and ambitious Americans to spend time in Germany, studying with the leading scholars of the era. Attracted to the laboratory of Wilhelm Wundt, Mead began a course of study for the PhD in Berlin. His visit to Germany might have had another reason. While staying with his friend Henry Castle, George became engaged to Mary Castle, who had accompanied her brother to Germany. They were married shortly afterwards in Berlin.

In the event, he did not complete his PhD. He returned to an instructorship at the University of Michigan, Ann Arbor, where he met and became fast friends with **John Dewey** (pp. 226–232). In 1892, Dewey was offered the job of setting up the philosophy department at the new University of Chicago, and insisted that he should bring Mead with him. Dewey eventually moved to Columbia University in New York, leaving Mead to carry on the school of the 'Chicago pragmatists'. He remained there until his death on 26 April 1931.

During this rather uneventful life, Mead continued to write but he published very little. His lectures were attended by many of those who became influential in their own turn, though more as sociologists than psychologists. Mead is remembered as a social psychologist, but this pigeonholing does not do justice to the breadth of his insights into the nature and sources of the human mind.

What did he contribute?

Mead, it must be said, hardly ever finished anything substantial. Apart from a few papers that found their way into print in his lifetime he published nothing that reflected the scale and scope of his views on psychology. The book for which he is famous, *Mind, Self and Society* (Mead, 1934), is a compilation of student notes. Nevertheless, he must rank as one of the most profound thinkers of the 20th century.

G. H. Mead was the very archetype of the philosopher-psychologist. His contributions to psychology were the result of critical reflection on some of the central concepts of the nature and conditions of the mental and emotional lives people actually led. He did no experiments nor did he conduct any studies. He drew analogies from observations of other species, though he was not at all given to biological reductionism. Nevertheless, he argued that 'because ... we have experience that is individual ... private, and ... have a common world [we do not have] two separate levels of existence' (Mead, 1934: 41). 'Psychology is not something that deals with consciousness; psychology deals with the experience of the individual in its relation to the conditions under which the experience goes on' (Mead, 1934: 40). How is this possible? What is the nature of that which is both private and public? It is the 'significant symbol'. Gestures bring about adjustments of one animate being to another, as successive stimulations elicit further responses in an interpersonal 'chain'. In the case of human beings, 'gestures' have expressive meaning but also make it possible for another person to see the gesture as expressing intentions ('ideas'). When this occurs 'we have a significant symbol' (Mead, 1934: 45). The existence of significant symbols makes thinking possible. Moreover, since these symbols had a public and social origin in gestures, they have a common meaning for all the members of a society. Language carries just this content in greater measure.

The central concept of human psychology is surely the 'self' or person, though Mead emphasizes that many exercises of human intelligence do not involve it. Each human being experiences him or herself as a singularity, living through a trajectory in space and time. Yet, at the same time, one's skills, memories, plans, and so on, are forever changing. Even as you read these lines, dear reader, you are changing in all sorts of ways. However, there is a 'you' which does not change, the very being who can, if in a reflective mood, register one's earlier and later states as different, the grounds of the perception of a life in time. What is this complex entity 'the self'? What are its origins? Mead proposes, in a striking anticipation of one of the main principles of discursive psychology, that 'the very process of thinking is ... an inner conversation' (Mead, 1934: 141). Using the example of a game, Mead argues that an individual's sense of self is not just a matter of taking account of the actions and attitudes of the others in the game. 'The organized community ... which gives to the individual his unity of self may be called the "generalized other"' (Mead, 1934: 154). Development of self moves from constitution by reference to other individuals to the 'generalized other', the characteristics of which are included as elements in the structure of the self.

Perhaps Mead's best known distinction is between the 'I' and the 'me'. The 'I' is aware of the social 'me'. This awareness becomes salient in the way that what a person does is not always quite what he or she intended. 'That moment into the future [in which a person takes cognizance of what was a feature of his or her self as "me"] is the step, so to speak, of the ego, of the "I". It is something that is not given in the "me"' (Mead, 1934: 177). The 'I' gives one a sense of freedom, of initiative, of agency. Summing up the analysis Mead declares that 'the self is essentially a social process going on with these two distinguishable phases' (Mead, 1934: 178). In a further refinement of the distinction, Mead makes clear that the 'I' appears retrospectively as memory, in reflecting on and responding to the attitude of the community. Any novel reply to the community constitutes the 'I'. These personal reactions and replies in their turn change the community which called them forth.

Mead's answers to the universal conundrums 'What is meaning?' and 'What is the self' now seem to be very much in tune with contemporary thinking on these matters. His forward-looking views came from attending to the language by means of which the experience of self-hood was expressible both to others and to oneself. It was in and through the acquisition of the necessary linguistic devices in public discourse that the individual sense of self was forged. This, in turn, depended in ways that **Ludwig Wittgenstein** (pp. 240–246) later made much clearer on the natural expressions of the human form of life.

Here is a neat summary of Mead's leading insight:

> The essence of Mead's so-called 'social behaviorism' is his view that mind is an emergent out of the interaction of organic individuals in a social matrix. Mind is not a substance located in some transcendental realm, nor is it merely a series of events that takes place within the human physiological structure. ... Without the peculiar character of the human central nervous system, internalization by the individual of the process of significant communication would not be possible; but without the social process of conversational behaviour, there would be no significant symbols for the self to internalize. (Cronk, 2000: 6)

Further Reading

Primary Source

Mead, G. H. (1934) *Mind, Self and Society*. Chicago: University of Chicago Press.

Secondary Source

Sheffler, I. (1974) *Four Pragmatists*. London: Routledge and Kegan Paul.

Biography

Cronk, G. (2000) George Herbert Mead. *Internet Encyclopedia of Philosophy*.

Edmund Husserl (1859–1938)

Phenomenology is a school of psychology which came into prominence in the first quarter of the 20th century. Its origins are philosophical. The project of phenomenology, the close study of conscious experience, was inaugurated by Edmund Husserl. The methodology he developed was quite unlike the experimental techniques we have been following in the main sections of this book. Among his followers were Alfred Schutz (1962) and Maurice Merleau-Ponty (1962). His best known student was Martin Heidegger (1957). While the psychologists of perception tried to understand the processes by which human beings perceived the world to which their senses gave them access, the phenomenologists attempted to analyse our personal experience of that world to bring to light how it came to be an experience of a common world.

Who was Edmund Husserl?

He was born on 8 April 1859 in Prossnitz, in Moravia, then a province in the Austro-Hungarian Empire. The family was very well off. His father had a successful clothing business. The fact that both Jews and Germans were in a minority in the predominantly Slavic town of Prossnitz and, furthermore, together made up the prosperous middle class of the town, threw the two communities together. The family was Jewish, but at that time many well-off Jews were converting to Christianity, and Edmund himself eventually converted. Breaking from the traditional educational path of provincial Jews, he did not attend the local Jewish high school. When he was 10, he was sent away to Vienna to the Realgymnasium. For some reason he left after only one year, returning to the provinces, to the Staatsgymnasium in Olmütz.

After completing his high school studies in 1876, he went to Leipzig to study mathematics and the physical sciences. The Austrian educational system, like that of Germany, encouraged students to adopt a rather peripatetic lifestyle. Husserl left Leipzig after two years to continue his studies in Berlin, finally taking his doctorate in Vienna in 1883. After another short spell in Berlin he returned to Vienna to attend the lectures of Franz Brentano (1838–1917).

By 1886 he was in Halle, working on his Habilitation, the necessary step to a career in academia. Successful completion of the work, a study of the concept of number, meant he was able to join the faculty at Halle, where he remained until 1901. During this period he was baptized, following the trend among the Austrian Jewish community at that time. He married a hometown girl, Malvine Steinschneider, who followed him into the Christian church. Their three children were born in Halle. There he worked on the foundations of mathematics and logic.

He moved to Göttingen in 1901, and began to develop the phenomenology for which he is now mostly remembered, and from which his influence on the development of psychology in the 20th century came. Over the next decade, he began publishing his phenomenological studies. The family had become to all intents and purposes German, and this led to a tragedy that affected him very deeply. His son, fighting in the German Army on the Western front, was killed during the savage fighting around the French fortress town of Verdun. Shortly afterwards Husserl moved again, this time to Freiburg where he remained for the rest of his academic career, retiring in 1928.

Though he was active in his phenomenological researches throughout his career, and continued to produce substantial manuscripts, these remained unpublished until after his death from pleurisy on 27 April 1938. His last years were dimmed by the advent of the Nazis and their anti-Semitic programme, though Husserl himself lived and died as a German Christian.

What did he contribute?

After a brief but promising career as a mathematician, including serving as assistant to the great Karl Weierstrass (1815–97) in Berlin, Husserl turned to philosophy as a student in Vienna with Franz Brentano. According to Brentano, all human experience was characterized by *intentionality*. The study of the domain of conscious awareness was the basic field for a scientific psychology. According to Brentano (1874: 15), 'Every mental phenomenon is characterized by what the scholastics in the Middle Ages called the intentional (and also mental) inexistence of an object, and what we could also, although in not entirely unambiguous terms, call the reference to a content, a direction upon an object.' Thoughts, perceptions and so on have this direction whether or not there really exists such an object as that to which the experience points.

Husserl seems to have accepted the general outlines of Brentano's point of view while at the same time being dissatisfied with his teacher's account of the relation between mental act and intentional object. Consciousness is directed. It is *as if of* an object whatever the status of that object might be. Surely the task of the philosopher/psychologist is to get to the bottom of what that 'as if of' relation might be.

Immanuel Kant (1724–1804) had emphasized the role of concepts in the genesis of perceived objects, shaping an inchoate flux of sensation into a determinate perception. Husserl too realized that somehow the mind brings it about that there are objects but without creating them. How can we explore what it is that is implicit in the structure of conscious experience that this should be possible? Sometimes it seems as if Husserl is necessarily locked within his own subjectivity, as he turns his attention exclusively to his own experience. Yet, he insists that he is not denying that a real world exists common to everyone, and that it is partially revealed by the human senses. His project is only to identify the marks in our experience that express that basic presupposition.

Persons in their fullness as conscious beings, each with a unique point of view on the common world, are as much givens as are material things. He bypasses the traditional problem of 'other minds' by insisting that his project is only to extract and make 'visible' the defining characteristics of our experience *as if of* people and things. However, given his insistence on the root character of the domain of personal conscious experience, it is not easy to see how Husserl could consistently take such a stand. Acknowledging the natural attitude to experience as if of an independent world leads to a conception of the *life world*, the world that human beings as centres of consciousness actually inhabit.

Husserl works with three basic concepts: *noema*, *noesis* and *hyle*. The directedness of acts of consciousness towards objects is a cluster of structural properties of experience. He calls this cluster the *noema*. Noematic structures are generic, and take specific form in particular thoughts and perceptions as *noesis*. Since noesis is particular, it is a process in time, while the noema is timeless. Husserl makes a point of emphasizing the possibility that many different noemata are compatible with any particular flux of sensations.

Noemata can be thought of as clusters of anticipations of further experience. Suppose a hundred years ago someone saw the moon as a sphere. The noema would have included the anticipated experience by a future astronaut of the curvature of its hidden side. When I speak to someone I know my taking my friend to be a person involves all sorts of anticipations of expression and action, including that of being a conscious being like me. The generality of noemata makes their projection as anticipations possible.

The third element in the scheme is *hyle*, derived from the Greek word for 'matter'. Not every logically possible noema is compatible with the conditions of experience. The flux of sensations is limited by the sort of stuff which a person is encountering. Water cannot be shaped into dinner plates, unless we freeze it.

Here then are the three 'elements' that are involved in the fullness of all experience *as if of* the world and its inhabitants, whatever their nature. However, we still lack a method by which these 'constituents' of mental acts could be brought to light. In our everyday lives we just carry on in the 'life world' performing our ordinary tasks, and never pausing to ask ourselves about the noemata that make our experiences *as if of* vegetables, guests and furniture.

Research into the constitution of experience consists in performing two kinds of *reductions*. An *eidetic* reduction is achieved as we turn our attention to the generic characteristics or essences of whatever it is the experience points to. The *transcendental* reduction or *epoché* is accomplished by turning our attention to the noemata, noeses, and hyle that are the structures of a certain act of consciousness. We 'bracket' what we have hitherto taken for granted, that there is a person in the other armchair. Setting aside that taken-for-granted aspect of experience *as if of* brings the relevant structures of consciousness to light. The method as a whole consists in the phenomenological reduction in which the transcendental and eidetic reductions are applied successively.

The last chapter of Husserl's *Cartesian Meditations* (1960) extends the analysis of experience to the moment in which I am enabled to see the Other as one for whom I am the Other. In this way there comes to be a life world for both of us, a common life world on which all sentient beings have a perspective. It might seem as if phenomenology 'lapses into transcendental solipsism' [there is no other world but mine] – however 'in my own experience, I experience not only myself but others.' '... the concretely apprehended transcendental ego [myself] grasps himself in his own primordial being, and likewise grasps the Others ... other transcendental egos ... appresentatively mirrored [and] ... appresented analogically (pp. 148–9).' In the first phase of entering into a common world one grasps the Other as a thing. The second phase follows in which by some sort of analogy or sympathetic understanding that thing becomes a You. It seems to me that this argument still leaves much to be desired as a route from my own sphere of consciousness to those of others.

Though he expressed himself in a notoriously obscure way, Martin Heidegger (1889–1976) realized that the knowledge of someone else's existence is given to us before our realization of our own individual existence. We are cast into a world in which language is always already there. So, 'Dasein [there-being] is essentially

Being-with' (Heidegger, 1957: 120). The Other, he says, is 'already with us in Being-in-the-world' (Heidegger, 1957: 116). Heidegger's treatment of the seeming problem of phenomenology, how one person's sphere of consciousness can encompass that of another person, is very similar to the main thrust of **Lev Vygotsky**'s (pp. 26–34) development psychology, and to **Ludwig Wittgenstein**'s (pp. 240–246) insights into the human form of life.

Husserl himself achieved his greatest success with this research method in studying the role of time in consciousness (Husserl, 1987). There is a back and forth between fulfilled and unfilled expectations and retrospective and prospective aspects of my conscious experience of any current state of affairs. In this lies the phenomenology of the temporality of experience.

Phenomenology has been very much more influential on the continent of Europe than in the English-speaking world. It has played a major role in the development of the idea of the social construction of reality (Berger & Luckmann, 1966). It was brought to North America by Alfred Schutz (1962) in his influential studies of the phenomenology of the taken-for-granted character of the social world. Though phenomenology is rarely found in the curricula of departments of psychology, there is a vigorous tradition of phenomenological research.

Further Reading

Primary Sources

Husserl, E. (1960) *Cartesian Meditations* (trans. D. Cairns). The Hague: Martinus Nijhoff.
Husserl, E. (1964) *The Idea of Phenomenology* (trans. W. P. Alston & G. Nakhmikian). The Hague: Nijhoff.
Husserl, E. (1987) *The Phenomenology of Internal Time Consciousness.* Ann Arbor, MI: UMI.

Secondary Sources

Berger, P. L. & Luckmann, T. (1966) *The Social Construction of Reality.* London: Penguin Books.
Brentano, F. (1874 [1973]) *Psychology from an Empirical Standpoint* (trans. A. C. Rancurrello, D. B. Terrell & L. L. McAlister). London: Routledge and Kegan Paul.
Heidegger, M. (1957) *Being and Time* (trans. W. McNeill). Oxford: Blackwell.
Merleau-Ponty, M. (1962) *The Phenomenology of Perception* (trans. C. Smith). London: Routledge and Kegan Paul.
Schutz, A. (1962) *The Phenomenology of the Social World* (trans. G. Walsh & F. Lehnert). Evanston, IL: Northwestern University Press.

Biography

Bell, D. (1990) *Husserl: The Arguments of the Philosophers.* London: Routledge.

Ludwig Wittgenstein (1889–1951)

Philosophy as conceptual analysis and psychology as the study of cognition are intimately interrelated in two ways. Cognition is mediated by concepts, and psychology as the study of cognition is concept driven, like any other science. Furthermore, the concepts we use in psychology are rooted in those with which we manage our everyday lives. For the most part these concepts are realized in language and other everyday symbolic systems. By the beginning of the 20th century both philosophers and psychologists were turning more and more to a realization of the key role that language plays at both levels: life as it is lived, and psychology as it is practised.

The turn of the century saw the rise of logicism in philosophy, pioneered in part by Bertrand Russell (1872–1970). Logicism is the idea that the underlying structure of all correct thinking must be found in logic, the formal science of correct reasoning. Not only did Russell believe that logic reflected the most general structure of the world, but he went on to try to derive mathematics from logic. The philosophers of the Vienna Circle, with their logical positivism, a philosophy of science that restricted scientific discourse to the concepts of direct experience and the machinery of logic, were tremendously influential on the development of psychology in the 20th century, through the support this ideal of science seemed to give to behaviourism.

Disenchanted with a philosophy based on the formal science of logic, though he had been one of its staunchest advocates, Wittgenstein began a long struggle to get clear about the nature of language and its influence on our thought and practice. At the same time, he forged an arsenal of weapons to overcome the illusions and mistakes that misunderstandings of our language lead us into. The work that ensued has profound implications for psychology, and has been a prime influence on the development of discursive psychology, cultural psychology and other realizations of the second cognitive revolution.

Who was Ludwig Wittgenstein?

He was born in Vienna on 26 April 1889, into a cultivated and wealthy family, the youngest of a family of eight. His father, Karl, was a leading industrialist and engineer, and one of the richest men in Austria. Though some of Karl's forebears were Jewish, Karl himself was a Protestant and Leopoldine, Ludwig's mother, was Catholic. Young Ludwig was brought up as a Catholic, and retained a strong attachment to Christianity as a way of life. He did not go to school until he was 14, studying at home with various tutors. He attended the Realschule at Linz from 1903 until 1906. By a curious chance, he was a classmate of a certain Adolf Hitler.

The family was exceptionally cultivated. The intellectual and musical elite of Vienna, then in its heyday as a centre of European civilization, were often visitors to the Wittgenstein 'palace'. Music was a particular interest of the Wittgensteins, and young Ludwig became a proficient clarinetist. His brother, who lost an arm in the First World War, was the Paul Wittgenstein for whom Ravel wrote the Sonata for the Left Hand.

After finishing his secondary education Ludwig, at the behest of his father, attended the Technical Hochschule in Berlin, studying the science and mathematics needed to equip himself as an engineer. In 1909, he enrolled in Manchester University to further his engineering training. He began research into the design of aircraft propellers. However, by 1911 he had begun to interest himself in the foundations of mathematics. He was advised to consult Bertrand Russell at Cambridge, if he wanted to pursue this interest further.

For the next two years he continued an intense and often emotional conversation with Russell. In the course of this passionate engagement he came to realize that Russell's views on logic were deeply unsatisfactory. In 1913, he made the first of his escapes from academic life to the isolation of a Norwegian fjord. In the same year, he inherited a fortune from his father, but he steadily rid himself of his wealth with gifts to his family and the needy. By the 1920s he began to suffer the chronic and self-induced poverty that he endured for the rest of his life.

At the outbreak of the First World War in 1914, he volunteered for the Austro-Hungarian Army, serving with distinction on the Eastern Front. By this time, his quest for an ethical and religious way of life had taken the dominant place in his thoughts that it was to hold for the rest of his life. He exulted in the exposure to danger in battle, as a test of his character. At the same time throughout the war he continued to write on logic, completing his first important book, the *Tractatus Logico-Philosophicus* (1921), while a prisoner of war in Italy.

He thought that the perfect language worked out in that book would bring all philosophy to an end. What mattered in life, personal relationships, religion, art and music could not be adequately expressed in language, if it was expressible at all. All that was left for him was a life of service.

After a teaching training course, he took up posts in various small villages, such as Trattenbach, but he kept in close touch with his family. His teaching career ended with complaints from parents about the ferocious discipline he maintained in the classroom. By 1926, he despaired of reaching the moral ideals of integrity and virtue that he had set himself, and returned to Vienna, to work as a technical assistant to an architect.

However, during this time he had been visited by Frank Ramsay, a Cambridge mathematics student, who later was instrumental in Wittgenstein's realization that his philosophy-as-logic approach was deeply mistaken. Finally, in 1929, he returned to Cambridge, submitting his now famous *Tractatus* as his doctoral dissertation. Shortly after his return, he formed a close attachment to Francis Skinner.

Over the next four or five years in lectures and discussions he began to forge a new approach to philosophy, the main thrust of which was his realization that the medium of cognition is not the formal algebra of logic, concealed within the word forms we use, but the language itself. It is both the instrument for living a human life, and at the same time full of pitfalls and temptations to error. During this time he wrote a great deal, building his new point of view, though these works were published only after his death. **Alan Turing** (pp. 82–86) was among those who attended his lectures and were destined for later fame.

In the 1930s, he made several attempts to flee from Cambridge. He tried to emigrate to the Soviet Union as a gardener and made long visits to the 'hut' he had had built in Norway.

When the Second World War began, he took up work as a hospital porter. Later he joined a research unit studying 'wound shock'. After the war, he returned to Cambridge, but he continued to find academic life oppressive. He left his professorship to take up life in remote places – the coast of Wales, the far west of Ireland and his retreat in Norway. During his last years, he formed a strong attachment to Ben Richards, a man much younger than himself. This relationship continued until he died.

In 1950, his continuing ill health was diagnosed as prostate cancer. He spent his last year mostly in the home of Elizabeth Anscombe, one of his former students. Finally he moved into the house of his doctor, Edward Bevan, where he died on 29 April 1951, still writing almost as vigorously as ever.

What did he contribute?

At first glance Wittgenstein's best known contributions seem very different from one another. In the *Tractatus* he sets out the most formal account of descriptive (scientific) language one could imagine. Meanings are reduced to the objects signified by words-as-names. The rules of the logic of true and false propositions are the only organizational principles allowed for the ordering of descriptive language to record all possible states of affairs in the material world. Complex propositions expressing all possible patterns of true or false descriptions are formed by the use of truth-functional connectives. These are formal versions of our familiar propositional connectives such as 'and', 'or' and so on. In the perfect language of the *Tractatus* they are defined by rules for computing the truth or falsity of the whole of a complex sentence given the true/false pattern of its component 'atomic propositions'.

In his disagreement with Russell, the status of the rules of logic was the prime issue. Russell had taken them to be super-empirical principles, necessarily true, and expressing the general character of the universe at large. For Wittgenstein they were rules for the construction of meaningful sentences. Violations of these rules result not in falsehood but in meaninglessness.

The idea of the main instrument of thought as language and of language as a computational system was not wholly Wittgenstein's invention. However, the popularity of the *Tractatus* had a lot to do with its influence. It is not hard to see a link, at least in spirit, between the logical grammar of the perfect Wittgensteinian language and the computational principles that lay behind **Alan Turing**'s (pp. 82–86) suggestion for a computational interpretation of cognition.

The main principles of the *Tractatus* view of language bear an uncanny resemblance to the Universal Symbol System hypothesis of **Allan Newell** and **Herbert Simon** (pp. 86–93), though it is unlikely either had read the *Tractatus*. For Wittgenstein sentences are arrays of objects. Some groups of words are true sentences because they can be matched one to one with objects in another array, the objects that realize a state of affairs in the material world. Logic consists of the rules for truth-preserving manipulations of the symbol patterns that realize the sentences of the perfect language. A set of rules for manipulating names seems very like a programme for manipulating symbols.

Some conclusions of moment follow from Wittgenstein's line in the *Tractatus*. Neither moral and religious attitudes and beliefs nor aesthetic experiences can be described in the 'perfect language' of the *Tractatus*. They can only be shown in how one conducts one's life.

The doctrine of showing also covers the relation between words and the objects they signify. That relation cannot be described either. If I to try explain a meaning by saying something like '"Dog" means dog', I have not reached out beyond language. Of course, I can begin to show what the word 'dog' means by pointing to a dog, though there will always remain some degree of ambiguity in the meaning thus created.

In the 1930s, the core of Wittgenstein's philosophy underwent a major revision. One could sum up Wittgenstein's later philosophy as the working out of the insight that we must enlarge the scope of norms beyond those controlling the stating of facts, and we must enlarge the concept of meaning beyond that of the relation of simple names to simple objects.

In his later philosophy, language comes to be seen as an instrument for living, including thinking, remembering, anticipating, giving orders, making pleas, praying and innumerable other human activities. Wittgenstein uses the metaphor of language as a tool kit to emphasize the practical work that we do with symbols. 'Grammars', normative principles of all sorts, displace the austere rules of logic. The standards of 'correct thought' become a multiple and ever-changing cluster of norms, sensitive to all sorts of contextual and historical considerations. Bringing out our meanings and extracting the loose systems of local and transitory rules with which we manage them gives us the best means for understanding human life. The main lines of this approach are laid out in the *Philosophical Investigations* (Wittgenstein, 1953: §§1–50).

However, when we abstract language from its actual uses in practical life, we readily fall into misinterpretations of key words, mistaking their grammatical character, and drawing all sorts of erroneous conclusions in consequence. Philosophers and psychologists, stepping back from life to subject it to scrutiny, are particularly prone to being caught in linguistic traps. Philosophy, properly employed, beginning with the study of words in use, that is in the everyday practices that Wittgenstein called 'language games', can be a therapy for conceptual confusion by reminding us how words are actually used.

One of the prime sources of conceptual confusions, according to Wittgenstein, is the assumption that because the same word is used in a variety of language games, contexts and situations, it must have a common underlying or essential meaning. Throughout his later writings he brings out case after case of confusions of thought arising from taking one of the many ways a word is used as the paradigm case, and generalizing it to all other uses. Thus, the word 'rule' is sometimes used for an instruction for how to proceed, and one consciously attends to the rule as if it were a command. In other uses the word 'rule' is used to draw attention to the mandatory character of a convention or custom, such as the grammar of one's mother tongue. Falling into the trap of linguistic essentialism, people are tempted to propose an unobservable, that is implicit or unconscious, process of mental rule following to explain the orderliness of customary acts. Cognitive psychologists are particularly prone to making this mistake. The uses of a word usually involve a field of family resemblances rather than a common linguistic essence. For example, if we look closely at how the word 'expect' is used we can see that while expecting is sometimes a state of mind, the word is also used to refer to a variety of other aspects of waiting for something. It would be a serious mistake to settle on just one of these uses and try to explicate all the others in its terms, particularly by inventing a 'hidden' version of the alleged common meaning. Insights like this have an obvious and immediate application to the setting up of research projects in cognitive psychology. In a particularly important analysis of the use of such words as 'hoping' or 'wishing for', Wittgenstein (1953: §437–444) shows how complex are the uses of these expressions. 'Hoping' can be a mental state tied to a local interpretation. That someone is hoping for something can be wholly a matter of a display of appropriate behaviour, such as setting out the tea cups while thinking of something else.

Wittgenstein exploits the metaphor of 'rule' to express the explicit formulation of the implicit standards of correctness that are displayed in the practices of a culture. This has another implication of importance for psychology. In explanations of the orderliness of streams of psychological phenomena such as decisions and actions, insults and apologies, bereavements and grieving, citation of norms should displace hypotheses of causes. For example, in trying to understand the relation between thought and action, in closely examining the role of intentions in human life, we see that the expression of an intention commits one to trying to perform a certain kind of action. It is not a prediction as to what one is about to do. Nor is it a cause of what one will do at some future time.

A major insight of great importance to neuropsychology is that subjective reports are a source of scientifically legitimate data (Pribram, 1971: 100). This principle links brain activity to subjective experience. It has been the basis of the work of **Wilder Penfield** (pp. 113–118), and many other neuropsychologists. However, it stands in need of justification. Wittgenstein's emphasis on a distinction between expressive and descriptive uses of language greatly clarifies the matter. If we were to try to account for the way that people can understand one another's talk about personal and subjective feelings as if it were descriptive, we would run straight into a paradox. Surely a word used to describe something must be learned by attending to a public exemplar of the thing signified. However, how could a word like 'pain', referring as it does to a private experience, be learned if its meaning had to be determined by pointing to an example? The only public items in the situation where such a word is used appropriately are groans and writhings, that is pain behaviour, not pain. However, to say 'I am in pain' does not mean 'I am groaning or writhing'.

A description is 'detachable' from that which it describes, since it can be true or false. An expression, however, is internally related to the subjectivity it expresses. If someone did not have a tendency to groan, the subjective experience would not be pain. A child learns the words for expressing subjective experiences by substituting verbal for natural expressions of such feelings. The words have the same 'grammar' as the cries and groans, laughter and tears of the natural expressions. That this use of language should be possible depends on the presumption of a common human ethology, a repertoire of natural expressions, a presumption which Wittgenstein was at pains to emphasize. However, this presumption licenses neither behaviourism nor reductive psychobiology. Psychology rests upon but does not reduce to the common human form of life.

The minds of other people are open to me, in that the conditions under which the relevant language games are acquired are public and social, while the topic of conversation, which the existence of such linguistic devices makes possible, is private and personal. Wittgenstein's use of the argument is directed, at least overtly, against a certain thesis in philosophy of language, that the meanings of words are fixed by attending to private experiences. In demonstrating the incoherence of this idea, he opened up a rich vein of analyses of the uses of mentalistic language, which gives strong support to the methodologies of **Wilder Penfield**, **Karl Pribram** (pp. 118–125) and a host of other neuropsychologists. This chapter in Wittgenstein's writings (1953: §243–317) has come to be called, somewhat misleadingly, the 'private language argument'. His intent was to show there could be no such thing as a private language, a language in which the meanings of the words was settled by inward pointing to private feelings.

Wittgenstein was as critical of the Cartesian hypothesis of an immaterial mind as the seat of thoughts and feelings as he was of the corresponding materialist thesis of reducing psychology to a study of the states of the brain. Neither could serve as *the* touchstone of psychological reality. In one of his most detailed analyses of the conceptual structure of a complex concept, he showed how the use of the concept of 'reading' is necessarily independent of subjective states of readers and of hypotheses about the neurological processes by which a person accomplishes this feat (Wittgenstein, 1953: §§156–172).

The discussion looks first at the conditions under which we would be prepared to say that some one could read a text aloud. These turn out to be matters of the display of skill in various conditions. In this way, we distinguish those who have learned a text off by heart and recite it as if they were reading, from those who have mastered the skill. Wittgenstein points out that the subjective accompaniments of adequate and inadequate performances could be just the same.

Could an examination of the state of the brains of readers and non-readers be substituted for the practical test of skillful performance? This will not do either. The distinction between being able to read and not being able to read must have been drawn by teachers long before any technology for examining brain processes was available. Furthermore, which brain processes are relevant could be known only from investigating what was going on neurologically in those who could read and those who had not yet mastered the skill. The concept 'able to read' could not be given an exclusively neurological interpretation.

The discussion is rounded off by a detailed study of the ways that written or printed marks could be said to guide someone's speaking. There are many uses of the word 'guide', including exerting a physical force on someone, paying conscious attention to a paradigm of what is required, to following some cue without paying any attention at all. Reading can involve any or all of these.

Looking back from the vantage point of the 21st century we can see how far Wittgenstein was ahead of much of the psychology of his time. He offers a powerful method of identifying psychological phenomena, and a prophylactic against the diseases that the intellect is particularly prone to when the concepts in some domain are extremely complex and subtle. Nevertheless, many of Wittgenstein's insights were anticipated by **Lev Vygotsky** (pp. 26–34) and paralleled by **Fritz Heider** (pp. 194–199) and **George Kelly** (pp. 62–68).

Further Reading

Primary Texts

Wittgenstein, L. (1921) [1961]) *Tractatus Logico-Philosophicus* (trans. D. R. Pears & B. F. McGuiness). London: Routledge and Kegan Paul.
Wittgenstein, L. (1953) *Philosophical Investigations* (trans. G. E. M. Anscombe). Oxford: Blackwell.

Secondary Texts

Harré, R. & Tissaw, M. A. (2005) *Wittgenstein and Psychology*. Aldershot: Ashgate.
Pribram, K. H. (1971) *Languages of the Brain*. Englewood Cliffs, NJ: Prentice-Hall.
Schulte, J. (1992) *Wittgenstein: An Introduction*. Albany: SUNY Press.

Biography

Monk, R. (1990) *The Duty of Genius*. London and New York: Penguin Books.

Michel Foucault (1926–84)

One finds very few explicit references to the writings of Foucault in the books and papers written by members of psychology departments in universities. However, these places are isolated islands in the great sea of 'psychology' in which our culture is embedded. If we look more broadly at ways of conceiving of human beings and explaining their conduct we find plenty of signs of the influence of Foucault. To put his main thesis simply, the main characteristics of human beings are the products of discursive practices. These are not fixed and universal, but in certain very important ways have changed since classical antiquity. Such central person-categories as criminality, madness and sexuality have been produced by changing discourses, ways of talking and writing about people, that have become means for the subtle exercise of power in the social order.

Foucault's method was empirical, that is he studied the records of the specific and concrete practices relevant to the constitution of these three central person cat-egories. For example, he showed how the practices of surveillance, which defined the change in the place of criminality in social life, were made possible by the architecture of the newly established penitentiaries of the 19th-century system of criminal justice.

Foucault's early writings are dense with historical allusions and develop complex analytical distinctions. His last work, *The History of Sexuality* (1976–84), presents a powerful case for rethinking contemporary ways of managing sexual categories in a more straightforward and lucid way.

Who was Michel Foucault?

Like many of those who have featured in this cluster of life stories, Michel Foucault came of a medical family. He was born on 15 June 1926. His father was a surgeon. Like the fathers of several of our characters, he would have liked his son to follow him into medicine. Michel's early education was at the St Stanilas School in Poitiers, but he was soon enrolled as a boarder in the Ecole Henri IV in Paris, the pre-eminent school in France. It was almost a foregone conclusion that he should go on in 1946 to the Ecole Normal Superieur, perhaps the premier uni-versity in France. There he came under the influence of the phenomenologist Maurice Merleau-Ponty. He graduated successively in philosophy in 1948, in psychology in 1950 and was awarded the diploma in psychopathology in 1952.

Unusually for a Frenchman of that background he spent the next three years teaching in other European countries, notably Sweden, Poland and Germany. During this time he was evidently very busy on his first major historico-philosophico-psychological treatise, *Madness and Civilization* (1961). In this book he brought into being a new kind of intellectual practice, the melding of historical and philosophi-cal analyses to throw light on a fundamental aspect of human psychology.

Foucault's life was shaped in important ways by his homosexuality. In 1960, on his return to France as head of the philosophy department at the University of Clermont-Ferrard, he met Daniel Defert. In 1966 Defert was sent to Tunisia for his two years of military service. In order to be near him Foucault took a teaching post there during the years 1966–8. Defert was active in politics and this seemed to have influenced Foucault's attitude to political matters. He was drawn into the stirring events of the 1968 student rebellion in France. He took an active part in setting up an institution for prisoners to make their voices heard outside the prison walls. Perhaps this was one of the influences that turned his attention to the nature of imprisonment.

In 1966 he had published a study of the development of the social and natural sciences in the 18th and 19th centuries well known in English translation as *The Order of Things*. The book was very successful and gave Foucault a nation-wide reputation. In France, the role of 'le philosophe' can be much more significant than it ever could be in the English-speaking world. In 1968 he was appointed head of the philosophy department of the University Paris VIII at Vincennes.

In 1969 his *Archaeology of Knowledge* appeared, setting out the principles of the historico-philosophico-psychological research programme that he had created and was later to develop in important ways.

In France the ultimate academic accolade is membership of the Collège de France. Foucault was elected to this august institution in 1970, to further his studies of the history of systems of thought. For the next five years he worked on his most influential book, *Discipline and Punish,* a study of the changing ways that the criminal justice system makes use of the bodies of those who are convicted of crimes. This work transformed our conception of the role of the prison and the nature of criminality.

The rest of his life was devoted to his massive study of sexuality, left unfinished at his death. Three volumes were published, however, before he died on 25 June 1984 of a cerebral tumour. His fame was such that it is said that 50,000 people turned out for his funeral.

What did he contribute?

Foucault's voluminous studies have displayed the way that what counts as bodies of knowledge and how human life is conceived in terms of them are historically unstable. Even such a seemingly universal concept, what it is to be a 'person', is subject to change when considered in relation to the institutions and the linguistic, legal and political practices of an age. The exercise of power is made possible and at the same time constrained by bodies of knowledge. So important did he take the role of knowledge in the exercise of power to be that he coined the compound noun 'power/knowledge' to express the intimate interweaving of the one with the other.

Foucault defined his project as a 'critical history of thought'. Thought is an act that posits a subject and an object along with their possible relations. Critical history will reveal the way something is a subject, a being having a certain body of knowledge, and, in complementary fashion, the way something is an object, about which there might be a body of knowledge. These are the modes of subjectivication and objectivication. It is a question of the forms according to which 'discourses are capable' of being declared true or false. Psychology and other humanist studies come into being if the subject posits himself as an object of knowledge. How does the subject appear as an object of knowledge – as a madman, a patient and so on?

How is one to carry out such a project? Foucault advises the abandonment of anthropological universals, and instead the close study of actual practices. This should reveal what is real to people who are constituted as knowing in a certain way. This requires attention to power relations, in so far as the person is constituted as 'object'. Indeed the uses of knowledge are exercises of power.

Foucault's first major study, *The Order of Things* (1966), begins with an analysis of the ubiquitous role of similarity relations in the thought of the 16th century. To understand the way Foucault thinks of the bodies of knowledge constituted by the use of a leading idea like 'similarity', we need to attend not only to knowledge in the sense of a body of propositions, what can be true or false (*savoir*), but also knowledge in the sense of knowing, being acquainted with (*conaissance*). Moreover, to get a grip on what people in the Renaissance 'knew', we must attend not only to the world as they saw it, shot through with similarities, but we must try to understand what sort of people there were who could see the world in this way. The knower and the known are mutually constituted. History does not reveal a common humanity with changing repertoires of what is taken to be knowledge, but a transformation of both poles of the knowledge relation.

In the development of the three major scientific bodies of knowledge or epistemes of the 18th century, biology, economics and linguistics, Foucault discerns a move to make 'man' the topic. Humanity appears as something independent of the rest of what might be known. He sees this as the beginning of the anthropomorphism of our current take on things. As it came, so it can go – the point of his famous claim that soon we will witness the 'death of man'. The fascination with humanity as an independent topic may simply fade away. This seems to be happening already in the attempts to biologize psychology.

Throughout his early book Foucault offers insights that have come to be almost commonplaces in the late 20th century. For example in his discussion of Classical discourse he finds the principle that meaning is naming shaping both philosophy as analysis and science as the laying out of a 'grid of a well-made language across the whole field of representations' (Foucault, 1966: 58). This suggests the possibility of a post-Classicism in which these ideas are abandoned or transformed. Foucault sees the doctrine of representation, something standing for something independent of it, as the root of Classicism, and the decline of this doctrine as the significant transition to the present era. To put it crudely, the insight that inspires the whole of his later work is that what is represented is, in important ways, a function of the means of representation. At the same time the people who have adopted a certain means of representation take on a specific character themselves. Science has no special claim to stand outside the pattern of power/knowledge. 'Thought' is whatever appears in every manner of acting and reflecting in which a human being acts as a knowing subject.

Foucault has a place in this book because he shows how the same principles govern the acquisition of bodies of knowledge about people, when our gaze turns on to ourselves. Just as the Renaissance categories of plants reflected the doctrine of signatures, so various ways of categorizing people reflect the doctrines of their times. Foucault applied the principle to his three major case studies, criminality, madness and sexuality. As we shall see, his topic is the human body as it appears in relation to the various ways of categorizing people within the three broad types. This goes along with the proviso that even at this abstract level of generality, the same objectivity-subjectivity pattern is discernible. Abstraction is remedied by studying the forms of experience from an analysis of practices, such as, for example, punishment for crimes, ways of dealing with madness and one's relation to oneself as a sexual being.

Foucault summed up the results of his investigations of madness in a lecture of 1970. There are four main areas of life from which people can be excluded: work, reproduction, speaking and the 'ludic', that is games and ceremonials. Each of these areas has its norms. So each has a penumbra of persons who, failing to adhere to the norms, are excluded. Whether in primitive tribes or in industrial civilization mad people are excluded from some or all of these areas. The idea that madmen ceased from being treated as criminals and took on the status of sufferers from illnesses at the end of the 18th century is, so Foucault asserts, overly simplistic. Instead there was a change in the excluding agency, from the family to the physicians. Of the four areas singled out as relevant to madness, violating the norms of sexuality was itself a way of identifying madness. The writings of madmen were sometimes excluded and sometimes admitted as contributions to literature during the 18th and 19th centuries. This again reflected the nature of the excluding agencies.

Before the industrialization of Europe all sorts of people were confined in institutions, excluded from ordinary life. During the 19th century many of the excluded were released to swell the labour force, but not the mad. They became patients. However great this change might have been, the status of the mad as the excluded remained unchanged. No one *discovered* that madness was an illness. The change was a recategorization succeeding other recategorizations, and no doubt to be succeeded by yet others. In each of these epochs we can see different ways of exercising power over the excluded.

In the project that engaged Foucault in his last years, a history of sexuality, he was concerned, he declares, not so much with domains of knowledge and systems of rules relevant to sexuality, nor with our sexual nature as a locus of experience, but with its value as a model for relations of the self to the self. His method is again historical. His plan was to trace the development of *discourses* of sex from the Renaissance. The first volume of the project, *The Will to Truth,* appeared in 1978.

Foucault's main argument is directed against the 'repression' hypothesis. He attacks the idea that in the industrialization of Europe sexuality was repressed in the interests of the capitalist way of life. On the contrary, he argues, this development took the form of an enhancement and realignment of the Christian practice of confession. Once a matter of a yearly self-scrutiny, confession not only became, at least in principle, a weekly occurrence, but the practice of self-scrutiny became a defining practice of modern life. As Foucault remarks (1978: 59): 'The confession has spread its effects far and wide. It plays a part in justice, medicine, education, family and love relationships. In the most ordinary affairs of everyday life, and in the most solemn rites; one confesses one's crimes, one's sins, one's thoughts and desires, one's illnesses and troubles.'

Thus, the will to truth, exemplified in the practice of confession, became the locus of a constraining power, but one of which we are unaware. The practice of confession in its various times and places has come to be taken for granted. 'The sexual misery of modernity', sex in the world of the bourgeoisie, so Foucault argues, is not the result of repression, but of positive mechanisms for the production of a certain mode of sexuality. Sex is 'put into discourse' (*mis en discours*). As he made clear in an interview, it is a complex of discourses and practices, supported by types of knowledge, which are the means of the productive power/knowledge nexus.

All this works to produce a certain experience of sex, the recognition of oneself as a sexual being, the characteristics of which are up for continuous scrutiny within a certain repertoire of discursive practices. The salience of sex as the prime product of the power/knowledge nexus comes about, he argues, because it is the central concern of 'self-techniques'. By that he means the use of culturally presented rules for sexual behaviour that make possible self-scrutiny.

As a historian he queried the taken-for-granted thesis that sexual austerity was a Christian invention. It had plenty of advocates in the ancient world, for example in the Roman conception of the family. However, he points out the class relativism in that period of the idea of sexual purity. Christianity not only codified sexual ethics but also universalized it across all classes of society. The nub of the matter is control, exercised via the practices of *self*-restraint. Here we have a perfect exemplar of the capillarity of power.

In the last four centuries there has been a shift from conceiving sexual matters within a framework of an art of pleasure towards a *scientia sexualis*, a 'complex machinery for producing true discourses of sex' (Foucault, 1978: 68). Sex as a fit topic for 'science' developed out of the shift in the confessional practices with respect to the legitimated recipient. Confessing one's misbehaviour to a priest activates a very different set of practices from confessing one's fantasies to Dr Freud, or one's erectile dysfunction to one's physician.

Commentators are united in their criticisms of the quality of Foucault's historical researches. What then could possibly recommend his claims about the historical formations of the concepts of crime and punishment, madness and its treatments, and sexuality to us, as they are incorporated in actual practices? However sloppy his history might have been he has brought us to realize how local are the particular forms that some leading psychologically significant concepts take. His work shows how large a role the constitutive power of historically-situated discourses have taken in shaping such important categories of human beings as men and women, mad and sane and criminal and innocent.

However, his way of conceiving of power changed. It modulated from the coercive and repressive exercise of influence of some people over others, the concept that appears in his studies of madness and the prison and the role of the body in punishment, to power as creative force, that which brings something into being. Power can do something other than repress. The crucial point is his emphasis on the minute processes of power, for which he coined the metaphor 'capillarity'. They seep through the social matrix carried by the discursive practices that provide what is the truth of a certain era. Societies are disciplinary, rich in practices through which, rather than by which, our lives are 'normalized'. The implication that society is by its very nature a complex of constitutive practices has been used against the plausibility of Foucault's doctrine (Merquior, 1985: 111–18). However, the idea of a person as embedded within an inescapable net of social practices, rather than being ordered about by some authority, does seem particularly apropos of the world as we know it now.

The upshot of Foucault's studies, whatever may be said about their academic quality, has been a reinforcement of the post-modernist claim that there is no such thing as a fixed and permanent human nature, the same at all times and places. Human nature has not been just superficially modified by culture and history. This insight has profound implications for the project of psychology. Psychological research *cannot* be revealing universal laws of cognitive functioning and social categorizing. If Foucault is right there can be no such a-historical project. If there is no universal human nature there can be no laws of it. We might say that psychologists mistake a local ethnography for a universal science.

Further Reading

Primary Texts

Foucault, M. (1966 [1970]) *The Order of Things.* London: Tavistock.
Foucault, M. (1969 [1972]) *The Archaeology of Knowledge.* London: Tavistock.
Foucault, M. (1975 [1977]) *Discipline and Punish.* London: Allen Lane.
Foucault, M. (1978) *The Will to Truth* (Vol. 1 of *The History of Sexuality*) (trans. R. Hurley). New York: Random House.

Secondary Texts[2]

Merquior, J. G. (1985) *Foucault.* London: Fontana/Collins.

Biographies

O'Farrell, C. (1989) *Foucault: Historian or Philosopher?* London: Macmillan.
Russell, P. (2002) (Ed.) Michel Foucault. In *The Gay 100*. London: Kensington Press.

Daniel Clement Dennett (1942–)

Philosophy and psychology are closely interwoven. There is an intimate relationship between conceptual and empirical studies of human life. The strongest part of contemporary psychology, the discursive analysis of actual psychological processes and phenomena, and the construction of computational models of the processes that underlie them, as a waystation on the route to an understanding of the brain as the tool of cognition, do not neglect philosophical insights. This in part accounts for the strength of these late 20th-century developments. Furthermore, analytical philosophy, particularly as practised by the Oxford school of the mid 20th century, is already a kind of cognitive psychology, tracking the way that words are used in performing cognitive tasks.

While it would be a fair bet to hazard a guess that the writings of Daniel Dennett have not been read by most mainstream academic psychologists, it is quite certain that they are read and appreciated and indeed influential at the cutting edge, particularly in the foundations of research programmes into how cognition and brain activity are to be understood within some comprehensive point of view. The desideratum being, of course, that neither neuroscience nor cognitive/discursive psychology colonizes and enslaves the other.

Choosing a representative from the many respected authors who have worked in the intermediate region between psychology and philosophy is not easy. Some 'philosophers of mind' rule themselves out by their neglect of psychology as an academic practice. Others, bemused by the misleading aura of clarity and 'rigour' that abstract logical and mathematical formulations seem to have, are ruled out by reason of the implausibility of their formal analyses of cognition. While Daniel Dennett has not had the personal influence of such heroic figures as **Lev Vygtosky** (pp. 26–34) and **Jerome Bruner** (pp. 54–62), nevertheless he has expressed with great clarity, consistency and verve a point of view that has proved increasingly influential.

Who is Daniel Dennett?

Daniel Clement Dennett, the third to bear the name, was born on 28 March 1942 in Beirut in the Lebanon. His mother and father were both the children of doctors, and both had chosen the humanities rather than follow their parents into medicine. After graduating with a master's degree in English from the University of Minnesota, his mother took up a post at the American Community School in Beirut, Lebanon. There she met Daniel C. Dennett, Jr., who was using the opportunity given by teaching in Lebanon to work on his Harvard PhD in Islamic history. During the Second World War the second Dan Dennett served as a secret agent for the OSS stationed in Beirut. He was killed in an aircraft crash in Ethiopia in 1947. With his mother and two sisters, the third generation Daniel Clement Dennett returned from Beirut to Winchester, New Hampshire, where, as he remarks (Dennett, 2005: 1), 'I grew up in the shadow of everybody's memories of a quite legendary father. I was blessed with the bracing presumption that I would excel, and few serious benchmarks against which to test it.'

His time at Winchester High School was enlivened by some excellent teachers, inspiring him with an interest in that profession. For his last two years at high school he moved to Phillips Exeter Academy, where he encountered an intense atmosphere of interest in things intellectual and literary.

Dennett entered Wesleyan University, and by a stroke of fortune enrolled in a mathematics course that actually focused on logic. This led him to read W. V. Quine's *From a Logical Point of View* (1953), and, in 1960, to transfer to Harvard where Quine (1908–2000) taught. Taking a course in philosophy of language brought him into contact with a gifted group of students.

His senior thesis topic involved a thorough critical study of Quine's views on language. In 1962, while still at Harvard, he married Susan Bell. Despite achieving some success in these surroundings where logicism was the favoured style, Dennett was drawn to the analytical approach to the philosophy of mind. He enrolled as a graduate student in Oxford to carry that interest further under the supervision of Gilbert Ryle, whose *Concept of Mind* (1949) he had read with appreciation.

He began his studies in Oxford in 1963, to work on the philosophy of mind. Even then he set himself the task of working out how a brain could be the source and support of mind. Already he had begun to think in terms of the distinction between what happens at the personal and at the subpersonal level. Perhaps a structure of insentient parts might be sentient. All this led him to transfer to the doctoral programme, not then much in favour in Oxford. His dissertation, involving a good deal of neuroscience, was accepted for the degree in 1965.

He took up an Assistant Professorship at the University of California at Irvine, where he found himself teaching the entire undergraduate philosophy curriculum aside from ethics. At Irvine he had the chance to carry further his interest in the relation between neuroscience and human cognition, as well as become acquainted with the new and contested field of artificial intelligence. At this time he first introduced the terminology of the 'intentional stance' as one of the ways one might address a complex entity, the behaviour of which was not explicable in simple causal terms. Another of his insightful metaphors from that period was the 'intuition pump', referring to a sequence of thought experiments with which to support an argument.

In 1971 he took up a post at Tufts University. Here he was able to pursue his interests despite the absence of a graduate school by the setting up of a Center for Cognitive Studies. He has remained at Tufts until the present day, apart from a year at the Center at Palo Alto, and a term in Oxford, delivering the John Locke Lectures on the topic of human agency, later published as *Elbow Room* (1984).

What has he contributed?

Dennett's project has been to steer a course between the traditional Cartesian conception of a science of mind and its updated variants and attempts to delete psychology from the sciences. He has resisted the claim that it has been made redundant by the development of neuroscience. The former requires that there must be an immaterial substance as the support of non-material attributes and processes. The latter makes the persistence in human life of all those practices that presume that there are cognitive processes that are not definable in the concepts of the physical sciences incredible.

He has been remarkably consistent in the line he has taken over these matters. The account of the nature of the psychological attributes of human beings that he presents in *Brainstorms* (1978) will serve as the basis for my exposition of his point of view in general.

To see how far one might want to go with Dennett's line and where one would perforce be likely to halt, his own account could hardly be a better starting point:

> If one insisted on giving a name to this theory, it could be called *type intentionalism*: every mental event is some functional, physical event or other, and the types [of these events] are captured not by any reductionist language but by a regimentation of the very terms we *ordinarily* use – we explain *what beliefs are* by systematizing the notion of a believing-system for instance. (Dennett, 1978: xix)

However, he rightly warns against taking type-intentionalism for granted for all the concepts deployed in ordinary languages. These concepts ought to be examined case by case. For example he argues that '*beliefs* and *pains* [are] not good theoretical *things*', as if this is what ordinary folks took them to be. However, as **Ludwig Wittgenstein** (pp. 240–246) demonstrated and Gilbert Ryle (1949) took further, for the most part such interpretations are foisted on common sense by philosophers, misled by the superficial grammar of these expressions. Of course, it is not always so. This shows how careful one must be in sorting out the limits of type-intentionalist taxonomies for use in psychology.

In his autobiography Dennett notes the degree to which his doctoral dissertation, the ancestor of his mature point of view, had been subtly influenced by the ideas of Gilbert Ryle, which in turn owed a great deal to **Ludwig Wittgenstein**'s sensitivity to the possibility of being misled by the overt grammatical category of some important and useful word. For example, 'belief' is surely a noun, but it is a mistake to interpret the referents of 'beliefs' as mental entities. So when Dennett tells us he means to eschew ordinary language as the technical vocabulary of psychology we must be careful to note that what he must have had in mind was one of the many philosophers' standard misinterpretations, errors which people going about their daily business do not make. Our first hypothesis in interpreting Dennett will be to suppose that the rejection of 'ordinary language' categories of psychological 'items' is an invitation to reject philosophers' mistaken interpretations and perhaps to work with 'Rylean' understandings, that is with how these expressions are actually used. This would make Dennett a precursor, perhaps even an anticipator, of the discursive or 'hybrid' approach to psychology that seems to be emerging in the 21st century. He declares that his project 'is about how to talk about the mind' (Dennett, 1978: 1). In effect, his proposal turns out to be a way of talking about mental activities, which does not presuppose any Cartesian supports in immaterial mind stuff.

His most important and lasting contribution to psychology is surely the high-lighting of three 'stances' one might take to some complex device with which one was interacting, and the activities of which one wanted to predict. Such a being might be a computer programmed to play chess. It might be a chimpanzee or it might be a human being. We can take the *intentional stance*, that is act as if the being acts for reasons. We can take the *design stance,* that is presume that it has a characteristic structure which makes its actions possible. We can take the *physical stance*, that is we can suppose it is a material entity made of material parts, interacting according to the causal laws of the natural sciences.

To adopt the 'intentional stance' is to treat 'the object whose behavior you want to predict as a rational agent with beliefs and desires ... exhibiting what Franz Brentano called intentionality' (Dennett, 1978: 15). 'Intentionality' is the non-material property we ascribe to something which 'points beyond itself', as a sign-post might point towards a distant lake, or an instruction towards the physical action required to perform a task. By coming to a conclusion about what an agent ought to do in the circumstances we can predict what an agent will do, if it is rational.

Dennett strips down adopting the intentional stance to the ascription of beliefs and desires to the being in question, presuming that the creature employs a meas-ure of rationality in employing them. Having done this we have a 'theory' or, if you like, a psychology. The concept of an intentional system is recommended as a 'source of order and organization in philosophical analyses of "mental" concepts' (Dennett, 1978: 16). Much can be learned about people by taking them to be inten-tional systems. It is in the move from taking an intentional stance to taking a design stance that Dennett locates the royal road towards a theory of cognition. Adopting the design stance towards something involves acting on the assumption that the object was designed to behave in a certain way. Knowing the design of a mecha-nism one can predict, leaving out concerns about breakdowns and so on, that the mechanism will do what it was designed to do.

In taking the physical stance to some object one tries to discover its material con-stitution. This allows one to use the laws of physics and chemistry to predict how the mechanism, highlighted by taking the design stance, will behave in this or that circumstance. The multiple and irreducible stances idea has been a guiding principle throughout Dennett's career.

Dennett's second major contribution to the philosophy of psychology is his attempt to given an account of consciousness. This is apparently the most obvious feature of the lives of human beings and yet the most puzzling for one who hopes to ground psychology in the organic nature of conscious beings. It seems anyone can distinguish between being unconscious of what he or she is doing (say 'sleep-walking'), doing something while one is awake without paying attention (say 'acting from habit') and doing something, paying attention to what one is doing and bearing in mind the goal at which one is aiming. One might offer the third of these cases as a paradigm for what it is like to be conscious.

Dennett's views have developed through the years, and take mature form in his *Consciousness Explained* (1991). To appreciate the strengths and limitations of his 'consciousness project' one needs to bear in mind the generally received view that the existence of conscious experience poses two problems:

1. Why should *this* kind of attribute, namely conscious awareness, emerge from this kind of neurological structure which sustains these kinds of processes, given that they have nothing in common? Conscious human experience seems to be unified, continuous and to display an 'I-structure', organized from a central origin. Cell structures and electrochemical processes do not exhibit any of these features.
2. What is the character of the material structures and processes from which consciousness emerges?

The second question can be answered without an answer having been found for the first. Some philosophers have thought that the first question has no answer. Dennett develops a speculative answer to the second question, through a cluster of metaphors that displace the Cartesian metaphors of mental substance as a way of talking about the domain of experience. There is no such domain. Dennett's proposal for a shift in the taken for granted underpinnings of the project of reaching a psychological understanding of consciousness is radical, and on that account difficult to grasp. The main insight is something like this:

Told to observe my consciousness, I find that I pay attention to trees, falling leaves, and other things outside my body, and twinges, throbs and so on inside my body, the orientation of my limbs in relation to the environment, and so on. After I have done all this you say, 'That's all very well, but you have left out the consciousness of all these things.' But having attended to all of them there is nothing left over that would be 'the consciousness of these feelings, things, events and so on'. There is nothing else to attend to but the various things I am aware of. In Dennett's own words, 'discrimination [of features] does not lead to a representation of the already discriminated feature for the benefit of the audience of the Cartesian Theater – for there is no Cartesian Theater' (Dennett, 1991: 113).

There *is* a genuine 'problem of consciousness' in that Dennett's account leaves two questions to be tackled: How well can I describe the way the various phenomena of perception and introspection fit together, in some sort of unity, with a pencil-like structure that seems to have its 'origin' in my bodily location in space and time? The second component involves finding out what is happening in my brain and nervous system as I see, hear, feel and sense all these things as a continuous and unified domain. This is not a domain of 'experiences', whatever they might be. It is a domain of things, events, itches and so on with which I am currently acquainted (*connaitre*). There are no experiences as such. The experience of a tree *is* seeing a tree or touching it, and so on. 'Consciousness', as such, has gone from the scene!

Rightly, Dennett argues that any answer to the second question must be global, and that there is no one place in the brain where non-conscious states are turned into conscious experiences, contrary to **Wilder Penfield**'s (pp. 113–118) claims about the role of the cerebellum in neuropsychology.

Following on from these insights Dennett developed a series of metaphors that reflect the move in computational models to parallel distributive processing, that is connectionism. (See the section on **Marvin Minsky** (pp. 93–98).) The brain as a computational device is processing all kinds of information at different rates and in different locations, producing, as Dennett calls them, 'multiple incomplete narrative drafts'. Somehow these are continually synthesized into a coherent but unstable narrative equilibrium.

There is no 'I' spot in the brain, so the sense of self must be a feature of this narrative equilibrium. In an earlier work Dennett (1978: 154) describes his project as 'to construct a full-fledged "I" out of subpersonal parts by exploiting subpersonal notions of access ...'. The three main modes of access are personal, computational (one subpersonal part has access to the output of another sub personal part), and public – the output of what is happening to the system. The key move is to shift to the design stance, and to sketch a device the design of which could implement the three forms of access.

There must be a 'public relations' box, the input to which consists of 'orders to perform speech-acts' and the output of which is just such speech-acts, providing public access to at least some states of the device. A system implementing this design must sustain a virtual machine of 'memes', in which the information patterns are processes. 'Meme' is the term introduced by Dawkins (1989) for the bearers of culture as genes are the bearers of human biology. Personal narratives, the stuff of consciousness in Dennett's scheme, involve memes, the cultural/historical forms of thought on which **Lev Vygotsky** (pp. 26–34) based his developmental psychology.

Dennett's argument in favour of this design as a solution to the psychological problem of consciousness is to take a number of features of consciousness and show how they could be realized in the structure and functioning of a brain. Given that some non-human realization of the design could perform like a person but have no inner life, what are we to conclude about the claim that persons are so designed? Dennett declares that 'immediate awareness' is not of thought processes, but of the outcome of thought processes. So we need only computational and public access to account for being aware of ourselves.

The argument shows the *possibility* of consciousness in a material thing structured in a certain way. Taking the design stance reveals how having that structure makes it a being fit to be conscious, that is to be aware of all sorts of goings on in its environment and in its own 'body'. Thus the materiality of the device does not preclude its having human cognitive powers. These come from the uniqueness of the structure and the processes it sustains. However, as critics have pointed out, it is clear that Dennett has not solved the first question. His argument is meant to show that there is no answer because the question is nothing but a muddle. Perhaps the brute fact that people and other animals have common kinds of experiences defines our place in the universe (McGinn, 1997).

It is easy to see how taking the design stance leads inexorably to Darwin. How did this structure, this 'design', which has been reproduced through thousands of generations, come about? Darwin showed how it could have arisen by material processes alone. The crown of Dennett's life work would have to be an account of Darwinian evolution as the origin of beings to which one could take the intentional stance (Dennett, 1995).

It is all very well to demonstrate how a structure of subpersonal units could sustain consciousness, but there is another key facet of human life as yet unaccounted for. Dennett's third major contribution to the philosophy of psychology is his attempt to give an account of acting freely, of choosing what one is to going to do, and doing it, the main topic of his John Locke Lectures. Once again he employs a familiar strategy to show how our everyday practices of deliberating make sense in a world in which the very deliberators are deterministic beings. The key distinction is between taking account of and sidelining those matters that are not 'up to me' and attending to those that are: '... any deliberator [must have an image of the world which] will include a partitioning of things into some that are to emerge as the results of the deliberator's deliberations – things that are thus "up to" the deliberator – and things, predictable or not, fixed or not, that are not up to the deliberator' (Dennett, 1984: 113). It is the 'possibility-for-all-one-knows' that provides the 'elbow room' required for deliberation.

Nevertheless, it seems that this account trades on the 'reality of some opportunities'. A real opportunity, declares Dennett, is an occasion in which a deliberator faces a situation 'in which the outcome of its subsequent "deliberation" will be a decisive factor' (Dennett, 1984: 118). The 'possibility of alternatives' plays a role in the deliberations that ultimately lead to action. It is the person who does the deliberating, and this gives sense to the crucial idea that whatever happens is 'up to him/her'. All this stands in contrast to the scientific account of the material world, which enters into deliberations in the distinction between 'what will happen unless we take certain steps' and 'what will happen because we take certain steps'. 'We cannot help acting under the idea of freedom ... We may be able to assess the rationality ... behind our way of deliberating ... by asking what constraints there are on the design of a finite, physical deliberator. ... we will assume determinism to be true, and see if anywhere we have to deny it to make sense of our enterprise' (Dennett, 1984: 108).

The final step in this argument is to examine the concept of an 'opportunity'. Here again we have the trademark Dennett move, to give an account of 'real opportunity' that gibes with the design stance of a physical deliberator. Thus he says: 'So a real opportunity is an occasion where a self-controller "faces" ... a situation in which the outcome of its subsequent "deliberation" will be a ... decisive factor. In such a situation more than one alternative is "possible" so far as the agent is concerned. ... the critical nexus passes through its deliberation' (Dennett, 1984: 118).

In the end why should we esteem free will with its moral and epistemological baggage? It is, says Dennett, rational to do so. He ties this back on to his larger scheme of cognition in a world of mechanisms. It is because this is the kind of design that we enjoy, as the beneficiaries of aeons of Darwinian selection.

Dennett shifts the point of attack in philosophy of psychology from futile attempts to reduce properties and attributes from one ontological status to another or to resist such reductions, to a discussion of the structures that must be realized for cognition and intentional action to be possible. This is a powerful and liberating move. The complement of this way of tackling the philosophy of psychological science must surely be an emergentist view of mental states and processes. The upshot of Dennett's programme, going back 20 years, is the preservation of the person-based concepts of the intentional stance, while allowing for the treatment of the human organism within the biological sciences.

If there is a weakness of Dennett's ample account it is in his tendency to locate cognition in and only in individual human beings. To fill out the Dennett programme with the kind of scope that a comprehensive theory would require, his cluster of 'theories' would need to find a place for **George Herbert Mead**'s (pp. 232–235) social emergence of the self, the essential shaping feature of consciousness in the course of symbolic interactions with others. It would also need to find a place for the insights of **Lev Vygotsky** (pp. 26–34) and others, that the primary location of cognition is in conversational interactions. None of these moves would be antithetical to the spirit of Dennett's philosophical project.

Further Reading

Primary Sources

Dennett, D. C. (1978) *Brainstorms*. Cambridge, MA: MIT Press.
Dennett, D. C. (1984) *Elbow Room*. Cambridge, MA: MIT Press.
Dennett, D. C. (1991) *Consciousness Explained*. Boston: Little, Brown.
Dennett, D. C. (1995) *Darwin's Dangerous Idea*. London: Allen Lane.

Secondary Sources

Brockman, J. (1995) *The Third Culture*. New York: Simon and Schuster.
Dawkins, R. (1989) *The Selfish Gene*. Oxford: Oxford University Press.
McGinn, C. (1997) *The Character of Mind*. Oxford: Oxford University Press.

Autobiography

Dennet, D. C. (2005) 'Autobiographical Essay', *Philosophy Now* (forthcoming).

Reflections

The writings of the philosophers I have chosen reflect the main lines of development of psychology in the 20th century as well as exemplifying trends in philosophy itself. **John Dewey**'s (pp. 226–232) 'pragmatism', with its explicit rejection of the technique of introducing unobservable states and processes into psychology, is clearly tied to behaviourism. Support too came from the philosophers of the Vienna Circle, though indirectly. J. B. Watson's elimination of all but directly and publicly observable phenomena from the domain of psychology seemed to have a sound philosophical foundation.

However, the interplay between the public/social domain and the personal/private domain of experience was strikingly illuminated by **George Herbert Mead**'s (pp. 232–235) way of linking selfhood, the most important characteristic of the conscious experiences of individuals, with the social processes in which they become persons. The opposite direction of research, from the characteristics of intrapersonal experience to the marks of the life world that exists for all sentient beings, was the leading thrust of **Edmund Husserl**'s (pp. 235–239) phenomenology. Only in the later work of **Ludwig Wittgenstein** (pp. 240–246) do we get an overview of all the ways that language and other symbolic systems are constitutive of the human form of life. Wittgenstein's insights not only support the psychology of **Lev Vygotsky** (pp. 26–34), but also legitimize the techniques of research upon which **Wilder Penfield**'s (pp. 113–118) discoveries in neuroscience were based. We can understand what someone tells us about his or her state of mind because the meaning of language of self-reports is expressive rather than descriptive in origin.

Taken together, the writings of Mead and Wittgenstein lead directly to a vision of the core of human life as symbolic, and psychology as the study of the ways people manage their lives with the use of symbols. Even if they do not establish the point to everyone's satisfaction, **Michel Foucault**'s (pp. 246–252) historical studies suggest that the symbolic, knowledge-defining practices of an era have had a historical point of origin, and may, in their turn, be displaced by something else.

The late 20th century saw the introduction of a model of cognition that has yet to be fully explored, the computational idea. In discussing the rise of scientific realism as the dominant philosophy of science in the second half of the 20th century, we noted the many layered conception of reality upon which it is based. Observable phenomena stand in need of explanation. However, the structures and processes which serve this role are for the most part theoretical. The natural sciences have flourished by virtue of the creation of formal representations of hidden generative processes, such as the familiar equations of chemistry, from which hypotheses about what really brings about the relevant phenomena can be developed and sometimes tested directly by giving these abstract symbols concrete interpretations. Dennett has shown what needs to go into a comprehensive conceptual system capable of comprehending the full scope of a similar programme in psychology. The ingredients are ready to hand. By making a critical use of the concepts with which people actually manage their lives we can develop an account of human life at the level of observable phenomena. Computational modeling, particularly in connectionist style, provides the necessary level of formal representations of the underlying cognitive processes from which observable thought and action proceed. Judicious interpretations of such models lead to questions about the workings of brain and nervous system to which neuroscience has already begun to find answers. All this can be made into a coherent and orderly research programme by the adoption of Dennett's conception of the three stances one can take to any of the complex and interesting beings one comes across, be it in the rainforest or the marketplace.

Notes

1 So far as I know there were no women authors among the 'empiricists'.
2 While not as much written about as Wittgenstein, nevertheless there are a large number of commentaries on Foucault's writings, taking very different stances to wherein lies their importance.

10

The Psychopathologists

Every society that we know of has had some conception of the normal range of bodily forms, of proper ways of behaving and of the limits of acceptable thoughts and feelings. Correspondingly there have been criteria for recognizing abnormalities, and procedures and practices of dealing with people on the margins. However, the range of acceptable ways of being has varied widely. So too have the explanations for deviant behaviour and strange thought ways. Madness has always been recognized, but who is to be counted as mad and for what reason has differed at different times and in different places. During the 19th century there were great changes in the ways of dealing with deviance. There were the beginnings of a scientific approach that paralleled the way physical medicine had developed on scientific lines. Psychopathology as the study of mental aberrations and strange conduct required a grounding in developments in psychology, just as the management of bodily diseases began to depend on the scientific study of the human organism and the assaults upon it.

By the beginning of the 20th century a broad distinction was drawn between psychoses, serious and perhaps incurable mental abnormalities, and neuroses, abnormalities in thought and behaviour of a less serious but still misery-inducing kind. The medical profession undertook to cure at least some neuroses. Psychoses were generally dealt with by isolating the person in an institution, saving them from themselves and of course saving other people from them.

As a branch of science, psychopathology required a system for classifying the phenomena and a powerful set of explanatory concepts, reaching into the underlying and often unobservable causes of mental troubles. Emil Kraepelin provided the former and Sigmund Freud believed he had provided the latter.

Emil Wilhelm Magnus Georg Kraepelin (1856–1926)

It was not until around 1900 that Emil Kraepelin's efforts at classifying mental diseases on a radically new basis became sufficiently established in his own mind to begin to exert an influence on psychiatry in general. The translations of certain sections of his *Psychiatry* began to appear in 1919. To my surprise I discovered that they have become rare books, much in need of reprinting. However, his system for classifying mental disorders has become the basis of our contemporary ways of identifying different kinds of mental troubles. Though his terminology has been modified, nevertheless our current vocabulary of mental disorders is derived directly from his.

Who was Emil Kraepelin?

He was born on 15 February 1856 in Neustrelitz, near Mecklenburg in Germany. It has proved very difficult to find out the details of his family background and his schooling and childhood, though the particulars of his life from his student days are readily available.

Kraepelin began the study of medicine in Würzburg. As was the custom in those days he also studied for some time at Leipzig. There he met Wilhelm Wundt (1852–1920). While Kraepelin was still a student, Wundt encouraged him to undertake experiments in psychology. He decided to become a psychiatrist. Even before graduation he won a prize for an essay on the treatment of mental disorders. In 1877 he was appointed assistant to Franz von Rinecker, a leading specialist in the treatment of mental problems.

Kraepelin graduated from Würzburg in 1878 and took up an assistantship to Johann von Gudden in Munich. During his four years there he undertook a number of experimental projects, involving the effects of various external influences on the onset of mental illnesses. His studies included the effects of alcohol, of fatigue and of infectious diseases. He was already beginning to think in terms of the causes of mental disturbances rather than their content. This became the key idea behind his later efforts to develop a rational classification of mental illnesses. In attempting to separate endogenous from exogenous factors in the onset of mental disease, he was already using the techniques of experimentation that had been pioneered by Wundt and which he had learned from him.

These experimental studies were also a defining moment in his attitude towards the apparently harmless indulgences of ordinary people, in particular alcohol and tobacco. He became almost fanatical in his opposition to them. When he had charge of his own clinic in Munich, towards the end of his career, he expelled both alcohol and tobacco from the premises. People were offered 'Kraepellinsekt', his own brand of lemonade! He published his study of the effect of infectious diseases on the development of mental illnesses in 1881. Shortly afterwards he moved to Leipzig to a clinic headed by Paul Flechsig. Part of the attraction of the job was the presence of Wundt and his laboratory in that city. Kraepelin not only worked in the clinic but also began further experimental work in Wundt's laboratory. There were undoubtedly some tensions between Wundt and Flechsig. No man can serve two masters, and Kraepelin was dismissed from the clinic. He soon found another post with Wilhelm Erb in the Policlinic, where he could continue his double life as clinician and experimentalist.

The ordinary doctorate is not sufficient in Germany to ensure a permanent position in a university. That requires the passing of the 'habilitation', usually through the presentation of a major work for a higher doctorate. Obtaining his 'habilitation' in 1883, Kraepelin was admitted as a Dozent, a university teacher, and a career as a professor was now open to him.

The story of Kraepelin's marriage is curious. He became engaged at the age of 15 to Ina Schwabe, a woman five years older than himself. They eventually married in 1885. The union was blessed, as we say, with four daughters. He had moved back to Munich in 1883, to work again with Gudden. However, he remained close to Wilhelm Wundt, who, it seems, warned him against trying to make a career in psychology. The return to Munich was short lived and he soon took up a senior position in an asylum near Breslau in Silesia. By this time, he had begun to publish some of his ideas about the classification of mental disturbances in a *Compendium der Psychiatrie*. Once again he moved, first to Dresden and then to Estonia, to the University of Dorpat, now Tartu.[1] After several years in Tartu, he returned to Heidelberg, where he began a long collaboration with Alois Alzheimer.

In 1904 he moved again, this time to Munich, taking Alzheimer with him. There he became the director of Deutsche Forshungsanstalt für Psychiatrie, where he remained until his retirement in 1922. Here he was able to implement his life-long plan to link scientific research into the causes of psychiatric conditions with their diagnosis and treatment.

He died on 7 October 1926.

What did he contribute?

The underpinnings of any science must include a system or systems of classification with which the subject matter of the science is ordered into kinds and species. We can hardly imagine zoology or botany without the Linnaean taxonomy, or chemistry without the periodic table of the elements and the standard system for referring to inorganic and organic compounds. The taxonomies of the provinces of the mind have been many and various, strongly influenced by vernaculars, the everyday language of cultures, both literate and non-literate. They have also been influenced by myths, strange forms of explanation, religious concepts and practices, and many other non-scientific factors.

One of the most pervasive classification systems depended on the content of the thoughts and convictions of the people concerned. This was particularly prominent in the various ways for classifying unusual or mad behaviour, thoughts and feelings. For example it was thought important to distinguish religious insanity from more secular delusions. It was to the reform and reconstitution of taxonomies of madness that Kraepelin devoted his life. Many of his distinctions are with us today, sometimes having received new names. Even when one of his categories has been abandoned, the way he conceived of building a taxonomy of mental disorders has survived.

To gauge his importance we must glance at some of the ways madness was categorized in earlier centuries, at least in the Western world. The most famous textbook of psychiatry prior to the modern era is surely Robert Burton's *Anatomy of Melancholy* (1621). In the Renaissance the main classificatory categories or varieties of melancholy were defined by Marsilio Ficino. *Atra bilis*, obnoxious melancholy, covered much the same ground as our 'clinical depression', while *candida bilis*, congenial melancholy, was a desirable state of mind conducive to creative work in literature and the sciences. We seem to have lost this concept. Burton built on and refined Ficino's scheme.

Another source of classificatory concepts of the past is Canon Law. The Church had to deal with issues of insanity is such matters as guardianship and trusts, entering into contracts, particularly matrimony (Pickett, 1952). Contemporary Canon Law retains much from the Middle Ages, current prior to the Council of Trent of 1643–1665. In turn the major categories recognized in Canon Law can be traced back to Roman law. The basic distinction was between the absolutely mentally incapacitated (*amentes*), permanently deprived of the capacity for responsible action and correct thought, and the partially insane, particularly *dementes*, those with fixed ideas dominating their thinking in some domains but not disturbing the whole of a person's mental life. The category of *amentes* included *idiotae*, beings incapable of any degree of rational thought. Then there were the *stupidi* and the *fatui*, mental subnormals. The law treated each of these categories differently in respect to the problems mentioned above.

In the first half of the 19th century a somatic theory of insanity prevailed, especially in the United States. The reason seems paradoxical. It was based on a firm adherence to the mind-body dualism of the Cartesian tradition, and set in a religious context. Injury or defect in the soul cannot be the basis of madness since it is the seat of rationality, and, unlike a mortal being, is unchanging and unchangeable. Where ideas of 'moral insanity' prevailed it was put down wholly to defects in the brain. The soul must be immune from disorders (Dain, 1964).

Kraepelin's experience in psychological investigations gained in Wundt's laboratory led him to think of madness in terms of its causes. He framed his system with a basic distinction between endogenous conditions, due to some defect of the person, and exogenous conditions, external influences on the person. This was mapped onto a general distinction between neurosis and psychosis. Though Kraepelin's focus was firmly on psychoses, he took an interest in other degenerative conditions. His collaborator, Alois Alzheimer, had studied pre-senile dementia. Kraepelin gave the name 'Alzheimer's disease' to a certain kind of degeneration of cognitive skills.

Kraepelin was much concerned to define the limits of each disease he wished to identify. The four most important were dementia praecox (schizophrenia), paraphrenia (paranoid delusions or feelings that later develop into dementia praecox), manic-depressive insanity and paranoia proper. He believed that though there might be exogenous conditions that triggered or exacerbated these conditions, their sources were endogenous, morbidity in the human organism itself.

Noting that the classification 'endogenous dementias' is a preliminary step to a deeper classification, Kraepelin remarks that such dementias seem to have no external causes, and lead to a general decline in mental faculties. Typically, he argued that despite divergences in the outward manifestations of dementia praecox, he was convinced that 'they are the expression of a single morbid process' (Kraepelin, 1919: 3). Addressing the question of a name for the condition, Kraepelin decided to make use of the term 'dementia praecox' already used by Benedict Morel, but he expressed some dissatisfaction with it. For instance, some patients with the condition make a complete recovery.

The most important psychic symptom of dementia praecox is auditory illusions. Voices that are unpleasant and disturbing are common, though sometimes there are 'good voices'. More characteristic is the patient's belief 'that one's thoughts are being influenced. People speak to the patient in his thoughts, guide them, contradict him, "offer" him thoughts' and so on (Kraepelin, 1919: 12). Strange bodily feelings also occur, but neither memory nor consciousness is disturbed throughout the course of the condition. Good judgement is impaired, and combinations of ideas of persecution with exalted conceptions of self and situation also occur. Finally, after listing a great many other characteristics, Kraepelin comes to one of the greatest importance, namely disorders in the 'train of thoughts' (Kraepelin, 1919: 72). The disjunctions in the flow of ideas seem to be the result of non-semantic aspects of words taking over as ordering conditions, for example, picking words simply by rhyme.

In summing up his observations of a thousand cases, Kraepelin identifies two principal groups of disorders: weakening of the emotional mainsprings of action, and loss of the inner unity of intellect. Classifying cases by reference to clinical details presented difficulties because of the complex pattern of recurrences and elisions in the features set out above. Kraepelin expressed his dissatisfaction with his original scheme, dividing mental disturbances into hebephrenic, catatonic and paranoid forms. Instead, deriving his categories directly from case material, he suggested the following taxa: dementia simplex, a slow impoverishment of psychic life; 'silly' dementia, incoherence in thinking; simple depressive dementia, in which the overall decline begins with a period of depression; delusional depressive dementia, in which delusions are prominent; agitated dementia, which begins with a state of excitement; and periodic dementia; catatonia, stupor and excitement; and paranoid dementias, in which delusions appear very early in the course of the disease. I have set these out in some detail to illustrate the way that Kraepelin used very comprehensive accounts of the symptoms to try to tease out distinctive forms, at the same time as he maintained the conviction that each and every one was endogenous and the consequence of a common underlying morbidity. The descriptions of symptoms from pages 89 to 180 in Kraepelin's treatise (1919) are striking in their subtlety.

The course of the disease also presents difficulties for the taxonomist. Not only are there periods of complete remission, but sometimes one set of symptoms is displaced by another more severe set from another part of the repertoire (Kraepelin, 1919: 181). What counts as a 'recovery' also influences the basis of prognosis. In a large proportion of cases, at least 70%, there are permanent incurable terminal states, in which there is 'loss of mastery over volitional action' rather than any particular persistence of disorders of intellect or continuance of delusions (Kraepelin, 1919: 207). As to the causes of dementia praecox, there was, as Kraepelin notes, impenetrable darkness, except that the condition comes on in early adulthood as a rule. Furthermore, it is found in all civilized nations, as he says. We now know that it is found throughout the human race, in roughly the same percentages. With admirable detachment, Kraepelin ran through a catalogue of possible causes, dismissing each and every one as at best contributory. Nor, at his time, as he remarked, was there any light to be thrown on how to combat dementia praecox.

In the introductory essay to the volume on *Manic-Depression Insanity and Paranoia*, Kraepelin emphasizes the point that the variety of conditions he is about to describe 'represent manifestations of a single morbid process' (Kraepelin, 1921: 1). That is why he takes them to form a single taxonomic category. To support this proposal he offers the following observations: certain features occur in all conditions; the seemingly different patterns of symptoms can pass over one into the other and replace one another in the same patient; there is a uniform prognosis for all the conditions; and there seems to be an element of heredity. In general, the manic state is succeeded by the depressive state and so on in a cycle interrupted by periods of normality. However, Kraepelin pointed out that there are clinical conditions in which the patient displays both manic and depressive phenomena, requiring an intermediate category of 'mixed states'.

As in any taxonomy, the categories are delineated by characteristic properties. There are both psychic and bodily symptoms, which cluster into a recognizable syndrome, one phase of which is manic and the other depressive. Among the bodily symptoms, he found that body weight went up during the manic phase and went down during the depressive phase. The psychic conditions are familiar to us now, but Kraepelin's careful distinctions are worth following. Trains of ideas are seldom consistent, and difficult to hold on to. In the depressive phase delusions appear and there may be a strong sense of sin or failure. In the manic phase the patient typically entertains 'ideas of greatness', claiming to be a monarch or divine. There is 'lack of inner unity in the train of ideas' (Kraepelin, 1921: 55). Unless the condition is very mild, patients have a very poor understanding that their current state is abnormal. Mood is exalted and sexual excitement is enhanced. At a certain point, the symptoms may become acute.

A state of depression more or less mirrors the conditions of mania, including an inability to carry through very simple actions. Speech is slowed. It becomes monosyllabic. In a typical attention to detail, Kraepelin notes that the ability to read aloud is unaffected.

Kraepelin's intensive studies revealed that in both the manic and the depressed states sleep is 'encroached upon'. Pulse rate was elevated in both manic and depressed patients during an attack.

In the periods between the manic and depressive phases there are changes in the psychic life. This hints at a pathology that has little to do with external conditions.

The endogenous/exogenous distinction was one to which Kraepelin gave great prominence. This 'shows us that the real, the deeper cause of the malady is to be sought in a permanent morbid state which must continue to exist in the intervals between the attacks' (Kraepelin, 1921: 117). In about a third of patients, certain subtle features persist even during periods of seeming normality. There is such a thing as a permanent manic personality, in which mood is always elevated. In the general case, there is a cyclothymic temperament, which is manifested in manic to depressive fluctuations.

The key, according to Kraepelin, lay in the periodicity of the states, however the symptoms of the phases may appear. Are there states of depression isolated from the cycle? Kraepelin insisted that periodic depressed states are interspersed with elevated moods and behaviour which is not sufficiently marked to be diagnosed as manic. 'Periodic melancholy is a form of manic-depressive insanity' (Kraepelin, 1921: 187).

It was not long before the terminology changed. 'Dementia praecox', with which Kraepelin himself was dissatisfied, became 'schizophrenia', while 'manic-depression' became 'bipolar disorder'.

Kraepelin frequently offers percentages of patients with this or that version of some mental disorder. However, he wisely makes no attempt to 'do statistics' to arrive at some generalized attribute of a disorder. The logic of his methodology is the 'intensive design', providing detailed descriptions of particular cases, as typifying this or that type of mental disorder.

Having begun my account of the contributions Emil Kraepelin made to the psychology of psychiatry by a brief summary of some of the classificatory schemes of earlier times, the comparison of his taxonomy with current diagnostic manuals is in order.

Interest in classification and its importance for diagnosis and prognosis of mental disorders led to the publication of a much criticized but still essential medical tool, the *Diagnostic and Statistical Manual of Mental Disorders* or *DSM*. It has been frequently revised and reissued. The following is taken from *DSM III R* (1987). It echoes Kraepelin very closely in most respects. For example: 'At some phase of the illness Schizophrenia always involves delusions, hallucinations, or certain characteristic disturbances in affect and the form of thought' (p. 187). Thought disorders include delusions of being externally controlled or having thoughts inserted in one's head. Disorderly thought running through disconnected topics also occurs, a phenomenon described in detail by Kraepelin. The commonest hallucinations are auditory, including 'the many voices the person perceives as coming from outside his or her head. The voices may be familiar, and often make insulting remarks ...' (p. 188).

On the subject of manic-depressive disorder, now renamed 'bipolar disorder', once again the account in *DSM III R* is very close to Kraepelin's: 'The initial episode ... is usually manic. ... Frequently a Manic or Major Depressive Episode is immediately followed by a short episode of the other kind. In many cases there are two or more complete cycles (a Manic and a Major Depressive Episode that succeed one another without a period of remission)' (p. 225). The term 'cyclothymia' has continued to be used much as Kraepelin used it, for cases where there are numerous episodes of hypermania followed by a period of depressed mood that does not reach the severity of the major depressive episode.

Returning to Kraepelin's texts from *DSM*, one is struck by the vividness and living detail of his descriptions of the patients and their disorders. His role in setting psychiatry on the right path cannot be over-emphasized. The next steps that would tie his categories to the originating conditions in the person were initiated by Sigmund Freud. As we shall see, Freud interposed a 'mentalistic' model between symptoms and the neurological conditions that produced them. Kraepelin, though admitting his ignorance of the underlying neuropathology, presumed a simple link between abnormal thinking and acting and malfunctioning of the brain.

Further Reading

Primary Sources[2]

Kraepelin, E. (1919) *Dementia Praecox and Paraphrenia* (trans. R. M. Barclay). Edinburgh: E. & S. Livingstone.

Kraepelin, E. (1921) *Manic-Depressive Insanity and Paranoia* (trans. R. M. Barclay). Edinburgh: E. & S. Livingstone.

Secondary Sources

Burton, R. (1621 [1987]) *The Anatomy of Melancholy* (ed. J. Bamborough). Oxford: Clarendon Press.

Dain, N. (1964) *Concepts of Insanity in the United States, 1989–1865*. New Brunswick, NJ: Rutgers University Press.

Pickett, R. C. (1952) *Mental Affliction and Canon Law*. Ottawa: University of Ottawa Press.

Biography

In the absence of any full scale biography of Emil Kraepelin, I have taken the outline of life from the website, 'www.whonamedit.com' (O. D. Enerson, 2001), elaborated here and there from other sources.

Sigmund Freud (1856–1939)

Even more than half a century after his death, the mere mention of psychology suggests the name of Sigmund Freud to a great many people. Versions of many of Freud's concepts have entered folk psychology. People talk about 'the unconscious', 'repression', 'complexes', 'sublimation', 'the id', 'denial', and so on, in trying to make sense of the thoughts, feelings and behaviour of their fellow human beings, and of their own. Freud not only presented accounts of the development of adult personalities, but he worked out a therapeutic practice to make good defects in that development. His ideas for a general psychology have almost acquired the status of commonsense. The distinction between the conscious and the unconscious mind is now one of our cultural resources, as is the threefold distinction between the ego, id and superego.

Though a good deal of Freud's clinical observations and the development of his theories of character and personality were worked out in the late 19th century, his impact on psychology took place in the 20th century.

Locating Freud's life and work in the section on psychopathology reflects an estimate of how Freud would have thought of himself. However, he had a great influence on developmental psychology and indirectly on child-rearing practices and on educational methods. The grand scheme within which he developed his psychotherapy can stand by itself as a major alternative to both behaviourism and cognitivism, though it is much closer to the latter.

Who was Sigmund Freud?

In writing a short biography of Freud one is faced with the fact that there was a distinctly unpleasant strand in his character. The way he treated some of his collaborators and several of his patients was far from admirable. Matters such as these could perhaps be passed over in sketching the lives and personalities of other people who figure in this volume, but in Freud's case they cannot be omitted. They had consequences for the theories he proposed. We must see him 'warts and all'. He was not above bullying patients into accepting his interpretations of their troubles. On occasion, he seems to have 'massaged' the facts to fit his theories. Nevertheless, he was a man driven by an intense passion to understand the human mind. He was no charlatan, but his deep conviction of the rightness of his theories led to no small measure of self-deception.

Sigmund Freud was born on 6 May 1856 in Frieberg in the province of Moravia, in the Austro-Hungarian Empire. When he was four years old, his family moved to Vienna. His mother, Amalia, was Jacob Freud's third and much younger wife. The children by Jacob's first marriage were more or less the same age as Amalia. Young Sigmund, the first child of the third marriage, grew up with two older stepbrothers, six younger siblings and an adoring mother. At times, Sigmund and his brother and sisters were crammed into a tiny apartment. Jacob Freud was a somewhat unsuccessful wool merchant, and he had great difficulty providing for Amalia and the children.

In later life Sigmund seems to have invented a more encouraging story of the economic circumstances of his family than seems to have been the case. Though the move to Vienna led to a gradual improvement in the circumstances of the

Freuds, by the time Sigmund had become aware of these things it must have been evident to him that the family was poor. In 1866 Josef Freud, Sigmund's uncle, was convicted for dealing in counterfeit money. Peter Gay suggests that Jacob Freud may have been implicated as well.

Nevertheless, Sigmund Freud's childhood was typical of the aspiring middle class Jewish community of the time. He seems to have received a good elementary education, though he was wracked by their shaming poverty. The origins of his longing for fame and wealth must surely lie in his family circumstances.

In his wonderful biography of Sigmund Freud, Peter Gay (1988) comments on the complexities of the family life of the Freuds. Sigmund's elder half-brother had a family of his own, while the younger, Peter, was still unmarried. Freud later confessed to having entertained an unfocused fantasy in which his brother was revealed to have been the father of his sister Anna, Amalia's second child. Freud's nephew, John, was a year older than he, and his regular childhood companion. Amalia was a powerful influence in his life, and his affection for her was tinged with darker emotions, as he himself later confessed. As to his father, his evidently submissive and unheroic nature makes Sigmund's lifelong search for heroic stature in his own chosen undertakings intelligible.

Being Jewish in central Europe at the time had its own peculiar complications. Many Jews were baptized as Christians, abandoning the faith of their forefathers completely. Others, like Jacob Freud, gave up strict observances, and Sigmund himself declared that he had lived as a godless Jew.

Throughout Eastern Europe there were formal and informal barriers to Jews entering the professions, with the notable exception of medicine, as we have observed in other life stories in this book. However, the emancipation of the Jews in Austro-Hungary had proceeded far further than anywhere else in the region. It was by no means inevitable that Freud would enter the Medical School of the University of Vienna in 1873. It seems that he had little interest in the practice of physical medicine, and was already drawn to physiological research. Medicine was a practical route to a scientific career.

In some ways Freud remained a biologist throughout his life. He was fortunate in finding Ernst Brücke as a research director in his first essay into physiological science. He worked in the physiology laboratory of the university for six years. Brücke, the first of several mentors who exercised a permanent influence on Freud's way of thought, was one of the earliest promoters of the strict materialism that later flourished in Vienna among the philosophers and physicists of the Vienna Circle. Organic life is a matter of chemical and physical forces. However, Brücke was not a mechanist but an energeticist, following the trend in physics initiated by Helmholtz. Organisms are energy systems. Psychology, conceived biologically, would be a study of the transformations of energy in the human system.

Freud eventually took his medical degree in 1881, making a more lucrative career possible. There was little chance for a permanent research position in Vienna, so he took a job in the Vienna General Hospital in 1882. In 1885, supported by Brücke, young Dr. Freud set off for a year in Paris. He was fortunate in meeting

Jean Charcot, the most prominent French 'mad doctor'. Charcot's practice was largely concerned with hysteria, the presentation of distressing physical symptoms which had no evident physiological causes. His method involved hypnosis and it seems to have had some measure of success, at least enough to persuade Freud to try such a treatment when he returned to Vienna in late 1886.

By now Freud was in need of a professional career. His first job was in Berlin, as a hospital neurologist, but after a short time he returned to Vienna. In 1882 he had become engaged to Martha Bernays. By 1886 it was surely time to marry and settle down. Again, fortune favoured him in that he set up a neuropsychiatric practice with a well-established practitioner, Joseph Breuer. Just as in Paris, hysteria was a problem of prime concern to Breuer and Freud. Hypnosis proved ineffective as a permanent cure, so Freud took up Breuer's practice of encouraging the patients to talk freely about their early lives. This sometimes led to the relief of the symptoms.

From this phenomenon, Freud leapt to the conclusion that the ultimate source of the symptoms must be a traumatic event which had been forgotten but was still exercising a malign influence on the health of the patient. If the event could be recalled and confronted the patient would be cured. What sort of event would be forgotten but have such long-lasting effects? It must be something sexual. Though Freud published a book with Breuer, his exclusive emphasis on the sexual sources of hysteria was unacceptable to Breuer, and the partnership broke up. Thereafter Freud practised as a psychotherapist alone, still engaging in some physiological research.

He married his long-time fiancée in 1886. Through a series of encounters with colleagues and what he had learned from a small number of patients, he began to construct his complex and gradually evolving theory of the human mind. Freud's relations with colleagues and followers were dominated by his sometimes desperate need to be the leader. He needed to be recognized and honoured as the originator of all the ideas that went into his growing theoretical account of the development of the human personality and its pathological distortions. Unless a colleague accepted Freud's line in every detail the relationship was soon broken off, usually with some acrimony. This happened with Karl Jung and Adolf Adler, and most significantly for Freud's theorizing, with Wilhelm Fliess.

The Fliess affair, as we might call it, has been the subject of intensive researches by historians and has fuelled much controversy. Dogmatically convinced of his hypothesis that the symptoms of hysteria were the result of a 'forgotten' sexual experience, Freud first claimed that all his patients had been sexually assaulted as children. He went further, to assert that this was a commonplace occurrence among the Viennese in general. Paradoxically, it was evident, according to Freud, in the very fact that few people actually recalled these events. They wouldn't, would they – given the thesis that such events would be forgotten precisely because they would have been particularly distressing.

This has been called the 'seduction hypothesis' as to the causes of hysteria. It met with a good deal of scepticism, and Freud soon abandoned it. The next crucial insight, so Freud himself claimed – the insight that led to the Oedipus complex and his theory of personal development – was his realization that the stories of childhood seductions that some of his women patients had told him were not true. Why did they tell them? These fantasies were the key to psychosexual development. Now he had to make good a new claim, that Viennese women regularly entertained sexual fantasies in which their fathers figured as seducers.

However, it seems more than likely that the majority of the tales of seduction were actually influenced by Freud himself. This interpretation of the apparent ubiquity of seduction fantasies has come from a close study of his correspondence with Fliess. His letters offer several reasons for abandoning the hypothesis that the seductions were real, among which we find his claim to have realized that the seduction stories were fantasies. It seems that Freud either bullied his patients into telling seduction stories or, in some cases, even made up the stories himself. Perhaps he needed to do this to preserve his claims to have revealed the inner core of psychic development, through the display of childhood sexuality in fantasies directed towards the parents (Gay, 1988: 125–8).

In claiming to have discovered the domain of childhood sexuality he was also claiming the heroic status of the prime innovator of a new approach to psychology itself. However, there can be little doubt that he took this idea almost whole, from Fliess. Fliess wrote back, objecting to Freud's claim to be the originator of the idea. On this note the relations between the two ended.

How could Freud have ignored the fact that his patients either denied his suggestions or, in the case of Dora, fled? Why did he harass his patients into acknowledging what *he* had perceived to be the truth? So confident was he in his capacity to see into the hidden depths of the minds of others that he interpreted any resistance to his interpretations as defences against the truth. In some cases patients seem to have invented seduction stories to please him (Cioffi, 1974 [1998]).

In 1923 Freud was finally forced to acknowledge that he had developed a 'growth' in the back of his mouth. He was advised to have it removed. The operation was botched and it was by great good fortune that he survived. For the next 15 years he fought a long battle against cancer. The painful results of the incompetent treatment he received, and of course the effects of the tumours that continued to return, led him to regular use of cocaine as an analgesic, a therapy practised by no less a person than Queen Victoria.

The publications of the early years of the 20th century propelled Freud into worldwide fame. In his own home country his work was generally rejected, and even condemned as scandalous. However, it quickly became popular in the United States and Britain, and eventually became a dominant force in French culture (Moscovici, 1961). Freud gathered a small group of disciples around him, the members of the Psychoanalytic Society, who gathered for regular meetings. Dissent from the views of the master generally led to expulsion. The more heroic dissidents, such as Jung and Adler, founded alternative versions of psychodynamics.

During the next 40 years the small group around Freud expanded into a number of psychoanalytic societies in many places. The expansion was accompanied by a biennial congress which served to give some coherence to the ideas of the growing population of 'Freudians'. However, there was something about psychodynamics itself that led to internecine quarrels that could become quite vicious. Rumbling on through the years there was a tide of dissent from Freud's views about women, and the psychology of the feminine. In this and other ways he remained a typical representative of the Viennese bourgeoisie. The story of Freud's troubled personal relationships is far too complex for such a sketch as this, but it can be followed in detail in Peter Gay's excellent biography.

However, Freud's character is germane to the ultimate assessment of the scientific status of his approach. From our vantage point it appears that Freud exerted an unacceptable amount of pressure on his patients to provide him with confirmation of his hypotheses. He seems to have fallen into a scientifically faulty habit of revising his empirical material to fit his theoretical predilections more closely than the material would properly allow. The case of 'Dora' has often been analysed. A more extensive treatment of this contentious issue can be found in Isbister (1985: 149–60).

Hitler came to power in Germany in 1933. Almost immediately he instituted an anti-Jewish policy that ranged from forced exile and confiscation of property to murder. The death camps came later. For a while, safe in Austria, Freud paid no more than passing attention to the rise of the Nazis, even expressing the hope that the regime would collapse. By 1938, however, it became clear that the Nazi takeover of Austria was immanent. In the early months of that year gangs of Nazis were openly attacking Jews and Jewish properties in Vienna. On 12 March the German army entered Austria to bring about the unification of the two Germanic nations. The subsequent unleashing of anti-Semitic violence was extraordinary. Freud's international fame protected him from the worst of it, but for how long? His apartment was searched a few days after the Anschluss, though Freud himself was unmolested. His friends began a concerted effort to bring him to England. Despite Freud's resistance to the plan he was finally persuaded to leave, taking the train westwards on 4 June 1938.

His time in England was spent completing a psychoanalytic study of Moses and making a start on an *Outline of Psychoanalysis*. In September he was operated on for a recurrence of the throat cancer that had plagued him earlier. By February of the following year cancer of the mouth and throat had returned in an inoperable way. He finally died on 23 September 1939, after the war that was to rid the world of the Nazis had already begun.

What did he contribute?

The theories that had gestated in Freud's early life found their public and eventually international presentation in the 20th century. *The Interpretation of Dreams* appeared in 1900, *The Psychopathology of Everyday Life* in 1901 and *Three Essays on the Theory of Sexuality* in 1905. These works presented the Freudian conception of the human mind and its vagaries together with his account of the origin of character and personality. He expounded the general theory on which the whole edifice depended in a series of lectures, delivered during the years 1915 to 1917.

Perhaps the best way to get a just appreciation of Freud's psychology is to see it as nothing less than a proposal for a new science of human mentality, psychodynamics. He proposed a new way of looking at the mind. It is not an entity, immaterial or material, nor is it any kind of substance, but a flow of psychic energy. The source of psychic energy in each individual is the instinctive need for sensual pleasure, gathered under a common category, 'sex'. This source, ultimately instinctual and biological, is the id. The flow of psychic energy is modulated and transformed both by life events and by acquiring the conventions and practices of the local social world, forming the superego. The main process of transformation of the originating psychic energy is through the resolution of the tensions induced by a child's unacknowledged sexual feelings for its parents.

From the very beginning Freud seems to have taken up the idea of an unconscious mind, parallel to but inaccessible from consciousness. Presuming the existence of unconscious mental processes allowed him to make sense of the aetiology of neurotic symptoms for which his patients could offer no explanation. We should not read him as reviving the Cartesian notion of a *res cogitans*, the mind as a substance, since he took the basis of mind to be biological. Nevertheless, his vocabulary was strongly mentalistic. Though there was no mental stuff, there was mental energy.

The contents of the unconscious are inaccessible as such. Unpleasant memories are repressed and fuse with other unconscious material into complexes. Freud called this the 'primary process'. However, this material can become conscious, but always transformed in such a way that its original content is concealed. In Lecture XVIII of his presentation of a theory of neuroses he remarks that while one of his patients 'had been aware of [her obsessional behaviour] ... in a normal mental fashion, ... none of the mental determinants of this effect came to the knowledge of her consciousness' (Freud, 1901, vol. 16: 277). This is the sort of situation when, he says, 'we speak of the existence of *unconscious mental processes*'. Crediting Breuer with the discovery that 'the symptoms disappear when we have made their unconscious predeterminants conscious', Freud goes on to emphasize that this can only happen when the patient's resistance to acknowledging the true sense of the repressed material has been overcome.

Freud likens the 'discovery' of the role of the unconscious as the main force in our mental lives to the Copernican revolution in astronomy and Darwin's proof of the descent of human beings from the animal kingdom. It is a third blow to human self-esteem. We are not in absolute control of our thoughts, feelings and actions. This, he believes, accounts for the ferocity of the attacks upon psychodynamics and psychoanalysis.

How can the content of the unconscious be discovered? The analysis of dreams can be a route to the unconscious because, according to Freud (1900, vol. 4: 121): 'when the work of interpretation has been completed, we perceive that a dream is the fulfillment of a wish'. Why is there need for an interpretation? According to Freud, though every dream is a fulfillment of a wish, it often may appear otherwise. A dream has a latent as well as a manifest content. The dream is not a true representation of the repressed material, the latent content, but expresses it symbolically. The art of the interpreter of dreams is to reveal the true meaning of the dream content. There are other ways in which repressed material reappears, for example as slips of the tongue, such as the case of the woman intent on repressing the memory of an attempted seduction who said 'Berglende' (hill-thigh) when she meant 'Berglehne' (hill-slope). Forgetting words can also be revealing (Freud, 1901, vol. 6: Ch. 5).

By 1923 Freud was giving more structure to the sources and transforming forces that his psycho-energetics required. The ego displays resistance to concerning itself with the repressed, but it is unconscious of this. So the resistance behaves like the repressed material itself. Though 'ego' includes that which is conscious and that which is unconscious, the latter is complex. This elaborates the unconscious, since the resistance does not itself consist of repressed material, though someone may not be conscious of their actions as resistance.

Consciousness is the surface of the mental apparatus, consisting of that which can be perceived whether reflexively in the mind or in the material and social environment. The unconscious is unknown. Instead of seeing the source of neuroses in a simple tension between conscious and unconscious thought, Freud added the preconscious, a domain of thoughts that can become conscious. Something can become known if it 'can be connected with word-presentations', and this is the domain of the preconscious. (Freud, 1901, vol. 6: 20). These verbal processes are vital to the dynamics of the mind, since it is through them that thought processes can be perceived. In a very illuminating passage Freud lines up his scheme for an architecture of the mind with the thesis that the ego is passive, that we are 'lived by' powerful forces. All that which is native to the person as a human organism and remains an unconscious source of psychic energy is the 'id'. It is the 'great reservoir of libido', the demand for sensual gratification. It is joined by repressed material as the unconscious expands through the vicissitudes of life (Freud, 1901, vol. 6: 30).

The third main component of the self is the superego, which, with the ego-ideal, plays a crucial role in the repression of the Oedipus complex of improper sexual desires within the family. There is an identification both with the father and with the mother, which joins with cultural influences, such as religion and schooling, to form the superego. It gives 'permanent expression to the influence of the parents' (Freud, 1901, vol. 6: 35).

A somewhat stripped down form of Freud's three aspect scheme has become part of our common ways of speaking about the human psyche. The mature Freudian model of the mind is a good deal more complex and dynamic than the simple picture of the conscious and unconscious regions coupled with the trio of id, ego and superego. Even from the above account, which has been shorn of many of Freud's subtleties, it should be clear that the popular scheme is at best a caricature. The id is seen as the source of instinctive forces that drive us to seek sensual gratification. The superego consists of the rules and conventions of social and civilized life taken up during the assimilation of the infant into the surrounding social world, and particularly the family. The ego, the self, is the point of intersection between the forces of the id and the constraints of the superego. The exact status of these 'entities' is not entirely clear. At times they appear as psychic beings, at other times as mere fields of force. The latter interpretation fits with Freud's Helmholtzian energetics.

The development of a stable and mature individual, whether male or female, requires the resolution of the Oedipus complex. The little boy develops a 'sexual' attraction to his mother, and identifies with his father. Soon he comes to see his father as a rival and would like to replace him. Resolution begins as the boy begins to develop his own identity as a man like his father. In some cases the identification may go towards the mother, resulting in a different kind of person at maturity. The development of girls follows a similar pattern. Having had to give up her father as love object, a girl may emphasize the masculine aspect of her character, identifying with the father, or she may emphasize the feminine side, identifying with the mother. What happens in any individual case, Freud asserts, depends on the balance of masculine and feminine characteristics in the initially bisexual child. This in broad outline is the Freudian story of how most boys come to be rough and tough, and most girls so sweet and neat. Guys usually like guns, gals usually like dolls.

Freud's categories of personality have also become part of our common ways of talking about people. According to Freud's theory, adult personalities are the products of events that occur very early in the lives of individuals. Like the developmental psychology of **Jean Piaget** (pp. 34–43), the Freudian account of personality and character development is based on an inevitable sequence of stages. The stage progression through infancy to adulthood is driven by the permanently active 'sex' drive, a need for bodily pleasure in general. Some parts of the body are more pleasure giving than others. These are the erogenous zones. Three bodily zones – the mouth, the anus and the genitals – fix the sequence. The zone that is predominant in pleasure seeking at each age defines a stage. There are, therefore, three stages: *oral, anal* and *phallic*.

In each stage pleasure is achieved by the appropriate activity: sucking, defecating and masturbation. Freud added a *latent* stage, during the middle years of schooling and prior to adolescence, in which the 'sexual drive' is overshadowed by the demands of schooling. Finally, post-adolescence, comes the *genital* stage, where pleasure migrates to sexual intercourse.

Suppose for some reason a person becomes 'stuck' at a certain stage of psychosexual development, through the long-term effects of problems at one or other of the stages. This gives Freud the basis for his system of categories. Oral-passive people, not weaned early enough, are dependent on others and favour oral gratifications such as smoking. Oral-aggressive people, weaned too soon, are aggressive and chew on pencils, pipe stems and so on. Anal-aggressive people, cajoled in potty training, are excessive in their social responses, both friendly and aggressive. Anal-retentive people, disciplined strictly during potty training, are perfectionists and mean.

Boys rejected by their mothers lack sexual confidence and may become reclusive or macho and aggressive. Girls rejected by their fathers may follow a similar pair of feminine stereotypes. Boys favoured by their mothers may be either arrogant or effeminate, while girls favoured by their fathers may be either vainly feminine or put on a masculine style. Much of the vocabulary that Freud used to describe these character types has been incorporated into everyday talk. However, the theory itself does not seem to figure prominently in current discussions of personality, such as those discussed in Chapter 7.

Why was Freud's theory at the same time so shocking and yet so rapidly taken up in many places? Consider the culture of upper middle class Vienna at the turn of the 19th century. Freud drew his patients from this stratum of society, a stratum which he aspired to join himself. Almost all the features of Freud's theory would have been among the unmentionables among that class of persons. There is no doubt Freud enjoyed the opportunity to shock the Viennese in the name of science. However, here was a catalogue of mysteries. Why were some people generous and others mean? Why were some girls wallflowers and others brazen hussies? Why do some people chew their fingernails, and why do others smoke? Why are some men wimps and others heroes? What is the source of neurotic symptoms and how can they be cured? His explanations of these *mysteries* were based on a matching catalogue of *unmentionables*. Perhaps the sense of mystery about the origins of these human traits simply lay in the unmentionability of their sources.

During the latter part of his career Freud turned his attention to larger forms of life, such as the role of religion in culture, and to the general question of the forces that led to civil society.

Psychodynamics has flourished far more in the consulting rooms of psychotherapists than in the psychology departments of universities. The 'talking cure' is still widely practised. It may not always have an explicitly Freudian label but its ancestry lies in Vienna at the turn of the 20th century. However, the question of its efficacy relative to other forms of psychotherapy has inevitably been raised. In a massive comparative study **Hans Eysenck** (pp. 175–179) (Eysenck & Wilson, 1973) demonstrated beyond reasonable doubt that people who had been through a course of Freudian analysis in the search for hidden childhood traumas recovered from neurotic troubles at about the same rate as those who had not. At best we can say that the time of recovery was more agreeably spent on the psychiatrist's couch than it might otherwise have been.

The three major postulates of Freud's psychodynamics have not remained unscathed (Cioffi, 1998). The concept of the 'unconscious mind' has been criticized from many sides, though sometimes unfairly. Freud's mentalism was surely a metaphor for certain neural structures and processes in the brain, the material bases of memory. Freud himself is likely to have interpreted it this way. The tripartite mind, id, ego and superego, no doubt points to the importance of the interplay between biological impulses and the demands and consequences of the embedment of the person in patterns of local social relations, not least in the family. However, it looks simplistic alongside the **Lev Vygotsky** (pp. 26–34) inspired conceptions of the social constructionists. Finally, the shock for a late Victorian society of the acknowledgement of childhood sexuality has long since dissipated, to be replaced by the cultural sophistication of such studies as **Michel Foucault**'s (pp. 246–252) *History of Sexuality*.

Further Reading[3]

Primary Sources

Freud, S. (1900) *The Interpretation of Dreams* in *The Complete Psychological Works of Sigmund Freud* (vols. 4 and 5). London: The Hogarth Press.
Freud, S. (1901) *The Psychopathology of Everyday Life* in *The Complete Psychological Works of Sigmund Freud* (vol. 6). London: The Hogarth Press.
Freud, S. (1905) *The Ego and the Id* in *The Complete Works Psychological Works of Sigmund Freud* (vol. 19). London: The Hogarth Press.

Secondary Sources

Cioffi, F. (1974 [1998]) *Was Freud a Liar?* in *Freud and the Question of Pseudoscience* (pp. 199–204). Chicago: Open Court.
Eysenck, H. J. & Wilson, G. (1973) *The Experimental Study of Freudian Theories*. London: Methuen.
Leahey, T. H. (2001) *A History of Modern Psychology* (Ch. 4). Upper Saddle River, NJ: Prentice Hall.
Moscovici, S. (1961) *La Psychoanalyse: Son image et Sa Publique*. Paris: Presses Universitaires de France.

Biographies

Gay, P. (1988) *Freud: A Life for Our Time*. New York and London: W. W. Norton.
Isbister, J. N. (1985) *Freud: An Introduction to His Life and Work*. Cambridge: Polity Press.

Reflections

If we take the contributions of Kraepelin and Freud together we find we have assembled an essential part of a scientific psychiatry. Remember what is required for a project to be scientific, in the sense of the natural sciences. There must be a conceptual scheme for identifying and classifying the phenomena that make up the domain of the relevant research projects. We have just such a scheme worked out with superb clarity and detail by Kraepelin. Then there must be a 'formal' model which represents the structure of the processes by which the phenomena come into being, change and so on. It leaves open the question of the unobservable processes that in reality sustain the phenomena. Freud's story of id, ego and superego, of repressed complexes in the unconscious and so on, is a fine example of a non-mathematical but powerful construction of such a model based on the analogy of flows of energy. Both Kraepelin and Freud understood that though neither was in a position to complete the work of creating a scientific psychiatry, the next step would be the opening up of knowledge of the relevant aspects of the human brain and nervous system. This must conform to what had been sketched in the working model, in this case Freud's psychodynamics.

Freud was well aware that this pattern must be fulfilled in the construction if a scientific psychiatry is to be brought off. He sketched out a version of the pattern in his *Project* (1895: 2). 'The intention [of this project],' he said, 'is to furnish a psychology that shall be a natural science'. Whatever we may think about the specifics of his psychodynamics, the project as a whole fulfills the demands of scientific method rather well. Reminding ourselves of the pattern that has emerged in chemistry, there we find a conceptual system based on the periodic table for identifying and classifying chemical phenomena, that is substances and reactions, an intermediate formal model of what the generative processes might be, the familiar chemical equations, with the final step in which chemistry is grounded in atomic and molecular physics.

Neuroscience is engaged at this very moment in laying the foundations of psychiatry as a science by establishing the third component, the base level of the *Project*, more or less as Freud outlined it a hundred years ago. As the editor remarks in his introduction to the *Project*, though most of the methods of psychoanalysis are not yet formulated in that early work, Freud's conception of the relation of the brain to thought is remarkably prescient. 'Freud's attempted approach ... to a description of mental phenomena in physiological terms might well seem to bear a resemblance to regarding the workings of the nervous system as similar to or even identical with an electronic computer – both of them machines for the reception, storage, processing and output of information' (Freud, 1895: 292). A careful reading of the *Project* suggests rather more of a link to the energetics of Helmholtz than the forward-looking view suggested by Strachey. However, it is worth remarking that Freud was careful to maintain a place for consciousness, the quality of experience, in a neuronal structure the input to which has only quantitative characteristics.

Freud's mature point of view seems to anticipate the threefold requirement of any scientific account of a domain of phenomena, in that his psychological mechanisms mediate between a phenomenological description of human experience and the picture of the workings of the brain offered by neuroscience. In that sense, his scheme as a whole comes very close to the logic of computational modelling and its relation to neuroscience.

Notes

1 Kraepelin's tenure at the University of Tartu is still remembered in Estonia.

2 I am particularly grateful to the medical librarians at Georgetown University for making these rare books available to me.

3 There is a vast secondary literature about Freud and his psychological theories. Gay's biography is magnificent, covering not only the events of Freud's life but also the development of his psychology.

Reference

Freud, S. (1895 [1966]) *Project for a Scientific Psychology* (trans. J. Strachey). In *The Complete Psychological Works of Sigmund Freud* (vol. 1). London: The Hogarth Press.

Name Index

Unless family members exerted a notable influence on the work of our cast of characters, their names have not been included in this index.

Subject Index